FTCE Chemistry 6

Teacher Certification Exam

By: Sharon Wynne, M.S.
Southern Connecticut State University

"And, while there's no reason yet to panic, I think it's only prudent that we make preparations to panic."

XAMonline, INC.

Boston

Copyright © 2008 XAMonline, Inc.
All rights reserved. No part of the material protected by this copyright notice may be reproduced or utilized in any form or by any means, electronic or mechanical, including photocopying, recording or by any information storage and retrievable system, without written permission from the copyright holder.

To obtain permission(s) to use the material from this work for any purpose including workshops or seminars, please submit a written request to:

XAMonline, Inc.
21 Orient Ave.
Melrose, MA 02176
Toll Free 1-800-509-4128
Email: info@xamonline.com
Web www.xamonline.com
Fax: 1-781-662-9268

Library of Congress Cataloging-in-Publication Data

Wynne, Sharon A.
 Chemistry 6-12: Teacher Certification / Sharon A. Wynne. -2nd ed.
 ISBN 978-1-58197-046-3
 1. Chemistry 6-12.   2. Study Guides.   3. FTCE
 4. Teachers' Certification & Licensure.   5. Careers

Disclaimer:
The opinions expressed in this publication are the sole works of XAMonline and were created independently from the National Education Association, Educational Testing Service, or any State Department of Education, National Evaluation Systems or other testing affiliates.

Between the time of publication and printing, state specific standards as well as testing formats and website information may change that is not included in part or in whole within this product. Sample test questions are developed by XAMonline and reflect similar content as on real tests; however, they are not former tests. XAMonline assembles content that aligns with state standards but makes no claims nor guarantees teacher candidates a passing score. Numerical scores are determined by testing companies such as NES or ETS and then are compared with individual state standards. A passing score varies from state to state.

Printed in the United States of America   œ-1

FTCE: Chemistry 6-12
ISBN: 978-1-58197-046-3

About the Subject Assessments

FTCE™: Subject Assessment in the Chemistry 6-12 examination

Purpose: The assessments are designed to test the knowledge and competencies of prospective secondary level teachers. The question bank from which the assessment is drawn is undergoing constant revision. As a result, your test may include questions that will not count towards your score.

Test Version: There is one version of subject assessment for Chemistry examination in Florida. The exam emphasizes comprehension in knowledge of the nature of matter, knowledge of energy and its interaction with matter; knowledge of bonding and molecular structure; knowledge of chemical reactions and stoichiometry; knowledge of atomic theory and structure; knowledge of the nature of science; knowledge of measurement; and knowledge of appropriate laboratory use and procedures. The Chemistry 6-12 study guide is based on a typical knowledge level of persons who have completed a _bachelor's degree program_ in Chemistry.

Time Allowance: You will have 2½ hours to finish the exam.

Additional Information about the FTCE Assessments: The FTCE™ series subject assessments are developed *Florida Department of Education* of Tallahassee, FL. They provide additional information on the FTCE series assessments, including registration, preparation and testing procedures and study materials such topical guides.

Table of Contents

189 (handwritten annotation)

5%

Great Study and Testing Tips!

What to study in order to prepare for the subject assessments is the focus of this study guide but equally important is *how* you study.

You can increase your chances of truly mastering the information by taking some simple, but effective steps.

Study Tips:

1. <u>**Some foods aid the learning process.**</u> Foods such as milk, nuts, seeds, rice, and oats help your study efforts by releasing natural memory enhancers called CCKs (*cholecystokinin*) composed of *tryptophan*, *choline*, and *phenylalanine*. All of these chemicals enhance the neurotransmitters associated with memory. Before studying, try a light, protein-rich meal of eggs, turkey, or fish. All of these foods release the memory enhancing chemicals. The better the connections, the more you comprehend.

Likewise, before you take a test, stick to a light snack of energy boosting and relaxing foods. A glass of milk, a piece of fruit, or some peanuts all release various memory-boosting chemicals and help you to relax and focus on the subject at hand.

2. <u>**Learn to take great notes.**</u> A by-product of our modern culture is that we have grown accustomed to getting our information in short doses (i.e. TV news sound bites or USA Today style newspaper articles.)

Consequently, we've subconsciously trained ourselves to assimilate information better in <u>neat little packages</u>. If your notes are scrawled all over the paper, it fragments the flow of the information. Strive for clarity. Newspapers use a standard format to achieve clarity. Your notes can be much clearer through use of proper formatting. A very effective format is called the *"Cornell Method."*

> Take a sheet of loose-leaf lined notebook paper and draw a line all the way down the paper about 1-2" from the left-hand edge.
>
> Draw another line across the width of the paper about 1-2" up from the bottom. Repeat this process on the reverse side of the page.

Look at the highly effective result. You have ample room for notes, a left hand margin for special emphasis items or inserting supplementary data from the textbook, a large area at the bottom for a brief summary, and a little rectangular space for just about anything you want.

3. Get the concept, then the details. Too often we focus on the details and don't gather an understanding of the concept. However, if you simply memorize only dates, places, or names, you may well miss the whole point of the subject.

A key way to understand things is to put them in your own words. If you are working from a textbook, automatically summarize each paragraph in your mind. If you are outlining text, don't simply copy the author's words.

Rephrase them in your own words. You remember your own thoughts and words much better than someone else's, and subconsciously tend to associate the important details to the core concepts.

4. Ask Why? Pull apart written material paragraph by paragraph and don't forget the captions under the illustrations.

Example: If the heading is "Stream Erosion", flip it around to read "Why do streams erode?" Then answer the questions.

If you train your mind to think in a series of questions and answers, not only will you learn more, but it also helps to lessen the test anxiety because you are used to answering questions.

5. Read for reinforcement and future needs. Even if you only have 10 minutes, put your notes or a book in your hand. Your mind is similar to a computer; you have to input data in order to have it processed. *By reading, you are creating the neural connections for future retrieval.* The more times you read something, the more you reinforce the learning of ideas.

Even if you don't fully understand something on the first pass, *your mind stores much of the material for later recall.*

6. Relax to learn, so go into exile. Our bodies respond to an inner clock called biorhythms. Burning the midnight oil works well for some people, but not everyone.

If possible, set aside a particular place to study that is free of distractions. Shut off the television, cell phone, pager and exile your friends and family during your study period.

If you really are bothered by silence, try background music. Light classical music at a low volume has been shown to aid in concentration over other types. Music that evokes pleasant emotions without lyrics are highly suggested. Try just about anything by Mozart. It relaxes you.

Testing Tips:

1. **Get smart, play dumb.** **Don't read anything into the question.** Don't make an assumption that the test writer is looking for something else than what is asked. Stick to the question as written and don't read extra things into it.

2. **Read the question and all the choices *twice* before answering the question.** You may miss something by not carefully reading, and then re-reading both the question and the answers.

If you really don't have a clue as to the right answer, leave it blank on the first time through. Go on to the other questions, as they may provide a clue as to how to answer the skipped questions.

If later on, you still can't answer the skipped ones . . . *Guess.* The only penalty for guessing is that you *might* get it wrong. Only one thing is certain; if you don't put anything down, you will get it wrong!

3. **Turn the question into a statement.** Look at the way the questions are worded. The syntax of the question usually provides a clue. Does it seem more familiar as a statement rather than as a question? Does it sound strange?

By turning a question into a statement, you may be able to spot if an answer sounds right, and it may also trigger memories of material you have read.

4. **Look for hidden clues.** It's actually very difficult to compose multiple-foil (choice) questions without giving away part of the answer in the options presented.

In most multiple-choice questions you can often readily eliminate one or two of the potential answers. This leaves you with only two real possibilities and automatically your odds go to Fifty-Fifty for very little work.

5. **Trust your instincts.** For every fact that you have read, you subconsciously retain something of that knowledge. On questions that you aren't really certain about, go with your basic instincts. **Your first impression on how to answer a question is usually correct.**

6. **Mark your answers directly on the test booklet.** Don't bother trying to fill in the optical scan sheet on the first pass through the test.

Just be very careful not to miss-mark your answers when you eventually transcribe them to the scan sheet.

7. **Watch the clock!** You have a set amount of time to answer the questions. Don't get bogged down trying to answer a single question at the expense of 10 questions you can more readily answer.

Periodic Table of the Elements

Group	1 IA	2 IIA	3 IIIB	4 IVB	5 VB	6 VIB	7 VIIB	8	9 VIIIB	10	11 IB	12 IIB	13 III IIIA	14 IV IVA	15 V VA	16 VI VIA	17 VII VIIA	18 VIII VIIIA
Period 1	hydrogen 1 H 1.0079																	helium 2 He 4.0026
2	lithium 3 Li 6.941	beryllium 4 Be 9.0122											boron 5 B 10.811	carbon 6 C 12.011	nitrogen 7 N 14.007	oxygen 8 O 15.999	fluorine 9 F 18.998	neon 10 Ne 20.180
3	sodium 11 Na 22.990	magnesium 12 Mg 24.305											aluminum 13 Al 26.982	silicon 14 Si 28.086	phosphorus 15 P 30.974	sulfur 16 S 32.065	chlorine 17 Cl 35.453	argon 18 Ar 39.948
4	potassium 19 K 39.098	calcium 20 Ca 40.078	scandium 21 Sc 44.956	titanium 22 Ti 47.867	vanadium 23 V 50.942	chromium 24 Cr 51.996	manganese 25 Mn 54.938	iron 26 Fe 55.845	cobalt 27 Co 58.933	nickel 28 Ni 58.693	copper 29 Cu 63.546	zinc 30 Zn 65.409	gallium 31 Ga 69.723	germanium 32 Ge 72.64	arsenic 33 As 74.922	selenium 34 Se 78.96	bromine 35 Br 79.904	krypton 36 Kr 83.798
5	rubidium 37 Rb 85.468	strontium 38 Sr 87.62	yttrium 39 Y 88.906	zirconium 40 Zr 91.224	niobium 41 Nb 92.906	molybdenum 42 Mo 95.94	technetium 43 Tc [98]	ruthenium 44 Ru 101.07	rhodium 45 Rh 102.91	palladium 46 Pd 106.42	silver 47 Ag 107.87	cadmium 48 Cd 112.41	indium 49 In 114.82	tin 50 Sn 118.71	antimony 51 Sb 121.76	tellurium 52 Te 127.60	iodine 53 I 126.90	xenon 54 Xe 131.29
6	cesium 55 Cs 132.91	barium 56 Ba 137.33	57-71 *	hafnium 72 Hf 178.49	tantalum 73 Ta 180.95	tungsten 74 W 183.84	rhenium 75 Re 186.21	osmium 76 Os 190.23	iridium 77 Ir 192.22	platinum 78 Pt 195.08	gold 79 Au 196.97	mercury 80 Hg 200.59	thallium 81 Tl 204.38	lead 82 Pb 207.2	bismuth 83 Bi 208.98	polonium 84 Po [209]	astatine 85 At [210]	radon 86 Rn [222]
7	francium 87 Fr [223]	radium 88 Ra [226]	89-103 **	rutherfordium 104 Rf [261]	dubnium 105 Db [262]	seaborgium 106 Sg [266]	bohrium 107 Bh [264]	hassium 108 Hs [277]	meitnerium 109 Mt [268]	darmstadtium 110 Ds [271]	roentgenium 111 Rg [272]							

*Lanthanoids

lanthanum 57 La 138.91	cerium 58 Ce 140.12	praseodymium 59 Pr 140.91	neodymium 60 Nd 144.24	promethium 61 Pm [145]	samarium 62 Sm 150.36	europium 63 Eu 151.96	gadolinium 64 Gd 157.25	terbium 65 Tb 158.93	dysprosium 66 Dy 162.50	holmium 67 Ho 164.93	erbium 68 Er 167.26	thulium 69 Tm 168.93	ytterbium 70 Yb 173.04	lutetium 71 Lu 174.97

**Actinoids

actinium 89 Ac [227]	thorium 90 Th 232.04	protactinium 91 Pa 231.04	uranium 92 U 238.03	neptunium 93 Np [237]	plutonium 94 Pu [244]	americium 95 Am [243]	curium 96 Cm [247]	berkelium 97 Bk [247]	californium 98 Cf [251]	einsteinium 99 Es [252]	fermium 100 Fm [257]	mendelevium 101 Md [258]	nobelium 102 No [259]	lawrencium 103 Lr [262]

Atomic mass values from IUPAC review (2001): http://www.iupac.org/reports/periodic_table/

COMPETENCY 1.0 – 10%   KNOWLEDGE OF CONCEPTS OF MATTER

"Nothing in life is to be feared, it is only to be understood. Now is the time to understand more, so that we may fear less." - Marie Curie

Skill 1.1   Differentiate between pure substances, homogeneous mixtures and heterogeneous mixtures.

The word "matter" describes everything that has physical existence, i.e. has mass and takes up space. However, the make-up of matter allows it to be separated into categories. The two main classes of matter are **pure substance and mixture.** Each of these classes can also be divided into smaller categories such as element, compound, homogeneous mixture or heterogeneous mixture based on composition.

PURE SUBSTANCES: A pure substance is a form of matter with a definite composition and distinct properties. This type of matter can not be separated by ordinary processes like filtering, centrifuging, boiling or melting.

Pure substances are divided into elements and compounds.

> **Elements:** A single type of matter, called an atom, is present. Elements can not be broken down any farther by ordinary chemical processes. They are the smallest whole part of a substance that still represents that substance. Examples are hydrogen and oxygen.

> **Compounds:** Two or more elements chemically combined are present. A compound may be broken down into its elements by processes that cause chemical change such as electrolysis. Compounds have a uniform composition regardless of the sample size or source of the sample.
>
> Examples are salt and pure water.

Comp 1 pp 1-36 Matter
2   40-65 Energy
3 67-115 Structure
4 120-177 Stoichiometry
5 181-211 Periodic Table atomic property
6. 212-236 Empirical design graph evidence
7 236-247 Units of measurement
8 248-271 Lab Safety

Unit 1
Unit 2
Unit 3

MIXTURES: Two or more substances that are not chemically combined. Mixtures may be of any proportions of the components and can be physically, or mechanically, separated by processes like filtering, centrifuging, boiling, or melting. The components do not form new chemical bonds to each other.

Mixtures are either homogeneous or heterogeneous: They can be classified according to particle size.

solution
< 1 nm

Homogeneous Mixtures: Homogeneous mixtures have the same composition and properties throughout the mixture and are also known as solutions. They have a uniform color and distribution of solute and solvent particles throughout the mixture. A homogeneous mixture exists in a single phase. **Solutions** are homogeneous mixtures. See Skill 1.4. Particle size is less than 1 nm, about the size of an atom or molecule. Examples are salt dissolved in water and air which is a mixture of gases.

colloid
1 – 1000 nm

Suspension
> 1000 nm

Heterogeneous Mixtures: Heterogeneous mixtures do not have a uniform distribution of particles throughout the mixture. The different components of the mixture can easily be identified and separated. **Colloidal dispersions** are heterogeneous mixtures. Colloids have particles in the 1 to 1000 nm size, larger than in a solution but smaller than in a suspension. Jelly, milk and blood are examples. **Suspensions** are heterogeneous mixtures in which the particles of at least one component are larger than 1000 nm. The components will settle out if left long enough. These particles show the **Tyndall effect** of scattering light. An example is sand in water.

Skill 1.2   Determine the effects of changes in temperature, volume, pressure or quantity on an ideal gas.

These relationships were found by experimental observation and may be explained by the kinetic molecular theory. See Skill 2.2.

Molecules have **kinetic energy (**they move around), and they also have **intermolecular attractive forces** (they stick to each other). The relationship between these two determines whether a collection of molecules will be a gas, liquid, or solid.

A **gas** has an indefinite shape and an indefinite volume. The kinetic model for a gas is a collection of widely separated molecules, each moving in a random and free fashion, with negligible attractive or repulsive forces between them. Gases will expand to occupy a larger container so there is more space between the molecules. Gases can also be compressed to fit into a small container so the molecules are less separated. **Diffusion** occurs when one material spreads into or through another. Gases diffuse rapidly and move from one place to another.

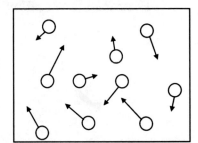

A **liquid** assumes the shape of the portion of any container that it occupies and has a specific volume. The kinetic model for a liquid is a collection of molecules attracted to each other with sufficient strength to keep them close to each other but with insufficient strength to prevent them from moving around randomly. Liquids have a higher density and are much less compressible than gases because the 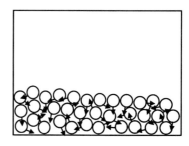 molecules in a liquid are closer together. Diffusion occurs more slowly in liquids than in gases because the molecules in a liquid stick to each other and are not completely free to move.

A **solid** has a definite volume and definite shape. The kinetic model for a solid is a collection of molecules attracted to each other with sufficient strength to essentially lock them in place. Each molecule may vibrate, but it has an average position relative to its neighbors. If these positions form an ordered pattern, the solid is called **crystalline**. Otherwise, it is called **amorphous**. Solids have a high density and are almost incompressible because the molecules are close together. Diffusion occurs extremely slowly because the molecules almost never alter their position.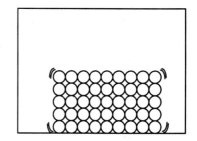

In a solid, the energy of intermolecular attractive forces (such as ionic or covalent bonds) is much stronger than the kinetic energy of the molecules. As temperature increases in a solid, the vibrations of individual molecules grow more intense and the molecules spread slightly further apart, decreasing the density of the solid.

In a liquid, the energy of intermolecular attractive forces (such as dipole=dipole and London dispersion forces) is about as strong as the kinetic energy of the molecules. Therefore, both play a role in the properties of liquids. Liquids will be discussed in detail in Skill 1.8.

In a gas, the energy of intermolecular forces is much weaker than the kinetic energy of the molecules. Kinetic molecular theory is most commonly used to understand gases and is best applied by imagining ourselves shrinking down to become a molecule and picturing what happens when we bump into other molecules and into container walls.

Gas **pressure** results from molecular collisions with container walls. The **number of molecules** striking an **area** on the walls and the **average kinetic energy** per molecule are the only factors that contribute to pressure. A higher **temperature** increases speed and kinetic energy. There are more collisions at higher temperatures, but the average distance between molecules does not change, and thus density does not change in a sealed container.

Kinetic molecular theory explains how pressure and temperature influences behavior of gases by making a few assumptions, namely:

1) The energies of intermolecular attractive and repulsive forces may be neglected.
2) The average kinetic energy of the molecules is proportional to absolute temperature.
3) Energy can be transferred between molecules during collisions and the collisions are elastic, so the average kinetic energy of the molecules doesn't change due to collisions.
4) The volume of all molecules in a gas is negligible compared to the total volume of the container.

Strictly speaking, molecules also manifest some kinetic energy by rotating or experiencing other motions. The motion of a molecule from one place to another is called **translation**. Translational kinetic energy is the form that is transferred by collisions, and kinetic molecular theory ignores other forms of kinetic energy because they are not proportional to temperature.

The following table summarizes the application of kinetic molecular theory to an increase in container volume, number of molecules, and temperature:

Effect of an **increase** in one variable with other two constant	Impact on gas: − = decrease, 0 = no change, + = increase						
	Average distance between molecules	Density in a sealed container	Average speed of molecules	Average translational kinetic energy of molecules	Collisions with container walls per second	Collisions per unit area of wall per second	Pressure (P)
Volume of container (V)	+	−	0	0	−	−	−
Number of molecules	−	+	0	0	+	+	+
Temperature (T)	0	0	+	+	+	+	+

Additional details on the kinetic molecular theory may be found at http://hyperphysics.phy-astr.gsu.edu/hbase/kinetic/ktcon.html. An animation of gas particles colliding is located at http://comp.uark.edu/~jgeabana/mol_dyn/.

The kinetic molecular theory describes how an ideal gas behaves when conditions such as temperature, pressure, volume or quantity of gas are varied within a system. An **ideal gas** is an imaginary gas that obeys all of the assumptions of the kinetic molecular theory. While an ideal gas does not exist, most gases will behave like an ideal gas except when at very low temperatures or very high pressures.

Charles's law states that the volume of a fixed amount of gas at constant pressure is directly proportional to absolute temperature, or increasing the temperature causes a gas to expand, in a mathematically proportional manner:

$$V \propto T.$$

Or V=kT where k is a constant. This gives a mathematical equation $\dfrac{V_1}{T_1} = \dfrac{V_2}{T_2}$.

Changes in temperature or volume can be found using Charles's law.

Example: What is the new volume of gas if 0.50 L of gas at 25°C is allowed to heat up to 35°C at constant pressure?

Solution: This is a volume-temperature change so use Charles's law. Temperature must be on the Kelvin scale. K= °C + 273.

T_1= 298K (273 + 25)
V_1= 0.50 L
T_2= 308K (273 + 35)
V_2 = ?

Use the equation: $\dfrac{V_1}{T_1} = \dfrac{V_2}{T_2}$ and rearrange for $V_2 = \dfrac{T_2 V_1}{T_1}$.

Substitute and solve V_2=0.52 L.

Boyle's law states that the volume of a fixed amount of gas at constant temperature is inversely proportional to the gas pressure, or increasing the pressure causes a gas to contract in a mathematically proportional manner:

$$V \propto \dfrac{1}{P}.$$

Or V=k/P where k is a constant. This gives a mathematical equation $P_1V_1 = P_2V_2$. Pressure or volume changes (at a constant temperature) can be determined using Boyle's law.

Example: A 1.5 L gas has a pressure of 0.56 atm. What will be the volume of the gas if the pressure doubles to 1.12 atm at constant temperature?

Solution: This is a pressure-volume relationship at constant temperature so use Boyle's law.

P_1= 0.56 atm
V_1= 1.5 L
P_2= 1.12 atm
V_2=?

Use the equation $P_1V_1=P_2V_2$, rearrange to solve for $V_2 = \dfrac{P_1 V_1}{P_2}$.

Substitute and solve. V_2=0.75 L

Gay-Lussac's law states that the pressure of a fixed amount of gas in a fixed volume is proportional to absolute temperature, or increasing the temperature causes the pressure to increase in a mathematically proportional manner:

$$P \propto T.$$

Or $P=kT$ where k is a constant. This gives a mathematical equation $\dfrac{P_1}{T_1} = \dfrac{P_2}{T_2}$.

Changes in temperature or pressure (with a constant volume) can be found using Gay-Lussac's law.

Example: A 2.25 L container of gas at 25°C and 1.0 atm pressure is cooled to 15°C. How does the pressure change if the volume of gas remains constant?

Solution: This is a pressure-volume change so use Gay-Lussac's law.

P_1= 1.0 atm
T_1= 298 K (273 +25)
T_2= 288 K (273 + 15)

Change the temperatures to the Kelvin scale. K=°C+ 273.
Use the equation $\dfrac{P_1}{T_1} = \dfrac{P_2}{T_2}$ to solve. Rearrange the equation to solve for P_2, substitute and solve.

$P_2 = \dfrac{P_1 T_2}{T_1}$ = 0.97 atm

The **combined gas law** uses the above laws to determine a proportionality expression that is used for a constant quantity of gas:

$$V \propto \frac{T}{P}.$$

The combined gas law is often expressed as an equality between identical amounts of an ideal gas at two different states ($n_1=n_2$):

$$\frac{P_1V_1}{T_1} = \frac{P_2V_2}{T_2}.$$

Example: 1.5 L of a gas at STP is allowed to expand to 2.0 L at a pressure of 2.5 atm. What is the temperature of the expanded gas?

Solution: Since pressure, temperature and volume are changing use the combined gas law to determine the new temperature of the gas.

P_1= 1.0 atm
T_1= 273K
V_1= 1.5 L
V_2= 2.0L
P_2= 2.5 atm
T_2=?

Using this equation, $\frac{P_1V_1}{T_1} = \frac{P_2V_2}{T_2}$, rearrange to solve for T_2.

$$T_2= \frac{P_2V_2T_1}{P_1V_1}$$

Substitute and solve T_2=910 K or, after subtracting 273: 637 °C

Avogadro's hypothesis states that equal volumes of different gases at the same temperature and pressure contain equal numbers of molecules.
Avogadro's law states that the volume of a gas at constant temperature and pressure is directly proportional to the quantity of gas, or:

$$V \propto n \text{ where } n \text{ is the number of moles of gas.}$$

Avogadro's law and the combined gas law yield $V \propto \frac{nT}{P}$.

The proportionality constant R--the **ideal gas constant**--is used to express this proportionality as the **ideal gas law**:

$$PV = nRT.$$

The ideal gas law ($PV = nRT$) is useful because it contains all the information of Charles's, Avogadro's, Boyle's, and the combined gas laws in a single equality.

If pressure is given in atmospheres and volume is given in liters, a value for R of **0.08206 L-atm/(mol-K)** is used. If pressure is given in Pascal (newtons/m^2) and volume in cubic meters, then the SI value for R of **8.314 J/(mol-K)** may be used. This is because a joule is defined as a Newton-meter. A value for R of **8.314 m^3-Pa/(mol-K)** is identical to the ideal gas constant using joules.

Many problems are given at "**standard temperature and pressure**" or "**STP**." Standard conditions are *exactly* **1 atm** (101.325 kPa) and **0 °C (273.15 K)**. At STP, one mole of an ideal gas has a volume of:

$$V = \frac{nRT}{P}$$

$$= \frac{(1 \text{ mole})\left(0.08206 \ \frac{\text{L-atm}}{\text{mol-K}}\right)(273 \text{ K})}{1 \text{ atm}} = 22.4 \text{ L.}$$

The value of 22.4 L is known as the **standard molar volume of any gas at STP**.

Solving gas law problems using these formulas is a straightforward process of algebraic manipulation. **Errors commonly arise from using improper units**, particularly for the ideal gas constant R. An absolute temperature scale must be used (never °C) and is usually reported using the Kelvin scale, but volume and pressure units often vary from problem to problem. Temperature in Kelvin is found from:

$$T \text{ (in K)} = T(\text{in } °C) + 273.15$$

Tutorials for gas laws may be found online at: http://www.chemistrycoach.com/tutorials-6.htm. A flash animation tutorial for problems involving a piston may be found at: http://www.mhhe.com/physsci/chemistry/essentialchemistry/flash/gasesv6.swf.

Example: What volume will 0.50 mole an ideal gas occupy at 20.0 °C and 1.5 atm?

Solution: Since the problem deals with moles of gas with temperature and pressure, use the ideal gas law to find volume.

$$PV = nRT$$

$$V = nRT/P$$

$$V = 0.50 \text{ mol } (0.0821 \text{ atm L/mol K}) \ 293 \text{ K}/1.5 \text{ atm}$$

$$V = 8.0 \text{ L}$$

Example: At STP, 0.250 L of an unknown gas has a mass of 0.491 g. Is the gas SO_2, NO_2, C_3H_8, or Ar? Support your answer.

Solution: Identify what is given and what is asked to determine.

Given: T= 273K
P=1.0 atm
V= 0.250 L
Mass= 0.419 g

Determine: Identity of the gas. In order to do this, must find molar mass of the gas. $n = \dfrac{mass}{MM}$. Find the number of moles of gas present using PV=nRT and then determine the MM to compare to choices given in the problem.

Solve for $n = \dfrac{PV}{RT} = 0.011$ moles

$MM = \dfrac{mass}{n} = 38.1$ g/mol

Compare to MM of SO_2 (96 g/mol), NO_2 (46 g/mol), C_3H_8 (44 g/mol) and Ar (39.9 g/mol). It is closest to Ar, so the gas is probably Argon.

Skill 1.3 **Apply units of mass, volume, and moles to determine concentrations and dilutions of solutions.**

In a solution, the amount of solute dissolved in a given amount of solvent is called concentration. Solutions that cannot dissolve any additional solute are referred to as saturated solutions. Qualitative terms such as concentrated and dilute are used to describe solutions with relativity high or low solute concentrations, respectively. However, these expressions give very little information about the actual quantities present in the solution.

Expressions of percent by mass or volume, molarity, molality, as well as part per million give more information about the quantity of solute and solvent present in a solution.

Percent by mass or volume expresses the amount of solute present as a percentage of the total solution present, either by mass or by volumes.

$$\% \text{ by mass} = \frac{\text{mass of solute}}{\text{mass of solute} + \text{mass of solvent}} \times 100\%$$

$$\% \text{ by volume} = \frac{\text{volume of solute}}{\text{volume of solute} + \text{volume of solvent}} \times 100\%$$
$$\text{(or total volume of solution)}$$

Example: What is the percent by mass of a solution prepared by dissolving 4.0 g of CH_3COOH is 35.0 g of water?

Solution: $\% \text{ by mass} = \dfrac{\text{mass of solute}}{\text{mass of solute} + \text{mass of solvent}} \times 100\%$

$$= 4 \text{ g} / (4 \text{ g} + 35 \text{ g}) = 10\%$$

$$\% \text{ by volume} = \frac{\text{volume of solute}}{\text{volume of solute} + \text{volume of solvent}} \times 100\%$$

Example: The label on a 500 mL bottle of hydrogen perioxide, H_2O_2, says 3% by volume. How much hydrogen perioxide does it contain?

Solution: % by volume = $\dfrac{\text{volume of solute}}{\text{volume of solute + volume of solvent}}$ X 100%
(or total volume of solution)

volume of H_2O_2 = 0.03 (volume of solution) = 0.03 x 500 mL = 15 mL of H_2O_2 present.

Molarity, M, is an expression of concentration that compares the number of mole of solute present in the solution to the total volume in liters of the solution.

$$\text{Molarity} = \frac{\text{moles solute}}{\text{volume of solution in liters}}$$

Molarity is the most frequently used concentration unit in chemical reactions because it reflects the number of solute moles available. By using Avogadro's number, the number of molecules in a flask--a difficult image to conceptualize in the lab--is expressed in terms of the volume of liquid in the flask—a straightforward image to visualize and actually manipulate.

Example: What is the molarity of a 5.00 liter solution that was made with 10.0 moles of $CuCl_2$?

Solution: We can use the original formula. Note that in this particular example, where the number of moles of solute is given, the identity of the solute ($CaCl_2$) has nothing to do with solving the problem.

$$\text{Molarity} = \frac{\text{\# of moles of solute}}{\text{Liters of solution}}$$

Given: # of moles of solute = 10.0 moles
Liters of solution = 5.00 liters

Molarity = $\dfrac{\text{10.0 moles of } CaCl_2}{\text{5.00 Liters of solution}}$ = 2.00 M

Answer = 2.00 M

Example: A 250 ml solution is made with 0.50 moles of NaCl. What is the molarity of the solution?

Solution: In this case we are given ml, while the formula calls for L. We must change the ml to Liters as shown below:

$$250 \; \text{ml} \; \times \; \frac{1 \; \text{liter}}{1000 \; \text{ml}} = 0.25 \; \text{liters}$$

Now, solve the problem using the equation:

$$\text{Molarity} = \frac{\text{\# of moles of solute}}{\text{Liters of solution}}$$

Given: Number of moles of solute = 0.50 moles of NaCl
Liters of solution = 0.25 L of solution

$$\text{Molarity} = \frac{0.50 \; \text{moles of NaCl}}{0.25 \; \text{L}} = 2.0 \; \text{M solution}$$

Answer = 2.0 M solution of NaCl

Example: What is the molarity of 3.50 L of solution that contains 90.0 g of sodium chloride?

Solution: Here we use the molecular weight of NaCl, 58.5g/mol, to determine the molarity.

$$M = 90.0 \; \text{g NaCl} \times (1 \; \text{mol} / 58.5 \; \text{g}) / 3.50 \; \text{L} = 0.440 \; \text{M}$$

Rarely do we see or use concentrated solutions. The majority of solutions that we come across in our daily lives are dilute solutions. Molarity is useful for dilutions because the moles of solute remain unchanged if more solvent is added to the solution:

$$(\text{Initial molarity})(\text{Initial volume}) = (\text{molarity after dilution})(\text{final volume})$$

or

$$M_{initial}V_{initial} = M_{final}V_{final}$$

Example: How much water and how much 12 M HCl must be used to prepare 500 mL of a 1 M HCl solution?

$$V_i = \frac{M_f V_f}{M_i} = \frac{[M] \, 500mL}{12M} = 41.67 mL$$

Solution: $M_i V_i = M_f V_f$

$$V_i = (1 \text{ M})(500 \text{ mL})/ (12 \text{ M}) = M_f V_f/M_i = 41.7 \text{ mL}$$

Thus, 41.66 mL of 12 M HCl is added to enough water to make 500 mL of solution. (about 458.3 mL of water)

On the other hand, molality, m, compares the moles of solute present in the solution to the mass of the solvent in kilograms.

$$\text{Molality} = \frac{\text{moles solute}}{\text{mass of solvent in kilograms}}$$

Example: Calculate the molality when 75.0 grams of $MgCl_2$ is dissolved in 500.0 g of solvent.

Solution: Since $m = \dfrac{\text{\# mol solute}}{\text{Kg solvent}}$

First we need the number mol solute ($MgCl_2$)

\# mol = 75.0 g $MgCl_2$/ 95.3 g/mol = 0.787 mol

We also need kg of solvent so 500.0 g of solvent needs to be converted to kg.

Kg = 500.0 g x 1 kg/1000 g = 0.5000 kg

Now it is just a matter of substituting into the molality formula:

molality = 0.787 mol/0.5000 kg = 1.57 m

Example: What is the molality of a solution composed of 2.55 g of acetone, $(CH_3)_2CO$ dissolved in 200g of water?

Solution: MM = 58.0 g/mol   mol acetone = 2.55 g x 1 mol/ 58 g = 0.0440 mol

m = mol solute/ kg solvent

0.0440 mol/ .200 kg water = 0.220 m

Molality is used with calculating **colligative properties** such as boiling point elevation and freezing point depression. See Skill 1.5.

Parts per million, ppm, is used frequently when very small amounts of solute are present, like in dealing with contaminants in water. When dealing with small amounts of solute present, it is more convenient to use the expression parts per million or even parts per billion. A 1% saline or NaCl solution means that there is 1 part NaCl per one hundred. Remember, percent is based on one hundred so it could be said 1% is one part per hundred.

Well, $\dfrac{1}{100} = \dfrac{10}{1000} = \dfrac{100}{10000} = \dfrac{1000}{100000} = \dfrac{10000}{1000000} = \dfrac{10000000}{1000000000}$

or 1 pph = 10 ppt   =   1000 ppm = 10000000ppb

Example: What is the concentration of a solution in pph, ppm, and ppb that contains 10 g of NaCl dissolved in 90 grams of H_2O?

Solution The total mass of the solution is 10 g + 90 g = 100 g. Therefore:

Percent by weight = 10 g NaCl / 100 g solution = 0.1 x 100% = 10%

ppm = 10 g NaCl / 100 g solution = 0.1 x 1,000,000 = 100,000 ppm

ppb = 10 g NaCl / 100 g solution = 0.1 x 1,000,000,000 = 100,000,000 ppb

The **normality** (abbreviated N) of a solution is defined as the number of **equivalents** of a solute per liter of solution.

$$\text{Normality} = \frac{\text{equivalents solute}}{\text{volume of solution in liters}}$$

An equivalent is defined according to the type of reaction being examined, but the number of equivalents of solute is always a whole number multiple of the number of moles of solute, and so the normality of a solute is always a whole-number multiple of its molarity. An equivalent is defined so that one equivalent of one reagent will react with one equivalent of another reagent.

For acid-base reactions, an equivalent of an acid is the quantity that supplies 1 mol of H^+ and an equivalent of a base is the quantity reacting with 1 mol of H^+. For example, one mole of H_2SO_4 in an acid-base reaction supplies two moles of H+. The mass of one equivalent of H_2SO_4 is half of the mass of one mole of H_2SO_4, and its normality is twice its molarity. In a redox reaction, an equivalent is the quantity of substance that gains or loses 1 mol of electrons.

A **mole fraction** is used to represent a component in a solution as a portion of the entire number of moles present. If you were able to pick out a molecule at random from a solution, the mole fraction of a component represents the probability that the molecule you picked would be that particular component. The mole fractions for all components must add up to one and mole fractions have no units.

$$\text{Mole fraction of a component} = \frac{\text{moles of component}}{\text{total moles of all components}}$$

Skill 1.4   Analyze the effects of physical conditions on solubility and the dissolving process.

When two or more pure materials mix in a homogeneous way (with their molecules intermixing on a molecular level), the mixture is called a **solution**. Dispersions of small particles that are larger than molecules are called **colloids**. Liquid solutions are the most common, but any two phases may form a solution. When a pure liquid and a gas or solid form a liquid solution, the pure liquid is called the **solvent** and the non-liquids are called **solutes**. When all components in the solution were originally liquids, then the one present in the greatest amount is called the solvent and the others are called solutes. Solutions with water as the solvent are called **aqueous** solutions. The amount of solute in relation to the amount of solvent is called its **concentration**. A solution with a small concentration of solute is called **dilute**, and a solution with a large concentration of solute is called **concentrated**.

As more solid solute particles (circles in the figure to the right) dissolve in a liquid solvent (grey background), the concentration of solute increases, and the chance that dissolved solute (grey circles) will collide with the remaining undissolved solid (white circles) also increases. A collision may result in the solute particle either bouncing off the solid or reattaching itself to the solid. If it reattaches, the process is called **crystallization**, and is the opposite of the solution process. Particles in the act of dissolving or crystallizing are half-shaded in the figure. An animation of the solution process may be found here:

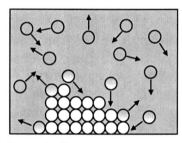

http://www.mhhe.com/physsci/chemistry/essentialchemistry/flash/molvie1.swf. } bit.ly?

Equilibrium occurs when no additional solute will dissolve because the rates of crystallization and solution are equal.

Dissolve

Solute + Solvent   ↔   **Solution**

Crystallize

A solution at equilibrium with non-dissolved solute is a **saturated** solution. The amount of solute required to form a saturated solution in a given amount of solvent is called the **solubility** of that solute. If less solute is present, the solution is called **unsaturated**. It is also possible under certain special conditions to have more solute than the equilibrium amount, resulting in a solution that is termed **supersaturated**.

Pairs of liquids that mix in all proportions are called **miscible**. Liquids that don't mix are called **immiscible**.

" mixable "

Gas solubility

Pressure does not dramatically alter the solubility of solids or liquids, but kinetic molecular theory predicts that **increasing the partial pressure of a gas will increase the solubility of the gas** in a liquid. If a substance is distributed between gas and solution phases and pressure is exerted, more gas molecules will impact the gas/liquid interface per second, so more will dissolve into the solution until a new equilibrium is reached at a higher concentration. **Henry's law** describes this relationship as a direct proportionality:

Think of:
$\uparrow T \downarrow$Sol.
$PV = nRT$ + Solubility
$\uparrow P \longleftrightarrow \uparrow$ solub.

$$\text{Solubility of gas in liquid (in } \frac{\text{mol solute}}{\text{L solution}}) \propto P_{gas}$$

Carbonated drinks are bottled under high CO_2 pressure, permitting the gas to dissolve into aqueous solution. When the bottle is opened, the partial pressure of CO_2 in the gas phase rapidly decreases to the value in the atmosphere, and the gas bubbles out of solution. When the bottle is closed again, CO_2 gas pressure builds until a saturated solution at equilibrium is again obtained. The solubility of gas in a liquid also increases in the bloodstream of deep-sea divers when they experience high pressures. If they return to atmospheric pressure too rapidly, large bubbles of nitrogen gas will form in their blood and cause a potentially lethal condition known as **the bends** or **decompression sickness**. The diver must enter a hyperbaric (high pressure) chamber to redissolve the nitrogen back into the blood.

Increasing temperature decreases the solubility of a gas in a liquid because kinetic energy opposes intermolecular attractions and permits more molecules to escape from the liquid phase. The vapor pressure of a pure liquid increases with temperature for the same reason. Greater kinetic energy will favor material in the gas phase.

Liquid and solid solubility

For solid and liquid solutes, the effects of temperature are dependent on whether the reaction absorbs heat (endothermic) or releases heat (exothermic). If a compound is dissolved in water and the solution becomes hot, the solution process is exothermic. If the solution becomes cold, the solution process is endothermic. For more on endothermic and exothermic, see Skill 2.5. The graphs show how the temperature of water may change upon the addition of an inorganic compound.

Exothermic

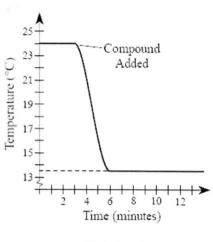

Endothermic

The energy change associated with the process in which a solute dissolves in a solvent is called the **heat of solution.** This energy change is the net result of two processes, the energy required to break the solute-solute bonds (crystal lattice energy) and the energy released when the solute particles bond with the solvent molecules (heat of hydration). For example, the heat of solution for KCl in water can be considered the sum of the two heat effects.

The crystal lattice energy of KCl, the energy necessary to break apart the KCl crystal lattice and form free ions is represented by:

$$KCl\ (s) \rightarrow K^{1+}\ (g)\ +\ Cl^{1-}\ (g) \qquad \Delta H\ =\ +\ 167.6\ kcal$$

The heat of hydration of KCl, the energy released when the free ions are hydrated, is represented by:

$$K^{1+}\ (g)\ +\ Cl^{1-}\ (g) \rightarrow K^{1+}\ (aq)\ +\ Cl^{1-}\ (aq) \qquad \Delta H\ =\ -163.5\ kcal$$

The overall reaction is endothermic, and the heat of solution is positive since more energy is required in the first step than is released by the second step.

Overall reaction: $KCl\ (s) \rightarrow K^{1+}\ (aq)\ +\ Cl^{1-}$

The following brief analysis is applicable for the effect of temperature on solutions.

Three processes occur when a solution is formed:

1) Solute particles are separated from each other, and heat is required to break these bonds.

2) Solvent particles are separated from each other to create space for solute particles, and heat is required to break these bonds also.

3) Solute and solvent particles interact with each other forming new bonds, and releasing heat.

If the heat required for the first two processes is greater than the heat released by the third, then the entire reaction may be written as an endothermic process:

$$\text{Solute} + \text{Solvent} + \text{Heat} \rightarrow \text{Solution}$$

According to Le Châtelier's principle, **solubility will increase with increasing temperature for an endothermic solution process**. This occurs for most salts in water, including NaCl. There is a large increase for potassium nitrate—KNO_3.

However, heat is released when many solutes enter solution, and the entire reaction is exothermic:

$$\text{Solute} + \text{Solvent} \rightarrow \text{Solution} + \text{Heat}$$

Solubility will decrease with increasing temperature for an exothermic solution process. This is the case for cerium(III) sulfate—$Ce_2(SO_4)_3$—in water.

Intermolecular forces in the solution process

Solutions tend to form when the intermolecular attractive forces between solute and solvent molecules are about as strong as those that exist in the solute alone or in solvent alone. NaCl dissolves in water because:

1) The water molecules interact with the Na^+ and Cl^- ions with sufficient strength to overcome the attraction between them in the crystal.
2) Na^+ and Cl^- ions interact with the water molecules with sufficient strength to overcome the attraction water molecules have for each other in the liquid.

The intermolecular attraction between solute and solvent molecules is known as **solvation**. When the solvent is water, it is known as **hydration**. The figure to the left shows a hydrated Na^+ ion.

Polar and nonpolar solutes and solvents

A nonpolar liquid like heptane (C_7H_{16}) has intermolecular bonds with relatively weak London dispersion forces. Heptane is immiscible in water because the attraction that water molecules have for each other via hydrogen bonding is strong in comparison. Unlike Na^+ and Cl^- ions, heptane molecules cannot break these bonds. Because bonds of similar strength must be broken and formed for solvation to occur, nonpolar substances tend to be soluble in nonpolar solvents, and ionic and polar substances are soluble in polar solvents like water. Polar molecules are often called **hydrophilic** and non-polar molecules are called **hydrophobic**. This observation is often stated as "**like dissolves like.**" Network solids (e.g., diamond) are soluble in neither polar nor nonpolar solvents because the covalent bonds within the solid are too strong for these solvents to break.

Electrolytes and precipitates

Compounds that are completely ionized in water are called **strong electrolytes** because these solutions easily conduct electricity. Most salts are strong electrolytes. For example, all NaCl is present in solution as ions. Other compounds (including many acids and bases) may dissolve in water without completely ionizing. These compounds are referred to as **weak electrolytes** (see **0019**) and their state of ionization is at equilibrium with the larger molecule (**0017** and **0018**). Those compounds that dissolve with no ionization (e.g., glucose, $C_6H_{12}O_6$) are called **nonelectrolytes**.

Particles in solution are free to move about and collide with each other, vastly increasing the likelihood that a reaction will occur compared with particles in a solid phase. Aqueous solutions may react to produce an insoluble substance that will fall out of solution as a solid or gas precipitate in a precipitation reaction. Aqueous solution may also react to form additional water, or a different chemical in aqueous solution.

Solubility rules for ionic compounds

Given a cation and anion in aqueous solution, we can determine if a precipitate will form according to some common solubility rules.

1) Salts with NH_4^+ or with a cation from group 1 of the periodic table are soluble in water.

2) Nitrates (NO_3^-), acetates ($C_2H_3O_2^-$), chlorates (ClO_3^-), and perchlorates (ClO_4^-) are soluble.

3) Cl^-, Br^-, and I^- salts are soluble except in the presence of Ag^+, Hg_2^{2+}, or Pb^{2+} with which they will form precipitates.

4) Sulfates (SO_4^{2-}) are soluble except in the presence of Ca^{2+}, Ba^{2+}, Ag^+, Hg_2^{2+}, or Pb^{2+}.

5) Hydroxides (OH^-) are insoluble except with cations from rule 1 or in the presence of Ca^{2+}, Sr^{2+}, or Ba^{2+}.

6) Sulfides (S^{2-}), sulfites (SO_3^{2-}), phosphates (PO_4^{3-}), and carbonates (CO_3^{2-}) are insoluble except with cations from rule 1.

Summary

The following table summarizes the impact of temperature and pressure on solubility:

	− = decrease, **0** = no/small change, **+** = increase, **++** = strong increase				
Effect on solution of an **increase** in one variable with the other constant	Gas solute in liquid solvent			Solid and liquid solutes	
	Average kinetic energy of molecules	Collisions of gas with liquid interface	Solubility	Solubility for an endothermic heat of solution	Solubility for an exothermic heat of solution
Pressure	0	++	+	0	0
Temperature	+	+	−	+	−

Skill 1.5   Evaluate problems relating colligative properties, molar mass, and solution concentrations.

A **colligative** property is a physical property of a solution that **depends on the number of solute particles present in solution** and usually not on the identity of the solutes involved. Colligative properties may be predicted by imagining ourselves shrinking down to the size of molecules in a solution and visualizing the impact of an increasing number of generic solute particles around us.

Vapor pressure lowering, boiling point elevation, freezing point lowering

After a nonvolatile solute is added to a liquid solvent, only a fraction of the molecules at a liquid-gas interface are now volatile and capable of escaping into the gas phase. The vapor consists of essentially pure solvent that is able to condense freely. This imbalance drives equilibrium away from the vapor phase and into the liquid phase and **lowers the vapor pressure** by an amount proportional to the solute particles present.

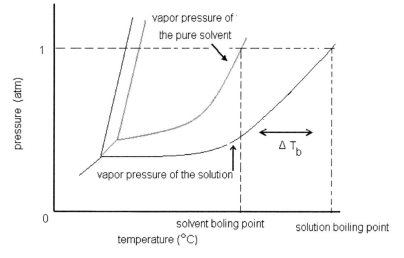

It follows from a lowered vapor pressure that a higher temperature is required for a vapor pressure equal to the external pressure over the liquid. Thus **the boiling point is raised** by an amount proportional to the solute particles present.

Solute particles in a liquid solvent are not normally soluble in the solid phase of that solvent. When solvent crystals freeze, they typically align themselves with each other to keep the solute out. This means that only a fraction of the molecules in the liquid at the liquid-solid interface are capable of freezing while the solid phase consists of essentially pure solvent that is able to melt freely. This imbalance drives equilibrium away from the solid phase and into the liquid phase and **lowers the freezing point** by an amount proportional to the solute particles present.

Boiling point elevation and freezing point depression are both caused by a lower fraction of solvent molecules in the liquid phase than in the other phase. For pure water at 1 atm there is equilibrium at the normal boiling and freezing points:

$$\text{At } 100\ ^\circ C,\ H_2O(l) \xrightleftharpoons[\text{condensation}]{\text{vaporization}} H_2O(g).$$

$$\text{At } 0\ ^\circ C,\ H_2O(l) \xrightleftharpoons[\text{melting}]{\text{freezing}} H_2O(s).$$

For water with a high solute concentration, equilibrium is not present:

$$\textbf{At } 100\ ^\circ C,\ \textbf{less interfacial } H_2O(l) \xrightleftharpoons[\text{condensation}]{\text{vaporization}} H_2O(g)$$

$$\text{At } 0\ ^\circ C,\ \text{less interfacial } H_2O(l) \xrightleftharpoons[\text{melting}]{\text{freezing}} H_2O(s).$$

Osmotic pressure

A **semipermeable membrane** is a material that permits some particles to pass through it but not others. The diagram shows a membrane that permits solvent but not solute to pass through it.

When a semipermeable membrane separates a dilute solution from a concentrated solution, the solvent flows from the dilute to the concentrated solution (i.e., from higher solvent to lower solvent concentration) in a process called **osmosis** until equilibrium is achieved.

The pressure required to prevent osmosis from a pure solvent into a solution is called **osmotic pressure**. Osmotic pressure is proportional to the molarity of the solution and thus it is a colligative property of solution. The osmotic pressure of a pure solvent is zero.

A simulation of solutes and solvent molecules interacting and an animation of osmotic flow between two flexible compartments are located here: http://physioweb.med.uvm.edu/bodyfluids/osmosis.htm.
A simulation of the osmotic pressure experiment above for NaCl, sucrose, and albumin (a protein) is found here: http://arbl.cvmbs.colostate.edu/hbooks/cmb/cells/pmemb/hydrosim.html.
Typical changes in a pressure/temperature phase diagram after adding a non-volatile solute are found here: http://chemmovies.unl.edu/ChemAnime/SOLND/SOLND.html.

Colligative Property Problems

Quantitative colligative property problems typically involve a change related to a solute concentration by a direct proportionality.

Raoult's law states that the vapor pressure of a solution with nonvolatile solutes is the mole fraction of solvent multiplied by the pure solvent vapor pressure:

$$P^{vapor}_{solution} = P^{vapor}_{pure\ solvent} \left(\text{mole fraction}\right)_{solvent}$$

Raoult's law is often used to describe the vapor pressure change from pure solvent using the solute concentration:

$$\Delta P^{vapor} = P^{vapor}_{solution} - P^{vapor}_{pure\ solvent} = P^{vapor}_{pure\ solvent}\left(\text{mole fraction}\right)_{solvent} - P^{vapor}_{pure\ solvent}$$

$$= -P^{vapor}_{pure\ solvent}\left(1 - \left(\text{mole fraction}\right)_{solvent}\right)$$

$$= -P^{vapor}_{pure\ solvent}\left(\text{mole fraction}\right)_{solute}$$

Different concentration units are used for other colligative properties to express a **change from pure solvent**. The following table summarizes these expressions for nonelectrolytes:

Colligative property	Equation for property X $\Delta X = X_{solution} - X_{pure\ solvent}$	Proportionality constant
Vapor pressure lowering	$\Delta P^{vapor} = -P^{vapor}_{pure\ solvent}\left(\text{mole fraction}\right)_{solute}$	Pure solvent vapor pressure
Boiling point elevation	$\Delta T_b = K_b\left(\text{molality}\right)$	Solvent-dependant constant K_b
Freezing point lowering	$\Delta T_f = -K_f\left(\text{molality}\right)$	Solvent-dependant constant K_f
Osmotic pressure	$P_{osmotic} = RT\left(\text{molarity}\right)$	(Gas constant) × (Temperature)

For solutions that contain electrolytes, the change from the pure solvent to solution is different from what is predicted by the above equations. Due to their ionic nature, these substances will dissociate to put many more ions in solution than their molal concentration would predict. The total number of ions affects the colligative properties just as the number of molecules would for a nonpolar solute.

The **van't Hoff factor** is an important factor in the extent of the change in boiling point or freezing point of a solution after solute has been added. The van't Hoff factor is symbolized by the lower-case letter i. It is a unitless constant directly associated with the degree of dissociation of the solute in the solvent.

This pattern continues for any number of particles into which a solute can dissociate:

Substances which do not ionize in solution, like sugar, have i = 1.
Substances which ionize into two ions, like NaCl, have i = 2.
Substances which ionize into three ions, like $MgCl_2$, have i = 3.

What this implies is exactly what van 't Hoff observed as he was compiling and examining boiling point and freezing point data. At the time, he did not understand what i meant. His use of i was strictly to try and make the data fit together.

He took a 1.0 molal aqueous solution of sugar, NaCl, and $MgCl_2$ and checked the boiling point temperature of each solution. He found that the NaCl had a boiling point elevation twice as high as that of the sugar and the $MgCl_2$ elevated the boiling point temperature three times higher than the sugar. Upon testing other substances, he found groups but he had no idea why until Svante Arrhenius' theory of electrolytic dissociation was published. The explanation seemed clear then.

Many colligative property problems compare one solution to another and may be solved without the use of the above expressions. All that is required for these comparison problems is knowledge of what the colligative properties are, how they are altered, and which solution contains the greater concentration of dissolved particles.

Example: One mole of each of the following compounds is added to water in separate flasks to make 1.0 L of solution.

> Potassium phosphate
> Silver chloride
> Sodium chloride
> Sugar (sucrose)

A. Which solution will exhibit the greatest change in the freezing point temperature?
B. Which solution will exhibit the least change in the boiling point temperature?

Be sure to explain you choices.

Solution:

Determine the molecular formulas and analyze the choices for solubility and dissociation:

Potassium phosphate	soluble in water → 4 ions K^+ PO_4^{3-}
Silver chloride	soluble in water → 2 ions Na^+ Cl^-
Sodium chloride	soluble in water → 2 ions Na^+ Cl^-
Sugar (sucrose)	soluble in water → 1 molecule (nonelectrolyte)

A. Of the choices, potassium phosphate forms the most ions so given the concentration of all of the choices is the same, K_3PO_4 will effect the boiling point temperature and the freezing point temperature the most. For every 1 mole of K_3PO_4 that dissolve, 4 moles of ions will be present in solution.

B. Sugar, a nonelectrolye, will have the least effect on the freezing point and boiling point temperatures due to the fact that it is a molecular substance and does not dissociate into ions. For every 1 mole of sugar in solution, only 1 mole of molecules will be present.

Changes to boiling point and freezing point may be determined by looking at the molal concentration of the solute, according to the equations in the table above.

Remember that a colligative property is one that depends only on the number of particles present, not their nature.

For **freezing point temperature changes**,

$$\Delta T_f = mk_f i$$

where m is the molal concentration of the solute, K_f is a constant specific to each solvent, and *i* is the number of particles or ions in solution. . For water, $K_f = -1.86\ °C/m$

For **boiling point temperature changes**,

$$\Delta T_b = mk_b i$$

where m is the molal concentration of the solute, K_b is a constant specific for each solvent and *i* is the number of particles or ions in solution. For water, $K_b = 0.52\ °C/m$

Example: How much of an increase in boiling point temperature will 31.5 grams of potassium chloride make when added to 225 g of water?

Solution:

KCl is an electrolyte so *i* = 2
Mass of water = 225 g = 0.225 kg
Mass KCl = 31.5 g, moles KCl = 0.423 mole
m = 0.423/0.225 kg = 1.88 m
$K_b = 0.52\ °C/m$

$\Delta T_b = mk_b i$
    = 1.88 m (0.56 °C/m) 2 = 1.96 °C

Example: How many grams of benzoic acid, $C_7H_6O_2$, a nonelectrolyte must be added to 178 g of water to increase the boiling point temperature 4°C?

Solution: First convert the units and identify the constants. Benzoic acid is a nonelectrolyte so $i = 1$.

Mass of water = 178 g = 0.178 kg
Molecular weight of benzoic acid = 122 g/mol
$\Delta T = 4$ °C
$K_b = 0.52$ °C/m

$\Delta T_b = mk_b i$

Rearranging the equation above and first solving for molality of benzoic acid:
$m = \Delta T_b / K_b i = 4/0.52$ °C/m (1) = 7.69 m

7.69 m = moles benzoic acid/0.178 kg water = 1.37 mole benzoic acid
Next, solve for grams of benzoic acid:

1.37 moles benzoic acid = x grams benzoic acid / 122 g/mol
167 g benzoic acid are needed.

Example: The mixture used to make ice cream does not "freeze" until the temperature reaches –15 to –18 °C. Using ice alone, the lowest temperature we can reach is 0°C. In order to reach the lower temperature needed to freeze the custard, sodium chloride, NaCl, is added to the ice. How much salt is needed to freeze the ice cream?

Solution: Each sodium chloride particle dissociates into a Na^+ ion and a Cl^- ion, making two solvated ions present for every one NaCl particle present. So, NaCl has an *i* value of 2.

The temperature change needed is -15°C and the K_f value for water is –1.86 °C/*m*.

Using the freezing point depression expression we can determine the *molality* of the salt-ice solution that will reach –15°C.

$\Delta T = K_f\, m\, i$ and rearranging

$$m = \frac{\Delta T}{K_f\, i} = \frac{-15°\ C}{-1.86°\ C/m \times 2} = 4.0\ m$$

Remember that $m = \frac{\text{\# moles solute}}{}$ so the moles of NaCl can be determined if we know the kilograms of ice used. In this case, 1 bag of ice is about 2.3 kg. So the number of moles of NaCl needed would be:

\# moles solute = *m* (kg solute) = 4.0 *mol/kg* (2.3 kg) = 9.3 mol of NaCl.

Now, the mass of NaCl needed can be found by using the relationship between moles and molar mass: \# mol = mass/ Molar Mass

In this case, mass = \# mol (Molar Mass) = 9.3 mol (58.5 g/mol) or about 544 g of NaCl is needed for every bag of ice used.

The most common errors in solving all types of colligative property problems arise from considering some value other than **the number of particles in solution**. Remember that one mole of glucose(*aq*) forms one mole of hydrated particles, but one mole of NaCl(*aq*) forms two moles of hydrated particles, and one mole of $Al_2(SO_4)_3$ (*aq*) forms five moles of them. We would expect a 0.5 M solution of glucose to have roughly the same colligative properties as a 0.25 M solution of sodium hydroxide and a 0.1 M solution of aluminum sulfate. Also remember that undissolved solids do not contribute to colligative properties.

Skill 1.6   Analyze the effects of forces between chemical species on properties (e.g., melting point, boiling point, vapor pressure, solubility, conductivity) of matter.

The impact of intermolecular forces on substances is best understood by imagining ourselves shrinking down to the size of molecules and picturing what happens when we stick more strongly to molecules nearby. It will take more energy (higher temperatures) to pull us away from our neighbors.

If two substances are being compared, the material with the **greater intermolecular attractive forces** (i.e. the stronger intermolecular bond) will have the following properties relative to the other substance:

For solids:
Higher melting point
Higher enthalpy of fusion
Greater hardness
Lower vapor pressure

For liquids :
Higher boiling point
Higher critical temperature
Higher critical pressure
Higher enthalpy of vaporization
Higher viscosity
Higher surface tension
Lower vapor pressure

For gases:
Intermolecular attractive forces are neglected for ideal gases.

Vapor Pressure

When a liquid is placed in an open container or a closed container that is not

entirely filled, there are always some molecules at the surface of the liquid (e.g., the half-shaded molecules to the left of the diagram) which have enough kinetic energy to overcome the attraction of their neighbors and escape into the gas above the liquid. This process is known as **evaporation**. In a closed container, these gas molecules develop a pressure until a dynamic equilibrium - the rate of their return to 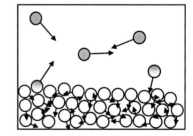 the liquid phase by **condensation** (e.g., the half-shaded molecule on the right in the diagram) equals the rate of their escape by evaporation - is achieved:

Evaporation

Liquid   ↔   **Vapor**

Condensation

At equilibrium, the partial pressure of the substance in the gas phase is at its **saturated vapor pressure**. Solids are also in equilibrium with vapor and have a saturated vapor pressure. There is no real difference between the terms *gas* and *vapor*, but *gas* is often used to describe a substance that appears in the gaseous state under standard temperature and pressure and *vapor* is normally used to describe the gaseous state of a substance that is ordinarily a liquid or solid at standard temperature and pressure.

A dynamic equilibrium consists of two **opposing reversible processes** that both occur at the **same rate**. *Balance* is a synonym for equilibrium. A system at equilibrium is stable; it does not change with time. Equilibria are drawn with a double arrow.

The saturated vapor pressure of a liquid is often simply called its **vapor pressure**. This term can sometimes lead to confusion when equilibrium is not present, but equilibrium is usually assumed.

An increase in temperature raises vapor pressure (making the liquid more **volatile**) because kinetic energy opposes intermolecular attractions and permits more molecules to escape from the liquid phase. See previous skills for a discussion of the kinetic theory and **Skill 2.3** for information on phase changes.

More information on vapor pressure may be found at: http://hyperphysics.phy-astr.gsu.edu/hbase/kinetic/vappre.html. A flash animation of liquid/vapor equilibrium showing how vapor pressure is measured is located at: http://www.mhhe.com/physsci/chemistry/essentialchemistry/flash/vaporv3.swf.

Surface Tension

There are very few molecules in the gas phase and so the intermolecular attractive force pulling a surface molecule (labeled in the diagram) towards that direction is very weak, but there are many molecules with intermolecular attractive forces in the liquid phase. This leads to an imbalance of forces and it makes the surface molecule stick to the liquid molecules nearby more strongly. There is a net inwards pull away from the interface to minimize its surface area. This is not the case for molecules in the interior of the liquid where the forces are balanced. **Surface tension** is the energy required to increase the surface area of a liquid by a unit amount. Because of surface tension, friction exists at the liquid-gas interface that makes it more difficult to move a solid object through the surface than to move it when it's completely submerged. It is as if there is a "film" at the interface that makes it more difficult for a solid object to "break through" the surface than to move around when it's already completely submerged.

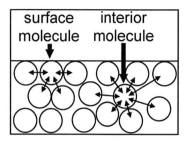

An increase in temperature decreases the surface tension because the kinetic energy acts in opposition to the intermolecular attractive forces. Chemicals with strong intermolecular attractive forces have a high surface tension. Surface tension can also be altered by adding other substances. For example, NaOH added to water will raise its surface tension, and soap added to water lowers surface tension (because the soap acts as a surfactant).

Boiling Point as a Function of Pressure

For a liquid in an open container, vapor pressure increases with temperature until the vapor pressure is equal to the external pressure, and the boiling point occurs at that temperature. Boiling is defined as the process of vapor bubbles forming and escaping from the liquid by breaking the intermolecular attractive forces within the liquid. Substances with stronger intermolecular attractive forces have a higher boiling point. An increase in the surrounding pressure forces molecules closer together and increases their intermolecular attractive forces. More kinetic energy is then required to break these bonds, so the boiling point of a liquid increases with increases in pressure.

Critical Point

See **Skill 2.3** for phase diagrams and a complete discussion on phase changes and the critical point. Rising temperature at a gas-liquid interface increases vapor pressure and decreases surface tension. All the liquid will become a gas if left at the boiling point long enough, but if the external pressure is increased above the vapor pressure, some material will remain in the liquid phase and the boiling point will increase. A pressure cooker is a good example of this. Finally, however, a temperature is reached at which no amount of pressure will keep the material in a liquid state. The highest temperature at which a substance can exist as a liquid is its **critical temperature**. **Critical pressure** is the vapor pressure of a liquid at its critical temperature. Surface tension shrinks to zero and there is no longer a gas-liquid interface when critical conditions are reached.

Above its critical temperature and pressure, a substance takes the shape and fills the volume of its container like a gas, but it has a density and intermolecular attractive forces similar to a liquid. This phase is called a **supercritical fluid**. Like liquids and gases, they are able to flow from one place to another.

Summary

The following table summarizes the properties of a liquid as temperature and pressure are altered. The speed and kinetic energy of molecules are only dependent on temperature as discussed in **0007**.

Effect on a liquid of an **increase** in one variable with the other constant	– = decrease, **0** = no change, **+** = increase, **NA**=not applicable					
	Average speed of molecules	Average translational kinetic energy of molecules	Viscosity	Vapor pressure	Surface tension	Boiling point
Temperature	+	+	–	+	–	NA
External pressure	0	0	+/–[1]	NA[2]	NA[2]	+

[1]A slight increase for most materials but a slight decrease for water at some temperatures.
[2]Not applicable. For a pure substance in a closed container at equilibrium, external pressure forces more vapor into the liquid phase. The volume of each phase is altered but conditions at the interface remain unchanged.

Skill 1.7   Solve problems involving an intensive property (e.g., density, specific heat) of matter.

An **intensive property** is one that is independent of the amount of matter present in a sample. Some examples of intensive physical properties include density, specific heat, viscosity, malleability, conductivity, melting point temperature, and boiling point temperature. Luster is a shine like steel or silver. Conductivity is a measure of how well heat and electricity pass through the matter. A substance that is ductile can be drawn into wire while one that is malleable can be hammered into thin sheets.

Density

Density is a physical property that can be used to help identify a substance. If the density of an object is less than the density of a liquid, the object will float in the liquid. If the object is denser than the liquid, then the object will sink. Density (ρ) is defined as mass per unit volume. Density is calculated by dividing the mass of an object by its volume. This is shown in equation form, as follows:

Density = mass / volume

The unit for density is grams/cubic centimeters for solids and grams/ milliliters for liquids and gases.

To discover an object's density, first use a balance to find its mass. Then calculate its volume. If the object is a regular shape, you can find the volume by multiplying the length, width, and height together. However, if it is an irregular shape, you can find the volume by seeing how much water it displaces. Measure the water in the container before and after the object is submerged. The difference will be the volume of the object.

Example: A sample of kerosene has a mass of 36.4 g. Its volume is measured to be 45.6 mL. What is the density of the kerosene?

Solution: ρ=M/V   36.4 g/45.6 mL= 0.80 g/mL

Example: What is the volume in cubic meters of a femur (thigh bone) with a mass of 1.18 kg? The density of bone is 1.8 kg/m^3.

Solution: Volume= mass/density   or   1.18 kg / 1.8 kg/m^3= 0.66 m^3

Viscosity

Viscosity measures the ability of a liquid to flow. Liquids with high viscosity flow less easily because they have strong intermolecular forces relative to kinetic energy. The viscosity of liquids decreases with temperature because it is easier for rapidly moving molecules to flow into the spaces between them. For most liquids (water is an exception), viscosity increases with pressure because the molecules are squeezed together forcing a greater interaction, but this dependence is not as strong as the dependence on temperature.

Specific Heat

A substance's molar **heat capacity** is the heat required to **change the temperature of one mole of the substance by one degree**. Heat capacity has units of joules per mol-kelvin or joules per mol-°C. The two units are interchangeable because we are only concerned with differences between one temperature and another. A Kelvin degree and a Celsius are the same size.

The **specific heat** of a substance (also called specific heat capacity) is the heat required to **change the temperature of one gram or kilogram by one degree.** Specific heat has units of joules per gram or joules per kilogram.

These terms are used to solve thermochemistry problems involving a change in temperature by applying the formula:

A substance's **enthalpy of fusion** (ΔH_{fusion}) is the heat required to **change a substance from a solid to a liquid** by freezing. This is also the heat released from the substance when it changes from a liquid to a solid (melts).

$q = n \times C \times \Delta T$ where $q \Rightarrow$ heat added (positive) or evolved (negative)

$\qquad n \Rightarrow$ amount of material

$\qquad C \Rightarrow$ molar heat capacity if n is in moles, specific heat if n is a mass

$\qquad \Delta T \Rightarrow$ change in temperature $T_{final} - T_{initial}$

A substance's **enthalpy of vaporization** ($\Delta H_{vaporization}$) is the heat required to **change a substance from a liquid to a gas** or the heat released by condensation.

A substance's **enthalpy of sublimation** ($\Delta H_{sublimation}$) is the heat required to change the substance directly from a solid to a gas by sublimation or the heat released by deposition (transition from gas to solid).

These three values are also called "heats" or "latent heats" of fusion, vaporization, and sublimation. They have units of joules per mole, and are negative values when heat is released.

$$\text{Solid} \xrightarrow[\text{melting}]{\Delta H_{fusion}} \text{Liquid} \xrightarrow[\text{vaporization}]{\Delta H_{vaporization}} \text{Gas} \qquad \text{Solid} \xrightarrow[\text{sublimation}]{\Delta H_{sublimation}} \text{Gas}$$

$$\text{Gas} \xrightarrow[\text{condensation}]{-\Delta H_{vaporization}} \text{Liquid} \xrightarrow[\text{freezing}]{-\Delta H_{fusion}} \text{Solid} \qquad \text{Gas} \xrightarrow[\text{deposition}]{-\Delta H_{sublimation}} \text{Solid}$$

These terms are used to solve thermochemistry problems involving a change of phase by applying the formula:

$$q = n \times \Delta H_{change}$$

where $q \Rightarrow$ heat added (positive) or evolved (negative)

$\quad$ $n \Rightarrow$ amount of material

$\Delta H_{change} \Rightarrow$ enthalpy of fusion, vaporization, or sublimation for heat added

$\quad\quad \Rightarrow -$(enthalpy of fusion, vaporization, or sublimation) for heat evolved

Example: What is the change in energy of 10 g of gold at 25 °C when it is heated beyond its melting point to 1300 °C. You will need the following data for gold:

Solid heat capacity: 28 J/mol-K

Molten heat capacity: 20 J/mol-K

Enthalpy of fusion: 12.6 kJ/mol

Melting point: 1064 °C

Solution: First determine the number of moles used: $10 \text{ g} \times \dfrac{1 \text{ mol}}{197 \text{ g}} = 0.051 \text{ mol}$.

There are then three steps. 1) Heat the solid. 2) Melt the solid. 3) Heat the liquid. All three require energy so they will be positive numbers.

1) Heat the solid:

$$q_1 = n \times C \times \Delta T = 0.051 \text{ mol} \times 28 \ \frac{\text{J}}{\text{mol-K}} \times (1064 \ °C - 25 \ °C)$$

$$= 1.48 \times 10^3 \text{ J} = 1.48 \text{ kJ}$$

2) Melt the solid: $q_2 = n \times \Delta H_{fusion} = 0.051 \text{ mol} \times 12.6 \ \dfrac{\text{kJ}}{\text{mol}}$

$$= 0.64 \text{ kJ}$$

3) Heat the liquid:

$$q_3 = n \times C \times \Delta T = 0.051 \, \text{mol} \times 20 \frac{J}{\text{mol-K}} \times (1300 \, °C - 1064 \, °C)$$

$$= 2.4 \times 10^2 \, J = 0.24 \, kJ$$

The sum of the three processes is the total change in energy of the gold:

$$q = q_1 + q_2 + q_3 = 1.48 \, kJ + 0.64 \, kJ + 0.24 \, kJ = 2.36 \, kJ$$

$$= 2.4 \, kJ$$

Skill 1.8   Differentiate physical methods (e.g., chromatography, filtration, extraction) for separating the components of mixtures.

A mixture consists of two or more substances that when put together retain their individual physical and chemical properties. That is, no new substances are formed. Differences in physical and chemical properties of the components of the mixture can be used to separate the mixture. For example, salt and pepper have different colors and can be separated by physically moving the white crystals away from the dark particles. Alternatively, we could make use of the fact that salt dissolves in water while pepper does not. The salt and pepper could be separated by adding water to the mixture; the salt will dissolve while the pepper will float on top of the water. Skim off the pepper and then evaporate the water. The salt and pepper are now separated.

Common methods for separating mixtures include filtration, chromatography, distillation and extraction. **Filtering** relies on one of the substances being soluble in the solvent, and the other(s) being insoluble. The soluble substance ends up in the **filtrate** (the liquid that passes through the filter paper). The insoluble substance ends up in the filter paper as the **residue**.

solvent

filter paper

filter funnel

residue or insolubile solid

filtrate
soluble solid dissolved in solvent

Distillation and **fractional distillation** rely on the fact that the liquids in the mixture are different. Each liquid has its own unique **boiling point**. As the temperature rises, it reaches the lowest boiling point liquid and so this liquid boils. The temperature remains at that temperature until all of the liquid has boiled away. The vapor passes into a condenser and is cooled and so turns back into a liquid. The pure liquid is now in a different part of the apparatus and rolls down into a test tube. This liquid has been separated from the mixture.

Chromatography is a technique that is used to separate mixtures based on differential migration. Differential migration uses differences in physical properties such as solubility, molecular size and polarity to separate the substance. The mixture is placed in a solution, which becomes the mobile phase. This solution then passes over a stationary phase.

Different components of the mixture travel at different rates. After the separation, the time that component took to emerge from the instrument (or its location within the stationary phase) is found with a detector. These chromatographic separations have many different types of stationary phases including paper, silica on glass or plastic plates (thin-layer chromatography), volatile gases (gas chromatography) and liquids, (liquid chromatography including column and high-performance liquid chromatography or HPLC) as well as gels (electrophoresis).

The result is a **chromatogram** like the one shown below. The **identity of an unknown** peak can be found by comparing its location on the chromatogram to standards. The **concentration** of a component can also found using signal strength or peak area by comparison to calibration curves of known concentrations.

In **paper chromatography** and **thin layer chromatography (TLC)**, the sample rises up by capillary action through a solid phase.

In **gas chromatography (GC)**, the sample is vaporized and forced through a column filled with a packing material. GC is often used to separate and determine the concentration of **low molecular weight volatile organic** compounds.

In **liquid chromatography (LC)**, the sample is a liquid. It is either allowed to seep through an open column using the force of gravity or it is forced through a closed column under pressure. The variations of liquid chromatography depend on the identity of the packing material. For example, an ion-exchange liquid chromatograph contains a material with a charged surface. The mixture components with the opposite charge interact with this packing material and spend more time in the column. LC is often used to separate **large organic polymers** like proteins.

Each component in the mixture can be identified by its retention factor or retention time once it has been separated. Both retention factor, R_f, and retention time are quantitative indications of how far a particular compound travels in a particular solvent or how long the component is retained on the column before eluting with the mobile phase (for gas chromatography and liquid chromatography). By comparing the R_f of the components in the mixture to known values for substances, identification of the components in the mixture can be achieved.

R_f = distance the component color traveled from the point of application / distance the solvent front traveled from the point of application

Extraction is a method typically used to separate the desired product from impurities. This process, then, makes use of differences is solubilities to separate components in what is called a work-up. The work-up is a planned sequence of extracting and washing.

distances mixture components traveled

distance solvent front traveled

origin of mixture

The planning involves determining the two solvents. One is usually water, the aqueous layer, while the other is an organic solvent, the organic layer. The important feature here is that the two solvents are immiscible and the mixture is the partition between the two solvents. The mixture is then separated as its components are attracted to the solvents differently. Most charged particles and inorganic salts will move towards the aqueous layer and dissolve in it, while the neutral organic molecules will move towards the organic layer.

separatory funnel

two immiscible layers

collection flask

14% COMPETENCY 2.0 **KNOWLEDGE OF ENERGY AND ITS INTERACTION WITH MATTER**

"Energy is an abstract concept invented by physical scientists in the nineteenth century to describe quantitatively a wide variety of natural phenomena."
- David Rose, MIT

Skill 2.1 **Distinguish between different forms of energy (e.g., thermal, electrical, nuclear).**

Abstract concept it might be, but energy is one of the most fundamental concepts in our world. We use it to move people and things from place to place, to heat and light our homes, to entertain us, to produce food and goods and to communicate with each other. It is not some sort of magical invisible fluid, poured, weighed or bottled.

Technically, **energy is the ability to do work or supply heat.** Work is the transfer of energy to move an object a certain distance. It is the motion against an opposing force. Lifting a chair into the air is work; the opposing force is gravity. Pushing a chair across the floor is work; the opposing force is friction.

Heat, on the other hand, is a form of energy transfer.

This energy, according to the **First Law of Thermodynamics**, is conserved. That means **energy is neither created nor destroyed in ordinary physical and chemical processes (non-nuclear).** Energy is merely changed from one form to another. Energy in all of its forms must be conserved. In any system, $\Delta E = q + w$ (E = energy, q = heat and w = work).

Potential Energy

Kinetic Energy

Energy exists in two basic forms, potential and kinetic. Kinetic energy is the energy of a moving object. Potential energy is the energy stored in matter due to position relative to other objects.

In any object, solid, liquid or gas, the atoms and molecules that make up the object are constantly moving (vibrational, translation and rotational motion) and colliding with each other. They are not stationary.

Due to this motion, the object's particles have varying amounts of kinetic energy. A fast moving atom can push a slower moving atom during a collision, so it has energy. All moving objects have energy and that energy depends on the object's mass and velocity. Kinetic energy is calculated: $K.E. = \frac{1}{2}mv^2$, where m=mass of the object and v= velocity of the object.

The temperature of an object is proportional to the average kinetic energy of the particles in the substance. Increase the temperature of a substance and its particles move faster so their average kinetic energies increase as well. But temperature is NOT an energy, it is not conserved.

The energy an object has due to its position or arrangement of its parts is called potential energy. Potential energy due to position is equal to the mass of the object times the gravitational pull on the object times the height of the object, or:

$$PE = mgh$$

Where PE = potential energy; m = mass of object; g = gravity; and h = height.

Heat is energy that is transferred between objects caused by differences in their temperatures. Heat passes spontaneously from an object of higher temperature to one of lower temperature. This transfer continues until both objects reach the same temperature. Both kinetic energy and potential energy can be transformed into heat energy. When you step on the brakes in your car, the kinetic energy of the car is changed to heat energy by friction between the brake and the wheels. Other transformations can occur from kinetic to potential as well. Since most of the energy in our world is in a form that is not easily used, man has developed some clever ways of changing one form of energy into another form that may be more useful.

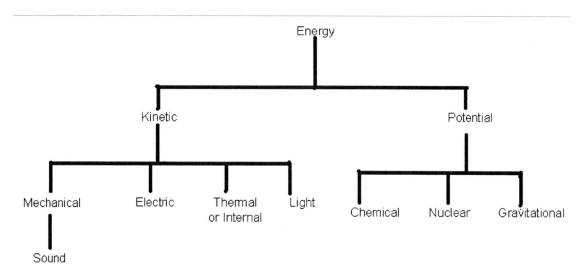

Gravitational Potential Energy

When something is lifted or suspended in air, work is done on the object against the pull of gravity. This work is converted to a form of potential energy called gravitational potential energy.

Nuclear Potential Energy

The energy trapped inside the atom is referred to as nuclear energy. When the atom is split, tremendous energy is released in the form of heat and light.

Chemical Potential Energy

The energy generated from chemical reactions in which the chemical bonds of a substance are broken and rearranged to form new substances is called chemical potential energy.

Electrical Kinetic Energy

The flow of electrons along a circuit is called electrical energy. The movement of electrons creates an electric current which gives us electricity.

Mechanical Kinetic Energy

Mechanical energy is the energy of motion doing work, like a pendulum moving back and forth in a grandfather clock.

Thermal Kinetic Energy

Thermal energy is defined as the energy that a substance has due to the chaotic motion of its molecules. Molecules are in constant motion, and always possess some amount of kinetic energy. It is also called Internal energy and is not the same as heat.

Light or Radiant Kinetic Energy

Radiant energy comes from a light source, such as the sun. Energy released from the sun is in the form of photons. These tiny particles, invisible to the human eye, move in a way similar to a wave.

Energy transformations make it possible for us to use energy to do work. Here are some examples of how energy is transformed to do work:

1. Different types of stoves are used to transform the chemical energy of the fuel (gas, coal, wood, etc.) into heat.

2. Solar collectors can be used to transform solar energy into electrical energy.

3. Wind mills make use of the kinetic energy of the air molecules, transforming it into mechanical or electrical energy.

4. Hydroelectric plants transform the kinetic energy of falling water into electrical energy.

5. A flashlight converts chemical energy stored in batteries to light energy and heat. Most of the energy is converted to heat, only a small amount is actually changed into light energy.

Skill 2.2 Relate temperature and heat to kinetic molecular theory.

Kinetic molecular theory says that the particles of a substance are in constant random motion. What causes this motion? Energy.

Heat energy is absorbed by atoms and molecules making up a substance that causes the atoms and molecules to move more. In the solid state, the motion is little more than a vibration. In melting; this vibration separates the atoms from each other, moving them apart, decreasing the force of attraction between the atoms or molecules, causing a phase change to liquid. As a liquid, the molecules still have attractive forces acting between them. The addition of more heat forces the atoms or molecules farther apart, weakening the forces to the point where they can no longer keep the atoms or molecules together. The substance has entered the gas phase.

How is the heat energy of the molecule measured? No device will measure heat energy directly. However, a property called **temperature** can give us an idea of the heat energy of the atoms or molecules.

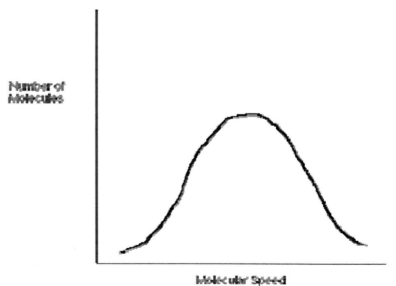

Temperature does not measure the individual temperature of the molecules but rather how fast the molecules are moving (kinetic energy) which is tied to the heat possessed by the molecules.

A thermometer in a beaker of water will determine the 'temperature' of the water. Place the beaker on a hot plate and slowly allow the 'heat' to increase, the 'temperature' increases. Place the beaker in ice water, the 'temperature' decreases. Why does the thermometer respond this way?

As heat energy is added to a system, the matter absorbs the heat. This increased heat causes the atoms or molecules to move more (increase of kinetic energy). Each water molecule has a kinetic energy equal to $1/2 \; m \cdot v^2$.

As the molecules move about they will bump into one another, the walls of the beaker and the thermometer. Some of the energy they possess is transferred to the bulb of the thermometer. The energy is transferred to the glass and, somehow, gets to the liquid inside the thermometer. The liquid is made of molecules. The increased energy of the molecules causes them to move faster and increase the liquid's volume. With only one place to go the liquid moves up through the space in the stem. The thermometer can't measure the individual energy of one molecule. It responds to all the molecules striking it. Some are moving faster than others. The observed temperature is the average kinetic energy of all the molecules striking the thermometer. The **temperature** of the water is a **measure of the average kinetic energy** of the water molecules involved in the process. How did the molecules get their kinetic energy? Heat.

The kinetic energy of molecules is unaltered during phase changes, but the freedom of molecules to move relative to one another increases dramatically. The following table summarizes the application of kinetic molecular theory to the addition of heat to ice, first changing it to liquid water and then to water vapor.

Effect at 1 atm of the addition of heat to:	0 = no change, + = increase, ++ = strong increase			
	Temperature	Average speed of molecules	Average translational kinetic energy of molecules	Intermolecular freedom of motion
Ice at less than 0 °C	+	+	+	+
Ice at 0 °C	0	0	0	++ (melting)
Liquid water at 0 °C	+	+	+	+
Liquid water at 100 °C	0	0	0	++ (boiling)
Water vapor at 100 °C	+	+	+	0 (complete freedom for an ideal gas)

Technically, heat is the measure of the internal energy gained or lost when two objects come in contact with one another and the temperature difference between the two objects is the measure of heat since it can not be directly determined.

The heat lost or gained is what is calculated.

$$Heat\ Loss = Heat\ Gained$$

$$m_{loss} \cdot c_{loss} \cdot \Delta T_{loss} = m_{gain} \cdot c_{gain} \cdot \Delta T_{gain}$$

where m= mass of substance undergoing temperature change,
c= heat capacity (specific heat) of the substance undergoing temperature change
and ΔT = change in temperature.

Skill 2.3   **Interpret a phase diagram of a pure substance.**

A **phase diagram** is a graphical way to summarize the conditions under which the different states of a substance are stable. The diagram is divided into three areas representing each state of the substance. The curves separating each area represent the boundaries of phase changes

Below is a typical phase diagram. It consists of three curves that divide the diagram into regions labeled "solid, liquid, and gas".

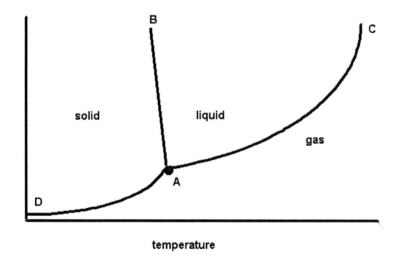

Curve **AB**, dividing the solid region from the liquid region, represents the conditions under which the solid and liquid are in equilibrium. Usually, the melting point is only slightly affected by pressure. For this reason, the melting point curve, AB, is nearly vertical.

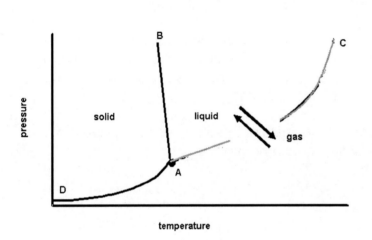

Curve **AC**, which divides the liquid region from the gaseous region, represents the boiling points of the liquid for various pressures.

Curve **AD**, which divides the solid region from the gaseous region, represents the vapor pressures of the solid at various temperatures.

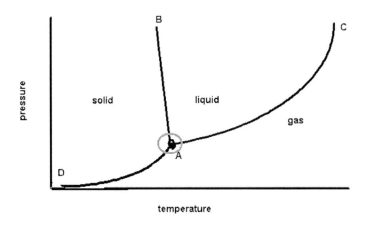

The curves intersect at **A**, the **triple point**, which is the temperature and pressure where three phases of a substance exist in equilibrium.

The temperature above which the liquid state of a substance no longer exists regardless of pressure is called the **critical temperature**.

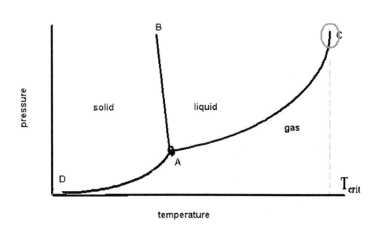

The vapor pressure at the critical temperature is called the **critical pressure**. Note that curve AC ends at the **critical point, C.**

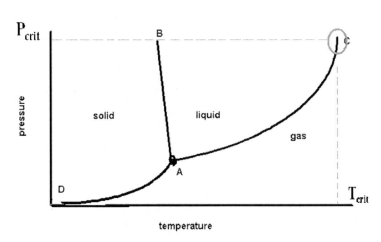

The phase diagram for water (shown on this page) is unusual. The solid/liquid phase boundary slopes to the left with increasing pressure because the melting point of water decreases with increasing pressure. Note that the normal melting point of water is lower than its triple point. The diagram is not drawn to a uniform scale. Many anomalous properties of water are discussed here: http://www.lsbu.ac.uk/water/anmlies.html.

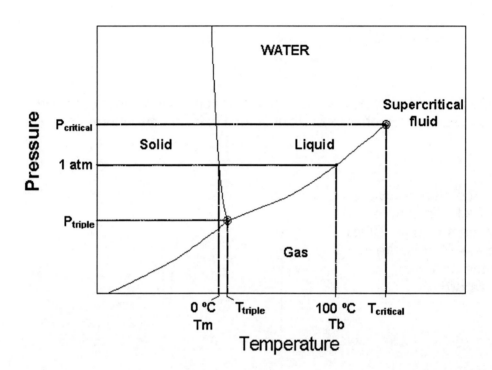

Normal melting point (T_m) and **normal boiling point** (T_b) are defined at 1 atm. Note that freezing point and melting point refer to an identical temperature approached from different directions, but they represent the same concept.

Solid lines dividing these regions are located at conditions under which two phases may exist at equilibrium and a phase change may occur. All three phases may coexist at the **triple point** of a substance. **Vapor pressure** at a given temperature is the pressure of the phase transition line to a gas at that temperature. **Normal melting point** (T_m) and **normal boiling point** (T_b) are defined at 1 atm. Note that freezing point and melting point refer to an identical temperature approached from different directions, but they represent the same concept. At temperatures and pressures above the **critical point**, the substance becomes too dense with too much kinetic energy for a gas-liquid interface to form. Matter under these conditions forms a **supercritical fluid** with properties of gases and of liquids.

This is the phase diagram for carbon dioxide, CO_2. It shows the same features, only at different temperatures and pressures.

The triple point pressure of CO_2 is greater than 1 atm, so dry ice sublimates at atmospheric pressure with no liquid phase.

Skill 2.4 Interpret a heating/cooling curve of a substance.

Kinetic models are used to describe gases, liquids, and solids. **Phase changes** occur when the relative importance of kinetic energy and intermolecular forces is altered sufficiently for a substance to change its state. See Skill 2.3.

The transition from gas to liquid is called **condensation** and from liquid to gas is called **vaporization**. The transition from liquid to solid is called **freezing** and from solid to liquid is called **melting**. The transition from gas to solid is called **deposition** and from solid to gas is called **sublimation**.

Heat removed from a substance during condensation, freezing, or deposition permits new intermolecular bonds to form, and heat added to a substance during vaporization, melting, or sublimation breaks intermolecular bonds. During these phase transitions, this **latent heat** is removed or added with **no change in the temperature** of the substance because the heat is not being used to alter the speed of the molecules or the kinetic energy when they strike each other or the container walls. Latent heat alters intermolecular bonds.

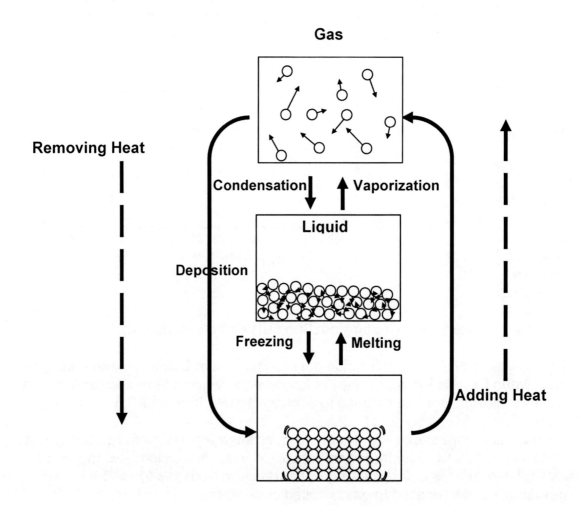

If a time graph was made of a pure substance being heated or cooled, it would look something like the following graph for the heating of water and be called a heating curve for water.

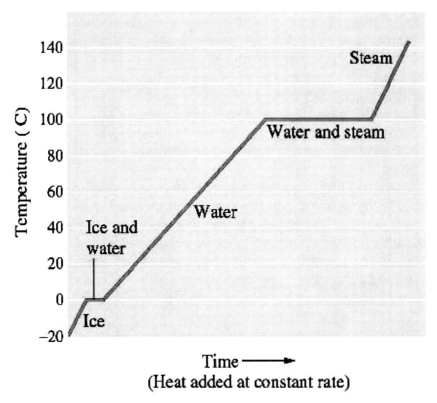

Time ————▶
(Heat added at constant rate)

Different changes are taking place during each interval on the graph.

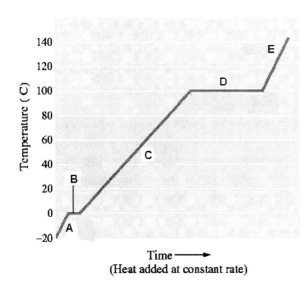

Time ————▶
(Heat added at constant rate)

When the system is heated, energy is transferred into it. In response to the energy it receives, the system changes, for example by increasing its temperature.

During the interval marked A on the graph, energy is being absorbed by the water molecules to increase the temperature to water's melting point, 0°C. The slope of the line for this interval shows the increase in temperature and is related to the heat capacity of the substance.

During the interval marked B on the graph, energy is still being added to the water but the temperature remains the same, at 0°C or water's melting point temperature. The additional energy is being used to overcome the intermolecular forces holding the water molecules in their solid pattern. This energy is moving the particles apart, breaking or weakening the forces of attraction trying to keep the water molecules aligned. The solid water (ice) is being converted to liquid water; a phase change is occurring. The temperature will not increase until every solid particle has melted and the entire sample is liquid.

Temperature again increases during interval C on the graph. Energy is being absorbed by the liquid water molecules. Notice that the slope of the line during this interval is different than the slope of the line during interval A. Again, this is due to differences in the heat capacity of ice and liquid water.

The flat line during interval D indicates that a phase change is occurring here. The additional energy is being used to overcome the attractive forces holding the liquid water molecules together. The water molecules increase their kinetic energies and move farther apart, changing to water vapor molecules. This occurs at the boiling point temperature, or 100°C in the case of water. The temperature stays at the boiling point temperature until all water molecules are converted to vapor molecules.

Once this conversion occurs, the temperature increases as energy is added, reflective of the heat capacity of the substance as a vapor.

Skill 2.5   Calculate thermal changes in chemical reactions, such as heats of reaction, heats of formation, and/or heats of combustion, from data.

Energy is the **driving force for change**. Energy has units of joules (J). Temperature remains constant during phase changes, so the **speed** of molecules and their **translational kinetic energy do not change** during a change in phase.

The **internal energy** of a material is the **sum of the total kinetic energy** of its molecules and the **potential energy** of interactions between those molecules. Total kinetic energy includes the contributions from translational motion and other components of motion such as rotation. The potential energy includes **energy stored in the form of resisting intermolecular attractions** between molecules.

The **enthalpy** (*H*) of a material is the **sum of its internal energy and the mechanical work** it can do by driving a piston. We usually don't deal with mechanical work in high school chemistry, so the differences between internal energy and enthalpy are not important. The key concept is that a change in the **enthalpy** of a substance is the total **energy** change caused by **adding/removing heat** at constant pressure.

When a material is heated and experiences a phase change, **thermal energy is used to break the intermolecular bonds** holding the material together. Similarly, bonds are formed with the release of thermal energy when a material changes its phase during cooling. Therefore, **the energy of a material increases during a phase change that requires heat and decreases during a phase change that releases heat**. For example, the energy of H_2O increases when ice melts and decreases when water freezes.

Hess's law states that energy changes are state functions. The amount of energy depends only on the states of the reactants and the state of the products, but not on the intermediate steps. Energy (enthalpy) changes in chemical reactions are the same, regardless whether the reactions occur in one or several steps. The total energy change in a chemical reaction is the sum of the energy changes in its many steps leading to the overall reaction.

A **standard** thermodynamic value occurs with all components at 25 °C and 100 kPa. This *thermodynamic standard state* is slightly different from the *standard temperature and pressure* (STP) often used for gas law problems (0 °C and 1 atm=101.325 kPa). Standard properties of common chemicals are listed in tables.

The **heat of formation, ΔH_f**, of a chemical is the heat required (positive) or emitted (negative) when elements react to form the chemical. It is also called the enthalpy of formation. The **standard heat of formation $\Delta H_f°$** is the heat of formation with all reactants and products at 25 °C and 100 kPa.

Elements in their **most stable form** are assigned a value of $\Delta H_f° = 0$ kJ/mol. Different forms of an element in the same phase of matter are known as **allotropes**.

Example: The heat of formation for carbon as a gas is:

$\Delta H_f°$ for $C(g) = 718.4 \ \dfrac{kJ}{mol}$. Carbon in the solid phase exists in three

allotropes. A C_{60} *buckyball* (one face is shown to the left), contains C atoms linked with aromatic bonds and arranged in the shape of a soccer ball. C_{60} was discovered in 1985. *Diamonds* (below left) contains single C–C bonds in a three dimensional network. The most stable form at 25 °C is *graphite* (below right). Graphite is composed of C atoms with aromatic bonds in sheets.

$\Delta H_f°$ for C_{60}(*buckminsterfullerene or buckyball*) $= 38.0 \ \dfrac{kJ}{mol}$

$\Delta H_f°$ for C_{∞} (*diamond*) $= 1.88 \ \dfrac{kJ}{mol}$

$\Delta H_f°$ for C_{∞} (*graphite*) $= 0 \ \dfrac{kJ}{mol}$.

Heat of combustion ΔH_c (also called enthalpy of combustion) is the heat of reaction when a chemical **burns in O_2** to form completely oxidized products such as **CO_2 and H_2O**. It is also the heat of reaction for **nutritional molecules that are metabolized** in the body. The standard heat of combustion ΔH_c° takes place at 25 °C and 100 kPa. **Combustion is always exothermic**, so the negative sign for values of ΔH_c is often omitted. If a combustion reaction is used in Hess's Law, the value must be negative.

The **standard molar entropy**, S°, is the absolute entropy of a chemical at 1 atm and 25 °C. The molar entropy of a substance is expressed in units of J/mol-K. (See Skill 2.6)

Chemical energy is an important source of energy. It is the energy stored in substances by virtue of the arrangement of atoms within the substance. When atoms are rearranged during chemical reactions, energy is either released or consumed. It is the energy released from chemical reactions that fuel our economy and power our bodies. Most of the electricity produced comes from chemical energy released by the burning of petroleum, coal and natural gas. ATP is the molecule used by our body to carry chemical energy form cell to cell.

The energy found in molecules is found in the bonds between the atoms in the molecule. To break these bonds requires energy. Once broken apart, the atoms, ions or molecules rearrange themselves to form new substances, making new bonds. Making new bonds releases energy.

If during a chemical reaction, more energy is needed to break the reactant bonds than released when product bonds form, the reaction is **endothermic** and heat is absorbed from the environment becomes colder.

On the other hand, if more energy is released due to product bonds forming than is needed to break reactant bonds the energy is **exothermic** and the excess energy is released to the environment as heat. The temperature of the environment goes up.

The total energy absorbed or released in the reaction can be determined by using bond energies. The total energy change of the reaction is equal to the total energy of all of the bonds of the products minus the total energy of all of the bonds of the reactants.

For example, propane , C_3H_8, is a common fuel used in heating homes and backyard grills. When burned, excess energy from the combustion reaction is released and used to cook our food.

$$C_3H_8 \text{ (g)} + 5\ O_2 \text{ (g)} \rightarrow 3\ CO_2 \text{ (g)} + 4\ H_2O\text{(l)}$$

The total energy of the products is from the bonds found in the carbon dioxide molecules and the water molecules.

$$3 \; O = C = O \; + \; 4 \; H {-} O {-} H$$

or 6 C=O bonds and 8 H-O bonds.

A table of bond energies gives the following information:

C=O   743 kJ/mol
H-O   463 kJ/mol

So for these molecules there would be: (6 x 743 kJ) + (8 x 463 kJ) =8162 kJ of energy released when these molecules form.

The reactants are these:

$$+ \; 5 \; O = O$$

or

2 C-C bonds
8 C-H bonds and
5 O=O bonds

These bonds require the following energy to break:

C-C   348 kJ/ mol
C-H   412 kJ/mol
O=O 498 kJ/mol

The total energy required for the reactants would be
     (2 x 348 kJ) + (8 x 412 kJ) +(5 x 498 kJ) = 6482 kJ of energy.

The total energy change that occurs during the combustion of propane is then:

8162 kJ – 6482 kJ = 680 kJ of energy is released for every mole of propane that burns in excess oxygen.

Skill 2.6 **Analyze entropy changes during solution formation, phase changes, and chemical reactions.**

Entropy may be thought of as **the disorder in a system** or as a measure of the **number of states a system may occupy**. Changes due to entropy occur in one direction with no driving force. For example, a small volume of gas released into a large container will expand to fill it, but the gas in a large container never spontaneously collects itself into a small volume. This occurs because a large volume of gas has more disorder and has more places for gas molecules to be. This change occurs because **processes increase in entropy** when given the opportunity to do so.

A brief definition will not help you master these concepts. But it is important that you can utilize them sufficiently to apply them to phase changes and to chemical reactions. Entropy has units of Joules/Kelvin.

For phase changes, examine the diagrams in **Skill 2.3**. In the solid phase, each molecule may vibrate a little, but it is otherwise locked into place in an ordered position and may only be in a relatively small number of locations. In the gas phase, however, each molecule could be almost anywhere and there is greater disorder. Therefore, **the entropy of a material increases during a phase change that raises the freedom of molecular motion and decreases during a phase change that prevents molecular motion.** Entropy also increases with temperature because molecules experience more disorder when they have a wider range of energy states to occupy.
Remember that gases are of greater entropy than liquids, liquids are of greater entropy than solids, and matter in the same state increases in entropy with temperature. Entropy is also an extensive property of matter. **A greater number of moles will have more entropy.**

If two different chemicals are at the same temperature, in the same state of matter, and they have the same number of molecules, their entropy difference will depend mostly on the number of ways the atoms within the two chemicals can rotate, vibrate, and flex. Most of the time, **the more complex molecule will have the greater entropy** because there are more energetic and spatial states in which it may exist.

At zero Kelvin (0 K), there is no energy available for a chemical to sample different states. The **absolute entropy**, S, of a pure crystalline solid at 0 K is zero. Absolute entropy may be measured and calculated for different substances at different temperatures.

The **entropy change of a reaction**, ΔS, is given by the sum of the absolute entropies of all the products multiplied by their stoichiometric coefficients minus the sum of all the reactants multiplied by their stoichiometric coefficients:

For the reaction below:

$$aA + bB \rightarrow pP + qQ$$

We can calculate the entropy to be:

$$\Delta S = pS(P) + qS(Q) - aS(A) - bS(B)$$

Skill 2.7 **Predict spontaneity of a chemical process given initial and final values of free energy, temperature, enthalpy, and/or entropy.**

Spontaneity

$$\Delta G = \Delta H - T\Delta S$$

(handwritten note: $-\Delta G$ is SPONTANEOUS + EXERGONIC)

A reaction with a negative ΔH and a positive ΔS causes a decrease in energy and an increase in entropy. **These reactions will always occur spontaneously.** A reaction with a positive ΔH and a negative ΔS causes an increase in energy and a decrease in entropy. These reactions never occur to an appreciable extent because the reverse reaction takes place spontaneously.

Whether reactions with the remaining two possible combinations (ΔH and ΔS both positive or both negative) occur depends on the temperature. If $\Delta H - T\Delta S$ (known as the **Gibbs Free Energy, ΔG**) is negative, the reaction will take place. If it is positive, the reaction will not occur to an appreciable extent. If $\Delta H - T\Delta S = 0$ exactly, then at equilibrium there will be 50% reactants and 50% products.

This chart will help identify four possible scenarios for the values of ΔH, ΔS and ΔG to predict spontaneity of the reaction.

ΔH	ΔS	ΔG
-	+	-, spontaneous
-	-	-, spontaneous
+	+	- if $|T\Delta S| < |\Delta H|$, spontaneous
+	-	- if $T\Delta S > \Delta H$

A spontaneous reaction is called *exergonic*. A non-spontaneous reaction is known as *endergonic*. These terms are used much less often than *exothermic* and *endothermic*.

Example (part 1): Determine the standard heat of formation ΔH_f° for ethylene:

$$2C(graphite)+2H_2(g) \rightarrow C_2H_4(g).$$

Use the heat of combustion for ethylene:

$$\Delta H_c^\circ = 1411.2\frac{kJ}{mol\ C_2H_4} \quad \text{for} \quad C_2H_4(g)+3O_2(g) \rightarrow 2CO_2(g)+2H_2O(l)$$

and the following two heats of formation for CO_2 and H_2O:

$$\Delta H_f^\circ = -393.5\frac{kJ}{mol\ C} \quad \text{for} \quad C(graphite)+O_2(g) \rightarrow CO_2(g)$$

$$\Delta H_f^\circ = -285.9\frac{kJ}{mol\ H_2} \quad \text{for} \quad H_2(g)+\frac{1}{2}O_2(g) \rightarrow H_2O(l).$$

Also find the standard change in entropy ΔS° for the formation of C_2H_4 given:

$$S^\circ(C(graphite)) = 5.7\frac{J}{mol\ K} \quad S^\circ(H_2(g)) = 130.6\frac{J}{mol\ K} \quad S^\circ(C_2H_4(g)) = 219.4\frac{J}{mol\ K}.$$

Example (part 2): Will graphite and hydrogen gas react to form C_2H_4 at 25 °C and 100 kPa?

Solution: Use Hess's Law after rearranging the given reactions so they cancel to yield the reaction of interest. Combustion is exothermic, so ΔH for this reaction is negative. We are interested in C_2H_4 as a product, so we take the opposite (endothermic) reaction. The given ΔH are multiplied by stoichiometric coefficients to give the reaction of interest as the sum of the three:

$$2CO_2(g) + 2H_2O(l) \rightarrow C_2H_4(g) + 3O_2(g) \quad \Delta H = 1411.2 \frac{kJ}{mol \ reaction}$$

$$2C(graphite) + 2O_2(g) \rightarrow 2CO_2(g) \quad \Delta H = -787.0 \frac{kJ}{mol \ reaction}$$

$$2H_2(g) + O_2(g) \rightarrow 2H_2O(l) \quad \Delta H = -571.8 \frac{kJ}{mol \ reaction}$$

$2\cancel{CO_2} + 2\cancel{H_2O} + 2C + \cancel{2O_2} + 2H_2 + \cancel{O_2} \rightarrow C_2H_4 + 3\cancel{O_2} + 2\cancel{CO_2} + 2\cancel{H_2O}$

$$2C(graphite) + 2H_2(g) \rightarrow C_2H_4(g) \quad \Delta H_f^{\circ} = 52.4 \frac{kJ}{mol}$$

-787.0 kJ/mol is found by multiplying 2 x 393.5 kJ/mol because 2 mol react. The same is true for the -571.8 kJ/mol; 2 mol react so it becomes 2 x -285.9 kJ/mol. The value for the first equation is not multiplied by 2 because the ΔH is for the equation as it is written.

The entropy change is found from:

PRODUCT – REACTANTS

$$\Delta S^{\circ} = S^{\circ}(C_2H_4) - 2S^{\circ}(C) - 2S^{\circ}(H_2) = 219.4 \frac{J}{mol \ K} - 2 \times 5.7 \frac{J}{mol \ K} - 2 \times 130.6 \frac{J}{mol \ K}$$

$$= -53.2 \frac{J}{mol \ K}.$$

This reaction is **endothermic** with a **decrease in entropy**, so it is **endergonic**. Graphite and hydrogen gas will not react to form C_2H_4.

In the diagram that follows, we look at the oxidation of carbon into CO and CO_2. The direct oxidation of carbon (graphite) into CO_2 yields an enthalpy of 393 kJ/mol. When carbon is oxidized into CO and then CO is oxidized to CO_2, the enthalpies are -110 and -283 kJ/mol respectively.

The sum of enthalpy in the two steps is exactly -393 kJ/mol, same as the one-step reaction.

The two reaction steps are:

$$C + \tfrac{1}{2} O_2 \to CO, \qquad \Delta H° = -110 \text{ kJ/mol}$$
$$CO + \tfrac{1}{2} O_2 \to CO_2, \qquad \Delta H° = -283 \text{ kJ/mol}.$$

Adding the two equations together and canceling out the intermediate, CO, on both sides leads to

$$C + O_2 \to CO_2, \qquad \Delta H° = (-110) + (-283) = -393 \text{ kJ/mol}.$$

Application of Hess's law enables us to calculate ΔH, $\Delta H°$, and ΔH_f for chemical reactions that are impossible to measure, providing that we have all the data of related reactions.

The enthalpy of combustion for H_2, C(graphite) and CH_4 are -285.8, -393.5, and -890.4 kJ/mol respectively. Calculate the standard enthalpy of formation ΔH_f for CH_4.

Using the equations and their ΔH values

(1) $H_2(g) + 0.5\, O_2(g) \to H_2O(l)$ $\Delta H = -285.8$ kJ/mol
(2) $C(graphite) + O_2(g) \to CO_2(g)$ $\Delta H = -393.5$ kJ/mol
(3) $CH_4(g) + 2O_2(g) \to CO_2(g) + 2H_2O(l)$ $\Delta H = -890.4$ kJ/mol

Find: $C + 2H_2 \rightarrow CH_4$

$2 \times (H_2(g) + 0.5\,O_2(g) \rightarrow H_2O(l))$ $2 \times (\Delta H = -285.8$ kJ/mol$)$

or $2H_2(g) + O_2(g) \rightarrow 2H_2O(l)$ $\Delta H = -571.6$ kJ

+ $C(graphite) + O_2(g) \rightarrow CO_2(g)$ $\Delta H = -393.5$ kJ

+ $CO_2(g) + 2H_2O(l) \rightarrow CH_4(g) + 2O_2(g)$ $\Delta H = +890.4$ kJ

$C(graphite) + 2H_2(g) \rightarrow CH_4(g)$ $\Delta H = -74.7$ kJ

From these data, we can construct an energy level diagram for these chemical combinations as follows:

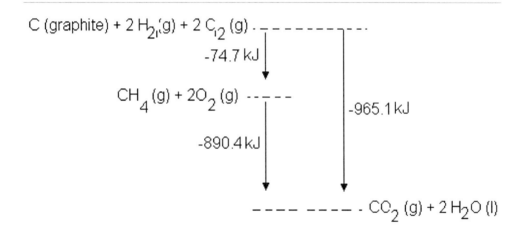

Skill 2.8 Relate regions of the electromagnetic spectrum to the energy, wavelength, and frequency of photons.

Rich Tall Men In loVe Use eXtra Gel Cream

The source of all our energy is the sun where fusion of nuclei takes place. Here matter is changed into electromagnetic radiation and travels out into space.

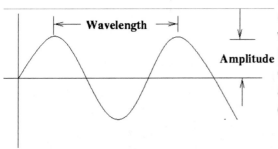

Some of this energy makes it to earth as sunlight or radiant energy, traveling as waves at a speed of 3.0×10^8 m/s. This energy exhibits properties of waves, having frequency, wavelength and amplitude.

Wavelength (λ): The distance between corresponding points on succeeding waves

Frequency (v): The number of wave cycles that pass a given point in a given amount of time, usually a second. Wave cycles / second = hertz (hz)

Amplitude (φ): The distance from the origin to the crest or trough of the wave.

Frequency and wavelength are inversely proportional to each other. That means if the wavelength decreases, the frequency of the wave cycles increases. The relationship between wavelength and frequency is:

$$c = \lambda v$$

Where c = the speed of light in a vacuum, 3.0×10^8 m/s.

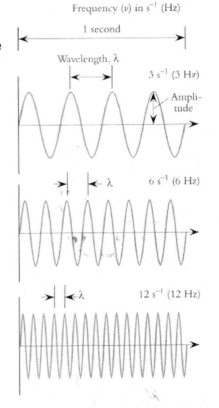

Yellow light has a wavelength of 560 nm. Its frequency is:

$$c = \lambda v$$

$c = 3.0 \times 10^8$ m/s

$\lambda = 560$ nm $= 5.60 \times 10^{-7}$ m

$v = c/\lambda$

$v = \dfrac{3.0 \times 10^8 \text{ m/s}}{5.60 \times 10^{-7} \text{ m}} = 5.36 \times 10^{14} \text{ s}^{-1}$

The energy carried by a specific type of electromagnetic radiation is directly proportional to its frequency or $E = hv$ where h is Planck's constant $= 6.36 \times 10^{-34}$ J·s and v is the frequency of the EMR.

For example: The yellow light in the problem above would have an energy of:

$E = hv$ or $E = 6.36 \times 10^{-34}$ J·s $(5.36 \times 10^{14} \text{ s}^{-1}) = 3.41 \times 10^{-19}$ J

$$E = hv = \frac{hc}{\lambda}$$

Skill 2.9   Relate regions of the electromagnetic spectrum to their effect on chemical or physical properties of matter.

Electromagnetic wave	Wavelength	Effects on matter	Examples
Radio waves	100 Mm to 100 cm	• Enhancement of a molecule's nuclear magnetic moment • Exploited by NMR spectroscopy	• Benign to the human body • Used for TV, phones, wireless networking
Microwaves	100 cm to 1000 μm	• Enhancement of chemical bond rotation	• Microwave ovens used to heat food • Low-frequency microwaves used in wi-fi
Far Infrared (far IR)	1000 to 10 μm	• Absorbed by rotational states of molecules	• Utilized primarily in astronomy
Infrared (IR)	10 μm to 400 nm	• Causes chemical bond stretches and vibrations	• Some animals use UV light to stalk their prey at night
Visible	400 to 700 nm	• Electron transitions promoting electrons to different energy states	• Light emitted by sun and stars
UV	700 nm to 10 nm	• Breakage of chemical bonds, causing ionization	• Sunburns result from UV damage to the skin • Used by honeybees to differentiate flower types

X-rays	10 to 10^{-2} nm	• Generated by electronic transitions involving the slowing of highly energetic inner electrons	• X-ray instruments used to image inner-body • Emitted by black holes and neutron stars
Gamma rays	<10^{-2} nm	• Electromagnetic radiation given off by the nucleus • Ionizing radiation, causes damage upon interactions with matter	• Produced by some radioisotopes

Skill 2.10   Analyze energy transformations in physical and biological systems (e.g., energy from the Sun to electricity, from food consumption to physical activity).

All energy transformations can be traced back to the sun -- the original source of energy for life on earth. The sun produces heat, light, and radiation through the process of fusion. The sun converts hydrogen to helium in a three-step process.

1. Two hydrogen atoms combine. This forms deuterium, also called heavy hydrogen.
2. Deuterium joins with another hydrogen atom. This forms a type of helium (helium-3).
3. Two helium-3 atoms collide, producing ordinary helium and two hydrogen atoms

Energy is released at every step. The energy comes in the form of tremendous heat, radiation that can kill us, and light that we need to survive. This energy forms in the core of the sun moves through several other layers to the photosphere and is emitted as light.

Once on earth, radiant energy (light) is transformed to the mechanical energy of wind and waves found in nature, through photosynthesis to the stored energy in plants, accumulated as chemical energy in deposits of coal, oil and gas.

Man uses mechanical, thermal and radiant energy to provide for his needs. Mechanical energy operates machines; thermal energy cooks food and heats homes while radiant energy provides light.

Plants capture the sunlight and through photosynthesis change it into chemical energy stored in carbohydrate (sugar) molecules in plant cells. The chlorophyll molecule found in plants captures light energy and uses it to build these carbohydrate molecules from the raw materials water, carbon dioxide and some minerals.

$$CO_2 \text{ (g)} + H_2O \text{ (g)} + chlorophyll + sunlight \rightarrow Oxygen \text{ (g)} + sugar.$$

This process produces oxygen and glucose, $C_6H_{12}O_6$. The sugar (glucose) is stored in the plant.

A person eats the plant. The chemical energy stored in the plant is transferred to the person. Body processes like digestion, circulation and respiration are fueled by cells converting stored chemical energy into work and heat.

Inside muscle cells, the chemical energy is converted to mechanical energy and heat. The muscle twitches and the body jumps to life. Stored chemical energy has been converted into kinetic energy. Energy not used immediately by the cells is stored as potential energy in fat cells.

Here are some other energy transformations:

Chemical   Mechanical

Chemical   Mechanical

Electrical   Thermal

Mechanical   Electrical

Radiant   Chemical

Chemical   Mechanical

COMPETENCY 3.0   KNOWLEDGE OF BONDING AND MOLECULAR STRUCTURE

18% (handwritten)

"Even the formal justification of the electron pair bond in the simplest case… requires a formidable array of symbols and equations. - Linus Pauling

Skill 3.1   Identify the basic theory and applications of spectroscopy (e.g., MRI, x-ray, mass spectrometry, UV, microwave, NMR, IR).

Spectroscopy can be broadly defined as the interaction between light and matter. It is a tool used by all types of chemists in the identification of substances based on the spectrum that results from the interaction of unique parts of molecules with light. There are three different types of light/matter interactions, detailed further below: scattering spectroscopy, absorption spectroscopy, and emission spectroscopy.

- **Scattering spectroscopy:** Light scattering spectroscopy is primarily used for particle size measurements. It relies on the amount of light scattered by a substance and is dependent on wavelength. The most common application of scattering spectroscopy is **Raman spectroscopy**, a technique that measures inelastic collisions between the atoms of a molecule and the scattered photons. Founded by Indian scientist Sir C.V. Raman in 1928, Raman spectroscopy utilizes monochromatic light to measure the difference in energy between the incident photon (incoming light) and the Raman scattered photon. This different is equal to the energy of a vibration of the scattering molecule. A plot of intensity of scattered light versus energy difference is a Raman spectrum.

- **Absorption spectroscopy:** As the name implies, absorption spectroscopy is a measurement of the light absorbed by a substance. When a molecule absorbs light, the absorption, A, can be ascertained from **Beer's Law: $A = \varepsilon bc$**, where ε = constant of absorbtivity, b = path length and c = concentration. Since different molecules absorb light of different wavelengths, the absorption spectrum will show different bands corresponding to structural groups within the molecule. There are several different types of absorption spectroscopy that are commonly used. These are discussed further below.

  A Becks Beer (handwritten)

  A = bEC (handwritten)

  - **UV/Vis Spectroscopy:** This type of absorption spectroscopy uses a combination of ultraviolet (UV) and visible light wavelengths to help ascertain the molecular structure of a substance. The absorption of light in this region corresponds to the excitation of outer shell electrons which occurs as ground state electrons (those in the lowest energy level) are promoted to excited states.

- o **IR Spectroscopy:** Similar in methodology to UV/Vis, IR spectroscopy uses infrared (IR) light (400 – 14,000 nm) to determine molecular structure based on the types of bonds present, rather than the types of atomic structure. This is possible due to the vibrational frequencies generated by the bonded atoms when light is absorbed. To measure a sample, a beam of infrared light is passed through the sample and the amount of energy absorbed at each wavelength is recorded. From this, an absorbance spectrum may be plotted. This shows at which wavelengths the sample absorbs the IR light and allows an interpretation of which bonds are present.

- **Emission Spectroscopy:** In contrast to absorption spectroscopy, where the properties of a substance can be determined from that molecule absorbing light, emission spectroscopy uses the energy given off *after* absorption to establish molecular structure. The molecule first absorbs energy, elevating electrons to higher energies. As these electrons return to their ground state, the substance radiates this energy as characteristic emissions that are directly related to the decrease in electron energy as it drops in orbitals.

- o **Fluorescence Spectroscopy:** Fluorescence spectroscopy uses high energy photons to excite a sample, which will then emit photons of another energy. In order for this to occur, a fluorophore is a necessary component of the molecule being tested. A fluorophore is a functional group which will absorb energy at one wavelength and emit it at another. The strength of this emission is measured as a function of wavelength.

- **Other:** Not all types of spectroscopy fit into the three above categories. Here are a few other examples.

- o **NMR spectroscopy:** Nuclear magnetic resonance (NMR) spectroscopy exploits the magnetic properties of atomic nuclei to obtain molecular structure. Although many different nuclei are NMR active, by far the most common NMR probes are ^{1}H and ^{13}C. NMR allows information to be garnered from a single atom and details the environment of that atom for structure determination. When placed in a magnetic field, NMR active nuclei resonate at different, and specific, frequencies. Since the resonance frequency is dependent on the strength of the magnetic field, it is reported as a chemical shift.

o **Mass spectroscopy:** Mass spectroscopy (MS) is a technique used to measure mass to charge ratios of ions generated in the instrument, based on the simple idea that different compounds have different masses. In the instrument, a sample is ionized, or broken down into the simplest ions of the substance. The spectrometer measures the relative abundances of each of the ions present and reports the abundance as a function of mass. The resulting spectrum is representative of the masses of the components of the substance and can be used to identify the parent compound.

Examples of Different Spectra for Acetic Acid

Infrared spectrum for acetic acid plotted as % transmittance vs. wavelength

Proton NMR spectrum plotted as intensity vs. ppm

Mass spectrum for acetic acid plotted as % abundance vs. m/z

Skill 3.2   Identify types and examples of metallic, ionic, and covalent (polar and nonpolar) bonds.

Chemical compounds form when two or more atoms join together. A stable compound occurs when the total energy of the combination of the atoms together is lower than the atoms separately. The combined state suggests an attractive force exists between the atoms. This attractive force is called a chemical bond.

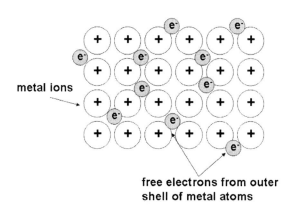

metal ions

free electrons from outer
shell of metal atoms

Metallic bonds occur when the bonding is between two metals. Metallic properties, such as low ionization energies, conductivity, and malleability, suggest that metals possess strong forces of attraction between atoms, but still have electrons that are able to move freely in all directions throughout the metal. This creates a "sea of electrons" model where electrons are quickly and easily transferred between metal atoms. In this model, the outer shell electrons are free to move. The metallic bond is the force of attraction that results from the moving electrons and the positive nuclei left behind. The strength of metal bonds usually results in regular structures and high melting and boiling points.

Ionic Bonds

An **ionic bond** describes the electrostatic forces that exist between particles of opposite charge. Elements that form an ionic bond with each other have a large difference in their electronegativity. Elements

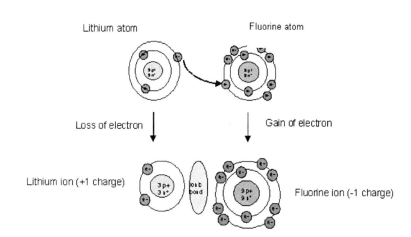

Lithium atom

Fluorine atom

Loss of electron

Gain of electron

Lithium ion (+1 charge)

Ionic bond

Fluorine ion (-1 charge)

Due to low ionization energies, metals have a tendency to lose valence electrons relatively easily, whereas non-metals, which have high ionization energies and high electronegativities, gain electrons easily. This produces cations (positively charged) and anions (negatively charged). Coulomb's Law says that opposites attract, and so do the oppositely charged ions. This *electrostatic interaction* between the anion and the cation results in an ionic bond. Ionic bonds will only occur when a metal is bonding to a non-metal, and is the result of the periodic trends (ionization energy and electronegativity). Elements that form an ionic bond with each other have a large difference in their electronegativity.

Anions and cations pack together into a crystal **lattice** as shown to the right for NaCl. Ionic compounds are also known as **salts**.

Single and multiple covalent bonds

A **covalent bond** forms when at least one pair of electrons is shared by two atoms. The shared electrons are found in the valence energy level and lead to a lower energy if they are shared in a way that creates a noble gas configuration (a full octet). Covalent, or molecular, bonds occur when a non-metal is bonding to a non-metal. This is due primarily to the fact that non-metals have high ionization energies and high electronegativities. Neither atom wants to "give up" electrons; both want to gain them. In order to satisfy both octets, the electrons can be shared between the two atoms.

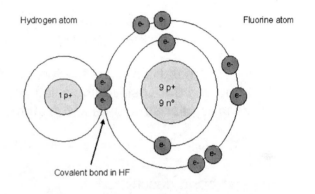

Sharing of electrons can be equal or unequal, resulting in a separation of charge (polar) or an even distribution of charge (non-polar). The polarity of a bond can be determined through an examination of the electronegativities of the atoms involved in the bond. The more electronegative atom will have a stronger attraction to the electrons, thus possessing the electrons more of the time. This results in a partial negative charge (δ^-) on the more electronegative atom and a partial positive charge (δ^+) on the less electronegative atom.

The simplest covalent bond is between two hydrogen atoms. Covalent bonds may be represented by an electron pair (a pair of dots) or a line as shown below. The shared pair of electrons provides each H atom with two electrons in its valence shell (the $1s$ orbital), so both have the stable electron configuration of helium.

$$H\cdot \ + \ \cdot H \longrightarrow \begin{array}{c} H\!:\!H \\ H\!-\!H \end{array}$$

Chlorine molecules have 7 electrons in their valence shell and share a pair of electrons so both have the stable electron configuration of argon.

$$:\overset{..}{\underset{..}{Cl}}\cdot \ + \ \cdot \overset{..}{\underset{..}{Cl}}: \longrightarrow :\overset{..}{\underset{..}{Cl}}:\overset{..}{\underset{..}{Cl}}:$$

$$:\overset{..}{\underset{..}{Cl}} - \overset{..}{\underset{..}{Cl}}:$$

In the previous two examples, a single pair of electrons was shared, and the resulting bond is referred to as a **single bond**. When two electron pairs are shared, two lines are drawn, representing a **double bond**, and three shared pairs of electrons represents a **triple bond** as shown below for CO_2 and N_2. The remaining electrons are in **unshared pairs**.

$$\overset{..}{\underset{..}{O}} :: C :: \overset{..}{\underset{..}{O}}$$

$$\overset{..}{\underset{..}{O}} = C = \overset{..}{\underset{..}{O}}$$

$$: N :: N :$$

$$: N \!\equiv\! N :$$

Polar/nonpolar covalent bonds

Electron pairs shared between **two atoms of the same element are shared equally**. At the other extreme, **for ionic bonding there is no electron sharing** because the electron is transferred completely from one atom to the other. Most bonds fall somewhere between these two extremes, and the electrons are **shared unequally (a polar bond)**.

The polarity of a bond can be determined through an examination of the electronegativities of the atoms involved in the bond. The more electronegative atom will have a stronger attraction to the electrons, thus possessing the electrons more of the time. This results in a partial negative charge (δ^-) on the more electronegative atom and a partial positive charge (δ^+) on the less electronegative atom as shown below for gaseous HCl. Such bonds are referred to as **polar bonds**. A particle with a positive and a negative region is called a **dipole**. A lower-case delta (δ) is used to indicate partial charge or an arrow is draw from the partial positive to the partial negative atom.

$$\begin{array}{cc} \delta+ & \delta- \\ H\!-\!Cl & \overset{\longrightarrow}{H\!-\!Cl} \end{array}$$

Skill 3.3   Apply electronegativity to bond type.

Electronegativity is a measure of the ability of an atom to attract electrons in a chemical bond. Metallic elements have low electronegativities and nonmetallic elements have high electronegativities. Relative values of electronegativity are shown in the table. Comparing the values allows us to determine the polarity of a bond, as described below.

Linus Pauling developed the concept of electronegativity and defined its relationship to different types of bonds in the 1930s.

A **large electronegativity difference** (greater than 1.7) results in an **ionic bond**. Any bond composed of two different atoms will be slightly polar, but for a **small electronegativity difference** (less than 0.4), the distribution of charge in the bond is so nearly equal that the result is called a **nonpolar covalent bond**. An **intermediate electronegativity difference** (from 0.4 to 1.7) results in a **polar covalent bond**. HCl is polar covalent because Cl has a very high electronegativity (it is near F in the periodic table) and H is a nonmetal (and so it will form a covalent bond with Cl), but H is near the dividing line between metals and nonmetals, so there is still a significant electronegativity difference between H and Cl. Using the numbers in the table above, the electronegativity for Cl is 3.2 and it is 2.2 for H. The difference of 3.2 – 2.2 = 1.0 places this bond in the middle of the range for polar covalent bonds.

Bond type is actually a continuum as shown in the following chart for common bonds. Note that the **C-H bond** is considered **nonpolar**.

Type of bonding	Electronegativity difference	Bond
		$Fr^+—F^-$
Very ionic		$Na^+—F^-$
	3.0	
⋮	⋮	⋮
Ionic		$Na^+—Cl^-$
	2.0	$Na^+—Br^-$
Mostly ionic		$Na^+—I^-$
Mostly polar covalent	1.5	$C^{\delta+}—F^{\delta-}$
		$H^{\delta+}—O^{\delta-}$
Polar covalent	1.0	$H^{\delta+}—Cl^{\delta-}$
		$C^{\delta+}=O^{\delta-}$
		$H^{\delta+}—N^{\delta-}$
		$C^{\delta+}—Cl^{\delta-}$
	0.5	$C^{\delta+}\equiv N^{\delta-}$
Mostly nonpolar covalent		C—H
Fully nonpolar covalent	0	H_2, N_2, O_2, F_2, Cl_2, Br_2, I_2, C—C, S—S

Increasing ionic character ⟹

Skill 3.4   Identify characteristics of simple organic compounds.

Many organic molecules contain functional groups which are groups of atoms in a particular arrangement that gives the molecule certain characteristics. Functional groups are named according to the composition of the group. The carboxyl group is the arrangement of -COOH atoms that tends to make a molecule exhibit acidic properties.

Some functional groups are polar and can ionize. For example, the hydrogen atom in the –COOH group can be removed (providing H^+ ions to a solution). When this occurs, the oxygen retains both the electrons it shared with the hydrogen and the molecule then has a negative charge.

If polar or ionizing functional groups are attached to otherwise hydrophobic molecules, the molecule may become hydrophilic due to the functional group. Some ionizing functional groups are: -COOH, -OH, -CO, and -NH$_2$.

Some common functional groups include:

Hydroxyl group:

The hydroxyl group, -OH, is the functional group identifying alcohols. The hydroxyl group makes the molecule polar which tends to increase the solubility of the compound in polar solvents.

Carbonyl group:

The carbonyl group is a -C=O.. It is found in aldehydes (carboxyl group on end of carbon chain) and ketones (carboxyl group in middle of chain).

Aldehyde   ketone

If the carbon is attached to two carbon chains, the molecule is a ketone.

The double bonded oxygen atom is highly electronegative so it creates a polar molecule and will exhibit properties of polar molecules.

Carboxyl group:

The –COOH group has the ability to donate a proton, thereby conferring acidic properties to the molecule.

Amino group:

An amino group contains an ammonia-like functional group composed of a nitrogen and two hydrogen atoms covalently bonded. The nitrogen atom has unshared electrons and so can bind free H^+ ions (proton). This gives the molecule basic properties. An organic compound that contains an amino group is called an amine. The amines are weak bases because the unshared electron pair of the nitrogen atom can form a coordinate bond with a proton. Another group of molecules that contains the amino group are amino acids. Every amino acids contains both a –NH_2 group and a –COOH group.

H–CH–COOH   This is the amino acid glycine.
    |
   NH$_2$

Sulfhydryl group:

A thiol is a compound that contains the functional group composed of a sulfur atom and a hydrogen atom (-SH). This functional group is referred to either as a *thiol group* or a *sulfhydryl group*. More traditionally, thiols have been referred to as *mercaptans*.

The small difference in electronegativity between the sulfur and the hydrogen atom produces a non-polar covalent bond. This in turn provides for no hydrogen bonding giving thiols lower boiling points and less solubility in water than alcohols of a similar molecular mass.

Phosphate group:

$$-O-\underset{\underset{O}{|}}{\overset{\overset{O}{\|}}{P}}-O$$

The phosphate ion is contained in a hydrocarbon chain making a phosphate group present in the molecule. This molecule is ideal for energy transfer reactions (such as those that occur with ATP) because of its symmetry and rotating double bond.

In biological systems, phosphates are most commonly found in the form of adenosine phosphates, (AMP, ADP and ATP) and in DNA and RNA.

Skill 3.5   Given the structural formula for a simple organic compound, identify the hybridization of the atoms.

Hybridization

Electron arrangements are built up by considering different energy levels for different subshells to explain spectroscopic data about individual atoms. However, when Lewis dot structures are drawn or molecular geometries are determined, all valence electrons are treated identically to explain the bonding between atoms regardless of whether the electrons once belonged to the *s* or the *p* subshell of their atom. Reconciling these views of the individual and the bonded atom requires a theory known as hybridization.

Hybridization describes the pre-bonding **promotion of one or more electrons** from a lower energy subshell to a higher energy subshell followed by a **combination** of the orbitals into degenerate **hybrid orbitals**.

Example: A boron atom has the valence electron configuration $2s^2 2p^1$ as shown to the right. Before bonding to three other atoms, the capability to form three equivalent bonds is achieved by hybridization. First a $2s$ electron is promoted to an empty p orbital. Next the occupied orbitals combine into three hybrid $2sp^2$ orbitals. Now three electrons in degenerate orbitals are available to create covalent bonds with three atoms.

Hybridization occurs for atoms with a valence electron configuration of ns^2, ns^2np^1, or ns^2p^2. For period 2, this corresponds with Be, B, C, and N in the NH_3^+ ion.

An atom joined to its neighbor by **multiple covalent bonds** is prepared for bonding by hybridization with incomplete combination. Electrons that remain in p orbitals can contribute additional bonds between the same two atoms.

Example: An isolated carbon atom has the valence electron configuration $2s^2 2p^2$. Hybridization to four $2sp^3$ orbitals occurs before bonding to four atoms. Three hybrid sp^2 orbitals form if there is a double bond so the C atom is bonded to three atoms and one electron remains in the p orbital. Two hybrid sp orbitals occur if there is a triple bond or two double bonds. In this case, C is bonded to two atoms with two electrons remaining in p orbitals.

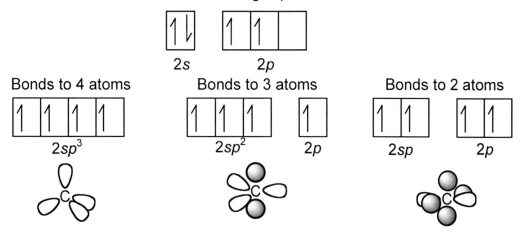

Note: p orbitals are shaded in the diagrams. These models are meant to illustrate the **locations** and **angles** of hybrid and p orbitals relative to the central atom. A mathematical solution would also show that each type of hybrid orbital (sp^3, sp^2, and sp) has a slightly different shape from the other two.

See
http://www.mhhe.com/physsci/chemistry/essentialchemistry/flash/hybrv18.swf for a flash animation tutorial of hybridization.

Skill 3.6   Identify sigma and pi bonds in a compound.

The electron configurations of isolated atoms are found in atomic orbitals; the configurations of atoms about to bond are represented by atomic and hybridized atomic orbitals; and the **electron configurations of molecules are represented by molecular orbitals**. Molecular orbital theory is an advanced topic, but it may be simplified to representing the **bonds between atoms as overlapping electron density shapes from atomic orbitals**. There are two typical locations for molecular orbitals.

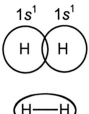

The **bonding sigma orbital** (σ) surrounds **a line drawn between the two atoms** in a bond. At least one electron pair in every bond is in a bonding σ orbital. Sigma bonds get their name from s orbitals because the spherical electron density shapes of two s orbitals overlap to form a σ orbital. A drawing of this overlap and the resulting molecular orbital is shown to the right for H_2. Hybrid or p atomic orbitals also form a σ orbital when they overlap such that the axis between the bonded atoms runs through the center of the combined electron density.

The **bonding pi orbital** (π) follows regions **separate from a line drawn between the two atoms** in a bond. Two overlapping p orbitals will form π bonds to contain the additional shared electrons in molecules with double or triple bonds. π bonds prevent atoms from rotating about the central axis between them.

In CH_4, the electron density of the four sp^3 orbitals of C each overlap with an s orbital of H to form four σ bonds. In C_2H_4 (an alkene), two sp^2 orbitals on each C overlap with H, the remaining sp^2 orbitals overlap with each other in a σ bond, and the p orbitals (drawn as shaded shapes) overlap with each other above and beneath the carbons in a π bond (also drawn as shaded shapes). In CO_2, the C atom has two sp hybrid orbitals and two p orbitals. These form one bond and one π bond with the two unfilled p orbitals on each O atom. In C_2H_2 (an alkyne), a triple bond forms with one σ and two π.

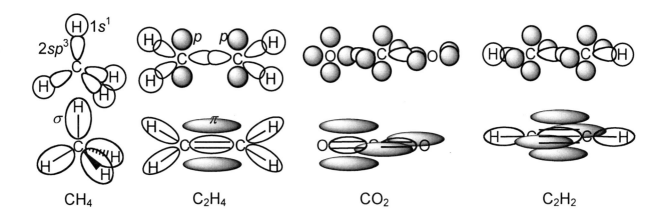

| CH₄ | C₂H₄ | CO₂ | C₂H₂ |

Skill 3.7 **Interpret the information derived from the following models: Lewis electron dot structures, valence shell electron pair repulsion (VSEPR) theory, and molecular orbital (M/O) theory.**

Lewis dot structures are used to keep track of each atom's valence electrons in a molecule. Drawing Lewis structures is a three-step process:

1) Determine the number of valence shell electrons for each atom. If the compound is an anion, add the charge of the ion to the total electron count because anions have "extra" electrons. If the compound is a cation, subtract the charge of the ion.

2) Write the symbols for each atom and show how the atoms within a molecule are bound to each other.

3) Draw a single bond (one pair of electron dots or a line) between each pair of connected atoms. Place the remaining electrons around the atoms as unshared pairs. If every atom has an octet of electrons except H atoms with two electrons, the Lewis structure is complete. Shared electrons count towards both atoms. If there are too few electron pairs to do this, draw multiple bonds (two or three pairs of electron dots between the atoms) until an octet is around each atom (except H atoms with two). If there are too many electron pairs to complete the octets with single bonds then the octet rule is broken for this compound.

Example: Draw the Lewis structure of HCN.

Solution:

1) From the periodic table, we know that each atom contributes the following number of electrons: H - 1, C - 4, N - 5. Summing these numbers, we see that this molecule will have a total of 10 valence electrons (because it has no net charge we do not add to or subtract from this number).

2) The atoms are connected with C at the center and will be drawn as: H C N. Having H as the central atom is impossible because H has one valence electron and will always only have a single bond to one other atom. If N were the central atom then the formula would probably be written as HNC.

3) Connecting the atoms with 10 electrons in single bonds gives the structure to the right. H has two electrons to fill its valence subshells, but C and N only have six each. A triple bond between these atoms fulfills the octet rule for C and N and is the correct Lewis structure.

$$H : \overset{..}{C} : \overset{..}{\underset{..}{N}}$$

$$H : C ::: \overset{..}{\underset{.}{N}}$$

Molecular Orbital Theory

Review Skill 3.6

The electron configurations of isolated atoms are found using atomic orbitals; the configurations of atoms about to bond are represented by atomic and hybridized atomic orbitals; and the electron configurations of molecules are represented by molecular orbitals. Molecular orbital theory is an advanced topic, but it may be simplified to representing the bonds between atoms as overlapping electron density shapes from atomic orbitals. There are two typical locations for molecular orbitals.

The bonding sigma orbital (σ) surrounds a line drawn between the two atoms in a bond. At least one electron pair in every bond is in a bonding σ orbital. Sigma bonds get their name from s orbitals because the spherical electron density shapes of two s orbitals overlap to form a σ orbital. A drawing of this overlap and the resulting molecular orbital is shown to the right for H_2. Hybrid or p atomic orbitals also form a σ orbital when they overlap such that the axis between the bonded atoms runs through the center of the combined electron density.

The bonding pi orbital (π) occurs in the region of a line drawn between the two atoms in a bond. Two overlapping p orbitals will form π bonds to contain the additional shared electrons in molecules with double or triple bonds. π bonds prevent atoms from rotating about the central axis between them.

In CH_4, the electron density of the four sp^3 orbitals of C each overlap with an s orbital of H to form four σ bonds. In C_2H_4 (an alkene), two sp^2 orbitals on each C overlap with H, the remaining sp^2 orbitals overlap with each other in a σ bond, and the p orbitals (drawn as shaded shapes) overlap with each other above and beneath the carbons in a π bond (also drawn as shaded shapes). In CO_2, the C atom has two sp hybrid orbitals and two p orbitals. These form one bond and one π bond with the two unfilled p orbitals on each O atom. In C_2H_2 (an alkyne), a triple bond forms with one σ and two π.

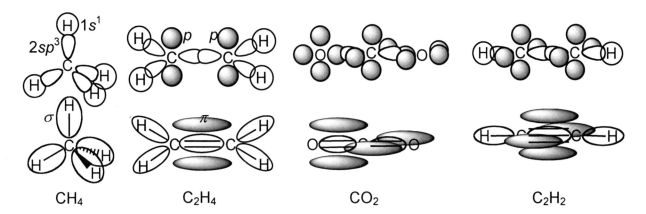

| CH₄ | C₂H₄ | CO₂ | C₂H₂ |

Molecules with double bonds next to each other and aromatic molecules based on benzene contain more than two π orbitals on adjacent atoms. The bonds and the entire molecules are described as being conjugated. Electrons in these molecules are free to move from one bond to the next on the same molecule and so are delocalized. Delocalized electrons are found throughout the entire substance in materials dealing with metallic bonds.

Resonance

O_2 contains a total of 12 valence electrons and the following Lewis structure:

$$\ddot{\text{O}}\!=\!\ddot{\text{O}}$$

Ozone, O_3, has a total of 18 valence electrons, and two Lewis structures are possible for this molecule

Equivalent Lewis structures are called **resonance forms**. A double-headed arrow is used to indicate resonance. The actual molecule does not have a double bond on one bond and a single bond on the other. The **molecular structure is in an average state between the resonance forms**.

Benzene (C_6H_6) has the following resonance forms:

Each carbon atom in benzene bonds to three atoms, so their electrons are in three sp^2 orbitals and one p orbital as we've seen for C_2H_4. The p orbitals are shown as the shaded shapes below on the left (only the C-C bonds are shown). The p atomic orbitals combine to form molecular orbitals with delocalized electrons as shown in the bonding π molecular orbital below to the right.

 Aromatic molecules are often drawn with a circle in the center of their benzene rings (shown to the left) to show delocalized π electrons. The atoms of a benzene molecule are all located in the same plane. This is in contrast to molecules that contain only σ bonds as shown to the right for cyclohexane, C_6H_{12}.

Molecular orbital theory also predicts **antibonding orbitals** that **prevent bonding** because they are at a higher energy level than the electrons in individual atoms. Antibonding electrons play a role in explaining why molecules like H_2 form while molecules like He_2 do not, but they are not required to predict molecular structures. For more on this aspect of molecular orbital theory, see http://www.chem.ufl.edu/~chm2040/Notes/Chapter_12/theory.html

For information on valence shell electron pair repulsion (VSEPR) theory please see Skill 3.9.

Skill 3.8   **Select the most probable Lewis electron dot structure for an ionic or covalent formula (e.g., CO_2, Na_2CO_3) that follows the octet rule.**

To select the most probable Lewis dot structure for a compound or molecule that follows the octet rule, review the structures and compare to the method for constructing Lewis dot structures given above.

Example: Which of the electron-dot structures given below for nitrous oxide (laughing gas), N_2O, is/are acceptable?

$$\text{I. } \overset{..}{:} \text{N} :: \overset{..}{\text{N}} : \overset{..}{\text{O}} :$$
$$ \underset{..}{}$$

$$\text{II. } : \overset{..}{\text{N}} : \text{N} :: \overset{..}{\text{O}} :$$

$$\text{III. } : \text{N} ::: \text{N} :: \overset{..}{\text{O}} :$$

Solution: Both nitrogen and oxygen follow the octet rule so the Lewis structure should show each atom in the molecule with 8 electrons, either unshared or shared. Upon examination, only choice I provides each atom in the molecule with 8 electrons. Choice II has only 6 electrons around each of the nitrogen atoms and choice III has 10 electrons around the center nitrogen atom.

Skill 3.9   **Predict geometry of simple molecules (e.g., symmetry elements).**

Electron Pairs

Molecular geometry is predicted using the valence-shell electron-pair repulsion or VSEPR model. VSEPR uses the fact that electron pairs repel each other. Imagine you are one of two pairs of electrons in bonds around a central atom (like a bonds in BeH_2 in the table below). You want to be as far away from the other electron pair as possible, so you will be on one side of the atom and the other pair will be on the other side. There is a straight line (or a 180° angle) between you to the other electron pair on the other side of the nucleus. In general, electron pairs lie at the largest possible angles from each other.

Electron pairs	Geometrical arrangement		Predicted bond angles	Example
2		Linear	180°	
3		Trigonal planar	120°	
4		Tetrahedral	109.5°	
5		Trigonal bipyramidal	120° and 90°	
6		Octahedral	90°	

X represents a generic central atom. Lone pair electrons on F are not shown in the example molecules.

Unshared Electron Pairs

The shape of a molecule is given by the location of its atoms. These are connected to central atoms by shared electrons, but unshared electrons on a central atom also have an important impact on molecular shape. Unshared electrons also repel one another and so can alter the expected angles between atoms. Molecular shapes in the following table take into account total pairs and unshared electrons.

Electron pairs	Molecular shape				
	All shared pairs	1 unshared pair	2 unshared pairs	3 unshared pairs	4 unshared pairs
2	A—X—A Linear				
3	Trigonal planar	Bent			
4	Tetrahedral	Trigonal pyramidal	Bent		
5	Trigonal bipyramidal	Seesaw or sawhorse	T-shaped	Linear	
6	Octahedral	Square pyramidal	Square planar	T-shaped	Linear

X represents a generic central atom bonded to atoms labeled A.

Altered Bond Angles

Unpaired electrons also have a less dramatic impact on molecular shape. Imagine you are an unshared electron pair around a molecule's central atom. The shared electron pairs are each attracted partially to the central atom and partially to the other atom in the bond, but you are different. You are attracted to the central atom, but there's nothing on your other side, so you are free to expand in that direction. That expansion means that you take up more room than the other electron pairs, and they are all squeezed a little closer together because of you. Multiple bonds have a similar effect because more space is required for more electrons. In general, unshared electron pairs and multiple bonds decrease the angles between the remaining bonds. A few examples are shown in the following tables.

Compound	CH_4	NH_3	H_2O
Unshared electrons	0	1	2
Shape	H | H—C^{••••}H H 109.5 Tetrahedral	•• N^{••••}H H H 107 Trigonal pyramidal	•• O H 104.5 H •• Bent

Compound	BF_3	C_2H_4 (ethylene)
Multiple bonds	0	1
Shape	F 120 120 B—F F 120 Trigonal planar	H H 121.5 117 C==C 117 121.5 H H Trigonal planar

Summary

In order to use VSEPR to predict molecular geometry, perform the following steps:

1) Write out Lewis dot structures.

2) Use the Lewis structure to determine the number of unshared electron pairs and bonds around each central atom counting multiple bonds as one (for now).

3) The second table of this skill gives the arrangement of total and unshared electron pairs to account for electron repulsions around each central atom.

4) For multiple bonds or unshared electron pairs, decrease the angles slightly between the remaining bonds around the central atom.

5) Combine the results from the previous two steps to determine the shape of the entire molecule.

http://www.shef.ac.uk/chemistry/vsepr/ is a good site for explaining and visualizing molecular geometries using VSEPR.

http://cowtownproductions.com/cowtown/genchem/09_16T.htm provides some practice for determining molecular shape

Skill 3.10   Predict polarity of simple compounds.

A polar molecule has positive and negative regions. Bond polarity is necessary but not sufficient for molecular polarity. A molecule containing polar bonds will still be nonpolar if the most negative and most positive location occurs at the same point. In other words, in a polar molecule, bond polarities must not cancel one another.

To determine if a molecule is polar perform the following steps.

1) Draw the molecular structure.
2) Assign a polarity to each bond with an arrow (remember C-H is nonpolar). If none of the bonds are polar, the molecule is nonpolar.
3) Determine if the polarities cancel each other in space. If they do, the molecule is nonpolar. Otherwise the molecule is polar.

Examples: Which of the following are polar molecules: CO_2, CH_2Cl_2, CCl_4 ?

Solution: 1)

CO_2	CH_2Cl_2	CCl_4

2)

3)	charges cancel	net dipole	charges cancel

nonpolar	polar	nonpolar

The polarity of molecules is critical for determining a good solvent for a given solute. Additional practice on the topic of polar bonds and molecules is available at http://cowtownproductions.com/cowtown/genchem/09_17M.htm.

Skill 3.11   Predict physical or chemical properties based upon the type of bonding involved.

The physical properties of substances usually result from the strength of the intermolecular forces between its molecules. The reactivity of substances is based on stability considerations that are often a result of high or low electronegativity. The reactivity of large molecules is often localized to the most polar regions or charged regions of the molecule.

The bonds in this skill are listed from strongest to weakest. (Also see Skill 3.2)

Covalent bonds in a network solid

A covalent network solid may be considered one large molecule connected by covalent bonds. These materials are very **hard**, **strong**, and have **a high melting point**. Diamond, C_n or C_∞, and quartz, $(SiO_2)_n$ or $(SiO_2)_\infty$, are two examples.

Ionic bonds

All common salts (compounds with ionic bonds) are **solids** at room temperature. Salts are **brittle**, have a **high melting point**, and **do not conduct electricity** because their ions are not free to move in the crystal lattice. Salts do conduct electricity in molten form. The formation of a salt is a highly exothermic reaction between a metal and a nonmetal.

Salts in solid form are generally stable compounds, but in molten form or in solution, their component ions often react to form a more stable salt. The reactivities of these ions vary with the electronegativity of the respective elements as described in Skill 3.3.

Some salts decompose to form more stable salts, as in the decomposition of molten potassium chlorate to form potassium chloride and oxygen:
$$2KClO_3(l) \rightarrow 2KCl(s) + 3O_2(g).$$

Metallic bonds

The physical properties of metals are attributed to the electron sea model of metallic bonds shown on the right. Metals **conduct heat and electricity** because their electrons are not incorporated into specific bonds between specific atoms. Rather, they are able to flow through the material. They are called **delocalized** electrons. Metals are **lustrous** because electrons at their surface reflect light at many different wavelengths.

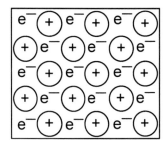

Metals are **malleable** and **ductile** because the electrons are able to rearrange their positions to maintain the integrity of the solid when the metallic lattice is deformed, acting like glue between the cations. The strengths of different metallic bonds can be related to the relative amounts and positions of electrons present.

Alkali metals contain only one valence electron ("less glue"), and that electron is a considerable distance away from the nucleus ("weaker glue"). The result is a weak metallic bond and a low melting point. Heavier alkali metals contain a valence electron even further from the nucleus, resulting in a very weak metallic bond and a lower melting point. With two valence electrons and smaller atoms, alkaline earth metals form stronger metallic bonds than the alkali metals. This explains some of the periodic trends described in Skill 5.4.

The metal with the weakest metallic bonds is mercury. Hg is a liquid at room temperature because Hg atoms hold on tightly to a stable valence configuration of full s, f, and d subshells. Fewer electrons are shared to create bonds than in other metals.

The reactivity of metals increases with lower electronegativity in reactions with nonmetals to form ionic bonds.

The following bonds are typically weaker than metallic bonds, and are called intermolecular forces.

Ion-dipole interactions

Salts tend to dissolve in several polar solvents. An ion with a full charge in a polar solvent will orient nearby solvent molecules so that their opposite partial charges are pointing towards the ion. In aqueous solution, certain salts react to form solid precipitates if a combination of their ions is insoluble. For example, table salt is NaCl. In water, it ionizes to Na+ and Cl –. The Na+ ions will tend to be attracted to the O end of the H_2O molecule, while the Cl – ions will tend to orient toward the H atoms in the H_2O molecule. The polarity of the water molecule makes it easier for the ionic compound to dissolve, as it helps pull the ions apart.

Hydrogen bonds

Hydrogen bonds are particularly strong dipole-dipole interactions that form between the H-atom of one molecule and an F, O, or N atom of an adjacent molecule. The partial positive charge on the hydrogen atom is attracted to the partial negative charge on the electron pair of the other atom. The hydrogen bond between two water molecules is shown as the dashed line below:

Dipole-dipole interactions

The intermolecular forces between polar molecules are known as dipole-dipole interactions. The partial positive charge of one molecule is attracted to the partial negative charge of its neighbor.

Ion-induced dipole

When a nonpolar molecule (or a noble gas atom) encounters an ion, its electron density is temporarily distorted resulting in an induced dipole that will be attracted to the ion. Intermolecular attractions due to induced dipoles in a nonpolar molecule are known as London forces or Van der Waals interactions. These are very weak intermolecular forces.

For example, carbon tetrachloride, CCl_4, has polar bonds but is a nonpolar molecule due to the symmetry of those bonds. An aluminum cation will draw the unbonded electrons of the chlorine atom towards it, distorting the molecule (this distortion has been exaggerated in the figure) and creating an attractive force as shown by the dashed line below.

Dipole-induced dipole

The partial charge of a permanent dipole may also induce a dipole in a nonpolar molecule resulting in an attraction similar to—but weaker than—that created by an ion.

London dispersion force: induced dipole-induced dipole

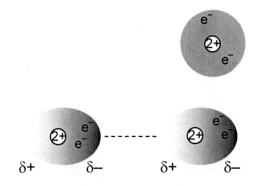

The above two interactions required a permanent charge to induce a dipole in a nonpolar molecule. A nonpolar molecule may also induce a temporary dipole on its identical neighbor in a pure substance. These forces occur because at any given moment, electrons are located within a certain region of the molecule, and the instantaneous location of electrons will induce a temporary dipole on neighboring molecules. For example, an isolated helium atom consists of a nucleus with a 2+ charge and two electrons in a spherical electron density cloud. An attraction of He atoms due to London dispersion forces (shown below by the dashed line) occurs because when the electrons happen to be distributed unevenly on one atom, a dipole is induced on its neighbor. This dipole is due to intermolecular repulsion of electrons and the attraction of electrons to neighboring nuclei.

The strength of London dispersion forces increases for larger molecules because a larger electron cloud is more easily polarized. The strength of London dispersion forces also increases for molecules with a larger surface area because there is greater opportunity for electrons to influence neighboring molecules if there is more potential contact between the molecules. Paraffin in candles is an example of a solid held together by weak London forces between large molecules. These materials are **soft**.

Skill 3.12   Identify an inorganic chemical formula (ionic or molecular), given the name.

The IUPAC is the **International Union of Pure and Applied Chemistry**, an organization that formulates naming rules for chemical elements and compounds. **Organic compounds contain carbon**, and they have a separate system of nomenclature but some of the simplest molecules containing carbon also fall within the scope of inorganic chemistry.

Naming rules depend on whether the chemical is an ionic compound or a molecular compound containing only covalent bonds. There are special rules for naming acids. The rules below describe a group of traditional "semi-systematic" names accepted by IUPAC.

Ionic compounds: Cation

Ionic compounds are named with the **cation (positive ion) first**. Nearly all cations in inorganic chemistry are **monatomic**, meaning they just consist of one atom (like Ca^{2+}, the calcium ion.) This atom will be a **metal ion**. For common ionic compounds, the **alkali metals always have a 1+ charge** and the **alkali earth metals always have a 2+ charge.**

Many metals may form cations of more than one charge. In this case, a Roman numeral in parenthesis after the name of the element is used to indicate the ion's charge in a particular compound. This Roman numeral method is known as the **Stock system**. An older nomenclature used the suffix –ous for the lower charge and –ic for the higher charge and is still used occasionally.

Example: Fe^{2+} is the iron(II) ion and Fe^{3+} is the iron(III) ion.

The only common inorganic **polyatomic cation** is **ammonium: NH_4^+.**

Ionic compounds: Anion

The **anion** (negative ion) is named and written last. Monatomic anions are formed from nonmetallic elements and are named by **replacing the end of the element's name with the suffix –ide.**

Examples: Cl^- is the chloride ion, S^{2-} is the sulfide ion, and N^{3-} is the nitride ion.

These anions also end with –ide:

C_2^{2-}	N_3^-	O_2^{2-}	O_3^-	S_2^{2-}	CN^-	OH^-
carbide or acetylide	azide	peroxide	ozonide	disulfide	cyanide	hydroxide

Oxoanions (also called oxyanions) **contain one element in combination with oxygen.** Many common polyatomic anions are oxoanions that **end with the suffix –ate.** If an element has two possible oxoanions, the one with the element at a lower oxidation state **ends with –ite.** This anion will also usually have **less oxygen per atom.** See **Skill 4.16** for a discussion of oxidation numbers. Additional oxoanions are named with the prefix *hypo-* if they have a lower oxidation number than the –ite form and the prefix *per–* if they have a higher oxidation number than the –ate form. Note the chlorate series of hypochlorite (ClO^-), chlorite (ClO_2^-), chlorate (ClO_3^-), and perchlorate (ClO_4^-).

Common examples:

			$CO_3{}^{2-}$	carbonate		
	$SO_3{}^{2-}$	sulfite	$SO_4{}^{2-}$	sulfate		
	$PO_3{}^{3-}$	phosphite	$PO_4{}^{3-}$	phosphate		
$N_2O_2{}^{2-}$ hyponitrite	$NO_2{}^{-}$	nitrite	$NO_3{}^{-}$	nitrate		
ClO^- hypochlorite	$ClO_2{}^{-}$	chlorite	$ClO_3{}^{-}$	chlorate	$ClO_4{}^{-}$	perchlorate
BrO^- hypobromite	$BrO_2{}^{-}$	bromite	$BrO_3{}^{-}$	bromate	$BrO_4{}^{-}$	perbromate
			$MnO_4{}^{2-}$	manganate	$MnO_4{}^{-}$	permanganate
			$CrO_4{}^{2-}$	chromate	$CrO_8{}^{3-}$	perchromate

Note that manganate/permanganate and chromate/perchromate are exceptions to the general rules because there are –*ate* ions but no –*ite* ions and because the charge changes.

Other polyatomic anions that end with –*ate* are:

$C_2O_4{}^{2-}$	$Cr_2O_7{}^{2-}$	SCN^-	$HCO_2{}^{-}$	$CH_3CO_2{}^{-}$
oxalate	dichromate	thiocyanate	formate	acetate

$HCO_2{}^{-}$ and $CH_3CO_2{}^{-}$ are condensed **structural formulas** because they show how the atoms are linked together. Their molecular formulas would be $CHO_2{}^{-}$ and $C_2H_3O_2{}^{-}$

If an H atom is added to a polyatomic anion with a negative charge greater than one, the word *hydrogen* or the prefix *bi-* are used for the resulting anion. If two H atoms are added, *dihydrogen* is used.

Examples: bicarbonate or hydrogen carbonate ion: $HCO_3{}^{-}$
dihydrogen phosphate ion: $H_2PO_4{}^{-}$

Ionic compounds: Hydrates

Water molecules often occupy positions within the lattice of an ionic crystal. These compounds are called **hydrates**, and the water molecules are known as **water of hydration**. The water of hydration is added after a centered dot in a formula. In a name, a number-prefix (listed below for molecular compounds) indicating the number of water molecules is followed by the root –*hydrate*.

Ionic compounds: Putting it all together

We now have the tools to name most common salts given a formula and to write a formula for them given a name. To determine a formula given a name, the number of anions and cations that are needed to achieve a neutral charge must be found.

Example: Determine the formula of cobalt(II) phosphite octahydrate.

Solution: For the cation, find the symbol for cobalt (Co) and recognize that it is present as Co^{2+} ions from the Roman numerals. For the anion, remember the phosphite ion is PO_3^{3-}. A neutral charge is achieved with 3 Co^{2+} ions for every 2 PO_3^{3-} ions. Add eight H_2O for water of hydration for the answer:

$$Co_3\left(PO_3\right)_2 \bullet 8H_2O.$$

Molecular compounds

Molecular compounds (compounds making up molecules with a neutral charge) are usually composed entirely of nonmetals and are named by placing the **less electronegative atom first**. See **Skill 3.3** for the relationship between electronegativity and the periodic table. The suffix –*ide* is added to the second, more electronegative atom, and prefixes indicating numbers are added to one or both names if needed.

Prefix	*mono-*	*di-*	*tri-*	*tetra-*	*penta-*	*hexa-*	*hepta-*	*octa-*	*nona-*	*deca-*
Meaning	1	2	3	4	5	6	7	8	9	10

The final "o" or "a" may be left off these prefixes for oxides.

The electronegativity requirement is the reason the compound with two oxygen atoms and one nitrogen atom is called nitrogen dioxide, NO_2 and not dioxygen nitride O_2N. The hydride of sodium is NaH, sodium hydride, but the hydride of bromine is HBr, hydrogen bromide (or hydrobromic acid if it's in aqueous solution). Oxygen is only named first in compounds with fluorine such as oxygen difluoride, OF_2, and fluorine is never placed first because it is the most electronegative element.

Examples: N_2O_4, dinitrogen tetroxide (or tetraoxide)
Cl_2O_7, dichlorine heptoxide (or heptaoxide)
ClF_5 chlorine pentafluoride

Acids

There are special naming rules for acids that correspond with the **suffix of their corresponding anion** if hydrogen were removed from the acid. Anions ending with –*ide* correspond to acids with the prefix *hydro*– and the suffix –*ic*. Anions ending with –*ate* correspond to acids with no prefix that end with –*ic*. Oxoanions ending with –*ite* have associated acids with no prefix and the suffix –*ous*. The *hypo*– and *per*– prefixes are maintained. Some examples are shown in the following table:

anion	anion name	acid	acid name
Cl^-	chloride	$HCl(aq)$	hydrochloric acid
CN^-	cyanide	$HCN(aq)$	hydrocyanic acid
CO_3^{2-}	carbonate	$H_2CO_3(aq)$	carbonic acid
SO_3^{2-}	sulfite	$H_2SO_3(aq)$	sulfurous acid
SO_4^{2-}	sulfate	$H_2SO_4(aq)$	sulfuric acid
ClO^-	hypochlorite	$HClO(aq)$	hypochlorous acid
ClO_2^-	chlorite	$HClO_2(aq)$	chlorous acid
ClO_3^-	chlorate	$HClO_3(aq)$	chloric acid
ClO_4^-	perchlorate	$HClO_4(aq)$	perchloric acid

Example: What is the molecular formula of phosphorous acid?

Solution: If we remember that the *–ous* acid corresponds to the *–ite* anion, and that the *–ite* anion has one less oxygen than (or has an oxidation number 2 less than) the *–ate* form, we only need to remember that phosphate is PO_4^{3-}. Then we know that phosphite is PO_3^{3-} and phosphorous acid is H_3PO_3.

For additional resources, see:
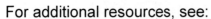
http://chemistry.alanearhart.org/Tutorials/Nomen/nomen-part7.html has thousands of sample questions. Don't do them all in one sitting.

http://www.iupac.org/reports/provisional/abstract04/connelly_310804.html - IUPAC's latest report on inorganic nomenclature

Skill 3.13   Select the name of an inorganic chemical compound (ionic or molecular), given its formula.

Properly written and named formulas

Proper formulas will follow the rules of the previous skill. Here are some ways to identify improper formulas that are emphasized below by underlining them.

In all common names for **ionic compounds, number prefixes are not used** to describe the number of anions and cations.

Examples: $CaBr_2$ is calcium bromide, not calcium dibromide.
$Ba(OH)_2$ is barium hydroxide, not barium dihydroxide.
Cu_2SO_4 is copper(I) sulfate, not dicopper sulfate or copper(II) sulfate or dicopper sulfur tetroxide.

All ionic compounds must have a **neutral charge in their formula** representations.

Example: MgBr is an improperly written formula because Mg ion always exists as 2+ and Br ion is always a 1– ion. $MgBr_2$, magnesium bromide, is correct.

Proper oxoanions and acids use the correct prefixes and suffixes.

Example: HNO_3 is nitric acid because NO_3^- is the nitrate ion.

In both ionic and molecular compounds, the **less electronegative element comes first**.

Example: CSi is an improperly written formula because Si is below C on the periodic table and therefore less electronegative. SiC, silicon carbide, is correct.

Skill 3.14   Identify properly named formulas for simple organic compounds.

The IUPAC is the **International Union of Pure and Applied Chemistry**. **Organic compounds contain carbon,** and have their own branch of chemistry because of the huge number of carbon compounds in nature, including nearly all the molecules in living things. The 1979 IUPAC organic nomenclature is used and taught most often today, and it is the nomenclature described here.

The simplest organic compounds are called **hydrocarbons** because they **contain only carbon and hydrogen**. Hydrocarbon molecules may be divided into the classes of **cyclic** and **open-chain** depending on whether they contain a ring of carbon atoms. Open-chain molecules may be divided into **branched** or **straight-chain** categories.

Hydrocarbons are also divided into classes called **aliphatic** and **aromatic**. Aromatic hydrocarbons are related to benzene and are always cyclic. Aliphatic hydrocarbons may be open-chain or cyclic. Aliphatic cyclic hydrocarbons are called **alicyclic**. Aliphatic hydrocarbons are one of three types: alkanes, alkenes, and alkynes.

Alkanes

Alkanes contain only single bonds. Alkanes have the maximum number of hydrogen atoms possible for their carbon backbone, so they are called **saturated**. Alkenes, alkynes, and aromatics are **unsaturated** because they have fewer hydrogens.

Straight-chain alkanes are also called **normal alkanes**. These are the simplest hydrocarbons. They consist of a linear chain of carbon atoms. The names of these molecules contain the suffix *–ane* and a **root based on the number of carbons in the chain** according to the table on the following page. The first four roots, *meth–*, *eth–*, *prop–*, and *but–* have historical origins in chemistry, and the remaining alkanes contain common Greek number prefixes. Alkanes have the general formula C_nH_{2n+2}.

A single molecule may be represented in multiple ways. Methane and ethane in the table are shown as three-dimensional structures with dashed wedge shapes attaching atoms behind the page and thick wedge shapes attaching atoms in front of the page.

Number of carbons	Name	Formula	Structure
1	Methane	CH_4	
2	Ethane	C_2H_6	
3	Propane	C_3H_8	
4	Butane	C_4H_{10}	
5	Pentane	C_5H_{12}	
6	Hexane	C_6H_{14}	
7	Heptane	C_7H_{16}	
8	Octane	C_8H_{18}	

Additional ways that pentane might be represented are:

n-pentane (the *n* represents a *normal* alkane)
$$CH_3CH_2CH_2CH_2CH_3$$
$$CH_3(CH_2)_3CH_3$$

If one hydrogen is removed from an alkane, the residue is called an **alkyl** group. The *–ane* suffix is replaced by an *–yl–* infix when this residue is used as **functional group**. Functional groups are used to systematically build up the names of organic molecules.

Branched alkanes are named using a four-step process:

1) Find the longest continuous carbon chain. This is the parent hydrocarbon.
2) Number the atoms on this chain beginning at the end near the first branch point, so the lowest locant numbers are used. Number functional groups from the attachment point.
3) Determine the numbered locations and names of the substituted alkyl groups. Use *di–*, *tri–*, and similar prefixes for alkyl groups represented more than once. Separate numbers by commas and groups by dashes.
4) List the locations and names of alkyl groups in alphabetical order by their name (ignoring the *di–*, *tri–* prefixes) and end the name with the parent hydrocarbon.

Example: Name the following hydrocarbon:

Solution:
1) The longest chain is seven carbons in length, as shown by the bold lines below. This molecule is a heptane.
2) The atoms are numbered from the end nearest the first branch as shown:

3) Methyl groups are located at carbons 2 and 3 (2,3-dimethyl), and an ethyl group is located at carbon 4.
4) "Ethyl" precedes "methyl" alphabetically. The hydrocarbon name is:
   4-ethyl-2,3-dimethylheptane.

The following branched alkanes have IUPAC-accepted common names:

Structure	Systematic name	Common name
	2-methylpropane	isobutane
	2-methylbutane	isopentane
	2,2-dimethylpropane	neopentane

The following alkyl groups have IUPAC-accepted common names. The systematic names assign a locant number of 1 to the attachment point:

Structure	Systematic name	Common name
	1-methylethyl	isopropyl
	2-methylpropyl	isobutyl
	1-methylpropyl	sec-butyl
	1,1-dimethylethyl	tert-butyl

Alkenes

Alkenes contain one or more double bonds. Alkenes are also called olefins. The suffix used in the naming of alkenes is –*ene*, and the number roots are those used for alkanes of the same length.

A number preceding the name shows the location of the double bond for alkenes of length four and above. Alkenes with one double bond have the general formula C_nH_{2n}. Multiple double bonds are named using –*diene*, –*triene*, etc. The suffix –*enyl*– is used for functional groups after a hydrogen is removed from an alkene. Ethene and propene have the common names **ethylene** and **propylene**. The ethenyl group has the common name **vinyl** and the 2-propenyl group has the common name **allyl**.

Examples:

H_2C══CH_2 is ethylene or ethene. H_2C══CH is a vinyl or ethenyl group.

is propylene or propene.   is an allyl or 2-propenyl group.

is 2-hexene.

is 2-methyl-1,3-butadiene (common name: isoprene).

Cis-trans isomerism is often part of the complete name for an alkene. Note that isoprene contains two adjacent double bonds, so it is a **conjugated** molecule.

Note that isoprene contains two adjacent double bonds, so it is a **conjugated** molecule

Alkynes and alkenynes

Alkynes contain one or more triple bonds. They are named in a similar way to alkenes. The suffix used for alkynes is –*yne*. Ethyne is often called **acetylene**. Alkynes with one triple bond have the general formula C_nH_{2n-2}. Multiple triple bonds are named using –*diyne*, –*triyne*, etc. The infix –*ynyl*– is used for functional groups composed of alkynes after the removal of a hydrogen atom.

Hydrocarbons with **both double and triple bonds are known as alkenynes**. The locant number for the double bond precedes the name, and the locant for the triple bond follows the suffix –*en*– and precedes the suffix –*yne*.

Examples: $HC\equiv CH$ is acetylene or ethyne.

$HC\equiv C—CH_2—CH_3$ is 1-butyne.

$HC\equiv C—C\equiv C—CH_3$ is 1,3-pentadiyne.

is a 4-hexynyl group.

is 1-buten-3-yne. This compound has the common name of vinylacetylene

Cycloalkanes, –enes, and –ynes

Alicyclic hydrocarbons use the prefix *cyclo–* before the number root for the molecule. The structures for these molecules are often written as if the molecule lay entirely within the plane of the paper even though in reality, these rings dip above and below a single plane. When there is more than one substitution on the ring, numbering begins with the first substitution listed in alphabetical order.

Cis-trans isomerism is often part of the complete name for a cycloalkane

Examples:

is cyclopropane

or

is methylcyclohexane.

or

is 1,3-cyclohexadiene.

is 1-ethyl-3-propylcyclobutane.

Aromatic hydrocarbons

Aromatic hydrocarbons are structurally related to benzene or made up of benzene molecules fused together. These molecules are called **arenes** to distinguish them from alkanes, alkenes, and alkynes. All atoms in arenes lie in the same plane. In other words, aromatic hydrocarbons are flat. Aromatic molecules have electrons in delocalized π orbitals that are free to migrate throughout the molecule.

Substitutions onto the benzene ring are named in alphabetical order using the lowest possible locant numbers. The prefix *phenyl–* may be used for C_6H_5- (benzene less a hydrogen) attached as a functional group to a larger hydrocarbon residue. Arenes in general form aryl functional groups. A phenyl group may be represented in a structure by the symbol Ø. The prefix *benzyl–* may used for $C_6H_5CH_2-$ (methylbenzene with a hydrogen removed from the methyl group) attached as a functional group.

Examples:

is benzene.

is 2-isopropyl-1,4-dimethylbenzene.

is 3-phenyloctane or (1-ethylhexyl)benzene.

The most often used common names for aromatic hydrocarbons are listed in the following table. Naphthalene is the simplest molecule formed by fused benzene rings.

Structure	Systematic name	Common name
	methylbenzene	toluene
	1,2-dimethylbenzene	ortho-xylene or o-xylene
	1,3-dimethylbenzene	meta-xylene or m-xylene
	1,4-dimethylbenzene	para-xylene or p-xylene
	ethenylbenzene	styrene
		naphthalene

Skill 3.15   Identify common organic functional groups.

Hydrocarbons consist entirely of nonpolar C-H bonds with no unpaired electrons. These compounds are relatively unreactive. The substitution of one or more atoms with unpaired electrons into the hydrocarbon backbone creates a **hydrocarbon derivative**. The unpaired electrons result in polar or charged portions of these molecules. These atoms fall into categories known as **functional groups**, and they create **local regions of reactivity**. Alkyl, alkenyl, alkynyl, and aryl groups may also be considered functional groups in some circumstances as described in the previous skill.

Two types of names are often used for the same hydrocarbon derivative. For **substitutive names**, the hydrocarbon name is written out and the correct prefix or suffix is added for the derivative group. For **functional class names**, the hydrocarbon is written as a functional group and the derivative is added as a second word. Skill 3.4 also contains information on functional groups.

Examples: CH_3Br may be called bromomethane (substitutive name) or methyl bromide (functional class name). CH_3CH_2OH is ethanol (substitutive name) or ethyl alcohol (functional class name).

In the tables on the following pages, the symbols R and R' represent hydrocarbons in covalent linkage to the functional group. Many derivatives are named in a similar manner to alkenes and alkynes, but the location and suffix of the functional group is used in place of –ene and –yne.

The **acyl group** is

There are non-systematic number roots for hydrocarbon derivatives containing acyl groups or derived from acyl groups. These are the ketones, carboxylic acids, esters, nitriles, and amides:

Number of carbons (including the acyl carbon)	Systematic prefix	Accepted prefix for acyl and nitrile functional groups
1	meth–	form–
2	eth–	acet–
3	prop–	propion–
4	but–	butyr–
5	pent–	pent–
6 and above	same for larger numbers	

Several functional groups utilize oxygen.

Class of molecule	Functional group	Structure	Affix	Example
Alcohol	Hydroxyl ——OH	**primary** R—CH$_2$—ÖH **secondary** R$_1$R$_2$CH—ÖH **tertiary** R$_1$R$_2$R$_3$C—OH	–ol	H$_3$C—CH$_2$—OH ethanol
Ether	Oxy	R$_1$—Ö—R$_2$	–oxy–	H$_3$C—O—CH$_2$—CH$_3$ methoxyethane or ethyl methyl ether
Aldehyde	Carbonyl	R—C(=Ö)—H	–al	O=C(H)—CH$_2$—CH$_3$ propionaldehyde or propanal
Ketone		R$_1$—C(=Ö)—R$_2$	–one	H$_3$C—C(=O)—CH$_3$ acetone
Carboxylic acid	Carboxyl	R—C(=Ö)—ÖH	–oic acid	HC(=O)—OH formic acid or methanoic acid

Class of molecule	Functional group	Structure	Affix	Example
Ester	Oxycarbonyl		–yl –oate	methyl butyrate or methyl butanoate
Acid anhydride	Carbonyloxycarbonyl		–oic anhydride	acetic anhydride or ethanoic anhydride

Derivatives utilizing other atoms are also common.

Class of molecule	Functional group	Structure	Affix	Example
Nitrile	Cyanide $-C\equiv N$	$R-C\equiv N:$	–nitrile	$H_3C-C\equiv N$ acetonitrile or ethanonitrile
Amine	Amino $-N-$	primary $R-\overset{..}{N}-H$ with H below; secondary $R_1-\overset{..}{N}-H$ with R_2 below; tertiary $R_1-\overset{..}{N}-R_3$ with R_2 below	–amine	$H_3C-\overset{H_2}{C}-NH_2$ ethanamine
Amide	Aminocarbonyl	primary secondary tertiary amide structures	–amide	propionamide or propanamide
Alkyl halide	Halide $-X$ (where X is F, Cl, Br, or I)	$R-\overset{..}{\underset{..}{X}}:$	fluoro– chloro– bromo– iodo–	2-bromobutane

Hydrocarbon derivatives and functional groups may be identified using the tables found in the previous skill. One way to memorize the derivatives utilizing oxygen is to divide them into pairs with a hydrogen atom in the first element of the pair replaced by a hydrocarbon in the second element. These pairs are:

1) alcohol/ether.
2) aldehyde/ketone.
3) carboxylic acid/ester.

A final word about IUPAC organic nomenclature

"IUPAC nomenclature" has become a synonym for "correct nomenclature," but the most recent IUPAC recommendations for organic nomenclature are ignored in most textbooks and curricula in the United States. This situation is similar to the nomenclature for inorganic chemistry in that the older nomenclature is "systematic enough" to be taught and to avoid most errors, but is a poor choice to name new compounds in an unambiguous way.

Two important differences between the 1979 and more recent nomenclature involve the use of locant numbers:

1) The 1979 nomenclature usually places locant numbers before the name of the entire compound, but the 1993 recommendations suggest placing locant numbers immediately before the group that they represent.
2) The 1979 nomenclature always assigns a locant number of 1 to the attachment point of groups, but the 1993 nomenclature recommends stating the attachment point explicitly before "–yl–." This decreases the complexity of hydrocarbon residues.

The 1993 nomenclature permits the 1979 nomenclature as "naming method a" and presents the newer method as a "method b." In provisional 2004 recommendations, the newer "method b" names are usually explicitly preferred. The newer method is more commonly used in Europe and elsewhere. These differences are shown below for some of the hydrocarbons described in skills 3.14 and 3.15

Structure	Systematic name (1979)	Systematic name (2004)	Common name
	2-hexene	hex-2-ene	
	1-buten-3-yne	but-1-en-3-yne	vinylacetylene
	1-methylethyl	propan-2-yl	isopropyl
	2-methylpropyl	2-methylpropan-1-yl	isobutyl
	1-methylpropyl	butan-2-yl	sec-butyl
	1,1-dimethylethyl	2-methylpropan-2-yl	tert-butyl
	3-phenyloctane or (1-ethylhexyl)benzene	octan-3-ylbenzene	

Provisional IUPAC recommendations from 2004 discuss a single "preferred IUPAC name". for organic compounds, and this nomenclature may be taught in the classrooms of the future, but the rules in **Skill 3.14** and **Skill 3.15** corresponding to 1979 conventions are what nearly everyone means by IUPAC organic nomenclature today, and they are what you should learn and teach while being aware of the more recent changes.

Many IUPAC rules for organic chemistry may be found on-line here: http://www.acdlabs.com/iupac/nomenclature/.

The complete recent IUPAC provisional recommendations may be found here: http://www.iupac.org/reports/provisional/abstract04/favre_310305.html

Skill 3.16 Differentiate between the structures of common biochemical compounds, such as lipids, amino acids, carbohydrates, and nucleic acids.

Lipids

Lipids typically have **large hydrocarbons** as part of their structure and are **insoluble in water**. Animal fats and vegetable oils are **complex lipids** called **triacylglycerides**. These molecules contain three ester groups.

Fats, such as the molecule shown above, may be broken apart to yield **glycerol** and long-chain carboxylic acids known as **fatty acids**. Glycerol is shown to the right and two fatty acids are shown below.

Classes of hydrocarbons are often applied to the corresponding fatty acid. **Saturated fat** refers to fatty acids containing a hydrocarbon chain with only single bonds as shown above on the right. **Unsaturated fat** refers to fatty acids containing one or more alkene group. If one alkene linkage is present on the hydrocarbon, it is **monounsaturated**. If more than one is present, it is **polyunsaturated**. Unsaturated fats are also described as *cis*– or *trans*– and may be conjugated. The molecule above on the left is a monounsaturated *cis*-fatty acid. Unsaturated fat in processed food is often converted to saturated fat by **hydrogenation**.

Simple lipids such as cholesterol (shown below) do not contain ester groups:

Many lipids like the fatty acids above have a long non-polar hydrocarbon "tail" region and a small polar "head" region. The hydrocarbon region of the molecule is **hydrophobic** and the polar region is **hydrophilic**. Hydrophobic means water hating while hydrophilic means water loving.

Soaps and synthetic **detergents** clean materials because their molecules have these two regions. When they are dispersed in water, the hydrophilic heads face the water in an attempt to dissolve, but the hydrophobic tails are attracted to each other and surround any grease particulates. These spherical clusters are called **micelles**. The net effect is to disperse grease in water where it can be washed away.

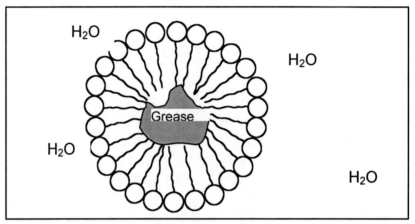

Lipid molecules in the membranes of cells form a **lipid bilayer** by lining up tail-to-tail in order to separate the space inside the cell from the extracellular environment.

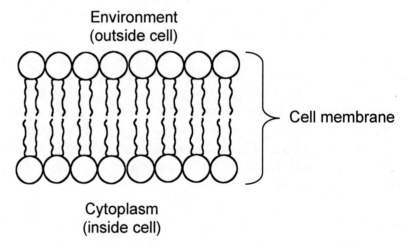

Proteins

Proteins play a role in nearly every process in living organisms and are the most important and diverse molecules in living things. **Amino acids form the building blocks of proteins**. Amino acids contain both an amine and a carboxylic acid.

Each of the 20 different common amino acids uses a different **side chain** for R. Side chains may be nonpolar or polar. The polar side chains may be acidic or basic. Side chains may also be aromatic or aliphatic.

The carbonyl carbon atom of one amino acid bonds to the amine nitrogen of another to form an amide group. This bond is called a peptide bond:

The molecule to the left is a **dipeptide** because it contains two amino acids. Many amino acids strung together form a **polypeptide**, and the term **protein** is used for these larger chains.

Interactions among specific sequences of side chains give each protein a certain shape with unique chemical properties. A common shape found within many proteins is an α-**helix** shown to the right. Physical properties of the protein follow from the way individual protein molecules interact with water and with each other.

A protein called **keratin** is insoluble in water but binds to other keratin molecules to form hard structures. Proteins like keratin are known as **structural proteins** or **fibrous proteins**. Keratin is the main component in hair and fingernails. A different protein called **insulin** is soluble in water and achieves a certain shape as an individual molecule. Proteins like insulin are known as **globular proteins**. Insulin in the bloodstream regulates glucose metabolism.

Globular proteins called **enzymes** act as catalysts to increase the rate of biochemical reactions. The names of enzymes often end with the suffix –*ase*. Many other protein names end with the suffix –*in*. Heating a protein or changing its chemical environment may cause it to lose its shape without breaking any covalent bonds. This loss of structure is called **denaturation**.

Carbohydrates

Monosaccharides (also known as **simple sugars**) **form the building blocks of carbohydrates**. The empirical formula for simple sugars is CH_2O. The name *carbohydrate* is derived from "hydrate of carbon" based on this formula. The names of monosaccharides use the suffix *–ose*. A monosaccharide contains multiple hydroxyl groups and may be an **aldose** or a **ketose** depending on whether it contains an aldehyde or a ketone group.

Organisms use the bonds in carbohydrates to store energy in chemical form. The most important monosaccharide is glucose. Glucose is a **hexose** because it contains six carbon atoms. Glucose has the formula $C_6H_{12}O_6$. It is also an aldose. Like many monosaccharides, the carbonyl group of glucose may react with one of its hydroxyl groups. This creates an **equilibrium between open chain and ring forms**. These two forms of glucose are shown below:

Two simple sugars may be joined together by a **glycosidic bond**.

The molecule to the left is the **disaccharide** sucrose. Many sugars linked together will form a **polysaccharide**, and the term **complex carbohydrate** is used for these structures. More than two glycosidic bonds may attach to a simple sugar, so complex carbohydrates often contain branch-like structures. This is in contrast to proteins where building blocks are strung together in a linear fashion.

Starch and **cellulose** are two examples of glycosidic complex carbohydrates.

Nucleic Acids

Nucleotides form the building blocks of nucleic acids. A nucleotide is made up of a phosphate, a sugar, and an amine "base." An example is shown below:

Living things use nucleic acids to carry genetic information based on the identity of the amine base present. This information is used to determine the amino acid sequence of every protein in the organism, and it provides a blueprint for how the organism is made.

The phosphate of one nucleotide may form a covalent bond with the sugar residue of another to form a **dinucleotide** as shown on the left. Sugar-phosphate groups link to each other to form a helix "backbone" with the amine bases protruding outwards. Many nucleotides linked together in this way form **ribonucleic acid (RNA)** if the sugar is ribose, and others will form **deoxyribonucleic acid (DNA)** if the sugar is ribose lacking a hydroxyl group.

Amine bases on one nucleic acid molecule may form hydrogen bonds with bases on a second strand. For DNA, these two strands form the familiar **double-helix**.

COMPETENCY 4.0   KNOWLEDGE OF CHEMICAL REACTIONS AND STOICHIOMETRY

21%

"Was not all the knowledge / Of the Egyptians writ in / mystic symbols?"
                                        - Ben Johnson, *The Alchemist*

Skill 4.1   Balance chemical equations.

A properly written chemical equation must contain properly written formulas and must be **balanced**. Chemical equations are written to describe a certain number of moles of reactants becoming a certain number of moles of products. Chemical equations obey the law of conservation of mass in that no atoms are created or destroyed, so each element has the same number of total atoms on the left of the arrow as it has on the right of the arrow when the equation is balanced. The number of moles of each compound is indicated by its **stoichiometric coefficient**. The number of atoms of an element is determined by multiplying the coefficient by the subscript, with subscripts outside of parentheses being multiplied by subscripts inside the parenthesis. This is done for each element in each compound. Then all the atoms of that element on that side of the arrow are added together.

Example: In the reaction

$$2H_2(g) + O_2(g) \rightarrow 2H_2O(l),$$

hydrogen has a stoichiometric coefficient of two, oxygen has a coefficient of one, and water has a coefficient of two because 2 moles of hydrogen react with 1 mole of oxygen to form two moles of water.

The number of atoms of hydrogen on the left is 4 which is found by multiplying the coefficient of 2 by the subscript of 2. The number of atoms of hydrogen on the right is found in the same way to be 4. The number of atoms of oxygen on the left is 2 since the coefficient of 1 is multiplied by the subscript of 2. Using the same method on the right, the coefficient of 2 is multiplied by the subscript of 1 (no subscript means there is one) to obtain a total of 2 atoms of oxygen. Therefore, this reaction is balanced.

In a balanced equation, the stoichiometric coefficients are chosen so that the equation contains an **equal number of each type of atom on each side**. In our example, there are four H atoms and two O atoms on both sides. Therefore, the equation is balanced with respect to atoms.

Balance properly written chemical equations.

Balancing equations is a multi-step process.

1. Determine the **correct formulas** for all compounds.

2. Write an **unbalanced equation**. This requires knowledge of the proper products which can be predicted from the reactants. Reactants are written on the left and products are written on the right.

3. Determine the **number of each type of atom on each side** of the equation to determine if the equation is already balanced. Under the reactants, list all the elements in the reactants starting with metals, then nonmetals, listing oxygen last and hydrogen next to last. Under the products, list all the elements in the same order as those under the reactants – preferably, straight across from them.

4. Count the atoms of each element on the left side and list the numbers next to the elements. Repeat for products. Don't forget that subscripts outside a parenthesis multiply subscripts inside the parenthesis. If each element has the same number of atoms on the right that it has on the left, the equation is balanced. If not, proceed to Step 5.

5. For the first element in the list that has unequal numbers of atoms, use a coefficient (whole number to the left of the compound or element) on either the left of the arrow or the right of the arrow to give an equal number of atoms. NEVER change the subscripts to balance an equation.

6. Go to the next unbalanced element and balance it, moving down the list until all are balanced.

7. Start back at the beginning of the list and actually count the atoms of each element on each side of the arrow to make sure the number listed is the actual number. Re-balance and re-check as needed.

Example: Balance the chemical equation describing the combustion of methanol (CH_4O) in oxygen to produce only carbon dioxide and water.

Solution:

1) The structural formula of methanol is CH_3OH, so its molecular formula is CH_4O. The formula for carbon dioxide is CO_2. Therefore the unbalanced equation is:

$$CH_4O + O_2 \rightarrow CO_2 + H_2O.$$

2) On the left there are 1 C, 4 H, and 3 O atoms. On the right, there are 1 C, 2 H, and 3 O atoms. The equation is close to being balanced, but there is still work to do.

3) Assuming that CH_4O has a stoichiometric coefficient of one means that the left side has 1C and 4H that also must be present on the right. Therefore the stoichiometric coefficient of CO_2 will be 1 to balance C and the stoichiometric coefficient of H_2O will be 2 to balance H. Now we have:

$$CH_4O + ?O_2 \rightarrow CO_2 + 2H_2O.$$

and only oxygen remains unbalanced. There are 4 O on the right and one of these is accounted for by methanol leaving 3 O to be accounted for by O_2. This gives a stoichiometric coefficient of 3/2 and a balanced equation:

$$CH_4O + \frac{3}{2}O_2 \rightarrow CO_2 + 2H_2O.$$

4) Whole-number coefficients are achieved by multiplying by two:

$$2CH_4O + 3O_2 \rightarrow 2CO_2 + 4H_2O.$$

Reactions among ions in aqueous solution may be represented in three ways. When solutions of hydrochloric acid and sodium hydroxide are mixed, a reaction occurs and heat is produced. The **molecular equation** for this reaction is:

$$HCl(aq) + NaOH(aq) \rightarrow H_2O(l) + NaCl(aq).$$

It is called a molecular equation because the **complete chemical formulas** of reactants and products are shown. But in reality, both HCl and NaOH are strong electrolytes and exist in solution as ions. This is represented by a **complete ionic equation** that shows all the dissolved ions:

$$H^+(aq) + Cl^-(aq) + Na^+(aq) + OH^-(aq) \rightarrow H_2O(l) + Na^+(aq) + Cl^-(aq).$$

Because $Na^+(aq)$ and $Cl^-(aq)$ appear as both reactants and products, they play no role in the reaction. Ions that appear in identical chemical forms on both sides of an ionic equation are called **spectator ions** because they aren't part of the action. When spectator ions are removed from a complete ionic equation, the result is a **net ionic equation** that shows the actual changes that occur to the chemicals when these two solutions are mixed together:

$$H^+(aq) + OH^-(aq) \rightarrow H_2O(l)$$

An additional requirement for **redox** reactions (see **Skill 4.17**) is that the equation contains an **equal charge on each side**. In the example above, the positive charge on the H+ ion cancels out the negative charge on the OH– ion, giving an overall neutral charge for both sides of the equation. Redox reactions may be divided into half-reactions which either gain or lose electrons.

Skill 4.2   Given common chemical species and reaction conditions, predict probable reaction products.

There are chemical reactions occurring all around us everyday. So many different chemical reactions would be very difficult to understand. However, the millions of chemical reactions that take place each and every day fall into only a few basic categories. Using these categories can help predict products of reactions that are unfamiliar or new.

Once we have an idea of the **reaction type**, we can make a good prediction about the products of chemical equations, and also balance the reactions. **General reaction types** are listed in the following table. Some reaction types have multiple names.

Reaction type	General equation	Example
Combination / Synthesis	$A + B \rightarrow C$	$2H_2 + O_2 \rightarrow 2H_2O$
Decomposition	$A \rightarrow B + C$	$2KClO_3 \rightarrow 2KCl + 3O_2$
Single substitution / Single displacement / Single replacement	$A + BC \rightarrow AB + C$	$Mg + 2HCl \rightarrow MgCl_2 + H_2$
Double substitution / Double displacement / Double replacement / Ion exchange / Metathesis	$AC + BD \rightarrow AD + BC$	$HCl + NaOH \rightarrow NaCl + H_2O$

Isomerization	$A \rightarrow A'$	

Example: Determine the products of a reaction between Cl_2 and a solution of NaBr.

Solution: The first step is to write:
$$Cl_2 + NaBr(aq) \rightarrow ?$$

Now examine the possible choices from the table. Decomposition and isomerization reactions require only one reactant. It also can not be a double substitution reaction because one of the reactants is an element.

A synthesis reaction to form some NaBrCl compound would require very unusual valences! The most likely reaction is the remaining one: Cl replaces Br in aqueous solution with Na:

$\left(\begin{array}{c} single \\ substitution \end{array} \right)$ $Cl_2 + NaBr(aq) \rightarrow NaCl(aq) + Br_2$

After balancing, the equation is:
$$Cl_2 + 2NaBr(aq) \rightarrow 2NaCl(aq) + Br_2$$

Many **specific reaction types** also exist. Always determine the complete ionic equation for reactions in solution. This will help you determine the reaction type. The most common specific reaction types are summarized in the following table:

Reaction type	General equation	Example
Precipitation	Molecular: $AC(aq) + BD(aq) \rightarrow AD(s \text{ or } g) + BC(aq)$ Net ionic: $A^+(aq) + D^-(aq) \rightarrow AD(s \text{ or } g)$	Molecular: $NiCl_2(aq) + Na_2S(aq) \rightarrow NiS(s) + 2NaCl(aq)$ Net ionic: $Ni^{2+}(aq) + S^{2-}(aq) \rightarrow NiS(s)$
Acid-base neutralization	Arrhenius: $H^+ + OH^- \rightarrow H_2O$	Arrhenius: $HNO_3 + NaOH \rightarrow NaNO_3 + H_2O$ $H^+ + OH^- \rightarrow H_2O$ (net ionic)
	Brønsted-Lowry: $HA + B \rightarrow HB + A$	Brønsted-Lowry: $HNO_3 + KCN \rightarrow HCN + KNO_3$ $H^+ + CN^- \rightarrow HCN$ (net ionic)
	Lewis: $A + {:}B \rightarrow A{:}B$	Lewis:
Redox	Full reaction: $A + B \rightarrow C + D$	$Ni + CuSO_4 \rightarrow NiSO_4 + Cu$ $Ni + Cu^{2+} \rightarrow Ni^{2+} + Cu$ (net ionic)
	Half reactions: $A \rightarrow C + e^-$ and $e^- + B \rightarrow D$	$Ni \rightarrow Ni^{2+} + 2e^-$ $2e^- + Cu^{2+} \rightarrow Cu$
Combustion	organic molecule $+ O_2 \rightarrow CO_2 + H_2O + heat$	$2C_2H_6 + 7O_2 \rightarrow 4CO_2 + 6H_2O$

Whether precipitation occurs among a group of ions—and which compound will form the precipitate—may be determined by the solubility rules on the following page. (There is a simplified list of solubility rules in Skill 1.4)

Ion	Solubility	Exception
All compounds containing alkali metals	All are soluble	
All compounds containing ammonium, NH_4^+	All are soluble	
All compounds containing nitrates, NO_3^-	All are soluble	
All compounds containing chlorates, ClO_3^- and perchlorates, ClO_4^-	All are soluble	
All compounds containing acetates, $C_2H_3O_2^-$	All are soluble	
Compounds containing Cl^-, Br^-, and I^-	Are soluble	Except halides of Ag^+, Hg_2^{2+}, and Pb^{2+}
Compounds containing F^-	Are soluble	Except fluorides of Mg^{2+}, Ca^{2+}, Sr^{2+}, Ba^{2+}, and Pb^2
Compounds containing sulfates, SO_4^{2-}	Are soluble	Except sulfates of Mg^{2+}, Ca^{2+}, Sr^{2+}, Ba^{2+}, and Pb^2
All compounds containing carbonates, CO_3^{2-}	Are insoluble	Except those containing alkali metals or NH_4^+
All compounds containing phosphates, PO_4^{3-}	Are insoluble	Except those containing alkali metals or NH_4^+
All compounds containing oxalates, $C_2O_4^{2-}$	Are insoluble	Except those containing alkali metals or NH_4^+
All compounds containing chromates, CrO_4^{2-}	Are insoluble	Except those containing alkali metals or NH_4^+
All compounds containing oxides, O^{2-}	Are insoluble	Except those containing alkali metals or NH_4^+
All compounds containing sulfides, S^{2-}	Are insoluble	Except those containing alkali metals or NH_4^+
All compounds containing sulfites, SO_3^{2-}	Are insoluble	Except those containing alkali metals or NH_4^+
All compounds containing silicates, SiO_4^{2-}	Are insoluble	Except those containing alkali metals or NH_4^+
All compounds containing hydroxides	Are insoluble	Except those containing alkali metals or NH_4^+, or Ba^{2+}

If protons are available for combination or substitution, then they are likely being transferred from an acid to a base. An unshared electron pair on one of the reactants may form a bond in a Lewis acid-base reaction.

The possibility that oxidation numbers may change among the reactants indicates an electron transfer and a redox reaction. (See Skill 4.17 for redox reactions) Combustion reactants consist of an organic molecule and oxygen.

Example: Determine the products, and write a balanced equation for the reaction between sodium iodide and lead(II) nitrate in aqueous solution.

Solution: We know that sodium iodide is NaI and lead(II) nitrate is $Pb(NO_3)_2$.
The reactants of the complete ionic equation are:
$$Na^+(aq) + Pb^{2+}(aq) + I^-(aq) + NO_3^-(aq) \rightarrow ?$$

The solubility rules indicate that lead iodide is insoluble and will form as a precipitate. The unbalanced net ionic equation is then:
$$Pb^{2+}(aq) + I^-(aq) \rightarrow PbI_2(s)$$

and the unbalanced molecular equation is:
$$NaI(aq) + Pb(NO_3)_2(aq) \rightarrow PbI_2(s) + NaNO_3(aq).$$

Balancing the equation yields:
$$2NaI(aq) + Pb(NO_3)_2(aq) \rightarrow PbI_2(s) + 2NaNO_3(aq).$$

Skill 4.3 Solve mass-mass stoichiometry problems.

The mole is the chemist's counting unit. Working with the mole should become second nature since they are very important in mass-mass stoichiometry, and the balanced equation provides mole ratios not mass ratios.

Mass to moles

First determine the molar mass of the substance by adding the masses for each element in the substance and multiplying by the number of atoms present.

Example: What is the molar mass of $CuSO_4$?

Solution:
(1 mole of Cu = 63.5 g) + (1 mol of S = 32 g) + (4 mol O = 4 x 16 = 48 g) = 143.5 g/mol $CuSO_4$

Then determine the number of moles present using the molar mass conversion 1 mol = molar mass of substance, for example: 1 mol $CuSO_4$ = 143.5 g $CuSO_4$

Example: 315 g of $CuSO_4$ is how many moles of $CuSO_4$?

315 g x 1 mol/143.5 g = 2.20 mol $CuSO_4$

Mole to grams conversions are the reverse

Solving these problems is a three-step process:

1) Grams of the given compound (known mass) are converted to moles (known moles) using molecular mass.
2) The moles of the given compound (known moles) are related to moles of the second compound (unknown moles) by relating their stoichiometric coefficients.
3) The moles of the second compound (unknown moles) are converted to grams (unknown mass) using the molecular mass of the compound.

These steps are often combined in one series of multiplications, which may be described as **"grams to moles to moles to grams."** Another way to look at them is **"grams of known to moles of known to moles of unknown to grams of unknown."**

Example: What mass of oxygen is required to consume 95.0 g of ethane in the following reaction?

$$2C_2H_6 + 7O_2 \rightarrow 4CO_2 + 6H_2O$$

Solution:

$$95.0 \text{ g } C_2H_6 \times \underbrace{\frac{1 \text{ mol } C_2H_6}{30.1 \text{ g } C_2H_6}}_{\text{step 1}} \times \underbrace{\frac{7 \text{ mol } O_2}{2 \text{ mol } C_2H_6}}_{\text{step 2}} \times \underbrace{\frac{32.0 \text{ g } O_2}{1 \text{ mol } O_2}}_{\text{step 3}} = 359 \text{ g } O_2$$

By expressing the molecular mass of the first or given compound as moles per gram, the grams of the known cancel. By putting the moles of the known compound on the bottom with the molecular coefficient of the unknown compound on top in the second conversion the moles of the known are canceled and converted to moles of unknown. And finally, by expressing the molecular mass of the second compound as grams per mole, its moles are converted to grams for the final answer and the units (by canceling) end up as grams of the unknown

Calculate percent yield

The **yield of a reaction is the amount of product** obtained. This value is nearly always less than what would be predicted from a stoichiometric calculation because side-reactions may produce different products, the reverse reaction may occur, and some material may be lost during the procedure. The yield from a stoichiometric calculation on the limiting reagent is called the theoretical yield.

Percent yield is the actual yield divided by the theoretical yield times 100%:

$$\text{Percent yield} = \frac{\text{Actual yield}}{\text{Theoretical yield}} \times 100\%.$$

Example: 387 g $AlBr_3$ are produced by the reaction described in the previous example. What is the percent yield?

Solution: $\dfrac{387 \text{ g } AlBr_3}{445 \text{ g } AlBr_3} \times 100\% = 87.0\% \text{ yield.}$

Skill 4.4   Solve mass-gas volume stoichiometry problems.

The progress of reactions that produce or consume a gas may be described by measuring gas volume instead of mass. If the gas is at STP (standard temperature and pressure), then the equivalency 22.4 liters = 1 mole can be used.

Example: How many liters of nitrogen are needed to produce 34.0 grams of NH_3?

Solution: Write and balance the equation: $N_2 + 3 H_2 \rightarrow 2 NH_3$

List what is given and what is unknown:

Mass NH_3: 34.0 g	Mass N_2: unknown
GFM NH_3: 17.0 g/mol	GFM N_2: 28.0 g/mol
Moles NH_3: 2 (coefficient)	Moles N_2: 1 (no coefficient)

Use the 3-step label canceling method:

$$\frac{34.0 \text{ g } NH_3}{} \cdot \frac{1 \text{ mole } NH_3}{17.0 \text{ g } NH_3} \cdot \frac{1 \text{ mole } N_2}{2 \text{ moles } NH_3} \cdot \frac{22.4 \text{ liters } N_2}{1 \text{ mole } N_2} \quad \begin{matrix} -- \\ -- \end{matrix}$$

For 34.0 L of NH_3 to be formed, 17.0 L of N_2 would be needed.

If you need to get the number of molecules or formula units, use Avogadro's number of 6.02 x 10^{23} particles per mol in the equation.

If the gas is not at STP, the best way to solve these problems is to use the ideal gas equation to convert between volume and moles.

$$n = \frac{PV}{RT} \quad \text{and} \quad V = \frac{RT}{nP}$$

If a volume is given, the steps are "**volume of known to moles of known to moles of unknown to grams of unknown**." If a mass is given, the steps will be "**grams of known to moles of known to moles of unkown to volume of unknown**."

Example: What volume of oxygen, in liters, is generated at 40° C and 1 atm by the decomposition of 280 g of potassium chlorate in the following reaction?

$$2KClO_3 \rightarrow 2KCl + 3O_2(g)$$

Solution: We are given a mass and are asked to find volume, so the steps in the solution will be "grams to moles to moles to volume."

Thus we convert grams to moles:

$$280 \text{ g KClO}_3 \times \frac{1 \text{ mol KClO}_3}{122.548 \text{ g KClO}_3} \times \frac{3 \text{ mol O}_2}{2 \text{ mol KClO}_3} = 3.427 \text{ mol O}_2$$

Then we use the ideal gas law and convert to volume, in liters.

$$PV = nRT$$
$$V = \frac{nRT}{P}$$

$$V = \frac{RT}{nP} = \frac{\left(0.08206 \frac{\text{L-atm}}{\text{mol-K}} \right)(273.15 + 40)\text{K}}{(3.427 \text{ mol O}_2)(1 \text{ atm})} = \boxed{7.50 \text{ L O}_2} \quad \text{WRONG}$$

$$= \frac{3.427 \text{ mol O}_2 \, . \, 08206 \frac{L \cdot atm}{mol \cdot K} \, 313 \, K}{1 \, atm} = 88.02 \text{ L}$$

Skill 4.5   Solve solution stoichiometry problems.

Solving stoichiometry problems involving a solution requires that the moles of solute for each solution to be determined. This is done using the molarity definition. Once the moles of solute are determined, the problem becomes a mole-mole stoichiometry problem or a limiting reactant problem.

Avogadro's law states that the volume of a gas, at constant temperature and pressure, will be proportional to the number of moles. All components of a reaction are usually in the same vessel at the same temperature and pressure.

Therefore, **stoichiometric coefficients may be used directly for volumes just as they are used for moles**.

Example: How many m^3 of water vapor are produced when 8.2 m^3 of hydrogen are consumed in this reaction: $2H_2(g) + O_2(g) \rightarrow 2H_2O(g)$?

Solution:

$$8.2 \text{ m}^3 \text{ H}_2 \times \frac{2 \text{ m}^3 \text{ H}_2O}{2 \text{ m}^3 \text{ H}_2} = 8.2 \text{ m}^3 \text{ H}_2O$$

Example: How much of a 0.50 M $Pb(NO_3)_2$ solution is required to completely react with 25 g of KI?

$$Pb(NO_3)_2 \text{ (aq)} + \ 2 \text{ KI (s)} \ \rightarrow \ PbI_2 \text{ (s)} \ + 2 \text{ KNO}_3 \text{ (aq)}$$

Solution:

    1. Find the moles of KI reacting:
        25 g KI x 1 mol KI/166 g/mol= 0.15 mol

    2. Use the mol ratio from the balanced equation to find the required amount of moles:
        0.15 mole KI x 1 mol $Pb(NO_3)_2$/ 2 mol KI = 0.075 mol $Pb(NO_3)_2$

    3. Use molarity to determine the volume of $Pb(NO_3)_2$ required.
        M = mol solute/ L solution
    L solution = mol solute/M = 0.075 mol/0.50 M =0.15 L or 150 mL

Skill 4.6   Solve stoichiometry problems with limiting reactants.

The **limiting reagent** of a reaction is the **reactant that runs out first**. This reactant **determines the amount of products formed**, and any **other reactants remain unconverted** to product and are called **excess reagents**.

Example: Consider the reaction $3H_2 + N_2 \rightarrow 2NH_3$ and suppose that 3 mol H₂ and 3 mol N₂ are available for this reaction. What is the limiting reagent?

Solution: The equation tells us that 3 mol H₂ will react with one mol N₂ to produce 2 mol NH₃. This means that H₂ is the limiting reagent because when it is completely used up, 2 mol of N₂ will still remain.

The limiting reagent may be determined by **dividing the number of moles of each reactant by its stoichiometric coefficient**. This determines the moles of reactant if each reactant were limiting. The **lowest result** will indicate the actual limiting reagent. Remember to use moles and not grams for these calculations.

Example: 50.0 g Al and 400. g Br_2 react according the following equation:

$$2Al + 3Br_2 \rightarrow 2AlBr_3$$

until the limiting reagent is completely consumed. Find the limiting reagent, the mass of $AlBr_3$ formed, and the excess reagent remaining after the limiting reagent is consumed.

Solution: First convert both reactants to moles:

$$50.0 \text{ g Al} \times \frac{1 \text{ mol Al}}{26.982 \text{ g Al}} = 1.853 \text{ mol Al} \text{ and } 400. \text{ g Br}_2 \times \frac{1 \text{ mol Br}_2}{159.808 \text{ g Br}_2} = 2.503 \text{ mol Br}_2.$$

The final digits in the intermediate results above are italicized because they are insignificant. Dividing by stoichiometric coefficients gives:

$$1.853 \text{ mol Al} \times \frac{\text{mol reaction}}{2 \text{ mol Al}} = 0.9265 \text{ mol reaction if Al is limiting}$$

$$2.503 \text{ mol Br}_2 \times \frac{\text{mol reaction}}{3 \text{ mol Br}_2} = 0.8343 \text{ mol reaction if Br}_2 \text{ is limiting.}$$

Br_2 is the lower value and is limiting reagent.

The reaction is expected to produce:

$$2.503 \text{ mol Br}_2 \times \frac{2 \text{ mol AlBr}_3}{3 \text{ mol Br}_2} \times \frac{266.694 \text{ g AlBr}_3}{\text{mol AlBr}_3} = 445 \text{ g AlBr}_3.$$

The reaction is expected to consume:

$$2.503 \text{ mol Br}_2 \times \frac{2 \text{ mol Al}}{3 \text{ mol Br}_2} \times \frac{26.982 \text{ g Al}}{\text{mol Al}} = 45.0 \text{ g Al.}$$

50.0 g Al − 45.0 g Al = 5.0 g Al, which will remain

Skill 4.7   Determine empirical formulas from experimental data.

If we know the chemical composition of a compound, we can calculate an **empirical formula** for it. An empirical formula is the **simplest formula** using the smallest set of integers to express the **ratio of atoms** present in a molecule.

The percent composition of a substance is the percentage by mass of each element. Chemical composition is used to verify the purity of a compound in the lab. An impurity will make the actual composition vary from the expected one.

To determine percent composition from a formula, follow these steps:

Write down the **number of atoms each element contributes** to the formula.
1) Multiply these values by the molecular weight of the corresponding element to determine the **grams of each element in one mole** of the formula

2) Add the values from step 2 to obtain the **formula mass**.

3) Divide each value from step 2 by the formula mass from step 3 and multiply by 100% to obtain the **percent composition of each element**.

The first three steps are the same as those used to determine formula mass, but we use the intermediate results to obtain the composition.

Example: What is the chemical composition of ammonium carbonate $(NH_4)_2CO_3$?

Solution:
1) One $(NH_4)_2CO_3$ contains 2 N, 8 H, 1 C, and 3 O.

2) $\dfrac{2 \text{ mol N}}{\text{mol } (NH_4)CO_3} \times \dfrac{14.0 \text{ g N}}{\text{mol N}} = 28.0 \text{ g N/mol } (NH_4)CO_3$

$8(1.0) = 8.0 \text{ g H/mol } (NH_4)CO_3$

$1(12.0) = 12.0 \text{ g C/mol } (NH_4)CO_3$

$3(16.0) = 48.0 \text{ g O/mol } (NH_4)CO_3$

Sum is $\quad 96.0 \text{ g } (NH_4)CO_3/\text{mol } (NH_4)CO_3$

3) $\%N = \dfrac{28.0 \text{ g N/mol } (NH_4)_2CO_3}{96.0 \text{ g } (NH_4)_2CO_3/\text{mol } (NH_4)_2CO_3} = 0.292 \text{ g N/g } (NH_4)_2CO_3 \times 100\% = 29.2\%$

4) $\%H = \dfrac{8.0}{96.0} \times 100\% = 8.3\%$ $\%C = \dfrac{12.0}{96.0} \times 100\% = 12.5\%$ $\%O = \dfrac{48.0}{96.0} \times 100\% = 50.0\%$

If we know the chemical composition of a compound, we can calculate an **empirical formula** for it. An empirical formula is the **simplest formula** using the smallest set of integers to express the **ratio of atoms** present in a molecule.

To determine an empirical formula from a percent composition, follow these steps:

1) Change the "%" sign to grams for a basis of 100 g of the compound.
2) Determine the moles of each element in 100 g of the compound.
3) Divide the values from step 1 by the smallest value to obtain ratios.
4) Multiply by an integer if necessary to get a whole-number ratio.

Example: What is the empirical formula of a compound with a composition of 63.9% Cl, 32.5% C, and 3.6% H?

Solution:

1) We will use a basis of 100 g of the compound containing 63.9 g Cl, 32.5 g C, and 3.6 g H.

2) In 100 g, there are: $63.9 \text{ g Cl} \times \dfrac{\text{mol Cl}}{35.45 \text{ g Cl}} = 1.802 \text{ mol Cl}$

$$32.5/12.01 = 2.706 \text{ mol C}$$

$$3.6/1.01 = 3.56 \text{ mol H}$$

3) Dividing these values by the smallest yields:

$$\dfrac{2.706 \text{ mol C}}{1.802 \text{ mol Cl}} = 1.502 \text{ mol C/mol Cl}$$

$$\dfrac{3.56 \text{ mol H}}{1.802 \text{ mol Cl}} = 1.97 \text{ mol H/mol Cl}$$

Therefore, the elements are present in a ratio of C:H:Cl=1.50:2.0:1

4) Multiply the entire ratio by 2 because you cannot have a fraction of an atom. This corresponds to a ratio of 3:4:2 for an empirical formula of $C_3H_4Cl_2$.

The **molecular formula** describing the **actual number of atoms in the molecule** might actually be $C_3H_4Cl_2$ or it might be $C_6H_8Cl_4$ or some other multiple that maintains a 3:4:2 ratio.

Skill 4.8   **Analyze the effects of concentration, temperature, pressure, surface area, and the presence or absence of catalysts on the rates of reaction.**

In order for one species to be converted to another during a chemical reaction, the reactants must collide. The collisions between the reactants determine how fast the reaction takes place. However, during a chemical reaction, only a fraction of the collisions between the appropriate reactant molecules convert them into product molecules. This occurs for two reasons:

1) Not all collisions occur with a **sufficiently high energy** for the reaction to occur.
2) Not all collisions **orient the molecules properly** for the reaction to occur.

The **activation energy**, E_a, of a reaction is the **minimum energy to overcome the barrier to the formation of products** and allow the reaction to occur.

At the scale of individual molecules, a reaction typically involves a very small period of time when old bonds are broken and new bonds are formed. During this time, the molecules involved are in a **transition state** between reactants and products. A threshold of maximum energy is crossed when the arrangement of molecules is in an unfavorable intermediate state between reactants and products known as the **activated complex**. Formulas and diagrams of activated complexes are often written within brackets to indicate they are transition states that are present for extremely small periods of time.

The activation energy, E_a, is the difference between the energy of reactants and the energy of the activated complex.   The energy change during the reaction, ΔE, is the difference between the energy of the products and the energy of the reactants. The activation energy of the reverse reaction is $E_a - \Delta E$. These energy levels are represented in an **energy diagram** such as the one shown below.

$$NO_2 + CO \rightleftharpoons NO + CO_2$$

This is an exothermic reaction because products are lower in energy than reactants.

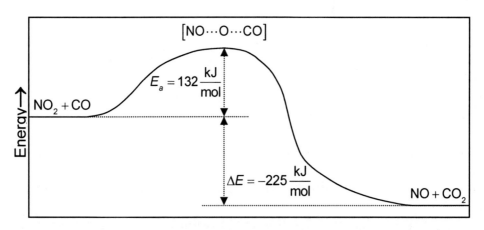

Reaction pathway $\rightarrow$

An energy diagram is a conceptual tool, so there is some variability in how its axes are labeled. The y-axis of the diagram is usually labeled energy (E), but it is sometimes labeled "enthalpy (H)" or (rarely) "free energy (G)." There is an even greater variability in how the x-axis is labeled. The terms "reaction pathway," "reaction coordinate," "course of reaction," or "reaction progress" may be used on the x-axis, or the x-axis may remain without a label.

The energy diagrams of an endothermic and exothermic reaction (See **Skill 2.1**) are compared below.

The rate of most simple reactions **increases with temperature** because a **greater fraction of molecules have the kinetic energy** required to overcome the reaction's activation energy. The chart below shows the effect of temperature on the distribution of kinetic energies in a sample of molecules. These curves are called **Maxwell-Boltzmann distributions**. The shaded areas represent the fraction of molecules containing sufficient kinetic energy for a reaction to occur. This area is larger at a higher temperature; so more molecules are above the activation energy and more molecules react per second.

http://www.mhhe.com/physsci/chemistry/essentialchemistry/flash/activa2.swf provides an animated audio tutorial on energy diagrams.

Kinetic molecular theory may be applied to reaction rates in addition to physical constants like pressure. **Reaction rates increase with reactant concentration** because more reactant molecules are present and more are likely to collide with one another in a certain volume at higher concentrations. The nature of these relationships determines the rate law for the reaction. For ideal gases, the concentration of a reactant is its molar density, and this varies with pressure and temperature as discussed in.

Kinetic molecular theory also predicts that **reaction rate constants (values for k) increase with temperature** because of two reasons:

1) More reactant molecules will collide with each other per second.
2) These collisions will each occur at a higher energy that is more likely to overcome the activation energy of the reaction.

A **catalyst** is a material that increases the rate of a chemical reaction without changing itself permanently in the process. Catalysts provide an alternate reaction mechanism for the reaction to proceed in the forward and in the reverse direction. Therefore, **catalysts have no impact on the chemical equilibrium** of a reaction. They will not make a less favorable reaction more favorable.

Catalysts reduce the activation energy of a reaction. This is the amount of energy needed for the reaction to begin. Molecules with such low energies that they would have taken a long time to react will react more rapidly if a catalyst is present.

The impact of a catalyst may also be represented on an energy diagram (as shown below). **A catalyst increases the rate of both the forward and reverse reactions by lowering the activation energy for the reaction**. Catalysts provide a different activated complex for the reaction at a lower energy state.

Reaction pathway→

There are two types of catalysts: **Homogeneous catalysts** are in the same physical phase as the reactants. Biological catalysts are called **enzymes**, and most are homogeneous catalysts. A typical homogenous catalytic reaction mechanism involves an initial reaction with one reactant followed by a reaction with a second reactant and release of the catalyst:

$$A + C \rightarrow AC$$

$$B + AC \rightarrow AB + C$$

$$\text{Net reaction: } A + B \xrightarrow{\text{catalyst C}} AB$$

Heterogeneous catalysts are present in a different physical state from the reactants. A typical heterogeneous catalytic reaction involves a solid surface onto which molecules in a fluid phase temporarily attach themselves in a way that favors a rapid reaction. Catalytic converters in cars utilize heterogeneous catalysis to break down harmful chemicals in exhaust.

Skill 4.9 **Assess the effects of changes in concentration, temperature, or pressure on a state of a system initially at equilibrium (Le Châtelier's principle).**

A system at equilibrium is in a state of balance because forward and reverse processes are taking place at equal rates. If equilibrium is disturbed by a change in concentration, pressure, or temperature, the state of balance is upset for a period of time before the equilibrium shifts to achieve a new state of balance. **Le Châtelier's principle states that equilibrium will shift to partially offset the impact of an altered condition.**

Change in reactant and product concentrations

If a chemical reaction is at equilibrium, Le Châtelier's principle predicts that **adding a substance**—either a reactant or a product—will shift the reaction so **a new equilibrium is established by consuming some of the added substance.** Removing a substance will cause the reaction to move in the direction that forms more of that substance.

Example: The reaction $CO + 2H_2 \rightleftharpoons CH_3OH$ is used to synthesize methanol. Equilibrium is established, and then additional CO is added to the reaction vessel. Predict the impact on each reaction component after CO is added.

Solution: Le Châtelier's principle states that the reaction will shift to partially offset the impact of the added CO. Therefore, the concentration of CO will decrease, and the reaction will "shift to the right." The concentration of H_2 will also decrease, and the concentration of CH_3OH will increase.

Change in pressure for gases

If a chemical reaction is at equilibrium in the gas phase, Le Chatelier's principle predicts that **an increase in pressure** will shift the reaction so **a new equilibrium is established by decreasing the number of moles of gas present**. A decrease in the number of moles partially offsets this rise in pressure. Decreasing pressure will cause the reaction to move in the direction that forms more moles of gas. These changes in pressure might result from altering the volume of the reaction vessel at constant temperature.

Example: The reaction, $N_2 + 3H_2 \leftrightarrow 2NH_3$ is used to synthesize ammonia. Equilibrium is established. Next the reaction vessel is expanded at constant temperature. Predict the impact on each reaction component after this expansion occurs.

Solution: The expansion will result in a decrease in pressure (Boyle's Law). Le Châtelier's principle states that the reaction will shift to partially offset this decrease by increasing the number of moles present. There are 4 moles of gas on the left side of the equation and 2 moles of gas on the right, so the reaction will shift to the left. N_2 and H_2 concentration will increase. NH_3 concentration will decrease.

Change in temperature

Le Châtelier's principle predicts that **when heat is added** at constant pressure to a system at equilibrium, **the reaction will shift in the direction that absorbs heat** until a new equilibrium is established. For an endothermic process, the reaction will shift to the right towards product formation. For an exothermic process, the reaction will shift to the left towards reactant formation. If you understand the application of Le Châtelier's principle to concentration changes, then writing "heat" on the appropriate side of the equation will help you understand its application to changes in temperature.

Example: $N_2 + 3H_2 \leftrightarrow 2NH_3$ is an exothermic reaction. First, equilibrium is established and then the temperature is decreased. Predict the impact of the lower temperature on each reaction component.

Solution: Since the reaction is exothermic, we may write it as:

$$N_2 + 3H_2 \leftrightarrow 2NH_3 + \text{heat}$$

To find the impact of temperature on equilibrium processes, we may consider heat as if it were a reaction component. Le Châtelier's principle states that after a temperature decrease, the reaction will shift to partially offset the impact of a loss of heat. Therefore more heat will be produced, and the reaction will shift to the right. N_2 and H_2 concentration will decrease. NH_3 concentration will increase.

A flash animation with audio that demonstrates Le Chatelier's principle is at
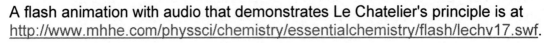 http://www.mhhe.com/physsci/chemistry/essentialchemistry/flash/lechv17.swf.

Skill 4.10   Determine rate laws from concentration and rate data.

Obtaining reaction rates from concentration data

The rate of any process is measured by its change per unit time. The speed of a car is measured by its change in position with time using units of miles per hour. The speed of a chemical reaction is usually measured by a change in the concentration of a reactant or product with time using units of **molarity per second** (M/s). The molarity of a chemical is represented in mathematical equations using brackets.

The **average reaction rate** is the change in concentration either reactant or product per unit time during a time interval:

$$\text{Average reaction rate} = \frac{\text{Change in concentration}}{\text{Change in time}}$$

Reaction rates are positive quantities. Product concentrations increase and reactant concentrations decrease with time, so a different formula is required depending on the identity of the component of interest:

$$\text{Average reaction rate} = \frac{\left[\text{product}\right]_{\text{final}} - \left[\text{product}\right]_{\text{initial}}}{\text{time}_{\text{final}} - \text{time}_{\text{iniial}}}$$

$$= \frac{\left[\text{reactant}\right]_{\text{initial}} - \left[\text{reactant}\right]_{\text{final}}}{\text{time}_{\text{final}} - \text{time}_{\text{iniial}}}$$

The **reaction rate** at a given time refers to the **instantaneous reaction rate**. This is found from the absolute value of the **slope of a curve of concentration vs. time**. An estimate of the reaction rate at time t may be found from the average reaction rate over a small time interval surrounding t. For those familiar with calculus notation, the following equations define reaction rate, but calculus is not needed for this skill:

$$\text{Reaction rate at time } t = \frac{d\left[\text{product}\right]}{dt} = -\frac{d\left[\text{reactant}\right]}{dt}.$$

Example: The following concentration data describes the decomposition of N_2O_5 according to the reaction below.

$$2N_2O_5 \rightarrow 4NO_2 + O_2$$

Time (sec)	[N_2O_5] (M)
0	0.0200
1000	0.0120
2000	0.0074
3000	0.0046
4000	0.0029
5000	0.0018
7500	0.0006
10000	0.0002

Time (sec)

Determine the average reaction rate from 1000 to 5000 seconds and the instantaneous reaction rate at 0 and at 4000 seconds.

Solution: Average reaction rate from 0 to 7500 seconds is found from:

$$\frac{[\text{reactant}]_{\text{initial}} - [\text{reactant}]_{\text{final}}}{\text{time}_{\text{final}} - \text{time}_{\text{iniial}}} = \frac{0.0120\ M - 0.0018\ M}{5000\ \text{sec} - 1000\ \text{sec}} = 2.55 \times 10^{-6}\ \frac{M}{s}.$$

Instantaneous reaction rates are found by drawing lines tangent to the curve, finding the slopes of these lines, and forcing these slopes to be positive values.

At 0 seconds:

$$\text{rate} = \text{slope} = \frac{0.0200\ M}{2000\ s}$$

$$= 1.00 \times 10^{-5}\ \frac{M}{s}.$$

At 4000 seconds:

$$\text{rate} = \text{slope} = \frac{0.0090\ M}{6000\ s}$$

$$= 1.5 \times 10^{-6}\ \frac{M}{s}.$$

Deriving rate laws from reaction rates

A **rate law** is an **equation relating a reaction rate to concentration**. The rate laws for most reactions discussed in high-school level chemistry are of the form:

$$\text{Rate} = k\,[\text{reactant 1}]^{a}\,[\text{reactant 2}]^{b}\,\ldots$$

In the above general equation, k is called the **rate constant**. a and b are called **reaction orders**. Most reactions considered in introductory chemistry have a reaction order of zero, one, or two. The sum of all reaction orders for a reaction is called the **overall reaction order**. Rate laws cannot be predicted from the stoichiometry of a reaction. They must be determined by experiment or derived from knowledge of reaction mechanism.

If a reaction is zero order for a reactant, the concentration of that reactant has no impact on the rate as long as some reactant is present. If a reaction is first order for a reactant, the reaction rate is proportional to the reactant's concentration. For a reaction that is second order with respect to a reactant, doubling that reactant's concentration increases reaction rate by a factor of four. Rate laws are determined by finding the appropriate reaction order describing **the impact of reactant concentration on reaction rate**.

Reaction rates typically have units of M/s (moles/liter-sec) and concentrations have units of M (moles/liter). For units to cancel properly in the expression above, the units of the rate constant k must vary with overall reaction order as shown in the following table. The value of k may be determined by finding the slope of a plot charting a function of concentration against time. These functions may be memorized or computed using calculus.

Overall reaction order	Units of rate constant k	Method to determine k for rate laws with one reactant
0	M/sec	−(slope) of a chart of [reactant] vs. t
1	sec^{-1}	−(slope) of a chart of ln[reactant] vs. t
2	$M^{-1}sec^{-1}$	slope of a chart of 1/[reactant] vs. t

As an alternative to using the rate constant k, the course of **first order reactions** may be expressed in terms of a **half-life**, $t_{halflife}$. The half-life of a reaction is the time required for reactant concentration to reach half of its initial value. First order rate constants and half-lives are inversely proportional:

$$t_{halflife} = \frac{\ln 2}{k_{first\ order}} = \frac{0.693}{k_{first\ order}}$$

Example: Derive a rate law for the reaction $2N_2O_5 \rightarrow 4NO_2 + O_2$ using data from the previous example.

Solution: Three methods will be used to solve this problem.

1) In the previous example, we found the following two **instantaneous reaction rates**:

Time (sec)	[N_2O_5] (M)	Reaction rate (M/sec)
0	0.0200	1.00×10^{-5}
4000	0.0029	1.5×10^{-6}

A decrease in reactant concentration to 0.0029/0.0200=14.5% of its initial value led to a nearly proportional decrease in reaction rate to 15% of its initial value. In other words, reaction rate remains proportional to reactant concentration. The reaction is first order:

$$Rate = k\left[N_2O_5\right].$$

We may estimate a value for the rate constant by dividing reaction rates by the concentration:

$$k_{first\ order} = \frac{Rate}{[N_2O_5]}.$$

Time (sec)	$[N_2O_5]$ (M)	Reaction rate (M/sec)	k (sec^{-1})
0	0.0200	1.00×10^{-5}	5.00×10^{-4}
4000	0.0029	1.5×10^{-6}	5.2×10^{-4}

2) We could estimate this rate constant by finding **average reaction rates** in each small time interval and assuming this rate occurs halfway between the two concentrations:

Time (sec)	$[N_2O_5]$ (M)	Average rate (M/sec)	Halfway $[N_2O_5]$ (M)	k (sec^{-1})
0	0.0200	8.00×10^{-6}	0.0160	5.00×10^{-4}
1000	0.0120	4.6×10^{-6}	0.0097	4.7×10^{-4}
2000	0.0074	2.8×10^{-6}	0.0060	4.7×10^{-4}
3000	0.0046	1.7×10^{-6}	0.0038	4.5×10^{-4}
4000	0.0029	1.1×10^{-6}	0.0024	4.7×10^{-4}
5000	0.0018	4.8×10^{-7}	0.0012	4.0×10^{-4}
7500	0.0006	2×10^{-7}	0.0004	4×10^{-4}
10000	0.0002			

3) If **concentration data** are given then no rate data needs to be found in order to determine a rate constant. For a first order reaction, chart the natural logarithm of concentration against time and find the slope.

Time (sec)	$[N_2O_5]$ (M)	$\ln[N_2O_5]$
0	0.0200	-3.91
1000	0.0120	-4.41
2000	0.0074	-4.90
3000	0.0046	-5.37
4000	0.0029	-5.83
5000	0.0018	-6.30
7500	0.0006	-7.39
10000	0.0002	-8.46

The slope may be determined from a best-fit method or it may be estimated from

$$\frac{-8.46-(-3.91)}{10000}=-5\times10^{-4}.$$

The rate law describing this reaction is:

$$\text{Rate}=\left(5\times10^{-4}\,\frac{M}{\text{sec}}\right)[N_2O_5]$$

Derive rate laws from simple reaction mechanisms

A **reaction mechanism** is a series of **elementary reactions** that explain how a reaction occurs. These elementary reactions are also called elementary processes or elementary steps. **A reaction mechanism cannot be determined from reaction stoichiometry**. Stoichiometry indicates the number of molecules of reactants and products in an **overall reaction**. Elementary steps represent a **single event**. This might be a collision between two molecules or a single rearrangement of electrons within a molecule.

The simplest reaction mechanisms consist of a single elementary reaction. The number of molecules required determines the rate laws for these processes. For a **unimolecular process:**

$$A\rightarrow\text{products}$$

the number of molecules of A that decompose in a given time will be proportional to the number of molecules of A present. Therefore unimolecular processes are first order:

$$\text{Rate}=k[A].$$

For **bimolecular processes**, the rate law will be second order.

For $A+A\rightarrow$ products, $\text{Rate}=k[A]^2$

For $A+B\rightarrow$ products, $\text{Rate}=k[A][B].$

Most reaction mechanisms are multi-step processes involving **reaction intermediates**. Intermediates are chemicals that are formed during one elementary step and consumed during another, but they are not overall reactants or products. In many cases one elementary reaction in particular is the slowest and determines the overall reaction rate. This slowest reaction in the series is called the **rate-limiting step** or rate determining step.

Example: The overall reaction:

$$NO_2(g) + CO(g) \rightarrow NO(g) + CO_2(g)$$

is composed of the following elementary reactions in the gas phase:

$$NO_2 + NO_2 \rightarrow NO + NO_3$$
$$NO_3 + CO \rightarrow NO_2 + CO_2.$$

The first elementary reaction is very slow compared to the second. Determine the rate law for the overall reaction if NO_2 and CO are both present in sufficient quantity for the reaction to occur. Also name all reaction intermediates.

Solution: The first step will be rate limiting because it is slower. In other words, almost as soon as NO_3 is available, it reacts with CO, so the rate-limiting step is the formation of NO_3. The first step is bimolecular. Therefore, the rate law for the entire reaction is:

$$Rate = k \left[NO_2 \right]^2.$$

NO_3 is formed during the first step and consumed during the second. NO_3 is the only reaction intermediate because it is neither a reactant nor a product of the overall reaction.

Skill 4.11   **Calculate either the equilibrium constant or concentration of a reaction species at equilibrium (e.g., K_a, K_b, K_{sp}, K_w, K_{eq}).**

The concentrations of reactants and products at equilibrium remain constant because the forward and reverse reactions take place at the same rate. This equilibrium responds to a perturbation in one concentration by altering every other concentration in a well-defined way until equilibrium is reestablished The mathematical relationship between the concentrations of the reactants and products of a system is called the law of mass action. It governs equilibrium expressions.

Consider the general balanced reaction:

$$mA + nB \leftrightarrow pR + qS$$

where m, n, p, and q are stoichiometric coefficients and A, B, R, and S are chemical species. An **equilibrium expression** relating the concentrations of chemical species at equilibrium is determined by the equation:

$$K_{eq} = \frac{[R]^p [S]^q}{[A]^m [B]^n}$$

where K_{eq} is a constant value called the **equilibrium constant**. Product concentrations raised to the power of their stoichiometric coefficients are placed in the numerator and reactant concentrations raised to the power of their coefficients are placed in the denominator.

Every reaction has a unique value of K_{eq} that varies only with temperature. Alternate subscripts are often given to the equilibrium constant. K_c or K with no subscript is often used instead of K_{eq} to represent the equilibrium constant. Other subscripts are used for specific reactions as describedl.

Example: Write the equilibrium expression for the following reaction.
$$2HI\ (g) \leftrightarrow H_2\ (g) + I_2\ (g)$$

Solution: $K_{eq} = \dfrac{[H_2][I_2]}{[HI]^2}$.

The units associated with equilibrium constants in the expression above are molarity raised to the power of an integer that depends on the stoichiometric coefficients of the reaction, but it is common practice to write these constants as dimensionless values. Multiplying or dividing the equilibrium expression by 1 M as needed achieves these dimensionless values. **The equilibrium expression for a reaction written in one direction is the reciprocal of the expression for the reaction in the reverse direction**.

For a heterogeneous equilibrium (a chemical equilibrium with components in different phases), reactants or products may be pure liquids or solids. The concentration of a pure liquid or solid in moles/liter cannot change. It is a constant property of the material, and these constants are incorporated into the equilibrium constant. Therefore the concentrations of pure liquids and solids are absent from equilibrium expressions for heterogeneous equilibria.

Example: Write the equilibrium expression for the redox reaction between copper and silver.

$$Cu\ (s) + 2Ag^+\ (aq) \leftrightarrow Cu^{2+}\ (aq) + 2Ag\ (s)$$

Solution: $K_{eq} = \dfrac{\left[Cu^{2+}\right]}{\left[Ag^+\right]^2}$. The solids do not appear in the equilibrium expression.

Calculation of unknown concentrations and concentration units

Many types of K_{eq} problems require the calculation of an unknown concentration at equilibrium from known quantities. These problems only require algebra to solve. Remember that equilibrium constants are dimensionless values. If all concentrations are represented in the same units, it is acceptable to be a little less cautious with units here than for other problems.

Example: The reaction:

$$N_2\left(g\right) + 3H_2\left(g\right) \rightleftharpoons 2NH_3\left(g\right)$$

achieves equilibrium in the presence of 0.27 M H_2 and 0.094 M N_2. What is the ammonia concentration, under these conditions, if the reaction at the given temperature has an equilibrium constant of $K_{eq} = 0.11$?

Solution: First we will solve this problem ignoring units since all concentrations are given in M.

$$K_{eq} = \frac{\left[NH_3\right]^2}{\left[N_2\right]\left[H_2\right]^3} = \frac{\left[NH_3\right]^2}{\left(0.094\right)\left(0.27\right)^3} = 0.11$$

Solving for [NH$_3$] yields:

$$\left[NH_3\right] = \sqrt{\left(0.11\right)\left(0.094\right)\left(0.27\right)^3} = 0.014\ M$$

This is the preferred method for solving these problems.

If units are to be treated rigorously, then a more explicit definition of K_{eq} should be written. This will achieve a dimensionless value for K_{eq} by repeatedly multiplying by 1 M.

$$K_{eq} = \frac{[NH_3]^2 (1\,M)^2}{[N_2][H_2]^3} = \frac{[NH_3]^2 (1\,M)^2}{(0.094\,M)(0.27\,M)^3} = 0.11$$

Solving for [NH$_3$] yields:

$$[NH_3] = \sqrt{(0.11)\frac{(0.094\,M)(0.27\,M)^3}{(1\,M)^2}} = 0.014\,M$$

Determining the directionality of a reaction

Some K_{eq} problems give every concentration value for a reaction that is not at equilibrium and ask which direction the reaction will proceed for a given equilibrium constant. Solving these problems is a two step process:

1) Insert the non-equilibrium reaction concentrations into the equilibrium expression to obtain a **reaction quotient**, Q.
2) If $Q<K_{eq}$, there are too many reactant molecules for the products, and the reaction proceeds to the right. If $Q>K_{eq}$, there are too many product molecules for the reactants, and the reaction proceeds to the left. If $Q=K_{eq}$, the reaction is at equilibrium.

Example: Predict the direction in which the reaction $H_2(g)+I_2(g) \rightleftharpoons 2HI(g)$ will proceed if initial concentrations are 0.004 mM H$_2$, 0.006 mM I$_2$, and 0.011 mM HI given K_{eq}=48.

Solution: 1) The reactant quotient is

$$Q = \frac{[HI]^2}{[H_2][I_2]} = \frac{(0.011)^2}{(0.004)(0.006)} = 5$$

2) The reactant quotient, which is 5, is less than K_{eq}, which is 48. Therefore, the numerator (products) of the reaction quotient is too small for the denominator (reactants). The trend towards equilibrium with time will increase the numerator in relation to the denominator until a ratio of 48 is achieved. More reactants will turn into products and the reaction will proceed to the right.

Special equilibrium constants

A few equilibrium constants are used often enough to have their own unique nomenclature.

The **solubility-product constant**, K_{sp}, is the equilibrium constant for an ionic solid in contact with a saturated aqueous solution. The two processes with equal rates in this case are dissolution and crystallization.

$$\text{ionic compound}(s) \rightleftharpoons p\ \text{Cation}^{+}(aq) + q\ \text{Anion}^{-}(aq)$$

$$K_{sp} = \left[\text{cation}^{+}\right]^{p}\left[\text{anion}^{-}\right]^{q}$$

Because this is an example of a heterogeneous equilibrium, the concentration of pure solid is not included as a variable. K_{sp} is a different quantity from solubility. K_{sp} is an equilibrium constant, and solubility is the mass of solid that is able to dissolve in a given quantity of water. See **Skill 1.4** for details about solubility processes.

Example: Solid lead chloride $PbCl_2$ is allowed to dissolve in pure water until equilibrium has been reached and the solution is saturated. The concentration of Pb^{2+} is 0.016 M. What is K_{sp} for $PbCl_2$?

Solution: For $PbCl_2(s) \rightleftharpoons Pb^{2+}(aq) + 2Cl^{-}(aq)$, $K_{sp} = \left[Pb^{2+}\right]\left[Cl^{-}\right]^{2}$. The only source of both ions in solution is $PbCl_2$, so the concentration of Cl^{-} must be twice that for Pb^{2+}, or 0.032 M. Therefore,

$$K_{sp} = (0.016)(0.032)^{2} = 1.6 \times 10^{-5}$$

The **acid-dissociation constant**, K_a, is the equilibrium constant for the ionization of a weak acid to a hydrogen ion and its conjugate base.

$$HX(aq) \rightleftharpoons H^{+}(aq) + X^{-}(aq) \qquad K_a = \frac{\left[H^{+}\right]\left[X^{-}\right]}{[HX]}$$

Polyprotic acids have unique values for each dissociation: K_{a1}, K_{a2}, etc.

Example: Hydrofluoric acid is dissolved in pure water until [H$^+$] reaches 0.006 M. What is the concentration of undissociated HF? K_a for HF is 6.8 X 10^{-4}.

Solution: $HF(aq) \rightleftharpoons H^+(aq) + F^-(aq)$, $\quad K_a = \dfrac{[H^+][F^-]}{[HF]}$

The principle source of both ions is dissociation of HF (autoionization of water is negligible). Therefore,

$$[F^-] = [H^+] = 0.006 \text{ M and } [HF] = \frac{[H^+][F^-]}{K_a} = \frac{(0.006)^2}{6.8 \times 10^{-4}} = 0.05 \text{ M}$$

The **base-dissociation constant**, K_b, is the equilibrium constant for the addition of a proton to a weak base by water to form its conjugate acid and an OH$^-$ ion. In these reactions, it is water that is dissociating as a result of reaction with the base:

$$\text{weak base}(aq) + H_2O(l) \rightleftharpoons \text{conjugate acid}(aq) + OH^-(aq)$$

$$K_b = \frac{[\text{conjugate acid}][OH^-]}{[\text{weak base}]}$$

The concentration of water is nearly constant and is incorporated into the dissociation constant.

For ammonia (the most common weak base), the equilibrium reaction and base-dissociation constant are:

$$NH_3(aq) + H_2O(l) \rightleftharpoons NH_4^+(aq) + OH^-(aq)$$

$$K_b = \frac{[NH_4^+][OH^-]}{[NH_3]}$$

Example: K_b for ammonia at 25 °C is 1.8 X 10^{-5}. What is the concentration of OH^- in an ammonia solution at equilibrium containing 0.2 M NH_3 at 25°C?

Solution: Let $x = \left[OH^-\right]$. The principle source of both ions is NH_3 (autoionization of water is negligible). Therefore $x = \left[NH_3^+\right]$ also.

$$K_b = \frac{\left[NH_4^+\right]\left[OH^-\right]}{\left[NH_3\right]} = \frac{x^2}{0.2} = 1.8 \times 10^{-5}$$

Solving for x yields: $x = \sqrt{(0.2)(1.8 \times 10^{-5})} = 0.002$ M OH^-

The **ion-product constant for water** (K_w) is the equilibrium constant for the dissociation of H_2O. Water molecules may donate protons to other water molecules in a process known as autoionization:

$$2H_2O(l) \rightleftharpoons H_3O^+(aq) + OH^-(aq)$$

A hydrated water molecule is often referred to as H^+ (aq), so the above equation may be rewritten as the following reaction that defines K_w. As with K_b, the concentration of water is nearly constant.

$$H_2O(l) \rightleftharpoons H^+(aq) + OH^-(aq)$$

$$K_w = \left[H^+\right]\left[OH^-\right] = 1.0 \times 10^{-14} \text{ at } 25°C.$$

Example: a) What is the concentration of OH^- in an aqueous solution with an H^+ concentration of 2.5X10^{-6} M?
   b) What is the concentration of H^+ when pure water reaches equilibrium?

Solution: a) $K_w = \left[H^+\right]\left[OH^-\right] = (2.5 \times 10^{-6})\left[OH^-\right] = 1.0 \times 10^{-14}$

Solving for $\left[OH^-\right]$ yields $\left[OH^-\right] = \dfrac{1.0 \times 10^{-14}}{2.5 \times 10^{-6}} = 4.0 \times 10^{-9}$.

b) The autoionization of pure water creates an equal concentration of the two ions:

$\left[H^+\right] = \left[OH^-\right]$. Therefore $K_w = \left[H^+\right]^2 = 1.0 \times 10^{-14}$.

Solving for $\left[H^+\right]$ yields $\left[H^+\right] = 1.0 \times 10^{-7}$.

Skill 4.12   Identify the characteristics of a chemical system in dynamic equilibrium.

A dynamic equilibrium consists of two **opposing reversible processes** that both occur at the **same rate**. *Balance* is a synonym for equilibrium. A system at equilibrium is stable; it does not change with time. Equilibria are drawn with a double arrow.

When a process at equilibrium is observed, it often doesn't seem like anything is happening, but **at a microscopic scale, two events are taking place that balance each other**. An example is presented on the right. Arrows in this diagram represent the movement of molecules. When water is placed in a closed container, the water evaporates until the air in the container is saturated. After this occurs, the water level no longer changes, so an observer at the macroscopic scale would say that evaporation has stopped, but the reality on a microscopic scale is that both evaporation and condensation are taking place at the same rate. All equilibria between different phases of matter have this dynamic character on a microscopic scale.

Liquid $\underset{\text{condensation}}{\overset{\text{evaporation}}{\rightleftharpoons}}$ Vapor

Chemical reactions often do not "go to completion." Instead, products are generated from reactants up to a certain point when the reaction no longer seems to occur, leaving some reactant unaltered. At this point, the system is in a state of **chemical equilibrium** because **the rate of the forward reaction is equal to the rate of the reverse reaction**. An example is shown to the right. Arrows in this diagram represent the chemical reactions of individual molecules. An observer at the macroscopic scale might say that no reaction is taking place at equilibrium, but at a microscopic scale, both the forward and reverse reactions are occurring at the same rate.

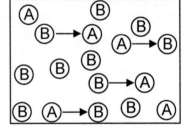

$A \rightleftharpoons B$

Homogeneous equilibrium refers to a chemical equilibrium among reactants and products that are all in the same phase of matter. **Heterogeneous equilibrium** takes place between two or more chemicals in different phases.

If a reaction at equilibrium is disturbed, changes occur to reestablish equilibrium. **Le Châtelier's principle** states that the equilibrium will be reestablished in a manner that counteracts the effect of the initial disturbance (see **Skill 4.9**).

A reaction at equilibrium contains a constant ratio of chemical species. The nature of these ratios is determined by an **equilibrium constant.** The mathematical relationship between the concentrations of the reactants and products of a system is called the law of mass action. It governs equilibrium expressions.

Skill 4.13   Identify major characteristics of strong and weak acids or bases.

It was recognized centuries ago that many substances could be divided into two general categories. **Acids** have a sour taste (as in lemon juice), dissolve many metals, and turn litmus paper red. **Bases** have a bitter taste (as in soaps), feel slippery, and turn litmus paper blue. The chemical reaction between an acid and a base is called **neutralization.** The products of neutralization reactions are neither acids nor bases. Litmus paper is an example of an **acid-base indicator,** a substance that changes color when added to an acid to a base.

Arrhenius definition of acids and bases

Svante **Arrhenius** proposed in the 1880s that **acids form H^+ ions and bases form OH^- ions in water.** The net ionic reaction for neutralization between an Arrhenius acid and base always produces water as shown below for nitric acid and sodium hydroxide:

$$HNO_3(aq) + NaOH(aq) \rightarrow NaNO_3(aq) + H_2O(l)$$

$$H^+(aq) + NO_3^-(aq) + Na^+(aq) + OH^-(aq) \rightarrow NO_3^-(aq) + Na^+(aq) + H_2O(l) \text{ (complete ionic)}$$

$$H^+(aq) + OH^-(aq) \rightarrow H_2O(l) \text{ (net ionic)}$$

The $H^+(aq)$ ion

In acid-base systems, **"protonated water" or "$H^+(aq)$" are shorthand for a mixture of water ions.** For example, HCl reacting in water may be represented as a dissociation:

$$HCl(aq) \rightarrow H^+(aq) + Cl^-(aq)$$

The same reaction may be described as the transfer of a proton to water to form H_3O^+:

$$HCl(aq) + H_2O(l) \rightarrow Cl^-(aq) + H_3O^+(aq)$$

H_3O^+ is called a **hydronium ion**. Its Lewis structure is shown below to the left. In reality, the hydrogen bonds in water are so strong that H^+ ions exist in water as a mixture of species in a hydrogen bond network. Two of them are shown below at center and to the right. Hydrogen bonds are shown as dashed lines.

Brønsted-Lowry definition of acids and bases

In the 1920s, Johannes **Brønsted** and Thomas **Lowry** recognized that **acids can transfer a proton to bases** regardless of whether an OH^- ion accepts the proton. In an equilibrium reaction, the direction of proton transfer depends on whether the reaction is read left to right or right to left, so **Brønsted acids and bases exist in conjugate pairs with and without a proton**. Acids that are able to transfer more than one proton are called **polyprotic acids**.

Examples:

1) In the reaction:
$$HF \ (aq) + H_2O \ (l) \leftrightarrow F^- \ (aq) + H_3O^+ \ (aq)$$

HF transfers a proton to water. Therefore HF is the Brønsted acid and H_2O is the Brønsted base. But in the reverse direction, hydronium ions transfer a proton to fluoride ions. H_3O^+ is the conjugate acid of H_2O because it has an additional proton, and F^- is the conjugate base of HF because it lacks a proton.

2) In the reaction:
$$NH_3 \ (aq) + H_2O \ (l) \leftrightarrow NH_4^+ \ (aq) + OH^- \ (aq)$$

water transfers a proton to ammonia. H_2O is the Brønsted acid and OH^- is its conjugate base. NH_3 is the Brønsted base and NH_4^+ is its conjugate acid.

3) In the reaction:

$$H_3PO_4 + HS^- \leftrightarrow H_2PO_4^- + H_2S$$

$H_3PO_4/H_2PO_4^-$ is one conjugate acid-base pair and H_2S/HS^- is the other.

4) H_3PO_4 is a polyprotic acid. It may further dissociate to transfer more than one proton:

$$H_3PO_4 \leftrightarrow H_2PO_4^- + H^+$$
$$H_2PO_4^- \leftrightarrow HPO_4^{2-} + H^+$$
$$HPO_4^{2-} \leftrightarrow PO_4^{3-} + H^+$$

Strong and weak acids and bases

Strong acids and bases are strong electrolytes, and weak acids and bases are weak electrolytes, so **strong acids and bases completely dissociate in water**, but weak acids and bases do not.

Example: $HCl(aq) + H_2O(l) \rightarrow H_3O^+(aq) + Cl^-(aq)$ goes to completion because HCl is a strong acid. The acids in the previous examples were all weak.

The aqueous dissociation constants K_a and K_b quantify acid and base strength. Another way of looking at acid dissociation is that strong acids transfer protons more readily than H_3O^+ transfers protons, so they protonate water, the conjugate base of H_3O^+. In general, **if two acid/base conjugate pairs are present, the stronger acid will transfer a proton to the conjugate base of the weaker acid**.

Acid and base **strength is not related to safety**. Weak acids like HF may be extremely corrosive and dangerous.

The most **common strong acids and bases** are listed here:

Strong acid		Strong base	
HCl	Hydrochloric acid	LiOH	Lithium hydroxide
HBr	Hydrobromic acid	NaOH	Sodium hydroxide
HI	Hydroiodic acid	KOH	Potassium hydroxide
HNO_3	Nitric acid	$Ca(OH)_2$	Calcium hydroxide
H_2SO_4	Sulfuric acid	$Sr(OH)_2$	Strontium hydroxide
$HClO_4$	Perchloric acid	$Ba(OH)_2$	Barium hydroxide

A flash animation tutorial demonstrating the difference between strong and weak acids is located at:
http://www.mhhe.com/physsci/chemistry/essentialchemistry/flash/acid13.swf.

Trends in acid and base strength

The strongest acid in a polyprotic series is always **the acid with the most protons** (e.g. H_2SO_4 is a stronger acid than HSO_4^-). The strongest acid in a series with the same central atom is always **the acid with the central atom at the highest oxidation number** (e.g. $HClO_4 > HClO_3 > HClO_2 > HClO$). The strongest acid in a series with different central atoms at the same oxidation number is usually **the acid with the central atom at the highest electronegativity** (e.g. the K_a of $HClO > HBrO > HIO$). This electronegativity trend stretches across the periodic table for oxides.

Lewis definition of acids and bases

The transfer of a proton from a Brønsted acid to a Brønsted base requires that the base accept the proton. When Lewis diagrams are used to draw the proton donation of Brønsted acid-base reactions, it is always clear that the base must contain an unshared electron pair to form a bond with the proton. For example, ammonia contains an unshared electron pair in the following reaction:

$$H^+ \; + \; \begin{array}{c} H \\ | \\ :N-H \\ | \\ H \end{array} \; \longrightarrow \; \left[\begin{array}{c} H \\ | \\ H-N-H \\ | \\ H \end{array} \right]^+ .$$

In the 1920s, Gilbert N. **Lewis** proposed that **bases donate unshared electron pairs to acids**, regardless of whether the donation is made to a proton or to another atom. Boron trifluoride is an example of a Lewis acid that is not a Brønsted acid because it is a chemical that accepts an electron pair without involving an H^+ ion:

$$\begin{array}{c} F \\ \diagdown \\ B-F \\ \diagup \\ F \end{array} \; + \; \begin{array}{c} H \\ | \\ :N-H \\ | \\ H \end{array} \; \longrightarrow \; \begin{array}{c} F \;\; H \\ | \;\;\; | \\ F-B-N-H \\ | \;\;\; | \\ F \;\; H \end{array} .$$

The Lewis theory of acids and bases is more general than Brønsted-Lowry theory, but Brønsted-Lowry's definition is used more frequently. The terms "acid" and "base" most often refer to Brønsted acids and bases, and the term "Lewis acid" is usually reserved for chemicals like BF_3 that are not also Brønsted acids.

Summary of definitions

A Lewis base transfers an electron pair to a Lewis acid. A Brønsted acid transfers a proton to a Brønsted base. These exist in conjugate pairs at equilibrium. In an Arrhenius base, the proton acceptor (electron pair donor) is OH^-. All Arrhenius acids/bases are Brønsted acids/bases and all Brønsted acids/bases are Lewis acids/bases. Each definition contains a subset of the one that comes after it.

Skill 4.14   Evaluate the properties of buffer systems.

A **buffer solution** is a solution that **resists a change in pH** after addition of small amounts of an acid or a base. Buffer solutions require the presence of an acid to neutralize an added base and also the presence of a base to neutralize an added acid. These two components present in the buffer also must not neutralize each other.

A **conjugate acid-base pair is present in buffers** to fulfill these requirements. Buffers are prepared by mixing together **a weak acid or base and a salt of the acid or base** that provides the conjugate.

Consider the buffer solution prepared by mixing together acetic acid ($HC_2H_3O_2$) and sodium acetate ($C_2H_3O_2^-$) and containing Na^+ as a spectator ion. The equilibrium reaction for this acid/conjugate base pair is:

$$HC_2H_3O_2 \leftrightarrow C_2H_3O_2^- + H^+$$

If H^+ ions from a strong acid are added to this buffer solution, Le Châtelier's principle predicts that the reaction will shift to the left and much of this H^+ will be consumed to create more $HC_2H_3O_2$ from $C_2H_3O_2^-$. If a strong base that consumes H^+ is added to this buffer solution, Le Châtelier's principle predicts that the reaction will shift to the right and much of the consumed H^+ will be replaced by the dissociation of $HC_2H_3O_2$. The net effect is that **buffer solutions prevent large changes in pH that occur when an acid or base is added to pure water** or to an unbuffered solution.

The amount of acid or base that a buffer solution can neutralize before large pH changes begins to occur is called its **buffering capacity**. Blood and seawater both contain several conjugate acid-base pairs to buffer the solution's pH and decrease the impact of acids and bases on living things.

An excellent flash animation with audio to explain the action of buffering solutions is found at
http://www.mhhe.com/physsci/chemistry/essentialchemistry/flash/buffer12.swf.

Skill 4.15   Interpret graphical and numerical titration data.

Standard titration

In a typical acid-base **titration, an acid-base indicator** (such as phenolphthalein) or a **pH meter** is used to monitor the course of a **neutralization reaction**. The usual goal of titration is to determine an unknown concentration of an acid (or base) by neutralizing it with a known concentration of base (or acid).

Initial buret volume

The reagent of known concentration is usually used as the **titrant**. The titrant is poured into a **buret** (also spelled burette) until it is nearly full, and an initial buret reading is taken. Buret numbering is close to zero when nearly full. A known volume of the solution of unknown concentration is added to a flask and placed under the buret. The indicator is added (or the pH meter probe is inserted). The initial state of a titration experiment is shown to the right above.

Unknown with indicator

The buret stopcock is opened, and titrant is slowly added until the solution permanently changes color, which indicates a rapid change in pH. This is the titration **endpoint**, and a final buret reading is made. The final state of a titration experiment is shown below, to the right. The endpoint occurs when the number of **acid and base equivalents in the flask are identical**.

$$N_{acid} = N_{base}. \text{ Therefore, } C_{acid}V_{acid} = C_{base}V_{base}.$$

The endpoint is also known as the titration **equivalence point**.

Volume added

Final volume

Titration data typically consist of:

$V_{inital} \Rightarrow$ Initial buret volume $V_{final} \Rightarrow$ Final buret volume

$C_{known} \Rightarrow$ Concentration of known solution

$V_{unknown} \Rightarrow$ Volume of unknown solution.

Color change at endpoint

To determine the unknown concentration, first find the volume of titrant added at the known concentration.

$$V_{known} = V_{final} - V_{initial}$$

At the equivalence point, $N_{unknown} = N_{known}$.

$$\text{Therefore, } C_{unknown} = \frac{C_{known}V_{known}}{V_{unknown}} = \frac{C_{known}\left(V_{final} - V_{initial}\right)}{V_{unknown}}.$$

Units of molarity may be used for concentration in the previous expressions **unless a mole of either solution yields more than one acid or base equivalent.** In that case, concentration must be expressed using **normality**.

Example: A 20.0 mL sample of an HCl solution is titrated with 0.200 M NaOH. The initial buret volume is 1.8 mL and the final buret volume at the titration endpoint is 29.1 mL. What is the molarity of the HCl sample?

Solution: Two solution methods will be used. HCl contains one acid equivalent and NaOH contains one base equivalent, so we may use molarity in all our calculations.

1) Calculate the moles of the known substance added to the flask:

$$0.200 \frac{mol}{L} \times \frac{1\,L}{1000\,mL} \times (29.1\,mL - 1.8\,mL) = 0.00546 \text{ mol NaOH}.$$

At the endpoint, this base will neutralize 0.00546 mol HCl. Therefore, this amount of HCl must have been present in the sample before the titration.

$$\frac{0.00546 \text{ mol HCl}}{0.0200\,L} = 0.273 \text{ M HCl}.$$

2) Utilize the formula: $C_{unknown} = \dfrac{C_{known}\left(V_{final} - V_{initial}\right)}{V_{unknown}}$

$$C_{HCl} = \frac{C_{NaOH}\left(V_{final} - V_{initial}\right)}{V_{HCl}} = \frac{0.200 \text{ M}\left(29.1\,mL - 1.8\,mL\right)}{20.0\,mL} = 0.273 \text{ M HCl}.$$

Titrating with the unknown

In a common variation of standard titration, an unknown is added to the buret as a titrant, and the reagent of known concentration is placed in the flask. The chemistry involved is the same as in the standard case, and the mathematics is also identical except for the identity of the two volumes. For this variation, V_{known} will be the volume added to the flask before titration begins and $V_{unknown} = V_{final} - V_{initial}$. Therefore:

$$C_{unknown} = \frac{C_{known}V_{known}}{V_{unknown}} = \frac{C_{known}V_{known}}{V_{final} - V_{initial}}$$

Example: 30.0 mL of a 0.150 M HNO_3 solution is titrated with $Ca(OH)_2$. The initial buret volume is 0.6 mL and the final buret volume at the equivalent point is 22.2 mL. What is the molarity of $Ca(OH)_2$ used for the titration?

Solution: The same two solution methods will be used as in the previous example. 1 mol $Ca(OH)_2$ contains 2 base equivalents because it reacts with 2 moles of H^+ via this reaction

$$Ca(OH)_2 + 2HNO_3 \rightarrow Ca(NO_3)_2 + 2H_2O.$$

Therefore, normality must be used in the formula for solution method 2.

1) First calculate the moles of the substance in the flask:

$$0.150 \frac{mol}{L} \times 0.0300 \text{ L} = 0.00450 \text{ mol } HNO_3.$$

This acid must be titrated with 0.00450 base equivalents for neutralization to occur at the end point. We calculate moles $Ca(OH)_2$ used in the titration from stoichiometry:

$$0.00450 \text{ base equivalents} \times \frac{1 \text{ mol } Ca(OH)_2}{2 \text{ base equivalents}} = 0.00225 \text{ mol } Ca(OH)_2.$$

The molarity of $Ca(OH)_2$ is found from the volume used in the titration:

$$\frac{0.00225 \text{ mol } Ca(OH)_3}{0.0222 \text{ L} - 0.0006 \text{ L}} = 0.104 \text{ M } Ca(OH)_3.$$

2) Utilize the formula: $C_{unknown} = \dfrac{C_{known} V_{known}}{V_{final} - V_{initial}}$ using units of normality.

For HNO_3, molarity=normality because 1 mol contains 1 acid equivalent.

$$C_{Ca(OH)_2} = \frac{C_{HNO_3} V_{HNO_3}}{V_{final} - V_{initial}} = \frac{\left(0.150 \text{ M} \times \frac{1 \text{ N}}{1 \text{ M}}\right)(30.0 \text{ mL})}{22.2 \text{ mL} - 0.6 \text{ mL}} = 0.208 \text{ N } Ca(OH)_2.$$

This value is converted to molarity. For $Ca(OH)_2$, normality is twice molarity because 1 mol contains 2 base equivalents.

$$0.208 \text{ N } Ca(OH)_2 \times \frac{1 \text{ M } Ca(OH)_2}{2 \text{ N } Ca(OH)_2} = 0.104 \text{ M } Ca(OH)_2.$$

(handwritten margin notes:)

$$C_k V_k = C_u V_u$$

$$C_u = \frac{C_k V_k}{V_u}$$

$$\frac{C_k V_k}{V_f - V_i}$$

Interpreting titration curves

A **titration curve** is a plot of a solution's **pH charted against the volume of an added acid or base**. Titration curves are obtained if a pH meter is used to monitor the titration, instead of an indicator. At the equivalence point, the titration curve is nearly vertical. This is the point where the most rapid change in pH occurs. In addition to determining the equivalence point, the **shape of titration curves** may be interpreted to determine **acid/base strength and the presence of a polyprotic acid.**

The pH at the equivalence point of a titration is the **pH of the salt solution obtained when the amount of acid is equal to amount of base**. For a strong acid and a strong base, the equivalence point occurs at the neutral pH of 7. For example, an equimolar solution of HCl and NaOH will contain NaCl(aq) at its equivalence point.

The salt solution at **the equivalence point of a titration involving a weak acid or base will not be at neutral pH**. For example, an equimolar solution of NaOH and hypochlorous acid HClO at the equivalence point of a titration will be a base because it is indistinguishable from a solution of sodium hypochlorite. A pure solution of NaClO(aq) will be a base because the ClO$^-$ ion is the conjugate base of HClO, and it consumes H$^+$(aq) in the reaction: ClO$^-$ + H$^+$ $\rightleftharpoons$ HClO.

In a similar fashion, an equimolar solution of HCl and NH$_3$ will be an acid because a solution of NH$_4$Cl(aq) is an acid. It generates H$^+$(aq) in the reaction: NH$_4^+$ $\rightleftharpoons$ NH$_3$ + H$^+$.

Contrast the following **titration curves for a weak acid or base** with those for a strong acid and strong base on the preceding page:

Titration of a polyprotic acid results in **multiple equivalence points** and a curve with more "bumps" as shown below for sulfurous acid and the carbonate ion.

Skill 4.16 Identify oxidation-reduction processes

Redox is shorthand for *reduction* and *oxidation*. **Reduction** is the **gain of an electron** by a molecule, atom, or ion. **Oxidation** is the **loss of an electron** by a molecule, atom, or ion. These two processes always occur together. Electrons lost by one substance are gained by another. In a redox process, the **oxidation numbers** of atoms are altered. Reduction decreases, or reduces, the oxidation number of an atom. Oxidation increases the oxidation number.

The easiest redox processes to identify are those involving monatomic ions with altered charges. For example, the reaction

$$Zn(s) + Cu^{2+}(aq) \rightarrow Zn^{2+}(aq) + Cu(s)$$

is a redox process because electrons are transferred from Zn to Cu.

However, many redox reactions involve the transfer of electrons from one molecular compound to another. In these cases, **oxidation numbers must be determined** as follows:

Oxidation numbers, sometimes called oxidation states, are signed (+ or -) numbers assigned to atoms in molecules and ions. They allow us to keep track of the electrons associated with each atom. Oxidation numbers are frequently used to write chemical formulas, to help predict properties of compounds, and to help balance equations in which electrons are transferred. Knowledge of the oxidation state of an atom gives us an idea about its positive or negative character. In themselves, oxidation numbers have no physical meaning; they are used to simplify tasks that are more difficult to accomplish without them.

Rules for determining oxidation state

1. Free elements are assigned an oxidation state of 0.

   Example: Al, Na, Fe, H_2, O_2, N_2, Cl_2 etc. have zero oxidation states

2. The oxidation state for any simple one-atom ion is equal to its charge.

   Example: The oxidation state of Na^+ is +1, Be^{2+}, +2, and of F^-, -1

3. The alkali metals (Li, Na, K, Rb, Cs and Fr) in compounds are always assigned an oxidation state of +1.

   Example: In LiOH, Li = +1; in Na_2SO_4, Na = +1

4. Fluorine in compounds is always assigned an oxidation state of -1.

Example: In HF_2^- and BF_2^-, F=-1

5. The alkaline earth metals (Be, Mg, Ca, Sr, Ba, and Ra) and also Zn and Cd in compounds are always assigned an oxidation state of +2. Similarly, Al & Ga are always +3.

Example: In $CaSO_4$, Ca = +2; in $AlCl_3$, Al = +3

6.   Hydrogen in compounds is assigned an oxidation state of +1, except in hydrides, where it is assigned -1.

Example: In H_2SO_4, H = +1; in LiH, H = -1

7.   Oxygen in compounds is assigned an oxidation state of -2. An exception is peroxide, where in H_2O_2, O = -1.

Example: In H_3PO_4, O = -2

8. The oxidation states of many other atoms may vary from compound to compound. However, their oxidation states can frequently be determined based on the following rule: the sum of the oxidation states of all the atoms in a species must be equal to the net charge on the species.

Example: The net charge of $HClO_4$ = 0. Applying the above rules, H = +1 and 4O = -2 x 4 = -8. Therefore, the oxidation state of Cl must be +7 so that the overall charge = 1 + -8 + 7 = 0.

Example: The net charge of CrO_4^{2-} = -2. Applying the above rules, 4O = -2 x 4 = -8. Therefore, the oxidation state of Cr must be +6 so that the overall charge = -8 + 6 = -2.

For example, the reaction:

$$H_2 + F_2 \rightarrow 2HF$$

is a redox process because the oxidation numbers of atoms are altered. The oxidation numbers of elements are always zero, and oxidation numbers in a compound are never zero. Fluorine is the more electronegative element, so in HF it has an oxidation number of −1 and hydrogen has an oxidation number of +1. This is a redox process where electrons are transferred from H_2 to F_2 to create HF.

In the reaction:

$$HCl + NaOH \rightarrow NaCl + H_2O$$

the H-atoms on both sides of the reaction have an oxidation number of +1, the Cl atom has an oxidation number of –1, the Na atom has an oxidation number of +1, and the O atom has an oxidation number of –2. **This is not a redox process because oxidation numbers remain unchanged** by the reaction.

Skill 4.17   Balance incomplete redox equations in acidic and basic solutions.

An **oxidizing agent** (also called an oxidant or oxidizer) has the ability to oxidize other substances by removing electrons from them. The **oxidizing agent is reduced** in the process. A **reducing agent** (also called a reductive agent, reductant or reducer) is a substance that has the ability to reduce other substances by transferring electrons to them. The **reducing agent is oxidized** in the process.

Redox reactions may always be written as **two half-reactions**, a **reduction half-reaction** with **electrons as a reactant** and an **oxidation half-reaction** with **electrons as a product**.

Example: The redox reactions considered in the previous skill:

$$Zn(s) + Cu^{2+}(aq) \rightarrow Zn^{2+}(aq) + Cu(s) \quad \text{and} \quad H_2 + F_2 \rightarrow 2HF$$

may be written in terms of the half-reactions:

$$2e^- + Cu^{2+}(aq) \rightarrow Cu(s) \quad \quad 2e^- + F_2 \rightarrow 2F^-$$
$$\text{and}$$
$$Zn(s) \rightarrow Zn^{2+}(aq) + 2e^-. \quad \quad H_2 \rightarrow 2H^+ + 2e^-.$$

An additional (non-redox) reaction, $2F^- + 2H^+ \rightarrow 2HF$, achieves the final products for the second reaction.

Determining whether a chemical equation is balanced (see **Skill 4.1**) requires an additional step for redox reactions because there must be a **charge balance.** For example, the equation:

$$Sn^{2+} + Fe^{3+} \rightarrow Sn^{4+} + Fe^{2+}$$

contains one Sn and one Fe on each side, but it is not balanced because the sum of charges on the left side of the equation is +5 and the sum on the right side is +6. A charge balance is obtained by considering each half-reaction separately before multiplying by an appropriate factor so that the number of electrons gained by one half-reaction is the same as the number lost in the other. The two half-reactions may then be combined again into one reaction.

From the example above, one electron is gained in the reduction half-reaction ($Fe^{3+} + e^- \rightarrow Fe^{2+}$), but two are lost in the oxidation half-reaction ($Sn^{2+} \rightarrow Sn^{4+} + 2e^-$). A charge balance is obtained by multiplying the reduction half-reaction by two to obtain the half-reactions:

$$2Fe^{3+} + 2e^- \rightarrow 2Fe^{2+}$$
$$Sn^{2+} \rightarrow Sn^{4+} + 2e^-.$$

The equation:

$$Sn^{2+} + 2Fe^{3+} \rightarrow Sn^{4+} + 2Fe^{2+}$$

is properly balanced because both sides contain the same sum of charges (+8) and electrons cancel from the half-reactions. .

Oxidation Number Method:

Redox reactions must be balanced to observe the **Law of Conservation of Mass.** This process is a little more complicated than balancing other reactions because the number of electrons lost must equal the number of electrons gained. Balancing redox reactions, then, conserves not only matter but also charge or electrons. It can be accomplished by slightly varying our balancing process.

Example: $Cr_2O_3(s) + Al(s) \longrightarrow Cr(s) + Al_2O_{3\,(s)}$

Solution: First, assign oxidation numbers to each atom in order to identify which are losing or gaining electrons.

$$Cr_2O_3(s) + Al(s) \longrightarrow Cr(s) + Al_2O_{3\,(s)}$$
$$3+ \ 2- 0 0 3+ \ 2-$$

Identify those atoms gaining and losing electrons

$$Cr^{3+} \longrightarrow Cr^0 \quad \text{gained 3 electrons (reduction)}$$
$$Al^0 \longrightarrow Al^{3+} \quad \text{lost 3 electrons (oxidation)}$$

Then, balance the atoms and electrons:

$$Cr_2O_3(s) \longrightarrow 2Cr(s) + 6 \text{ electrons}$$
$$2Al(s) + 6 \text{ electrons} \longrightarrow Al_2O_3(s)$$

Half reactions are balanced by adding missing elements. Ignore elements whose oxidation number does not change, and add an H_2O for oxygen and H^+ for hydrogen.

$$Cr_2O_3(s) \longrightarrow 2Cr(s) + 6 \text{ electrons} + \textbf{3 } \mathbf{H_2O}$$

There are 3 O atoms needed on the product side. This requires $6H^+$ on the reactant side.

$$Cr_2O_3(s) + \textbf{6 } \mathbf{H^+} \longrightarrow 2Cr(s) + 6 \text{ electrons} + \textbf{3 } \mathbf{H_2O}$$
$$2Al(s) + 6 \text{ electrons} + \textbf{3 } \mathbf{H_2O} \longrightarrow Al_{2}O_{3\,(s)} + \textbf{6 } \mathbf{H^+}$$

There are 3 O atoms required on the reactant side. This requires $6H^+$ on the product side.

Put the two half reactions together and add the species. Then, cancel out the species that occur in both the reactant and product sides of the equation.

$$Cr_2O_3(s) + 6\,H^+ + 2Al(s) + 6 \text{ electrons} + 3\,H_2O \longrightarrow$$
$$2Cr(s) + 6 \text{ electrons} + 3\,H_2O + Al_{2}O_{3\,(s)} + 6\,H^+$$

Therefore, the balanced equation is:

$$Cr_2O_3(s) + 2Al(s) \longrightarrow 2Cr(s) + Al_2O_{3\,(s)}$$

Example: Balance the following redox reaction:
$$AgNO_3 + Cu \longrightarrow Cu(NO_3)_2 + Ag$$

Solution: First, assign oxidation numbers to each atom in order to identify which are losing or gaining electrons.

$$AgNO_3 + Cu \longrightarrow Cu(NO_3)_2 + Ag$$
$$1+ \; 5+ \; 2- \quad 0 \qquad 2+ \; 5+ \; 2- \quad 0$$

Then identify the atoms that are gaining and losing electrons:

$$Ag^{1+} + 1\,e^- \longrightarrow Ag^0 \quad \text{1 electron gained (reduction)}$$
$$Cu^0 \longrightarrow Cu^{2+} + 2\,e^- \quad \text{2 electrons lost (oxidation)}$$

Balance each of the atoms and electrons:

$$AgNO_3 + 1\,e^- \longrightarrow Ag^0$$
$$Cu^0 \longrightarrow Cu(NO_3)_2 + 2\,e^-$$
$$Cu^0 \longrightarrow Cu^{2+} + 2\,e^-$$

There is one electron gained and two electrons lost. This must be balanced, so 2 electrons must be gained.

$$2\,[Ag + 1\,e^- \longrightarrow Ag^0] = \mathbf{2\,AgNO_3 + 2\,e^- \longrightarrow 2\,Ag^{0+}}$$

Reduction: $2\,AgNO_3 + 2\,e^- \longrightarrow 2\,Ag^{0+}$
Oxidation: $Cu^0 \longrightarrow Cu(NO_3)_2 + 2\,e^-$

Balance the half reactions by adding missing elements. Ignore elements whose oxidation number does not change. Add H_2O for oxygen and H^+ for hydrogen

$$2\,AgNO_3 + 2\,e^- \longrightarrow 2\,Ag^{0+} + 2\,NO_3$$
$$\mathbf{2NO_3} + Cu^0 \longrightarrow Cu(NO_3)_2 + 2\,e^-$$

Put the two half reactions together and add the species. Cancel out the species that occur in both the reactants and products.

Reduction: $2\,AgNO_3 + 2\,e^- \longrightarrow 2\,Ag^{0+} + 2\,NO_3$
Oxidation: $2NO_3 + Cu^0 \longrightarrow Cu(NO_3)_2 + 2\,e^-$

The balanced reaction is then:
$$2\,AgNO_3 + Cu \longrightarrow Cu(NO_3)_2 + 2\,Ag$$

Example: Balance the following redox reaction:

$$Ag_2S + HNO_3 \longrightarrow AgNO_3 + NO + S + H_2O$$

Solution: First, assign oxidation numbers to each atom:

$$Ag_2S + HNO_3 \longrightarrow AgNO_3 + NO + S + H_2O$$
$$1+ \; 2- \quad 1+ \; 5+ \; 2- \qquad 1+ \; 5+ \; 2- \quad 2+ \; 2- \quad 0 \quad 1+ \; 2-$$

Identify those atoms gaining and losing electrons:

Oxidation: $S^{2-} \longrightarrow S^0 + 2\,e^-$
Reduction: $N^{5+} + 3\,e^{-+} \longrightarrow N^{2+}$

Balance the atoms in the equation:

$$2\,NO_3 + Ag_2S \longrightarrow S + 2\,e^- + 2\,AgNO_3 \text{ (oxidation)}$$
$$3\,H^+ + HNO_3 + 3\,e^- \longrightarrow NO + 2\,H_2O \text{ (reduction)}$$

Balance the electrons that are lost or gained:
There are 2 electrons that are lost and 3 electrons that are gained. This must balance, so find the lowest multiple of the two numbers, which is 6 in this case.

Oxidation:

$$3[\,2\,NO_3 + Ag_2S \longrightarrow S + 2\,e^- + 2\,AgNO_3\,]$$
$$6\,NO_3 + 3\,Ag_2S \longrightarrow 3\,S + 6\,e^- + 6\,AgNO_3$$

Reduction:

$$2[\,3\,H^+ + HNO_3 + 3\,e^- \longrightarrow NO + 2\,H_2O\,]$$
$$6\,H^+ + 2\,HNO_3 + 6\,e^- \longrightarrow 2\,NO + 4\,H_2O$$

Finally, put the two half reactions together and add the species. Cancel out the species that occur on both the reactant and product sides of the equation.

$$6\,NO_3 + 3\,Ag_2S + 6\,H^+ + 2\,HNO_3 + 6\,e^- \longrightarrow$$
$$3\,S + 6\,e^- + 6\,AgNO_3 + 2\,NO + 4\,H_2O$$

Therefore, the balanced equation is:

$$3\,Ag_2S + 8\,HNO_3 \longrightarrow 6\,AgNO_3 + 2\,NO + 3\,S + 4\,H_2O$$

To balance a redox reaction which occurs in a basic solution is very similar to balancing a redox reaction which occurs in an acidic solution. First, balance the reaction as you would for an acidic solution and then make appropriate adjustments for the basic solution.

Example: Solid chromium(III) hydroxide, $Cr(OH)_3$, reacts with aqueous chlorate ions, ClO_3, in basic conditions to form chromate ions, CrO_4^{2-}, and chloride ions, Cl^-.

$$Cr(OH)_3(s) + ClO_3^-(aq) \rightarrow CrO_4^{2-}(aq) + Cl^-(aq) \quad \text{(basic)}$$

Solution:
1. Write each of the half-reactions:
   $Cr(OH)_3(s) \rightarrow CrO_4^{2-}(aq)$ and
   $ClO_3^-(aq) \rightarrow Cl^-(aq)$

2. Balance the atoms in each half-reaction. Use H_2O to add oxygen atoms and H^+ to add hydrogen atoms.
   $$H_2O(l) + Cr(OH)_3(s) \rightarrow CrO_4^{2-}(aq) + 5\,H^+(aq)$$

   $$6H^+(aq) + ClO_3^-(aq) \rightarrow Cl^-(aq) + 3\,H_2O(l)$$

3. Balance the charges of both half-reactions by adding electrons.

   $$H_2O(l) + Cr(OH)_3(s) \rightarrow CrO_4^{2-}(aq) + 5\,H^+(aq)$$

   has a charge of +3 on the right and 0 on the left. Adding 3 electrons to the right side will give that side a 0 charge as well.

   $$H_2O(l) + Cr(OH)_3(s) \rightarrow CrO_4^{2-}(aq) + 5\,H^+(aq) + 3e^-$$

   $$6H^+(aq) + ClO_3^-(aq) \rightarrow Cl^-(aq) + 3\,H_2O(l)$$

   has a charge of -1 on the right side and a +5 on the left. Six electrons need to be added to the left side to equal the -1 charge on the right side.

   $$6\,e^- + 6H^+(aq) + ClO_3^-(aq) \rightarrow Cl^-(aq) + 3\,H_2O(l)$$

4. The number of electrons lost must equal the number of electrons gained, so multiply each of the half-reactions by a number that will give an equal number of electrons lost and gained.

$$H_2O \ (l) + Cr(OH)_3(s) \rightarrow CrO_4^{2-}(aq) + 5 \ H^+ \ (aq) + 3e^-$$

$$6 \ e^- + 6H^+ \ (aq) + ClO_3^-(aq) \rightarrow Cl^-(aq) + 3 \ H_2O \ (l)$$

The first half reaction needs to be multiplied by 2 to equal the 6 electrons gained in the second half-reaction.

$$2[H_2O \ (l) + Cr(OH)_3(s) \rightarrow CrO_4^{2-}(aq) + 5 \ H^+ \ (aq) + 3e^-] =$$
$$2H_2O \ (l) + 2 \ Cr(OH)_3(s) \rightarrow 2 \ CrO_4^{2-}(aq) + 10 \ H^+ \ (aq) + 6e^-$$

5. Add the two half-reactions together; canceling out species that appear on both sides of the reaction.

$$2H_2O + \cancel{2}Cr(OH)_3(s) + \cancel{6e^-} + 6H^+(aq) + ClO_3^-(aq) \rightarrow 2 \ CrO_4^{2-}(aq) + \cancel{10} \ H^+ \ (aq) + \cancel{6e^-} + Cl^-(aq) + \cancel{3}H_2O$$

$$4 \ H^+ \ (aq) \qquad 1 \ H_2O \ (l)$$

6. Since the reaction occurs in a basic solution and there are 4 H^+ ions on the right side, 4 OH^- need to be added to both sides. Combine the H^+ and OH^- where appropriate to make water molecules.

$$4 \ OH^- \ (aq) + 2 \ Cr(OH)_3(s) + ClO_3^-(aq) \rightarrow$$

$$2 \ CrO_4^{2-}(aq) + 4 \ H^+ \ (aq) + Cl^-(aq) + 1H_2O \ (l) + 4 \ OH^- \ (aq)$$

$$4 \ H_2O \ (l)$$

7. Write final balanced equation:

$$4 \ OH^- \ (aq) + 2 \ Cr(OH)_3(s) + ClO_3^-(aq) \rightarrow$$

$$2 \ CrO_4^{2-}(aq) + Cl^-(aq) + 5 \ H_2O \ (l)$$

57 videos of redox experiments are presented here:
http://chemmovies.unl.edu/chemistry/redoxlp/redox000.html.

Skill 4.18   Determine the spontaneity of a chemical reaction using standard reduction potentials.

A **standard cell potential,** E_{cell}°, is the voltage generated by an electrochemical cell at **100 kPa and 25°C,** when all components of the reaction are pure materials (or solutes) at a **concentration of 1 M**. Older textbooks may use 1 atm instead of 100 kPa. Standard solute concentrations may differ from 1 M for solutions that behave in a non-ideal way, but this difference is beyond the scope of general high school chemistry.

Standard cell potentials are calculated from the **sum of the two half-reaction potentials** for the reduction and oxidation reactions occurring in the cell:

$$E_{cell}^{\circ} = E_{red}^{\circ}(\text{cathode}) + E_{ox}^{\circ}(\text{anode}$$

All half-reaction potentials are relative to the reduction of H^+ to form H_2. This potential is assigned a value of zero:

$$\text{For } 2H^+(aq \text{ at } 1 \text{ M}) + 2e^- \rightarrow H_2(g \text{ at } 100 \text{ kPa}), \quad E_{red}^{\circ} = 0 \text{ V}.$$

The standard potential of an oxidation half-reaction, E_{ox}°, **is equal in magnitude but has the opposite sign to the potential of the reverse reduction reaction.** Standard half-cell potentials are calculated as reduction potentials. These are sometimes referred to as **standard electrode potentials $E°$**. Therefore,

$$E_{cell}^{\circ} = E^{\circ}(\text{cathode}) - E^{\circ}(\text{anode}.$$

Example: Given

$$E°=0.34 \text{ V for } Cu^{2+}(aq)+2e^-\rightarrow Cu(s) \text{ and}$$
$$E°= -0.76 \text{ V for } Zn^{2+}(aq)+2e^-\rightarrow Zn(s),$$
what is the standard cell potential of the
system $Zn(s) + Cu^{2+}(aq) \rightarrow Zn^{2+}(aq) + Cu(s)$

Solution:
$$E_{cell}^{\circ} = E^{\circ}(\text{cathode}) - E^{\circ}(\text{anode})$$
$$= E^{\circ}\left(Cu^{2+}(aq) + 2e^- \rightarrow Cu(s)\right) - E^{\circ}\left(Zn^{2+}(aq) + 2e^- \rightarrow Zn(s)\right)$$
$$= 0.34 \text{ V} - (-0.76 \text{ V}) = 1.10 \text{ V}.$$

Spontaneity

When the value of $E°$ is positive, the reaction is spontaneous. If the $E°$ value is negative, an outside energy source is necessary for the reaction to occur. In the above example, the $E°$ is a positive 1.10 V, therefore this reaction is spontaneous.

Skill 4.19   Identify the characteristics of biochemical and fossil fuel combustion reactions.

Most combustion reactions are the oxidation of a fuel material with oxygen gas. Complete burning produces carbon dioxide from all the carbon in the fuel, and water from the hydrogen in the fuel. These reactions are used mainly for the production of heat energy. The fuel value is the energy released when 1 g of a material is combusted. This number is a positive number since energy is released, and it is measured by calorimetry.

Biochemical combustion involves the use of enzymes to lower the activation energy so that the combustion reaction can be carried out at lower temperatures, like body temperature (37°C). In our bodies, most of the energy comes from the combustion of carbohydrates and fats. Starch, a carbohydrate, is decomposed in the intestines into glucose, $C_6H_{12}O_6$. Glucose is soluble in blood and is transported to cells where it reacts with oxygen, producing carbon dioxide and water while releasing 2803 kJ/mol of energy.

$$C_6H_{12}O_6 \text{ (s)} + 6 \text{ } O_2\text{(g)} \rightarrow 6CO_2 \text{ (g)} + 6H_2O \text{ (l)} \qquad \Delta H = -2803 \text{ kJ}$$

Carbohydrates supply energy quickly due to their rapid breakdown. Storage of carbohydrates is limited, however.

Fats also undergo combustion in the cells to produce carbon dioxide and water.

$$2C_{57}H_{110}O_6 \text{ (s)} + 163 \text{ } O_2 \text{ (g)} \rightarrow 114 \text{ } CO_2 \text{ (g)} + 110 \text{ } H_2O \text{ (l)} \qquad \Delta H = -75.520 \text{ kJ}$$
(tristearin)

Fuel Values of Carbohydrates, Fats and Proteins	
	Fuel Value (kJ/g)
Carbohydrate	17
Fat	38
Protein	17

This energy is used to regulate body temperature, contract muscles, and build and repair tissues. Any excess energy is stored as fat. Fats are insoluble in water, and they produce more energy per gram than carbohydrates and proteins, so they are prefect for storing excess energy.

However, combustion in the body releases less energy than combustion in a calorimeter, since the products are slightly different. In the body, protein, which contains nitrogen, forms urea with the nitrogen, $(NH_2)_2CO$. But in the calorimeter, proteins form N_2 when combusted.

The combustion of fossil fuels releases energy as well. This energy is in the form of heat. Carbon dioxide and water are formed as the bonds in the fossil fuel rearrange themselves during the combustion reaction. Coal, petroleum and natural gas are known as fossil fuels and are formed from the decay of living matter. Natural gas is a gaseous type of hydrocarbon, primarily methane with small amounts of ethane, propane and butane, and it has a fuel value of 49 kJ/g. Petroleum, with a fuel value around 48 kJ/g for gasoline, is a liquid that contains mostly hydrocarbons, but also has some organic compounds containing sulfur, nitrogen or oxygen. These impurities result in air pollution when petroleum is burned. Coal is a solid that consists of large hydrocarbons, as well as some impurities of sulfur, nitrogen or oxygen. Again, it is these impurities that provide for the contaminants in air pollution when coal is burned. Anthracite coal has a fuel value of 31 kJ/g while bituminous coal has a fuel value of 32 kJ/g.

$$CH_4 \text{ (g)} + O_2 \text{ (g)} \rightarrow CO_2 \text{ (g)} + 2H_2O \text{ (g)} \qquad \Delta H = \text{-802 kJ}$$
The combustion of methane

Skill 4.20   Solve problems related to pH of strong acids or bases.

The concentration of $H^+(aq)$ ions is often expressed in terms of pH. **The pH of a solution is the negative base-10 logarithm of the hydrogen-ion molarity:**

$$pH = -\log\left[H^+\right] = \log\left(\frac{1}{\left[H^+\right]}\right).$$

A ten-fold increase in $[H^+]$ decreases the pH by one unit. $[H^+]$ may be found from pH using the expression:

$$\left[H^+\right] = 10^{-pH}.$$

Because $[H^+] = 10^{-7}$ M for pure water, **the pH of a neutral solution is 7**. In an **acidic solution**, $[H^+] > 10^{-7}$ M and **pH < 7**. In a basic solution, $[H^+] < 10^{-7}$ M and **pH > 7**.

The negative base-10 log is a convenient way of representing other small numbers used in chemistry by placing the letter "p" before the symbol. Values of K_a are often represented as pK_a, with $pK_a = -\log K_a$. The concentration of $OH^-(aq)$ ions may also be expressed in terms of pOH, with $pOH = -\log\left[OH^-\right]$.

The ion-product constant of water, $K_w = [H^+][OH^-] = 1.0 \times 10^{-14}$ at 25 °C. The value of K_w can used to determine the relationship between pH and pOH by taking the negative log of the expression:

$$-\log K_w = -\log[H^+] - \log[OH^-] = -\log(10^{-14}).$$

Therefore: $pH + pOH = 14$.

Example: An aqueous solution has an H^+ ion concentration of 4.0×10^{-9}. Is the solution acidic or basic? What is the pH of the solution? What is the pOH?

Solution: The solution is basic because $[H^+] < 10^{-7}$ M.

$$pH = -\log[H^+] = -\log 4 \times 10^{-9}$$

$$= 8.4.$$

$pH + pOH = 14$. Therefore $pOH = 14 - pH = 14 - 8.4 = 5.6$.

Skill 4.21   Analyze electrolytic and/or voltaic cells

Electrolytic cells use electricity to force nonspontaneous redox reactions to occur. **Electrochemical cells generate electricity** by permitting spontaneous redox reactions to occur. The two types of cells have some components in common.

Both systems contain two **electrodes**. An electrode is a piece of conducting metal that is used to make contact with a nonmetallic material. One electrode is an **anode**. An **oxidation reaction occurs at the anode**, so electrons are removed from a substance there. The other electrode is a **cathode.** A **reduction reaction occurs at the cathode**, so electrons are added to a substance there. Electrons flow from anode to cathode outside either device.

Electrolytic systems

Electrolysis is a chemical process **driven by a battery** or another source of electromotive force. This source pulls electrons out of the chemical process at the anode and forces electrons in the cathode. The result is a **negatively charged cathode and a positively charged anode**.

Oxidation
(e⁻ pulled out)

Reduction
(e⁻ forced in)

Electrolysis of pure water forms O_2 bubbles at the anode by the oxidation half-reaction:

$$2H_2O(l) \rightarrow 4H^+(aq) + O_2(g) + 4e^-$$

and forms H_2 bubbles at the cathode by the reduction half-reaction:

$$2H_2O(l) + 2e^- \rightarrow H_2(g) + 2OH^-(aq).$$

The net redox reaction is:

$$2H_2O(l) \rightarrow 2H_2(g) + O_2(g).$$

Neither electrode took part in the reaction described above. An electrode that is only used to contact the reaction and deliver or remove electrons is called an **inert electrode**. An electrode that takes part in the reaction is called an **active electrode**.

Electroplating is the process of **depositing dissolved metal cations,** in a smooth even coat, onto an object used as an active electrode. Electroplating can be used to protect metal surfaces or for decoration. For example, to electroplate a copper surface with nickel, a nickel rod is used for the anode and the copper object is used for the cathode. $NiCl_2(aq)$ or another substance with free nickel ions is used in the electrolytic cell. $Ni(s) \rightarrow Ni^{2+}(aq) + 2e^-$ occurs at the anode and $Ni^{2+}(aq) + 2e^- \xrightarrow{\text{onto Cu}} Ni(s)$ occurs at the cathode.

Electrochemical systems

An **electrochemical cell** separates the half-reactions of a redox process into two compartments or half-cells. Electrochemical cells are also called *galvanic cells* or *voltaic cells*.

A **battery** consists of one or more electrochemical cells connected together. Electron transfer from the oxidation to the reduction reaction may only take place through an external circuit.

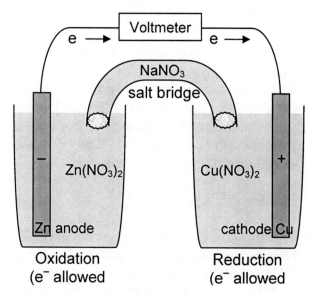

A Voltaic Cell

Electrochemical systems provide a **source of electromotive force**.
This force is called **voltage** or **cell potential** and is measured in **volts**. Electrons are allowed to leave the chemical process at the anode and permitted to enter at the cathode. The result is a **negatively charged anode and a positively charged cathode**.

Electrical neutrality is maintained in the half-cells by **ions migrating** through a **salt bridge**. A salt bridge in the simplest cells is an inverted U-tube filled with a non-reacting electrolyte and plugged at both ends with a material like cotton or glass wool that permits ion migration but prevents the electrolyte from falling out.

The spontaneous redox reaction: $Zn(s) + Cu^{2+}(aq) \rightarrow Zn^{2+}(aq) + Cu(s)$ generates a voltage in the cell pictured on the previous page. The oxidation half-reaction, $Zn(s) \rightarrow Zn^{2+}(aq) + 2e^-$, occurs at the anode. Electrons are allowed to flow through a voltmeter before they are consumed by the reduction half-reaction $Cu^{2+}(aq) + 2e^- \rightarrow Cu(s)$ at the cathode. Zinc dissolves away from the anode into solution, and copper from the solution builds up onto the cathode.

To maintain electrical neutrality in both compartments, positive ions (Zn^{2+} and Na^+) migrate through the salt bridge from the anode half-cell to the cathode half-cell and negative ions (NO_3^-) migrate in the opposite direction.

An animation of the cell described above is located at:
http://www.mhhe.com/physsci/chemistry/essentialchemistry/flash/galvan5.swf.

A summary of anode and cathode properties for both cell types is contained in the table below.

		Electrolytic cell	Electrochemical cell
Anode	Half-reaction	Oxidation	Oxidation
	Electron flow	Pulled out	Allowed out
	Electrode polarity	+	−
Cathode	Half-reaction	Reduction	Reduction
	Electron flow	Forced in	Allowed in
	Electrode polarity	−	+

The reducing and oxidizing agents in a standard electrochemical cell are depleted with time. In a **rechargeable battery** (e.g., lead storage batteries in cars) the direction of the spontaneous redox reaction is reversed, and **reactants are regenerated** when electrical energy is added into the system. A **fuel cell** has the same components as a standard electrochemical cell except that **reactants are continuously supplied**.

COMPETENCY 5.0 KNOWLEDGE OF ATOMIC THEORY AND STRUCTURE

12%

It was as if you fired a 15-inch shell at a sheet of tissue paper and it came back to hit you.

—Ernest Rutherford (after scattering alpha particles off gold foil)

Skill 5.1   Using the periodic table, determine the number of protons, neutrons, and electrons in a specific isotope of an atom or ion.

The first periodic table was developed in 1869 by Dmitri **Mendeleev** several decades before the nature of electron energy states in the atom was known. Mendeleev arranged the elements in order of increasing atomic mass into **columns of similar physical and chemical properties**. He then boldly **predicted the existence and the properties of undiscovered elements** to fill the gaps in his table. These interpolations were initially treated with skepticism until three of Mendeleev's theoretical elements were discovered and were found to have the properties he predicted. It is the correlation with properties—not with electron arrangements—that have placed the periodic table at the beginning of most chemistry texts.

In the modern periodic table, **the elements in a column are known as a group**, and groups are numbered from 1 to 18. Older numbering styles used Roman numerals and letters. These elements, known as a family, have similar properties due to their similar outermost electron arrangements. Each family or column has a group name. **A row of the periodic table is known as a period**, and periods of the known elements are numbered from 1 to 7. The lanthanoids are all in period 6, and the actinoids are all in period 7.

Today, the 115 named elements are organized into the Periodic Table. The design of this table provides much information about a particular element or group of elements. .

The identity of an **element** depends on the **number of protons** in the nucleus of the atom. This value is called the **atomic number** and it is sometimes written as a subscript before the symbol for the corresponding element. Atoms and ions of a given element that differ in number of neutrons have a different mass and are called **isotopes**. A nucleus with a specified number of protons and neutrons is called a **nuclide**, and a nuclear particle, either a proton or neutron, may be called a **nucleon**. The total number of nucleons is called the **mass number** and may be written as a superscript before the atomic symbol. The **mass number** of an atom is the total number of nucleons it contains. This is the **sum of the number of protons and neutrons** in the nucleus.

$$^{14}_{6}C$$ represents an atom of carbon with 6 protons and 8 neutrons.

Different isotopes have different natural abundances and have different nuclear properties, but an atom's chemical properties are almost entirely due to electrons.

The number of neutrons may be found by subtracting the atomic number from the mass number. For example, uranium-235 has 235 – 92 = 143 neutrons because it has 235 nucleons and 92 protons.

Atomic mass is a mass relative to carbon-12, and ^{12}C has an assigned value of exactly 12 u. This means that **the mass number of an atom is usually a good guess at the atom's atomic mass**, and for ^{12}C it is an exact value and not a guess at all. For example, uranium-238 has an atomic mass of 238.05 u.

But if ^{12}C is exactly 12 u, why does carbon have an atomic mass of 12.011 u in the periodic table? This is because 1.1% of carbon on Earth exists as the stable isotope carbon-13. This carbon that is heavier by 1 u and constitutes 1.1% of all carbon contributes the additional 0.011 g to the expected mass of a mole of carbon atoms that we'd find anywhere on this planet. In general, the **atomic mass** of an element is the average of the atomic masses of all stable isotopes of that element weighted by their abundance on Earth.

Atomic mass of element X = (Fraction of X as isotope A) (Atomic mass of isotope A) +
$$\text{(Fraction of X as isotope B) (Atomic mass of isotope B) +}$$
$$\text{(Fraction of X as isotope C) (Atomic mass of isotope C) +}$$
$$\vdots$$

Chlorine, for example, exists on Earth in two stable isotopes: ^{35}Cl and ^{37}Cl. 75.76% of the chlorine is ^{35}Cl which has an atomic mass of 34.969 u and 24.24% is ^{37}Cl which has an atomic mass of 36.966 u. Therefore,
Atomic mass of chlorine $= 0.7576 \times 34.969$ u $+ 0.2424 \times 36.966$ u $= 35.453$ u.

Elements with no stable isotopes are often listed in tables of atomic masses with a number in brackets. This value is the mass number of the isotope with the longest half-life. A list of isotopic compositions and atomic masses for all natural isotopes is at http://physics.nist.gov/cgi–bin/Compositions/stand_alone.pl.

Skill 5.2   Using the periodic table, relate the physical properties of atoms and ions to the elements' positions on the table.

The first periodic table was developed in 1869 by Dmitri Mendeleev. Mendeleev arranged the elements in order of increasing atomic mass into **columns of similar physical and chemical properties**. He then predicted the existence and the properties of undiscovered elements to fill the gaps in his table. These interpolations were treated with skepticism until three of Mendeleev's theoretical elements were discovered and were found to have the properties he predicted. It is the correlation with properties—not with electron arrangements—that have placed the periodic table at the beginning of most chemistry texts.

The elements in a column are known as a group, and groups are numbered from 1 to 18. Older numbering styles used roman numerals and letters. **A row of the periodic table is known as a period**, and periods of the known elements are numbered from 1 to 7. The lanthanoids are all in period 6, and the actinoids are all in period 7.

Metals, nonmetals, and atomic radius

Elements in the periodic table are divided into two broad categories, **metals** and **nonmetals**, with a jagged line separating the two as shown in the figure.

Seven elements near the line dividing metals from nonmetals exhibit some properties of each and are called **metalloids** or **semimetals**. These elements are boron, silicon, germanium, arsenic, antimony, tellurium and astatine.

The most metallic element is francium at the bottom left of the table. The most nonmetallic element is fluorine. The metallic character of elements within a group increases with period number. This means that **within a column, the more metallic elements are at the bottom**. The metallic character of elements within a period decreases with group number. This means that **within a row, the more metallic elements are on the left**. Among the main group atoms, **elements diagonal to each other** as indicated by the dashed arrows **have similar properties** because they have a similar metallic character. The noble gases are nonmetals, but they are an exception to the diagonal rule.

Physical properties relating to metallic character are summarized in the following table:

Element	Electrical/thermal conductivity	Malleable/ductile as solids?	Lustrous?	Melting point of oxides, hydrides, and halides
Metals	High	Yes	Yes	High
Metalloids	Intermediate. Altered by dopants (semiconductors)	No (brittle)	Varies	Varies (oxides). Low (hydrides, halides)
Nonmetals	Low (insulators)	No	No	Low

Malleable materials can **be beaten into sheets**. **Ductile** materials can **be pulled into wires**. **Lustrous** materials **have a shine**. Oxides, hydrides, and halides are compounds with O, H, and halogens respectively. Measures of intermolecular attractions other than melting point are also higher for metal oxides, hydrides, and halides than for the nonmetal compounds. A dopant is a small quantity of an intentionally added impurity. The controlled movement of electrons in doped silicon semiconductors carries digital information in computer circuitry.

The **size of an atom** is not an exact distance due to of the probabilistic nature of electron density, but we may compare radii among different atoms using some standard. As seen to the right, the sizes of neutral atoms increase with period

number and decrease with group number. This trend is similar to the trend described above for metallic character. The smallest atom is helium.

Atomic radius decreases left to right due to the electrons being pulled in tighter to the nucleus with the addition of each electron and proton. The atomic radius increases going down the periodic table due to the addition of another level of electrons with each row.

Group names, melting point, density, and properties of compounds

Groups 1, 2, 17, and 18 are often identified with the group names shown on the table below.

Seven elements are found as **diatomic molecules:** (**H_2, N_2, O_2, and the halogens: F_2, Cl_2, Br_2, and I_2**). Mnemonic devices to remember the diatomic elements are: "$Br_2I_2N_2Cl_2H_2O_2F_2$" (pronounced "Brinklehof") and "**H**ave **N**o **F**ear **O**f **I**ce **C**old **B**eer." Another way to remember them is by using the Rule of Sevens: 7 of them which form a 7 on the Periodic Table and 4 of the 7 are from Group 7. These molecules are attracted to one another using **weak London dispersion forces**.

Alkali metals

Alkaline earth metals

Halogens

Noble gases

Note that **hydrogen** is <u>not</u> an alkali metal. Hydrogen is a colorless gas and is the most abundant element in the universe, but H_2 is very rare in the atmosphere because it is light enough to escape gravity and reach outer space. Hydrogen atoms form more compounds than any other element.

Alkali metals are shiny, soft, metallic solids. They have **low melting points and low densities** compared with other metals (see squares in the following figures) because they have a weaker metallic bond. Measures of intermolecular attractions including their **melting points decrease further down the periodic table due to weaker metallic bonds** as the size of atoms increases.

Alkaline earth metals (group 2 elements) are grey, metallic solids. They are harder, denser, and have a higher melting point than the alkali metals (see asterisks in figures on the following page) but values for these properties are still low compared to most of the transition metals. Measures of metallic bond strength, such as melting points, do not follow a simple trend down the periodic table.

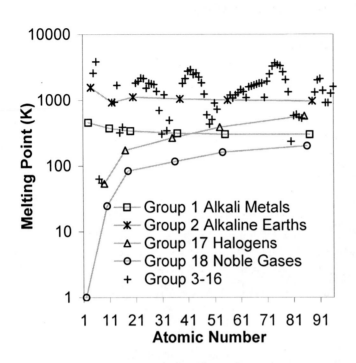

Halogens (group 17 elements) have an irritating odor. Unlike the metallic bonds between alkali metals, **London forces between halogen molecules increase in strength further down the periodic table**. Their melting points increase as shown by the triangles to the left. London forces make Br_2 a liquid and I_2 a solid at 25 °C. The lighter halogens are gases.

Noble gases (group 18 elements) have no color or odor and exist as **individual gas atoms** that experience London forces. These attractions also increase with period number as shown by the circles to the left.

The known **densities** of liquid and solid elements at room temperature are shown below. **Intermolecular forces contribute to density** by bringing nuclei closer to each other, so the periodicity is similar to trends for melting point. These group-to-group differences are superimposed on a general trend for **density** to **increase with period number** because heavier nuclei make the material denser.

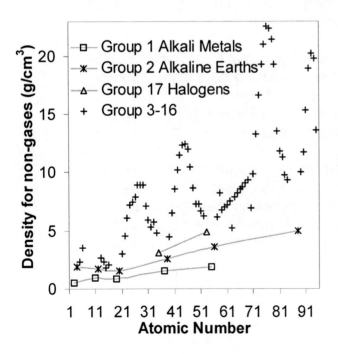

Trends among properties of **compounds** may often be deduced from **trends among their atoms**, but caution must be used. For example, the densities of three potassium halides are:

2.0 g/cm³ for KCl   2.7 g/cm³ for KBr
3.1 g/cm³ for KI.

We would expect this trend for increasing atomic mass within a group. We might also expect the density of KF to be less than 2.0 g/cm³, but it is actually 2.5 g/cm³ due to a change in crystal lattice structure.

Physics of electrons and stability of electron configurations

For an isolated atom, the **most stable system of valence electrons is a filled set of orbitals**. For the main group elements, this corresponds to group 18 (ns^2np^6 and $1s^2$ for helium), and, to a lesser extent, group 2 (ns^2).

The next most stable state is a set of degenerate half-filled orbitals. These occur in group 15 (ns^2np^3). The least stable valence electron configuration is a single electron with no other electrons in similar orbitals. This occurs in group 1 (ns^1) and to a lesser extent in group 13 (ns^2np^1).

An atom's first **ionization energy** is the **energy required to remove one electron** by the reaction $M(g) \rightarrow M^+(g) + e^-$. Periodicity is in the opposite direction from the trend for atomic radius. The most metallic atoms have electrons further from the nucleus, and these are easier to remove. Factors that affect ionization energy are:

    a. Nuclear charge – the larger the nuclear charge, the greater the IE
    b. Shielding effect – the greater the shielding effect, the less the IE
    c. Radius – the greater the distance between the nucleus and the outer electrons of an atom, the less the IE
    d. Sublevel – an electron from a sublevel that is more than half-full requires additional energy to be removed

An atom's **electron affinity** is the energy released when one electron is added by the reaction $M(g) + e^- \rightarrow M^-(g)$. A large negative number for the exothermic reaction indicates a high electron affinity. Halogens have the highest electron affinities.

Trends in **ionization energy and electron affinity** within a period reflect the **stability of valence electron configurations**. A stable system requires more energy to change and releases less when changed. Note the peaks in stability for groups 2, 13, and 16 to the right.

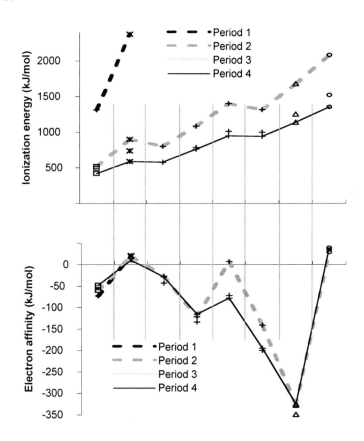

Skill 5.3   **Using the periodic table, relate the chemical reactivity of elements to their positions on the table.**

Much of chemistry consists of atoms **bonding** to achieve stable valence electron configurations. **Nonmetals gain electrons or share electrons** to achieve these configurations and **metals lose electrons** to achieve them.

Qualitative group trends

When cut by a knife, the exposed surface of an **alkali metal or alkaline earth metal** quickly turns into an oxide. These elements **do not occur in nature as free metals**. Instead, they react with many other elements to form white or grey water-soluble salts. With some exceptions, the oxides of group 1 elements have the formula M_2O, their hydrides are MH, and their halides are MX (for example, NaCl). The oxides of group 2 elements have the formula MO, their hydrides are MH_2, and their halides are MX_2, for example, $CaCl_2$.

Halogens combine with each other and also form a wide variety of oxides. They combine with hydrogen to form HX gases, and these compounds are also commonly used as acids (hydrofluoric, hydrochloric, etc.) in aqueous solution. Halogens form salts with metals by gaining electrons to become X^- ions. Astatine is an exception to many of these properties because it is an artificial metalloid.

Noble gases are **nearly chemically inert**. The heavier noble gases form a number of compounds with oxygen and fluorine such as KrF_2 and XeO_4

Electronegativity and reactivity series

Electronegativity measures the ability of an atom to attract electrons in a chemical bond. The most metallic elements have the lowest electronegativity. The most nonmetallic have the highest electronegativity.

The most powerful chemical reactions between elements occur between metals and non-metals. This also corresponds to reactions between the most and least electronegative elements. In a reaction with a metal, the most reactive chemicals are the **most electronegative elements** or compounds containing those elements. In a reaction with a nonmetal, the most reactive chemicals are the **least electronegative elements** or compounds containing them. The reactivity of elements may be described by a **reactivity series**: an ordered list with chemicals that react strongly at one end and nonreactive chemicals at the other. The following reactivity series is for metals reacting with oxygen:

Metal	K	Na	Ca	Mg	Al	Zn	Fe	Pb	Cu	Hg	Ag	Au
Reaction with O_2	Burns violently	Burns rapidly						Oxidizes slowly			No reaction	

Copper, silver, and gold (group 11) are known as the **noble metals** or **coinage metals** because they are very unreactive. The impact of electronegativity on chemical bonding is discussed in **Skill 3.3**.

Fluorine is the most electronegative element in the periodic table, so the elements decrease in electronegativity going right to left and from top to bottom with the halogens being the most reactive (electronegative) group.

Valence and oxidation numbers

The term **valence** is often used to describe the number of atoms that may react to form a compound with a given atom by sharing, removing, or losing **valence electrons**. A more useful term is **oxidation number**. The **oxidation number of an ion is its charge**. The oxidation number of an atom sharing its electrons is **the charge it would have if the bonding were ionic**. There are four rules for determining oxidation number:

1) The oxidation number of an element (i.e., a Cl atom in Cl_2) is zero because the electrons in the bond are shared equally.

2) In a compound, the more electronegative atoms are assigned negative oxidation numbers, and the less electronegative atoms are assigned positive oxidation numbers equal to the number of shared electron-pair bonds. For example, hydrogen may only have an oxidation number of –1 when bonded to a less electronegative element or +1 when bonded to a more electronegative element. Oxygen almost always has an oxidation number of –2. Fluorine always has an oxidation number of –1 (except in F_2).

3) The oxidation numbers in a compound must add up to zero, and the sum of oxidation numbers in a polyatomic ion must equal the overall charge of the ion.

4) The charge on a polyatomic ion is equal to the sum of the oxidation numbers for the species present in the ion. For example, the sulfate ion, SO_4^{2-}, has a total charge of -2. This comes from adding the -2 oxidation number for 4 oxygen (total -8) and the +6 oxidation number for sulfur.

Example: What is the oxidation number of nitrogen in the nitrate ion, NO_3^- ?

Solution: Oxygen has the oxidation number of –2 (rule 2), and the sum of the oxidation numbers must be –1 (rule 3). The oxidation number for N may be found by solving for x in the equation $x + 3 \times (-2) = -1$. The oxidation number of N in NO_3^- is +5.

There is a **periodicity in oxidation numbers** as shown in the table on the next page for examples of oxides with the maximum oxidation number. Remember that an element may occur in different compounds in several different oxidation states.

Group	1	2	13	14	15	16	17	18
Oxide with maximum oxidation number	Li_2O	BeO	B_2O_3	CO_2	N_2O_5		Cl_2O_7	XeO_4
	Na_2O	MgO	Al_2O_3	SiO_2	P_2O_5	SO_3	Br_2O_7	
Oxidation number	+1	+2	+3	+4	+5	+6	+7	+8

They are called "oxidation numbers" because oxygen was the element of choice for reacting with materials when modern chemistry began, and as a result, Mendeleev arranged his first table to look similar to this one.

Acidity/alkalinity of oxides

Metal oxides form basic solutions in water because the ionic bonds break apart and the O^{2-} ion reacts to form hydroxide ions:

metal oxide $\rightarrow$ metal cation(aq) $+O^{2-}(aq)$ and $O^{2-}(aq) + H_2O(l) \rightarrow 2\ OH^-(aq)$

Ionic oxides containing a large cation with a low charge (Rb_2O, for example) are most soluble and form the strongest bases.

Covalent oxides form acidic solutions in water by reacting with water. For example:

$$SO_3(l) + H_2O(l) \rightarrow H_2SO_4(aq) \rightarrow H^+(aq) + HSO_4^-(aq)$$
$$Cl_2O_7(l) + H_2O(l) \rightarrow 2HClO_4(aq) \rightarrow 2H^+(aq) + 2ClO_4^-(aq)$$

Covalent oxides at high oxidation states and high electronegativities form the strongest acids. Acids and bases are discussed in **Skill 4.13**. For this skill, note that the periodic trends for acid and base strength of the oxide of an element follows the same pattern that we have seen before.

http://jcrystal.com/steffenweber/JAVA/jpt/jpt.html contains an applet of the periodic table and trends.

http://www.webelements.com is an on-line reference for information on the elements.

http://www.uky.edu/Projects/Chemcomics/ has comic book pages for each element.

Summary

A summary of periodic trends is shown below. The properties tend to decrease or increase as shown depending on a given element's proximity to fluorine in the table.

Metallic character ⇓   Ionization energy ⇑
Ionic character of halides ⇓ Covalent character of halides ⇑
Atomic radius   ⇓   Electroneativity   ⇑
Alkalinity of oxides ⇓   Acidity of oxides   ⇑

*Note: Memorize the ones in italics; everything else increases top→bottom, left→right

Group Trends (top to bottom):

Increases: atomic radius, nuclear charge, ionic size, shielding effect, atomic number (number of protons, number of electrons), covalent character of halides, acidity of oxides

Decreases: ionization energy, electron affinity, electronegativity, metallic character, ionic character of halides, alkalinity of oxides

Period Trends (left to right):

Increases: electronegativity, nuclear charge, ionization energy, electron affinity, atomic number (number of protons, number of electrons), acidity of oxides

Decreases all the way across: atomic radius, metallic character, ionic character of halides, alkalinity of oxides

Decreases through cations (positive) and again through anions: ionic size

Stays the same left to right: shielding effect

Skill 5.4   Using the periodic table, determine electron configurations for main group and transition elements.

Quantum numbers

The quantum-mechanical solutions from the Schrödinger Equation utilize three quantum numbers (n, l, and m_l) to describe an orbital and a fourth (m_s) to describe an electron in an orbital. This model is useful for understanding the frequencies of radiation emitted and absorbed by atoms and chemical properties of atoms.

The **principal quantum number** n may have positive integer values (1, 2, 3, ...). n is a measure of the **distance** of an orbital from the nucleus, and orbitals with the same value of n are said to be in the same **shell**. This is analogous to the Bohr model of the atom. Each shell may contain up to $2n^2$ electrons. The highest quantum number n that any shell of an element has is the same as the number of the row of the periodic table in which the element is found.

The **azimuthal quantum number** l may have integer values from 0 to n-1. l describes the angular momentum of an orbital. This determines the orbital's **shape**. Orbitals with the same value of n and l are in the same **subshell**, and each subshell may contain up
to $4l + 2$ electrons. Subshells are usually referred to by the principle quantum number followed by a letter corresponding to l as shown in the following table:

Azimuthal quantum number l	0	1	2	3	4
Subshell designation	s	p	d	f	g

Therefore, s subshells may have 4 x 0 + 2 = 2 electrons, and p subshells may have 4 x 1 + 2 = 6 electrons. Helium is in the first row of the periodic table, and has only a single s subshell with two electrons. This subshell would be notated as 1s.

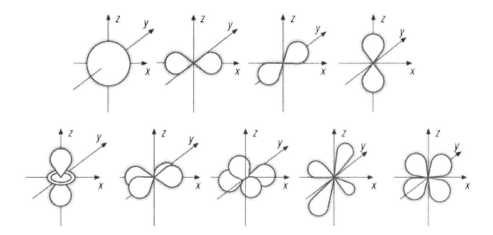

The **magnetic quantum number** m_l **or** m may have integer values from $-l$ to l. m_l is a measure of how an individual orbital responds to an external magnetic field, and it often describes an orbital's orientation. In any given shell, there is only one s orbital with an m value of 0. If p orbitals are present in a shell there will always be 3 p orbitals with values of -1, 0, and 1 (usually referred to as x, y, and z to denote 3-dimensional orientation). A subscript—either the value of m_l or a function of the x-, y-, and z-axes—is used to designate a specific orbital within a subshell For example, $n = 3$, $l = 2$, and $m_l = 0$ would be shown as the $3d_0$ orbital. Each orbital may hold up to two electrons.

The **spin quantum number** m_s **or** s has one of two possible values: $-1/2$ or $+1/2$. m_s differentiates between the two possible electrons occupying an orbital. Electrons moving through a magnet behave as if they were tiny magnets themselves spinning on their axes in either a clockwise or counterclockwise direction. These two spins may be described as $m_s = -1/2$ and $+1/2$ or as down and up.

The **Pauli exclusion principle** states that **no two electrons in an atom may have the same set of four quantum numbers**.

The following table summarizes the relationship among n, l, and m_l through $n=3$:

n	l	Subshell	m_l	Orbitals in subshell	Maximum number of electrons in subshell
1	0	1s	0	1	2
2	0	2s	0	1	2
	1	2p	−1, 0, 1	3	6
3	0	3s	0	1	2
	1	3p	−1, 0, 1	3	6
	2	3d	−2, −1, 0, 1, 2	5	10

Subshell energy levels

In single-electron atoms (H, He$^+$, and Li^{2+}) above the ground state, subshells within a shell are all at the same energy level, and an orbital's energy level is only determined by n. However, in all other atoms, multiple electrons repel each other. Electrons in orbitals closer to the nucleus create a screening or **shielding effect** on electrons further away from the nucleus, preventing them from receiving the full attractive force of the nucleus. **In multi-electron atoms, both n and l determine the energy level of an orbital.** In the absence of a magnetic field, **orbitals in the same subshell with different m_l all have the same energy** and are said to be **degenerate orbitals**.

The following list orders subshells by increasing energy level:
$1s < 2s < 2p < 3s < 3p < 4s < 3d < 4p < 5s < 4d < 5p < 6s < 4f < 5d < 6p < 7s < 5f < ...$

This list may be constructed by arranging the subshells according to n and l and drawing diagonal arrows as shown below:

```
1s
2s  2p
3s  3p  3d
4s  4p  4d  4f
5s  5p  5d  5f  5g
6s  6p  6d  6f  6g
7s  7p  7d  7f  7g
8s  8p  8d  8f  8g
```

Drawing electron arrangements

Electron arrangements (also called electron shell structures) in an atom may be represented using three methods: an **electron configuration**, an **orbital diagram**, or an **energy level diagram**. All three methods require knowledge of the subshells occupied by electrons in a certain atom. The **Aufbau principle** or **building-up rule** states that **electrons at ground state fill orbitals starting at the lowest available energy levels**.

An **electron configuration** is a **list of subshells** with superscripts representing the **number of electrons** in each subshell. For example, an atom of boron has 5 electrons. According to the Aufbau principle, two will fill the $1s$ subshell, two will fill the higher energy $2s$ subshell, and one will occupy the $2p$ subshell which has an even higher energy. The electron configuration of boron is $1s^2 2s^2 2p^1$. Similarly, the electron configuration of a vanadium atom with 23 electrons is:

$$1s^2 2s^2 2p^6 3s^2 3p^6 4s^2 3d^3.$$

Configurations are also written with their principle quantum numbers together:

$$1s^2 2s^2 2p^6 3s^2 3p^6 3d^3 4s^2.$$

Electron configurations are often written to emphasize the outermost electrons. This is done by writing the symbol in brackets for the element with a full p subshell from the previous shell and adding the **outer electron configuration** onto that configuration. The element with the last full p subshell will always be a noble gas from the right-most column of the periodic table. For the vanadium example, the element with the last full p subshell has the configuration $1s^2 2s^2 2p^6 3s^2 3p^6$. This is $_{18}Ar$. The configuration of vanadium may then be written as $[Ar]4s^2 3d^3$ where $4s^2 3d^3$ is the outer electron configuration.

Electron arrangements may also be written by noting the number of electrons in each shell. For vanadium, this would be:

$$2, 8, 11, 2.$$

Orbital diagrams assign electrons to individual orbitals so the energy state of individual electrons may be found. This requires knowledge of how electrons occupy orbitals within a subshell. **Hund's rule** states that **before any two electrons occupy the same orbital, other orbitals in that subshell must first contain one electron each with parallel spins**. Electrons with up and down spins are shown by half-arrows, and these are placed in lines of orbitals (represented as boxes or dashes) according to Hund's rule, the Aufbau principle, and the Pauli exclusion principle. Below is the orbital diagram for vanadium:

An **energy level diagram** is an orbital diagram that shows subshells with higher energy levels higher up on the page. The energy level diagram of vanadium is:

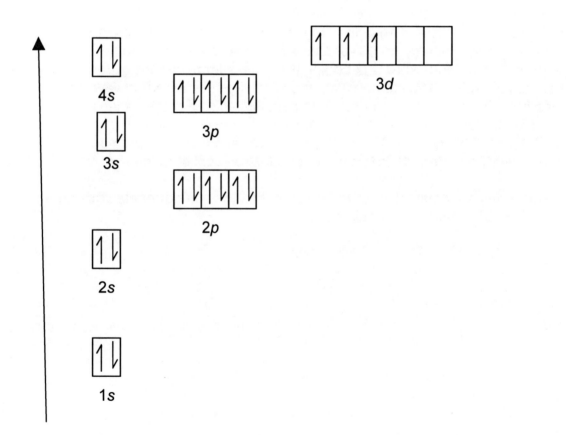

Valence shell electron arrangements and the periodic table

Electrons in the **outermost shell** are called **valence shell electrons**. For example, the electron configuration of Se is $[Ar]4s^2 3d^{10} 4p^4$, and its valence shell electron configuration is $4s^2 4p^4$.

The **periodic table** may be used to write down the electron configuration of any element. The table may be divided up into **blocks corresponding to the subshell** designation of the most recent orbital to be filled by the building-up rule. Elements in the s- and p-blocks are known as **main-group elements**. The d-block elements are called **transition metals.** The f-block elements are called **inner transition metals**.

The maximum number of electrons in each subshell (2, 6, 10, or 14) determines the number of elements in each block, and the order of energy levels for subshells creates the pattern of blocks. These blocks also usually correspond to the value of l for the **outermost electron** of the atom. This has important consequences for the physical and chemical properties of the elements. The outermost shell or valence shell principle quantum number (for example, 4 for Se) is also the period number for the element in the table.

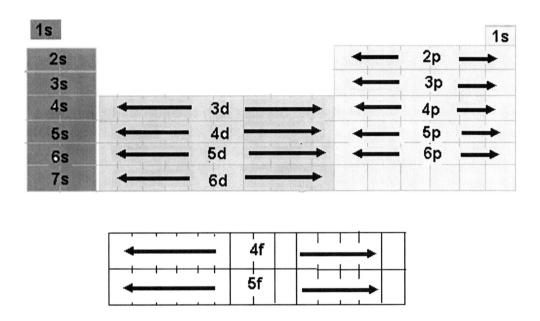

Atoms in the d- and f-blocks often have unexpected electron arrangements that cannot be explained using simple rules. Some heavy atoms have unknown electron configurations because the number of different frequencies of radiation emitted and absorbed by these atoms is very large.

http://www.cowtownproductions.com/cowtown/genchem/08_07T1.htm contains a brief tutorial on energy level diagrams.
http://www.colorado.edu/physics/2000/applets/a2.html contains (among other things) energy level diagrams and animations of electron shells and nuclei.
http://intro.chem.okstate.edu/WorkshopFolder/Electronconfnew.html animates the building up of energy level diagrams.

Skill 5.5   Relate chemical activity to electron configuration.

Nonmetals gain electrons or share electrons to achieve stable configurations and **metals lose electrons** to achieve them.

Valence electrons are the electrons involved in chemical reactions, and valence electron configuration has an affect on chemical activity. The octet rule states that when there are less than four valence electrons, the atom would want to lose electrons to go back to the previous energy level that was full. When the outer energy level is more than half full (more than 4 valence electrons), the atom would want to gain electrons to complete the valence energy level.

For example, aluminum has 13 electrons with a configuration of $1s^2, 2s^2, 2p^6, 3s^2, 3p^1$. There are only three electrons in the third energy level, and the octet rule states that there should be eight. Aluminum can try and find 5 more electrons to fill the 3 p orbital or lose the $3s^2$, and $3p^1$ electrons. It takes less energy to lose the three electrons. When these electrons are lost, an Al^{+3} ion forms with an electron configuration of $1s^2, 2s^2, 2p^6$, which has a complete octet in the outer shell.

With this in mind, you can notice that the families with valence configurations s^1, s^2 or s^2, p^1 tend to lose electrons to form ionic compounds. Families with valence configurations s^2, p^2; s^2, p^3; s^2, p^4; s^2, p^5 tend to gain electrons to form ionic compounds or share electrons to form molecular substances.

The noble gas family with a s^2, p^6 configuration has a complete octet in its valence shell, which causes them to be unreactive. However, the heavier noble gases form a number of compounds with oxygen and fluorine, such as KrF_2 and XeO_4. Remember that atoms with electrons in the "d" or "f" orbitals, have s^1 or s^2 in their valence configuration.

This information helps us to understand some other characteristics. For example, the elements in the alkali metal family are not found as free elements in nature. This is due to their high chemical activity. The one valence electron in the outermost energy level is highly unstable, and it tends to be easily lost, forming many different ionic compounds in the process. The halogen family consists of molecules, rather than free elements. The almost complete valence energy level is easily completed by two halogen atoms sharing electrons to form a covalently bonded molecule.

Skill 5.6   Identify characteristics of the wave and particle nature of matter

See Skill 2.8

Prior to the late 1800s, atoms were thought to be small, spherical and indivisible particles that made up matter. However, with the discovery of electricity and the investigations that followed, this view of the atom changed.

The ideas that pure materials called elements existed and that these elements were composed of fundamentally indivisible units called atoms were proposed by ancient philosophers even though they had little evidence. Modern atomic theory is credited to the work of **John Dalton** published in 1803-1807. Observations made by him and others about the composition, properties, and reactions of many compounds led him to develop the following postulates:

Dalton's table of atomic symbols and masses

1) Each element is composed of small particles called atoms.
2) All atoms of a given element are identical in mass and other properties.
3) Atoms of different elements have different masses and differ in other properties.
4) Atoms of an element are not created, destroyed, or changed into a different type of atom by chemical reactions.
5) Compounds form when atoms of more than one element combine.
6) In a given compound, the relative numbers and kinds of atoms are constant.

Dalton determined and published the known relative masses of a number of different atoms. He also formulated the law of partial pressures. Dalton's work focused on the ability of atoms to arrange themselves into molecules and to rearrange themselves via chemical reactions, but he did not investigate the composition of atoms themselves. **Dalton's model of the atom** was a tiny, indivisible, indestructible **particle** of a certain mass, size, and chemical behavior, but Dalton did not deny the possibility that atoms might have a substructure.

Joseph John Thomson, often known as **J. J. Thomson**, was the first to examine this substructure. In the mid-1800s, scientists had studied a form of radiation called "cathode rays" or "electrons" that originated from the negative electrode (cathode) when electrical current was forced through an evacuated tube. Thomson determined in 1897 that **electrons have mass**, and because many different cathode materials release electrons, Thomson proposed that the **electron is a subatomic particle**. **Thomson's model of the atom** was a uniformly positive particle with electrons contained in the interior. This has been called the "plum-pudding" model of the atom where the pudding represents the uniform sphere of positive electricity and the bits of plum represent electrons. For more on Thomson, see http://www.aip.org/history/electron/jjhome.htm.

Max Planck determined in 1900 that **energy is transferred by radiation in exact multiples of a discrete unit of energy called a quantum**. Quanta of energy are extremely small, and may be found from the frequency of the radiation, v, using the equation:

$$\Delta E = hv$$

where h is Planck's constant and hv is a quantum of energy.

Ernest Rutherford studied atomic structure in 1910-1911 by firing a beam of alpha particles at thin layers of gold leaf. According to Thomson's model, the path of an alpha particle should be deflected only slightly if it struck an atom, but Rutherford observed some alpha particles bouncing almost backwards, suggesting that **nearly all the mass of an atom is contained in a small positively charged nucleus**. **Rutherford's model of the atom** was an analogy to the sun and the planets. A small positively charged nucleus is surrounded by circling electrons and mostly by empty space. Rutherford's experiment is explained in greater detail in this flash animation: http://www.mhhe.com/physsci/chemistry/essentialchemistry/flash/ruther14.swf.

Niels Bohr incorporated Planck's quantum concept into Rutherford's model of the atom in 1913 to explain the **discrete frequencies of radiation emitted and absorbed by atoms with one electron** (H, He^+, and Li^{2+}). This electron is attracted to the positive nucleus and is closest to the nucleus at the **ground state** of the atom.

When the electron absorbs energy, it moves into an orbit further from the nucleus and the atom is said to be in an electronically **excited state**. If sufficient energy is absorbed, the electron separates from the nucleus entirely, and the atom is ionized:

$$H \rightarrow H^+ + e^-$$

The energy required for ionization from the ground state is called the atom's **ionization energy**. The discrete frequencies of radiation emitted and absorbed by the atom correspond (using Planck's constant) to discrete energies and in turn to discrete distances from the nucleus. **Bohr's model of the atom** was a small positively charged nucleus surrounded mostly by empty space and by electrons orbiting at certain discrete distances ("shells") corresponding to discrete energy levels. Animations utilizing the Bohr model may be found at the following two URLs: http://artsci-ccwin.concordia.ca/facstaff/a–c/bird/c241/D1.html and http://www.mhhe.com/physsci/chemistry/essentialchemistry/flash/linesp16.swf.

Bohr's model of the atom didn't quite fit experimental observations for atoms other than hydrogen. He was, however, on the right track. DeBroglie was the first to suggest that matter behaved like a wave. Until then, waves had wave properties of wavelength, frequency and amplitude while matter had matter properties like mass and volume. DeBroglie's suggestion was quite unique and interesting to scientists.

Depending on the experiment, radiation appears to have wave-like or particle-like traits. In 1923-1924, Louis de Broglie applied this **wave/particle duality to all matter with momentum**. The discrete distances from the nucleus described by Bohr corresponded to permissible distances where standing waves could exist. **De Broglie's model of the atom** described electrons as **matter waves in standing wave orbits** around the nucleus. The first three standing waves corresponding to the first three discrete distances are shown in the figure. De Broglie's model may be found here: http://artsci-ccwin.concordia.ca/facstaff/a-c/bird/c241/D1-part2.html.

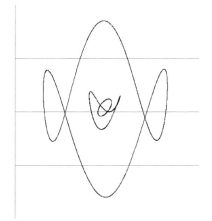

The realization that both matter and radiation interact as waves led **Werner Heisenberg** to the conclusion in 1927 that the act of observation and measurement requires the interaction of one wave with another This interaction results in an **inherent uncertainty** in the location and momentum of particles observed. This limitation in the measurement of phenomena at the subatomic level is known as the **Heisenberg uncertainty principle**, and it applies to the location and momentum of electrons in an atom. A discussion of the principle and Heisenberg's other contributions to quantum theory is located here: http://www.aip.org/history/heisenberg/.

When **Erwin Schrödinger** studied the atom in 1925, he replaced the idea of precise orbits with regions in space called **orbitals** where electrons were likely to be found. **Schrödinger's model of the atom** is a mathematical formulation of quantum mechanics that describes the electron density of orbitals. The **Schrödinger equation** describes the **probability** that an electron will be in a given region of space, a quantity known as **electron density** or Ψ^2.
This is the atomic model that has been in use from shortly after it was introduced up to the present. The diagrams below are surfaces of constant Ψ^2 found by solving the Schrödinger equation for the hydrogen atom $1s$, $2p_z$ and $3d_0$ orbitals. Additional representations of solutions may be found here: http://library.wolfram.com/webMathematica/Physics/Hydrogen.jsp.

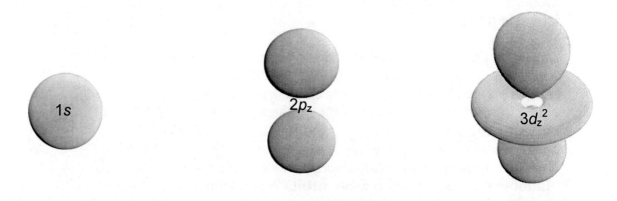

This model explains the movement of electrons to higher energy levels when exposed to energy. It also explains the movement of electrons to lower energy levels when the source of energy has disappeared. Accompanying this drop in energy level is the emission of electromagnetic radiation (light as one possibility).

Using Plank's equation, the frequency of that electromagnetic radiation, EMR, can be determined, radiation caused by the movement of matter.

Wolfgang Pauli helped develop quantum mechanics in the 1920s by developing the concept of spin and the **Pauli exclusion principle**, which states that if two electrons occupy the same orbital, they must have different spin (intrinsic angular momentum). This principle has been generalized to other quantum particles.

Friedrich Hund determined a set of **rules to determine the ground state** of a multi-electron atom in the 1920s. One of these rules is called **Hund's Rule** in introductory chemistry courses, and describes the order in which electrons fill orbitals and their spin.

Quantum numbers – See Skill 5.4

Skill 5.7 Identify characteristics of unstable nuclei and the particles and energies emitted.

Some nuclei are unstable and emit particles and electromagnetic radiation. These emissions from the nucleus are known as **radioactivity**; the unstable isotopes are known as **radioisotopes**; and the nuclear reactions that spontaneously alter them are known as **radioactive decay**. Particles commonly involved in nuclear reactions are listed in the following table:

Particle	Neutron	Proton	Electron	Positron	Alpha particle	Beta particle	Gamma rays
Symbol	^1_0n	^1_1p or ^1_1H	$^0_{-1}e$	^0_1e	$^4_2\alpha$ or ^4_2He	$^0_{-1}\beta$ or $^0_{-1}e$	$^0_0\gamma$

Skill 5.8 Given measurable quantities, calculate parameters of radioactive decay.

The **half-life** of a reaction is the **time required to consume half the reactant**. See **Skill 4.10** for the relationship between half-life and first order rate constants. The rate of radioactive decay for an isotope is usually also expressed as a half-life. Solving these problems is straightforward if the given amount of time is an exact multiple of the half-life. For example, the half-life of ^{233}Pa is 27.0 days. This means that of 200 grams of ^{233}Pa will decay according to this table:

Day	Number of half-lives	^{233}Pa remaining	^{233}Pa decayed since day 0
0	0	200 g	0 g
27.0	1	100 g	100 g
54.0	2	50.0 g	150.0 g
81.0	3	25.0 g	175.0 g
108.0	4	12.5 g	187.5 g

Regardless of whether the given amount of time is an exact multiple of the half-life, the following equation may be used:

$$A_{remaining} = A_{initially} \left(\frac{1}{2}\right)^{\frac{t}{t_{halflife}}}$$

where: $A_{remaining} \Rightarrow$ amount remaining

$A_{initially} \Rightarrow$ amount initially

$t \Rightarrow$ time

$t_{halflife} \Rightarrow$ half-life

For example:

Problem: An isotope of cesium (cesium-137) has a half-life of 30 years. If 1.0 mg of cesium-137 disintegrates over a period of 90 years, how many mg of cesium-137 would remain?

Solution: Using the equation

$$A_{remaining} = A_{initially} \left(\frac{1}{2}\right)^{\frac{t}{t_{halflife}}}$$

where: $A_{remaining} \Rightarrow$ amount remaining

$A_{initially} \Rightarrow$ amount initially

$t \Rightarrow$ time

$t_{halflife} \Rightarrow$ half-life

$A_{remaining}$ = X
$A_{initially}$ = 1.0 mg
t= 90 years
$t_{1/2}$ = 30 years

then $A_{remaining}$ = 1.0 mg $(1/2)^{90/30}$ = 0.125 mg

Example: A 2.5 gram sample of an isotope of strontium-90 was formed in a 1960 explosion of an atomic bomb at Johnson Island in the Pacific Test Site. The half-life of strontium-90 is 28 years. In what year will only 0.625 grams of this strontium-90 remain?

Solution: This is a little more challenging in that substuting into the above equation gives you: $0.625 \text{ g} = 2.5 (1/2)^{x/28}$. The solution requires simplifying and then taking the natural log of both sides:

ln (0.625/2.5) =ln 0.25= ln $(1/2^{x/28})$ x=56 years

Add 56 years to 1960 and the year will be 2016 when only 0.625 grams of Sr-90 remain from that test.

Skill 5.9   Balance simple nuclear equations.

Nuclear equations are balanced by equating the sum of mass numbers and the sum of atomic numbers on both sides of a reaction equation.

The electron is assigned an atomic number of -1 to account for the conversion during radioactive decay of a neutron to a proton and an emitted electron called a **beta particle**:

$$_0^1n \rightarrow {_1^1}p + {_{-1}^0}e \, .$$

Sulfur-35 is an isotope that decays by beta emission.

$$_{16}^{35}S \rightarrow {_{17}^{35}}Cl + {_{-1}^0}e$$

In most cases, nuclear reactions result in a **nuclear transmutation** from one element to another. Transmutation was originally connected to the mythical "philosopher's stone" of alchemy that could turn cheaper elements into gold. When Frederick Soddy and Ernest Rutherford first recognized that radioactive decay was changing one element into another, Soddy remembered saying, "Rutherford, this is transmutation!" Rutherford replied, "Soddy, don't call it transmutation. They'll have our heads off as alchemists."

Isotopes may also decay by **electron capture** from an orbital outside the nucleus.

$$_{79}^{196}Au + {_{-1}^0}e \rightarrow {_{78}^{196}}Pt$$

A **positron** is a particle with the small mass of an electron but with a positive charge. A positron emission converts a proton into a neutron. Carbon-11 decays by positron emission.

$$_6^{11}C \rightarrow {_5^{11}}B + {_1^0}e$$

Large isotopes often decay by **alpha particle** emission.

$$_{92}^{238}U \rightarrow {_{90}^{234}}Th + {_2^4}He$$

Gamma rays are high-energy electromagnetic radiation emissions. Gamma radiation is almost always emitted when other radioactive decay occurs. Gamma rays usually aren't written into equations because neither the mass number nor the atomic number is altered. One exception is the annihilation of an electron by a positron, an event that only produces gamma radiation.

$$_{-1}^0e + {_1^0}e \rightarrow 2{_0^0}\gamma$$

Nuclear equations, whether spontaneous or induced decay, must follow the law of conservation of matter as well as obeying conservation of charge.

Example: Balance the following nuclear transmutation:

$$^{14}_{6}C \rightarrow {}^{14}_{7}N + \underline{\hspace{1cm}}$$

Solution: 1) The sum of the mass numbers on both the left and right side of the arrow must be the same:

Left side	Right side
14	14

2) They are the same, so the particle emitted during decay has a mass of 0.

3) The sum of the charge must be the same on the left side and right side of the arrow.

Left side	Right side
6	7

4) The right side has one extra positive charge to balance the 6 positive charges on the left side. Adding -1 to the right side will make it balance with 6 positive charges.

5) Thus, the charge of the particle emitted during decay is -1. That particle is an electron. $^{0}_{-1}e$ and should be placed in the equation to complete.

$$^{14}_{6}C \rightarrow {}^{14}_{7}N + {}^{0}_{-1}e$$

Example: Complete the following nuclear transmutation:

$$^{234}_{90}\text{Th} \rightarrow\ ^{0}_{-1}\text{e} + \underline{\hspace{3cm}}$$

Solution: Again, the sum of the mass numbers on each side of the arrow must be the same as well as the sum of the charges on each side.

Left side	Right side
234	0

234 is needed on the right side to equal the left side.

Left side	Right side
90	-1

91 is needed on the right side to equal the left side, so the particle that forms from the decay of this isotope is $^{234}_{91}\text{Pa}$ and should be inserted to complete the transmutation.

$$^{234}_{90}\text{Th} \rightarrow\ ^{0}_{-1}\text{e} + ^{234}_{91}\text{Pa}$$

The same nucleons may arrange themselves within the nucleus in different ways with differing energies. This multiplicity is known as nuclear isomerism. Adding the letter "m" to their mass number designates nuclei with alternate arrangements. The "m" stands for "metastable," and "m1", "m2", and so on are used if additional nuclear isomers exist. Only gamma rays are produced when one nuclear isomer decays to another:

$$^{99m}_{43}\text{Tc} \rightarrow\ ^{99}_{43}\text{Tc} + ^{0}_{0}\gamma$$

Skill 5.10   Analyze the processes of nuclear fission and fusion, including interconversion of mass and energy.

When two nuclei collide, they sometimes stick to each other and synthesize a new nucleus. This **nuclear fusion** was first demonstrated by the synthesis of oxygen from nitrogen and alpha particles.

$$^{14}_{7}\text{N} + ^{4}_{2}\text{He} \rightarrow\ ^{17}_{8}\text{O} + ^{1}_{1}\text{H}$$

Fusion is also used to create new heavy elements, causing periodic tables to grow out of date every few years. In 2004, IUPAC approved the name roentgenium (in honor of Wilhelm Roentgen, the discoverer of X-rays) for the element first synthesized in 1994 by the following reaction:

$$^{209}_{83}\text{Bi} + ^{64}_{28}\text{Ni} \rightarrow ^{272}_{111}\text{Rg} + ^{1}_{0}\text{n}.$$

A heavy nucleus may also split apart into smaller nuclei by **nuclear fission.**

Nuclear power currently provides 17% of the world's electricity. Heat is generated by **nuclear fission of uranium-235 or plutonium-239**. This heat is then converted to electricity by boiling water and forcing the steam through a turbine. Fission of ^{235}U and ^{239}Pu occurs when **a neutron strikes the nucleus and breaks it apart into smaller nuclei and additional neutrons**. One possible fission reaction is:

$$^{1}_{0}\text{n} + ^{235}_{92}\text{U} \rightarrow ^{141}_{56}\text{Ba} + ^{92}_{36}\text{Kr} + 3\,^{1}_{0}\text{n}.$$

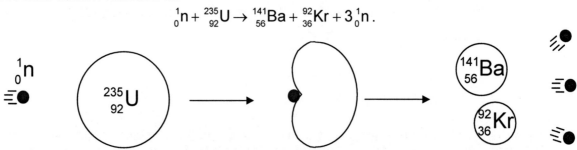

Gamma radiation, kinetic energy from the neutrons themselves, and the decay of the fission products (^{141}Ba and ^{92}Kr in the example above) all produce heat. The neutrons produced by the reaction strike other uranium atoms and produce more neutrons and more energy in a **chain reaction**. If enough neutrons are lost, the chain reaction stops and the process is called **subcritical**. If the mass of uranium is large enough that one neutron on average from each fission event triggers another fission, the reaction is said to be **critical**. If the mass is larger than this so that few neutrons escape, the reaction is called **supercritical**. The chain reaction then multiplies the number of fissions that occur and the violent explosion of an atomic bomb will take place if the process is not stopped. The concentration of **fissile material** in nuclear power plants is sufficient for a critical reaction to occur but too low for a supercritical reaction to take place.

The alpha decay of **Plutonium-238 is used as a heat source for localized power generation** in space probes and in heart pacemakers from the 1970s.

The most promising nuclear reaction for producing power by nuclear fusion is:

$$^{2}_{1}\text{H} + ^{3}_{1}\text{H} \rightarrow ^{4}_{2}\text{He} + ^{1}_{0}\text{n}.$$

Hydrogen-2 is called **deuterium** and is often represented by the symbol D. Hydrogen-3 is known as **tritium** and is often represented by the symbol T.

Nuclear reactions between very light atoms similar to the reaction above are the energy source behind the sun and the hydrogen bomb.

Interconversion of mass and energy

With nuclear reactions, the energies involved are so great that the changes in mass become easily measurable. One no longer can assume that mass and energy are conserved separately, but must take into account their interconversion via Einstein's relationship, $E = mc^2$. If mass is in grams and the velocity of light is expressed as $c = 3 \times 10^{10}$ cm sec^{-1}, then the energy is in units of g cm^2 sec^{-2}, or ergs. A useful conversion is from mass in amu to energy in million electron volts (MeV):

1 amu = 931.4 MeV

What holds a nucleus together? If we attempt to bring two protons and two neutrons together to form a helium nucleus, we might reasonably expect the positively charged protons to repel one another violently. Then, what keeps them together in the $^4_2$He nucleus?

The answer is that a helium atom is lighter than the sum of the mass of two protons, two neutrons, and two electrons. Some of the mass of the separated particles is converted into energy and dissipates when the nucleus is formed. Before the helium nucleus can be torn apart into its component particles, this dissipated energy must be restored and turned back into mass. Unless this energy is provided, the nucleus cannot be taken apart. This energy is termed the **binding energy** of the helium nucleus.

4.0331 amu

1.0073 amu

0.00055 amu   1.0087 amu

1.0073 amu   1.0087 amu

0.00055 amu

proton   electron   neutron

28.4 MeV energy given off

4.0026 amu

$^4_2$He atom is 0.0305 amu lighter than its components.

We must include electrons in this calculation because 4.0026 amu is the mass of the He atom, not just the nucleus. This missing mass corresponds to 0.0305 x 931.4 MeV = 28.4 MeV of energy. If we could put together a helium atom directly from two neutrons, two protons, and two electrons, then 28.4 MeV of energy would be given off for every atom formed:

$$2p + 2n + 2e^- \rightarrow {}^4_2He + 28.4 \text{ MeV of energy}$$

Compared to common chemical reactions, this is an enormous quantity of energy. Since 1 electron volt per atom is equivalent to 23.06 kcal per mole,

$$\text{binding energy} = 28.4 \text{ MeV atom}^{-1} \times \frac{23.06 \text{ kcal mole}^{-1}}{1 \text{ eV atom}^{-1}}$$
$$= 655,000,000 \text{ kcal mole}^{-1}$$

Compare this energy with the 83 kcal mole^{-1} required to break carbon-carbon bonds in chemical reactions.)

Every atomic nucleus is lighter than the sum of the masses of the nucleons from which it is built, and this mass loss corresponds to the binding energy of the nucleus. The relative stability of two nuclei with different numbers of nucleons can be assessed by comparing their **mass loss per nucleon**.

The binding energies are plotted above for nuclei from helium through uranium. After some initial minor irregularities in the first- and second-row elements, the values settle down to a smooth curve, which rises to a maximum at iron, then begins a long descending slope through uranium and beyond.

Iron is the most stable nucleus of all. For elements with smaller atomic numbers than iron, fusion of nuclei to produce heavier elements releases energy, because the products are lighter and more stable on a per-nucleon basis than the reactants. In contrast, beyond iron, fusion absorbs energy because the products are heavier on a per-nucleon basis than the reactants.

Example: What is the mass loss per nucleon for the $^{56}_{26}Fe$ atom, compared with its component protons, neutrons, and electrons?

Solution: The $^{56}_{26}Fe$ atom contains 26 protons, 26 electrons, and 30 neutrons, so the mass calculation is performed as follows:

Mass of 26 protons:	26 (1.0073) amu =	26.1898 amu
Mass of 30 neutrons:	30 (1.0087) amu =	30.261 amu
Mass of 26 electrons:	26 (0.00055) amu =	0.0143 amu
Total mass of components in iron-56		56.465 amu
Mass of iron-56 atom		55.93 amu
Total mass loss:		0.54 amu
Mass loss/nucleon:	0.54amu/56 =	0.0096 amu

Notice that the mass loss (and the binding energy) per nucleon is greater for iron (0.0096 amu) than for helium (0.0076 amu). This means that the iron nucleus is more stable, relative to protons and neutrons, than the helium nucleus is. If some combination of helium nuclei could be induced to produce an iron nucleus, energy would be given off, which would correspond to the increased stability of the product nucleus per nuclear particle.

Skill 5.11   Identify electron density distribution diagrams and characteristics for s, p, and d orbitals (e.g., nodes).

See Skill 5.4

COMPETENCY 6.0 KNOWLEDGE OF THE NATURE OF SCIENCE

10%

"There are and can be only two ways (inductive and deductive methods) of searching into and discovering truth. The one (deductive) flies from the senses and the particulars to the most general axioms and from these (principles); the truth it takes as fore settled and immovable proceeds to judgment and to the discovery of middle axioms and this way is now in fashion. The other (inductive) derives axioms from the senses and particulars rising by a gradual and unbroken assent, that it arrives at the most general axiom last of all. This is the true way."

Sir Francis Bacon

Skill 6.1 Identify the characteristics and components of scientific inquiry.

Modern science began around the late 16th century with a new way of thinking about the world. Few scientists will disagree with Carl Sagan's assertion that "science is a way of thinking much more than it is a body of knowledge" (Broca's Brain, 1979). Science is a process of inquiry and investigation. It is a way of thinking and acting, not just a body of knowledge to be acquired by memorizing facts and principles. This way of thinking, the scientific method, is based on the idea that scientists begin their investigations with observations. From these observations they develop a hypothesis, which is further developed into a prediction. The hypothesis is challenged through experimentation and further observations and is refined as necessary. Science has progressed in its understanding of nature through careful observation, a lively imagination, and increasingly sophisticated instrumentation. Science is distinguished from other fields of study in that it provides guidelines or methods for conducting research, and the research findings must be reproducible by other scientists in order for those findings to be valid.

It is important to recognize that scientific practice is not always this systematic. Discoveries have been made that are serendipitous and others have been predicted based on theory rather than observation of phenomena. Einstein's theory of relativity was developed not from the observation of data but with a kind of mathematical puzzle. Only later were experiments able to be conducted that validated his theory.

The Scientific Method is a logical set of steps that a scientist goes through to solve a problem. . The main purpose of using the Scientific Method is to eliminate, as much as possible, preconceived ideas, prejudices and biases by presenting an objective way to study possible answers to a question. Only by designing a way to study one variable at a time can each possible answer be ruled out or accepted for further study. There are as many different scientific methods as there are scientists experimenting. However, there seems to be some pattern to their work.

While an inquiry may start at any point in this method and may not involve all of the steps, the overall approach can be described as follows:

Making Observations

Scientific questions frequently result from observations of events in nature or events observed in the laboratory. An observation is not just a look at what happens. It also includes measurements and careful records of the event. Records could include photos, drawings, or written descriptions. The observations and data collection may provide answers, or they may lead to one or more questions. In chemistry, observations almost always deal with the behavior of matter.

Having arrived at a question, a scientist usually researches the scientific literature to see what is known about the question. Perhaps the question has already been answered, or another experimenter has found part of the solution. The scientist then may want to test or reproduce the answer found in the literature. Or, the research might lead to a new question.

Sometimes the same observations are made over and over again and are always the same. For example, one can observe that daylight lasts longer in summer than in winter. This observation never varies. Such observations are called **laws of nature**. For example, one of the most important laws in chemistry was discovered in the late 1700s. Chemists observed that no mass was ever lost or gained in chemical reactions. This law became known as the law of conservation of mass. Explaining this law was a major topic of chemistry in the early 19th century.

Developing a Hypothesis

If the question has not yet been answered, the scientist may prepare for an experiment by making a hypothesis. A hypothesis is a statement of a possible answer to the question. It is a tentative explanation for a set of facts and can be tested by experiments. Although hypotheses are usually based on observations, they may also be based on a sudden idea, intuition, or mathematical theory.

Conducting and Experiment

An experiment tests the hypothesis to determine whether it may be a correct answer to the question or a solution to the problem. Some experiments may test the effect of one thing on another under controlled conditions. Such experiments have two variables. The experimenter controls one variable, called the **independent variable**. The other variable, the **dependent variable**, shows the result of changing the independent variable. (See Skill 6.3)

For example, suppose a researcher wanted to test the effect of Vitamin A on the ability of rats to see in dim light. The independent variable would be the dose of Vitamin A added to the rats' diet. The dependent variable would be the intensity of light to which the rats respond. All other factors, such as time, temperature, age, water and other nutrients given to the rats are held constant.

Chemists sometimes do short experiments "just to see what happens" or to see what a certain reaction produces. Often, these are not formal experiments. Rather, they are ways of making additional observations about the behavior of matter.

When students are involved in designing experiments, they better understand what scientists are doing as well as the difficulty of designing appropriately controlled experiments. An ideal experiment at the high school level should not last more than 12-14 days.

In most experiments scientists collect **quantitative data**, which are data that can be measured with instruments. They also collect **qualitative data**, descriptive information from observations other than measurements. (Skill 6.9)

Interpreting data and analyzing observations are an important part of the scientific method. If data are not organized in a logical manner, incorrect conclusions can be drawn. Also, other scientists may not be able to follow or reproduce the results. (See Skills 6.5, 6.6, and 6.7) By placing data into charts and graphs, the scientist may see patterns or lack thereof. The scientist will also be able to understand if the experiment truly tested the hypothesis. Induction is drawing conclusions based on facts or observations. Deduction is drawing conclusions based on generalizations.

Drawing a Conclusion

Finally, a scientist must draw conclusions from the experiment. A conclusion must address the hypothesis on which the experiment was based. The conclusions state whether or not the data support the hypothesis. If not, the conclusion should state what the experiment did show. If the hypothesis is not supported, the scientist uses the observations from the experiment to make a new or revised hypothesis. Then, new experiments are planned.

Effective written communication is necessary to present the research to a teacher or to a scientific journal. Effective oral communication is needed to present the research to a group whether that group is a class or other scientists. Students must recognize that, in this age of communication, those who cannot communicate effectively will be left behind. Accordingly, the evaluation system of the use of the scientific method should make provision for communication skills and activities.

Defending results is as important as conducting an experiment. One can honestly defend one's own results only if the results are reliable, and experiments must be well-controlled and repeated at least twice to be considered reliable. It must be emphasized to the students that *honesty and integrity are the foundation for any type of investigation.*

Steps of the Scientific Method

Developing a Theory

When a hypothesis survives many experimental tests to determine its validity, the hypothesis may be developed into a **theory**. A theory explains a body of facts and laws that are based on the facts. A theory also reliably predicts the outcome of related events in nature. For example, the law of conservation of matter and many other experimental observations led to a theory proposed early in the 19th century . This theory explained the conservation law by proposing that all matter is made up of atoms which are never created or destroyed in chemical reactions, only rearranged. This atomic theory also successfully predicted the behavior of matter in chemical reactions that had not been studied at the time. As a result, the atomic theory has stood for 200 years with only minor modifications.

A theory also serves as a scientific **model**. A model can be a physical model made of wood or plastic, a computer program that simulates events in nature, or simply a mental picture of an idea. A model illustrates a theory and explains nature. For example, in your chemistry course, you will develop a mental (and possibly a physical) model of the atom and its behavior. Outside of science, the word theory is often used to describe an unproven notion. In science, theory means much more. It is a thoroughly tested explanation of things and events observed in nature.

A theory can never be proven true, but it can be proven untrue. All this requires is to demonstrate *one* exception to the theory.

Skill 6.2   Identify how the characteristics of scientific research differ from those of other areas of learning.

Throughout history, different ways of knowing have complimented each other and been used by all civilizations. Different fields of study require different skills, from mathematics and science to arts and crafts, from medicine and law to religion and philosophy.

There are four basic ways of gaining information: personal experience, a trusted source, intuition or inspiration, or reason or logical thinking. Science, it seems, is a combination of personal experience and logical thinking. Religion flows from a trusted source while philosophy comes from logical thinking.

Science, both the natural sciences like physics, biology and chemistry along with the social sciences like psychology and sociology, uses the scientific method for standards of proof. There is a well-established series of steps that must be followed, beginning with research and experimentation and ending with publication. These standards of proof make it difficult for science to be manipulated. However, this occurred in March of 1989, when Stanley Pons and Martin Fleischmann announced the achievement of cold fusion, a long-sought after phenomena which set the scientific community ablaze. This fire was extinguished quickly with accusations of fraud and incompetence, followed by the humiliation of those two scientists afforded by rushed and incomplete results along with errors in their data interpretation.

In other areas of knowledge, information is much more difficult to judge, since the evidence used for study is open to personal interpretation. For the most part, other areas of study use subjective explanations as proof. Religious knowledge relies on information from books or from a deity and passed down to mankind. It can come from a variety of translations, or it can come through prayer or meditation or association with other believers and followers. Philosophy is a belief accepted by some school or group and relies on public discourse for validation. Assessments of the same piece of literature can vary widely from one person to another. Learning about history uses primary and secondary sources, and again relies on a great deal of elucidation.

While no method for learning is perfect, each different way of learning is necessary to fill our senses and explain our world. They all work together to provide a full picture of the world in which we live.

Skill 6.3   Identify variables in a given experimental design.

The design of chemical experiments must include every step needed to obtain the desired data. In other words, the design must be **complete** and it must include all required **controls**.

Complete design

Familiarity with individual experiments and equipment will help you evaluate if anything is missing from the design. For data requiring a difference between two values, the experiment **must determine both values**. For data utilizing the ideal gas law, the experiment **must determine three of the values of P, V, n, or T** in order to determine the fourth, or one value and a ratio of the other two in order to determine the fourth. In general, whenever an equation is used to determine an unknown quantity, each of the other quantities in the equation must be measured or otherwise derived from the experiment.

Example: In a mercury manometer, the level of mercury in contact with a reaction vessel is 70.0 mm lower than the level exposed to the atmosphere. Use the following conversion factors:

$$760 \text{ mm Hg} = 1 \text{ atm} = 101.325 \text{ kPa}$$

What additional information is required to determine the pressure in the vessel in kPa?

Solution: The barometric pressure is needed to determine vessel pressure from an open-ended manometer. A manometer reading is always a **difference** between two pressures. One standard atmosphere is 760 mm mercury, but on a given day at a given location, the actual ambient pressure may vary. If the barometric pressure on the day of the experiment is 104 kPa, the pressure of the vessel is:

$$104 \text{ kPa} + 70.0 \text{ mm Hg} \times \frac{101.325 \text{ kPa}}{760 \text{ mm Hg}} = 113 \text{ kPa}.$$

Controls

Experimental **controls** prevent factors other than those under study from impacting the outcome of the experiment. A **test sample** in a controlled experiment is the unknown that is compared against one or more **control samples**. Control samples should be selected to be as identical to the test sample as possible in every way other than the one variable being tested.

A **negative control** is a control sample that is known to lack the effect. A **positive control** is known to contain the effect. Positive controls of varying strengths or concentrations are often used to generate a **calibration curve** (also called a **standard curve**).

For example, a scientist may wish to measure the level of arsenic in drinking water in a former mining area. A negative control would consist of water similar to that being tested that does not contain arsenic. This insures that there has been no cross-contamination during the experiment, and that the instruments are recording properly. Positive controls are also prepared consisting of water samples with increasing known concentrations of arsenic. The curve of concentration responses obtained is called a calibration curve, and is compared to past curves to ensure that the instrument is recording accurate and precise measurements across a wide concentration range.

When determining the concentration of a component in a mixture, an **internal standard** is a known concentration of a different substance that is added to the experimental sample. An **external standard** is a known concentration of the substance of interest. External standards are more commonly used. They are not added to the experimental sample; they are analyzed separately. These standards are frequently used to evaluate potential bias in the results, which may be caused by poor instrument calibration, interference from other compounds, or loss of the substance during sample pre-processing.

Replicate samples

Replicate samples characterize the degree of random error that is present. A mean may be taken of the results from replicate samples to obtain a best value, or replicate samples may be used in statistical testing to determine if one sample is likely to be part of the same population as another. If one replicate is obviously inconsistent with the results from other replicates, it may be discarded as an **outlier** and not counted as an observation when determining the mean. Discarding an outlier is equivalent to assuming the presence of a systematic error for that particular observation. In research, this must be done with great caution because some real-world behavior generates sporadically unusual results, and most natural populations contain occasional outliers.

Example: A pure chemical in aqueous solution is known to absorb light at 615 nm. What controls would best be used with a spectrophotometer to determine the concentration of this chemical when it is present in a mixture with other solutes in an aqueous solution?

Solution: The other solutes may also absorb light at 615 nm. The best negative control would be an identical mixture with the chemical of interest entirely absent. Known concentrations of the chemical could then be added to the negative control to create positive controls (external standards) and develop a calibration curve of the spectrophotometer absorbance reading at 615 nm as a function of concentration. Replicate samples of each standard and of the unknown should be read.

Example: Ethanol is separated from a mixture of organic compounds by gas chromatography. The concentration of each component is proportional to its peak area. However, the chromatograph detector has a variable sensitivity from one run to the next. Is an internal standard required to determine the concentration of ethanol?

Solution: Yes. The variable detector sensitivity may only be accounted for by adding a known concentration of a chemical not found in the mixture as an internal standard to the experimental sample and control samples. The variable sensitivity of the detector will be accounted for by determining the ratio of the peak area for ethanol to the peak area of the added internal standard.

Skill 6.4   Identify bias in an experimental design.

Experimental bias occurs when a researcher favors one particular outcome over another in an experimental setup. In order to avoid bias, it is imperative to set up each experiment under exactly the same conditions, including a **control experiment**, an experiment with a known negative outcome. Additionally, in order to avoid experimental bias, a researcher must not "read" particular results into data.

An example of experimental bias can be seen in the classic example of the mouse in the maze experiment. In this example, a researcher is timing mice as they move through the maze towards a piece of cheese. The experiment relies on the mouse's ability to smell the cheese as it approaches. If one mouse chases a piece of cheddar cheese, while another chases Limburger, or so called "stinky" cheese, clearly the Limburger mouse has a huge advantage over the mouse chasing cheddar. To remove the experimental bias from this experiment, the same cheese should be used in both tests.

See Skill 6.3 for other ways in which an experiment can contain bias

Skill 6.5   Evaluate, interpret, and predict from empirical data.

Galileo studied the behavior of falling bodies in the 1590's. Almost a century later, Newton followed up on his work and established calculus and physics which have governed mechanics for centuries. From that point on, science was on a new pathway. No longer would it merely be the philosophy of the ancient Greeks. It would be a qualitative and quantitative discourse.

Lavoisier made careful measurements in his conservation of mass experiments. Since then, data collection has become a central part of all science investigations. Data collected, however, takes varied forms depending of the scientific field and complexity of the inquiry.

Scientific data are initially organized into tables, spreadsheets, or databases. However, trends or patterns in data can be difficult to identify using tables of numbers. For example, here is a table of carbon dioxide concentrations taken over many years atop Mauna Loa Observatory in Hawaii, as compiled by the Carbon Dioxide Information Analysis Center (CDIAC).

Atmospheric CO_2 concentrations at Mauna Loa

Year	Jan.	Feb.	March	April	May	June	July	Aug.	Sept.	Oct.	Nov.	Dec.	Annual
1958	--	--	315.71	317.45	317.5	---	315.86	314.93	313.19	---	313.34	314.67	---
1959	315.58	316.47	316.65	317.71	318.29	318.16	316.55	314.8	313.84	313.34	314.81	315.59	315.98
1960	316.43	316.97	317.58	319.03	320.03	319.59	318.18	315.91	314.16	313.83	315	316.19	316.91
1961	316.89	317.7	318.54	319.48	320.58	319.78	318.58	316.79	314.99	315.31	316.1	317.01	317.65
1962	317.94	318.56	319.69	320.58	321.01	320.61	319.61	317.4	316.26	315.42	316.69	317.69	318.45
1963	318.74	319.08	319.86	321.39	322.24	321.47	319.74	317.77	316.21	315.99	317.07	318.36	318.99
1964	319.57	---	---	---	322.23	321.89	320.44	318.7	316.7	316.87	317.68	318.71	---
1965	319.44	320.44	320.89	322.13	322.16	321.87	321.21	318.87	317.81	317.3	318.87	319.42	320.03
1966	320.62	321.59	322.39	323.7	324.07	323.75	322.4	320.37	318.64	318.1	319.79	321.03	321.37
1967	322.33	322.5	323.04	324.42	325	324.09	322.55	320.92	319.26	319.39	320.72	321.96	322.18
1968	322.57	323.15	323.89	325.02	325.57	325.36	324.14	322.11	320.33	320.25	321.32	322.9	323.05
1969	324	324.42	325.64	326.66	327.38	326.7	325.89	323.67	322.38	321.78	322.85	324.12	324.62
1970	325.06	325.98	326.93	328.13	328.07	327.66	326.35	324.69	323.1	323.07	324.01	325.13	325.68
1971	326.17	326.68	327.18	327.78	328.92	328.57	327.37	325.43	323.36	323.56	324.8	326.01	326.32
1972	326.77	327.63	327.75	329.72	330.07	329.09	328.05	326.32	324.84	325.2	326.5	327.55	327.46
1973	328.54	329.56	330.3	331.5	332.48	332.07	330.87	329.31	327.51	327.18	328.16	328.64	329.68
1974	329.35	330.71	331.48	332.65	333.09	332.25	331.18	329.4	327.44	327.37	328.46	329.58	330.25
1975	330.4	331.41	332.04	333.31	333.96	333.59	331.91	330.06	328.56	328.34	329.49	330.76	331.15
1976	331.74	332.56	333.5	334.58	334.87	334.34	333.05	330.94	329.3	328.94	330.31	331.68	332.15
1977	332.92	333.42	334.7	336.07	336.74	336.27	334.93	332.75	331.58	331.16	332.4	333.85	333.9
1978	334.97	335.39	336.64	337.76	338.01	337.89	336.54	334.68	332.76	332.54	333.92	334.95	335.5
1979	336.23	336.76	337.96	338.89	339.47	339.29	337.73	336.09	333.91	333.86	335.29	336.73	336.85
1980	338.01	338.36	340.08	340.77	341.46	341.17	339.56	337.6	335.88	336.01	337.1	338.21	338.69
1981	339.23	340.47	341.38	342.51	342.91	342.25	340.49	338.43	336.69	336.85	338.36	339.61	339.93
1982	340.75	341.61	342.7	343.56	344.13	343.35	342.06	339.82	337.97	337.86	339.26	340.49	341.13
1983	341.37	342.52	343.1	344.94	345.75	345.32	343.99	342.39	339.86	339.99	341.16	342.99	342.78
1984	343.7	344.51	345.28	347.08	347.43	346.79	345.4	343.28	341.07	341.35	342.98	344.22	344.42
1985	344.97	346	347.43	348.35	348.93	348.25	346.56	344.69	343.09	342.8	344.24	345.56	345.9
1986	346.29	346.96	347.86	349.55	350.21	349.54	347.94	345.91	344.86	344.17	345.66	346.9	347.15
1987	348.02	348.47	349.42	350.99	351.84	351.25	349.52	348.1	346.44	346.36	347.81	348.96	348.93
1988	350.43	351.72	352.22	353.59	354.22	353.79	352.39	350.44	348.72	348.88	350.07	351.34	351.48
1989	352.76	353.07	353.68	355.42	355.67	355.13	353.9	351.67	349.8	349.99	351.3	352.53	352.91
1990	353.66	354.7	355.39	356.2	357.16	356.22	354.82	352.91	350.96	351.18	352.83	354.21	354.19
1991	354.72	355.75	357.16	358.6	359.34	358.24	356.17	354.03	352.16	352.21	353.75	354.99	355.59
1992	355.98	356.72	357.81	359.15	359.66	359.25	357.03	355	353.01	353.31	354.16	355.4	356.37
1993	356.7	357.16	358.38	359.46	360.28	359.6	357.57	355.52	353.7	353.98	355.33	356.8	357.04
1994	358.36	358.91	359.97	361.26	361.68	360.95	359.55	357.49	355.84	355.99	357.58	359.04	358.88
1995	359.96	361	361.64	363.45	363.79	363.26	361.9	359.46	358.06	357.75	359.56	360.7	360.88
1996	362.05	363.25	364.03	364.72	365.41	364.97	363.65	361.49	359.46	359.6	360.76	362.33	362.64
1997	363.18	364	364.57	366.35	366.79	365.62	364.47	362.51	360.19	360.77	362.43	364.28	363.76
1998	365.32	366.15	367.31	368.61	369.3	368.87	367.64	365.77	363.9	364.23	365.46	366.97	366.63
1999	368.15	368.86	369.58	371.12	370.97	370.33	369.25	366.91	364.6	365.09	366.63	367.96	368.29
2000	369.08	369.4	370.45	371.59	371.75	371.62	370.04	368.04	366.54	366.63	368.2	369.43	369.4
2001	370.17	371.39	372	372.75	373.88	373.17	371.48	369.42	367.83	367.96	369.55	371.1	370.89
2002	372.29	372.94	373.38	374.71	375.4	375.26	373.87	371.35	370.57	370.1	371.93	373.63	372.95

However, data is more commonly compiled into graphs. Graphs help scientists visualize and interpret the variation in data. There are many types of graphs, and the nature of the data will determine which is best to use. Bar graphs, pie charts and line graphs are just a few methods used to pictorially represent numerical data.

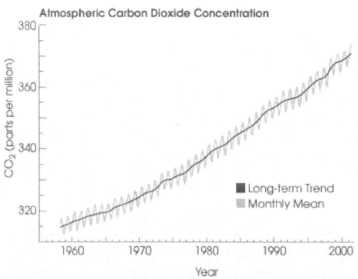

Atmospheric CO_2 measured at Mauna Loa
This is a famous graph called the Keeling Curve (courtesy NASA).

Interpretation of graphical data shows that on the x-axis is the variable of time in units of years and the y-axis represents the variable of CO_2 concentration in units of parts per million (ppm). The best fit line (solid dark line) shows the trend in CO_2 concentrations during the time period. The steady upward-sloping line indicates a trend of increasing CO_2 concentrations during the time period. However, the light blue line, which indicates monthly mean CO_2, levels shows a periodic trend in CO_2 levels during the year. This periodic trend is accounted for by the changes in the seasons. In the spring and summer, deciduous trees and plants undergo increased photosynthesis and remove more CO_2 from the atmosphere in the Northern Hemisphere than in the fall and winter when they have no leaves.

Skill 6.6   Interpret graphical data.

The interpretation of data and the construction and interpretation of graphs are central practices in science. Graphs are effective visual tools which relay information quickly and reveal trends easily. While there are several different types of graphical displays, extracting information from them can be described in three basic steps.

1. **Describe the graph:** What does the title say? What is displayed on the x-axis and y-axis, including the units.
   a. Determine the set-up of the graph.
   b. Make sure the units used are understood. For example, $g \cdot cm^3$ means g/cm^3
   c. Notice any symbols used and check for a legend or explanation.

2. **Describe the data:** Identify the range of data. Are patterns reflected in the data?

3. **Interpret the data:** How do patterns seen in the graph relate to other variables? What conclusions can be drawn from the patterns?

There are seven basic types of graphs.

Column Graphs

Column graphs, consist of patterned rectangles displayed along a baseline called the x-category or the horizontal axis. The height of the rectangle represents the amount of the variable shown on the y-axis. Column graphs best show:
• changes in data over time (short time series)
• comparisons of several items (relationship between two series)

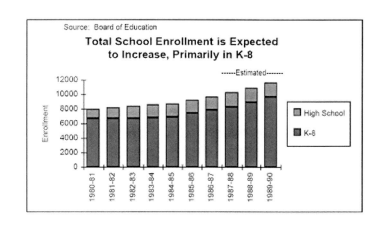

Bar Graphs

Bar graphs are column graphs in which the rectangles are arranged horizontally. The length of each rectangle represents its value. Bar graphs are sometimes referred to as histograms. Bar graphs best show data series with no natural order.

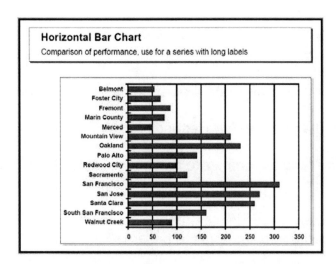

Bar graphs are good for looking at differences amongst similar things. If the data are a time series, a carefully chosen column graph is generally more appropriate but bar graphs can be used to vary a presentation when many column graphs of time series are used. One advantage of bar graphs is that there is greater horizontal space for variable descriptors because the vertical axis is the category axis.

Line Graphs

Line graphs show data points connected by lines; different series are given different line markings (for example, dashed or dotted) or different tick marks. Line graphs are useful when the data points are more important than the transitions between them. They are best at showing long series' of data points, general trends, or changes over time.

Pie Charts

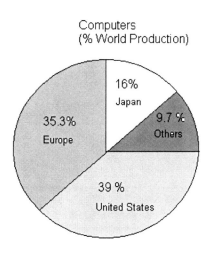

Computers
(% World Production)

16% Japan

9.7 % Others

35.3% Europe

39 % United States

A pie chart is a circle with radii connecting the center to the edge. The area between two radii is called a slice. Data values are proportionate to the angle between the radii. Pie charts best show parts of a whole. Be careful not to include too many slices, as this may result in a cluttered graph. Six slices are typically as many as can be handled on one pie.

Area Graphs

Area charts show the relative contributions over time that each data series makes to a whole picture and are
"stacked line graphs" in the sense that values are together (e.g., principal + interest = total payment). Unlike line graphs, the space between lines is filled with shadings to emphasize variation among the variables over time. Thus, the scale provides accurate measurements only for the lowest part of the graph. This can cause misinterpretation if not fully understood. If reasonable, consider putting the "flattest" graph on the bottom.

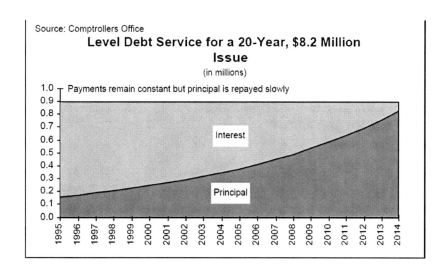

Source: Comptrollers Office
Level Debt Service for a 20-Year, $8.2 Million Issue
(in millions)

Payments remain constant but principal is repaid slowly

Interest

Principal

Scatter Graphs

A scatter plot is the simplest type of graph. It simply plots the data points against their values, without adding an connecting lines, bars or other stuff. The first variable is measured along the x-axis and the second along the y-axis. Because of this, scatter graphs do not have descriptors in the same sense as other graphs.

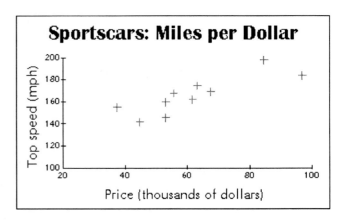

Scatter graphs best show possible relationships between two variables. The purpose of the graph is to try to decide if some partial or indirect relationship—a correlation—exists.

Skill 6.7   **Analyze the relationship between experimental observations and underlying assumptions, hypotheses, conclusions, laws, or theories.**

A law is the highest level that a scientific idea can achieve. Followed by laws (in order of importance) are theories and then hypotheses. The scientific method is the process by which data is collected, interpreted, and validated.

A **law** is a statement of an order or relation of phenomena that, so far as is known, is unchangeable under the given conditions. Everything we observe in the universe operates according to known natural laws. If the truth of a statement is verified repeatedly in a reproducible way over many decades, then the theory can reach the level of a natural law. Some well known and accepted natural laws of science are:

- First Law of Thermodynamics
- Second Law of Thermodynamics
- Law of Cause and Effect
- Law of Biogenesis
- Law of Gravity

A **theory** is, in contrast to a law, a scientific idea used to explain an observation or a set of observations. It is generally accepted to be true, though no real proof exists. The important thing about a scientific theory is that there are no experimental observations which prove it NOT to be true, and each piece of evidence that exists supports the theory. A theory is often accepted at face value, since they are often difficult to prove, and can be rewritten in order include the results of all experimental observations. An example of a theory is the big bang theory. While there is no experiment that can directly test whether or not the big bang actually occurred, there is no strong evidence indicating otherwise.

Theories provide a framework to explain the **known** information of the time, but are subject to constant evaluation and updating. There is always the possibility that new evidence will conflict with a current theory. Some examples of theories that have been rejected because they are now better explained by current knowledge include:

- theory of spontaneous generation
- inheritance of acquired characteristics
- blending hypothesis

As technology evolves and improves, giving the ability to measure things that previously were even unknown, the date to support or disprove theories becomes available.

Some theories were initially rejected because they fell outside of the accepted knowledge of the time, but are well-accepted today due to increased knowledge and data, which include:

- The sun-centered solar system
- Warm-bloodedness in dinosaurs
- The germ-theory of disease
- Continental drift

A **hypothesis** is a tentative assumption made in order to draw out and test its logical or empirical consequences. Many refer to a hypothesis as an educated guess about what will happen during an experiment. A hypothesis can be based on prior knowledge or prior observations. It will be proved true or false only through experimentation.

The **Scientific Method** is defined as principles and procedures for the systematic pursuit of knowledge involving: the recognition and formulation of a problem, the collection of data through observation and experiment, and the formulation and testing of hypotheses. The steps in the scientific method are found in Skill 6.1.

Experiments are designed and hypotheses are proposed to answer a question or better understand a phenomenon or process. If the hypothesis proves true for the first experiment, other experiments are designed to try to disprove it. If a variety of experiments over a period of time and done by a variety of scientists in different settings does not disprove the hypothesis, it can become a theory. In this way, most theories are the result of inductive reasoning.

On the other hand, a law is a broad generalization which often cannot have an experiment to prove or disprove it. It is an overarching concept based on years worth of observations. Therefore, it is the result of deductive reasoning. In some rare cases, however, a theory becomes elevated to the level of a law.

Skill 6.8   Relate experimental evidence to models.

A scientific model is a set of ideas that describes a natural process. Models are developed with empirical or theoretical objects which help scientists focus on basic, fundamental processes. They may be physical representations, such as a space-filling model of a molecule or a map, or they may be mathematical algorithms.

Whatever form they take, scientific models are based on what is known about the science systems or objects at the time that the models are constructed. Models usually evolve and are improved as scientific advances are made. Sometimes, a model must be discarded because new findings show it to be misleading or incorrect.

Proper use of models

Models are developed in an effort to explain how things in nature work. Because models are not the "real thing," they can never perfectly represent the system or object in all respects. The amount of detail that they contain depends upon how the model will be used, as well as the sophistication and skill of the scientist doing the modeling. If a model has too many details left out, its usefulness may be limited. But, too many details may also make a model useless by being too complicated. So, it is easy to see why models lack some features of the real system.

To overcome this difficulty, different models are often used to describe the same system or object. Scientists must then choose which model most closely fits the scientific investigation being carried out, which findings are being described, and, in some cases, which one is compatible with the sophistication of the investigation itself. For example, there are many models of atoms. The solar system model is adequate for some purposes (such as a junior high school classroom), since electrons have properties of matter. They have mass and charge and they are found in motion in the space outside the nucleus. However, a highly mathematical model based on the field of quantum mechanics is necessary when describing the energy (or wave) properties of electrons in the atom.

Scientific models are based on physical observations that establish some facts about the system or object of interest. Scientists then combine these facts with appropriate laws or scientific principles and hypotheses to produce a "picture" that mimics the behavior of the system or object to the greatest possible extent. It is on the basis of such models that science makes many of its most important advances, because such models provide a vehicle for making predictions about the behavior of a system or object. The predictions can then be tested as new measurements, technology or theories are applied to the subject. The new information may result in modification and refinement of the model. However, more complicated issues may remain unresolved by the model for years. The goal, though, is to continue to develop the model in such a way as to move it even closer to a true description of the natural phenomenon. In this way, models are vital to the scientific process.

Skill 6.9   Differentiate between the uses of qualitative and quantitative data.

Qualitative data refers to observations that are descriptive in nature. For example, "the sample was yellow," is descriptive and thus an example of qualitative data. Quantitative data is any observation collected that is numerical in nature. "The sample had a mass of 1.15 grams," is quantitative data. Both types of data have their place in scientific research.

Qualitative Data

The purpose of qualitative data analysis is a complete and detailed, though subjective, description. Qualitative research involves collecting, analyzing, and interpreting data by observing what the subject does.

Qualitative research is much more subjective than quantitative research and uses very different methods of collecting information. This type of data generates rich, detailed and valid observations that contribute to in-depth understanding of the experiment. For example, color change is a type of qualitative observation that is useful in chemistry. However, this is a subjective type of data, since two scientists may view the color change in different ways. Qualitative analysis allows for fine distinctions to be made because it is not necessary to force the data into a finite number of categories.

The main disadvantage of qualitative approaches to data analysis is that their findings can not be extended to other experiments with the same degree of certainty that quantitative analyses can. This is because the findings of the research are not tested to discover whether they are either statistically significant or due to chance.

Quantitative Data

Analysis of quantitative data involves taking objective measurements using standard instruments during an experiment and analyzing the data in an attempt to explain the experiment. These findings, then, can be repeated by other scientists and direct comparisons can be made between two data sets as long as valid scientific techniques have been used.

Most observations made during a scientific experiment will provide quantitative data. Any data point that involves a number obtained by an instrument is a piece of quantitative data. This includes temperature, pressure, mass, time, and many others.

Quantitative research generates reliable, generalizable data and is well suited to establishing cause-and-effect relationships, such as the ideal gas law. For example, we can observe that when the temperature of an ideal gas increases by a specific about, then the pressure will increase a specific, measurable amount (assuming the volume remains constant).

The decision of whether to choose a quantitative or a qualitative design is a philosophical question. Which methods to choose will depend on the nature of the experiment and the type of information needed.

It is important to keep in mind that these are two different types of data, not necessarily polar opposites. Elements of both designs can be used together in scientific observation. Combining qualitative and quantitative research is not uncommon.

It is advantageous for scientists to combine both types of research data for several reasons:
1. Research development (one approach is used to inform the other)
2. Increased validity (confirmation of results by means of different data sources)
3. Complementary (adding information such as, words to numbers and vice versa)
4. Creating new ideas (emerging fresh perspectives)

Quantitative data involves a number, and **qualitative** data does not. Qualitative data may be a description such as a slight/moderate/intense color change or a weak/strong/explosive reaction or it may simply be the absence/presence of an event.

Basically, quantitative research is objective; qualitative is subjective. Quantitative research seeks explanatory laws; qualitative research aims at in-depth description. Quantitative research measures what it assumes to be a static reality in hopes of developing universal laws and is well suited to establishing cause-and-effect relationships. Quantitative data are measurements that are numerical in nature. "The sample had a mass of 1.15 grams" is a quantitative data point. Qualitative research is an exploration of what is assumed to be a dynamic reality. It does not claim that what is discovered in the process is universal, and thus necessarily replicable.

A **lab notebook** is used as the **record of lab work and data collection as it occurs**. Researchers often use lab notebooks to document hypotheses and data analysis. A good lab notebook should allow another scientist to follow the same steps. Electronic lab notebooks are growing in popularity.

Skill 6.10   Analyze the relationship between basic scientific research and applied research, technology, the economy, and the public good.

The union of science, technology, and mathematics has shaped the world we live in today. Science describes the world. It attempts to explain all aspects of how nature works, from our own bodies to the tiny particles making up the world, from the entire earth to the universe beyond. Science lets us know in advance what will happen when a cell splits or when two chemicals react. Yet, science is ever-evolving. Throughout history, people have developed and validated many different ideas about the processes of the universe. Frequently, the development of new technology used in conducting experiments allows for new information and theories to emerge.

Technology makes use of scientific knowledge to solve real-world problems. For example, science is used to study the flow of electrons, but technology is required to channel the flow of electrons to create a supercomputer. **Basic research** generally refers to investigation of fundamental scientific principles.

Applied research is oriented toward making use of basic research in technology development. Applied research is dependent on basic research, and both are necessary for technology advancement. Mathematics, in turn provides the language that allows this knowledge to be communicated. It allows the creation models for scientists to use in explaining natural phenomena and is also the language of technology and computers.

The economy today is dependent upon the existence of technology. The job market changes as new technologies develop. For example, with the advent of computers, many trained workers in information science and technology are needed, moving our economy from a manufacturing-based economy to a knowledge-based economy. Industrial labs are being redefined or eliminated, creating a convergence between scientific disciplines and engineering and providing for new entrepreneur opportunities.

At the same time, advances in scientific knowledge and technology often present ethical dilemmas for society. Industrialization brought about the consumption of great amounts of energy, for example. This, in turn, created environmental problems, and even led to wars. It may result in a depletion of natural resources. Scientific knowledge tells us there is oil in shale that we have not accessed yet. Technological developments will allow us to reach the oil and power our economy. At the same time, new technologies will emerge providing for alternative power supplies like wind farms or biofuels. New types of skills will be needed to support these new technologies and the job market; education and our society will shift in response.

Skill 6.11   Identify how science and society influence each other.

Science and society are interconnected. Important discoveries in science influence and alter society. For example, the invention of the printing press caused a blurring of the classes of society and, at the same time, greatly increased scientific endeavors. The printing press allowed for the cheap production of books, so that common individuals, not just the wealthy, could access literary works. It made it easier to learn to read and write, increasing the education level of all classes. It also made it easier to dream of places, things, and worlds not yet discovered. Scientists could work from exactly the same book at the same time, with fewer errors.

The printing press also allowed for the scientific revolution to occur since scientists could communicate their research results much more quickly. Because knowledge could be spread easily, the printing press changed the way people thought and looked at their world.

The needs of society help to drive the direction of scientific investigation. World War II led the United States to begin developing its own atomic bomb. The need to end the war strengthened and hastened the need for the Manhattan Project to be successful. The creation of the atomic bomb changed the way society existed. It also changed the direction of science. Would we have discovered nuclear power, television, the computer, nuclear medicine and all of the millions of other discoveries that came from the work of the Manhattan Project scientists? Probably, but the pace and the development of such technologies might not have occurred so quickly.

The need for technological development drives science, and in turn discoveries in science influence society and allow new technologies to be developed. The first personal computers were mass-marketed by IBM and Apple in the late 1970s. The IBM 5100 had 16K of memory, a five-inch screen, and cost nearly $11,000 in 1975! A mere twenty-five years later, computers are more prevalent than notebooks, have gigabytes of memory and monitors larger than some televisions, and cost less than $2,000. Why did computers develop so quickly? It was the interconnection between science, technology, and society.

Skill 6.12 Identify evidence of the progressive development of science.

Probably one of the best examples of the progressive development of science would be the development of atomic theory. The ancient Greeks debated over the continuous nature of matter. Two schools of thought had emerged: matter was either continuous or matter was not continuous. The continuous idea was promoted by Aristotle, and due to his high regard among scholars, that was the idea that flourished. However, there was no effort made by the Greeks to prove or disprove this idea. During the dark ages, alchemists started experimenting and keeping records of their results, sending science on a pathway of experimentation and discovery. Robert Boyle and his famous J-tube experiment in 1661, gave the first experimental evidence for the existence of atoms. He even used words similar to Democritus to describe the results saying that the air consisted of atoms with a void between them. By increasing the pressure inside the J-tube, some of the void was squeezed out, decreasing the volume. Slowly, experimental evidence, including the work of Antoine Lavoisier and Joseph Priestley, began to mount, and in 1803, John Dalton proposed the Modern Atomic Theory which contained 5 basic postulates about the nature and behavior of matter.

Ben Franklin's discovery of electricity in 1746 sent scientists to work to understand it. J.J Thomson investigated a cathode ray tube and identified the negatively charged particle in the cathode ray in 1897. His work was closely followed by Robert Millikan who discovered that the electron had a -1 charge in his oil drop experiment.

Experiments were under way to understand how electricity and matter interact when the discoveries of x-rays and radioactivity were announced. Scientists trying to understand radioactivity experimented day and night. Ernest Rutherford was one of them. He tried to understand the nature of radioactivity and classified it into three basic types. While trying to find out more about radioactivity, he conducted his gold foil experiment that ultimately provided greater insight into the subatomic nature of the atom, by discovering the nucleus. He also identified the proton present in the nucleus.

Rutherford's graduate student, Neils Bohr, made slight alterations to Rutherford's model of the atom, to account for his experimental results. These changes helped Rutherford's model stand up to classical physics. However, scientists looking for other patterns and information proposed more changes to the planetary model of the atom. These changes fit with spectroscopy experiments and the quantum mechanical view of the atom was formed. About the same time that this new theory was emerging, James Chadwick, a collaborator of Rutherford's, announced in 1932, the discovery of the neutron within the nucleus. This discovery, ultimately led to the discovery of fission and the development of the nuclear bomb.

Skill 6.13   Analyze natural events for evidence of patterns.

The goal of science is to explain natural phenomena and use it to predict future events. That is only possible if the evidence collected in explaining the natural phenomena leads to a pattern or sequence that can be used in the prediction. Mendeleev noticed a repeating pattern of physical and chemical properties when he arranged the known elements according to increasing atomic mass. He even went so far as to leave spaces in his organization for elements that were not yet discovered. Using his organization and the patterns it was based on, Mendeleev predicted, with great accuracy, the properties of some of the missing elements.

Using natural events and their patterns has been an endeavor that mankind has used to help explain their world, as well as determine the direction their world takes. For example, early humans marked the wall of caves to keep track of the rising of the sun and the moon. This data pattern told them when to migrate to warmer or cooler climates and when to plant and when to harvest. Meteorologists use similar ideas to predict the weather. They rely on patterns, such as how a low pressure system off the coast of Africa develops to predict whether it will become an Atlantic hurricane and where it will cause damage.

Some patterns in nature are regular. That is, they follow a set logical pattern like the rising and setting of the sun, or what is seemingly a random sequence but is really an algorithm, called the Fibonacci sequence, 0,1,1,2,3,5,8,13,21,34,55, etc. The pattern of these numbers is that after two numbers, each subsequent number is the sum of the previous two. Thus, $0 + 1 = 1$, $1 + 1 = 2$, $2 + 1 = 3$, $3 + 2 = 5$, etc.

Nature has incorporated the Fibonacci sequence into many of its patterns. Look at a daisy and notice the pattern of the florets. They are arranged as two sets of intertwined logarithmic spirals. Each floret belongs to both a right-handed and a left-handed spiral. Now, carefully count the number of clockwise and counter-clockwise spirals, and you will find that they are consecutive Fibonacci numbers. Scientific controversies still exist over why such a scheme is found in flowers, pine cones, pineapples, and other structures, but their artistic beauty remains unquestioned.

Lately, much attention has been given to the study of fractals. A fractal is a mathematical formula of a pattern that repeats over a wide range of size and time scales. These patterns are hidden within more complex systems. A good example of a fractal is the branching system of a river. Small tributaries join to form larger and larger "branches" in the system, but each small piece of the system closely resembles the branching pattern as a whole. Recent studies have shown that by applying the concept of fractals to weather patterns, for example, weather predictions can be made more accurate and for a longer time interval.

COMPETENCY 7.0   KNOWLEDGE OF MEASUREMENT

10%

"Weights and measures may be ranked among the necessaries of life to every individual of human society. They enter into the economical arrangements and daily concerns of every family. They are necessary to every occupation of human industry; to the distribution and security of every species of property; to every transaction of trade and commerce; to the labors of the husbandman; to the ingenuity of the artificer; to the studies of the philosopher; to the researches of the antiquarian; to the navigation of the mariner, and the marches of the soldier; to all the exchanges of peace, and all the operations of war. The knowledge of them, as in established use, is among the first elements of education, and is often learned by those who learn nothing else, not even to read and write. This knowledge is riveted in the memory by the habitual application of it to the employments of men throughout life."

- John Quincy Adams, Report to the Congress, 1821

Skill 7.1   Convert between dimensional units for 1, 2, and 3 dimensional measurements.

Dimensional analysis is a structured way to convert units. It involves a conversion factor that allows the units to be cancelled out when multiplied or divided. A conversion factor is the same measurement written as an equivalency between two different units such as 1 meter = 100 centimeters.

One Dimension Unit Conversions

These are the steps to converting one dimension measurements.

1. Write the term to be converted, (both number and unit)

   6.0 cm = ? m

2. Write the conversion formula(s) needed for the involved units.   /

   100 cm = 1 m

3. Make a fraction of the conversion formula, such that:
   a. if the unit in step 1 is in the numerator, that same unit in this step must be in the denominator

$$\frac{1\ m}{100\ cm}$$

   b. if the unit in step 1 is in the denominator, that same unit in this step must be in the numerator

$$\frac{100\ cm}{1\ m}$$

Since both the numerator and denominator are equal in value, the fraction equals 1.

4. Multiply the term in step 1 by the correct fraction in step 3. Since the fraction equals 1, you can multiply by it without changing the size of the original term.

5. Cancel units : 6.0 cm x (1 m / 100 cm)

6. Perform the indicated calculation, rounding the answer to the correct number of significant figures.

$$6.0 \times 1 / 100 = 0.060 \text{ km (or } 6.0 \times 10^{-2} \text{ km)}$$

Two or Three Dimension Unit Conversions

The process is nearly the same for two and three dimension conversions.

Example: How many cm^3 is 1 m^3?

Solution: Remember, 100 cm = 1 m and that 1 m^3 is really 1m x 1m x 1m. Substituting in the 100 cm for every meter the problem can be rewritten as 100 cm x 100 cm x 100 cm or $1m^3$ = 1,000,000 cm^3

$$1 \text{ m}^3 \times 1,000,000 \text{ cm}^3/1m^3 = 1,000,000 \text{ cm}^3 \text{ (or } 1.0 \times 10^6 \text{ cm)}$$

Example: Convert 4.17 kg/m^2 to g/cm^2

Solution: First to convert from kg to g use 1000 g = 1.00 kg as the conversion factor.

$$4.17 \text{ kg/m}^2 \times 1000 \text{ g/1.00 kg} = 4170g /m^2$$

Then use 1.00 m = 100 cm to convert the denominator. Remember that m^2 is m x m and replacing m with 100 cm, the denominator becomes 100 cm x 100 cm. or 10 000 cm^2
The conversion factor for the denominator becomes $1.00m^2$ = 10 000 cm^2

$$4170 \text{ g/m}^2 \times 1.00 \text{ m}^2/10,000 \text{ cm}^2 = 0.417 \text{ g/cm}^2$$

Skill 7.2   Analyze the dimensional units of a mathematical formula.

Units are a part of every measurement. Without the units, the numbers could mean many things. For example, the distance 10 could mean 10 cm, 10 m, or 10 km. The units will even help solve mathematical problems.

Example: The density of gold is 19.3 g/cm^3. How many grams of gold would be found in 55 cm^3?

Solution: Using dimensional analysis, some unit must cancel. The answer needs to be in grams, so the cm^3 needs to cancel out. Multiply or divide the units so that the cm^3 cancel.

In this case:
g/cm^3 x cm^3 = g (or density unit x volume = weight)

This will cancel out the cm^3, and then we perform the calculations to obtain the answer.
19.3 g/c̶m̶^{3} x 55 c̶m̶^{3} = 1060 g of gold.

Skill 7.3   Identify prefixes (e.g., kilo-, milli-, nano-) used in scientific measurements.

SI is an abbreviation of the French *Système International d'Unités* or the **International System of Units**. It is the most widely used system of units in the world and is the system used in science. The use of many SI units in the United States is increasing outside of science and technology. There are two types of SI units, **base units** and **derived units**. The base units are:

Quantity	Unit name	Symbol
Length	meter	m
Mass	kilogram	kg
Amount of substance	mole	mol
Time	second	s
Temperature	kelvin	K
Electric current	ampere	A
Luminous intensity	candela	cd

Amperes and candelas are rarely used in chemistry. The name "kilogram" occurs for the SI base unit of mass for historical reasons. Derived units are formed from the kilogram, but appropriate decimal prefixes are attached to the word "gram." See **Skill 4.10** for reaction rate constant units.

Derived units measure a quantity that may be expressed in terms of other units. The derived units important for chemistry are:

Derived quantity	Unit name	Expression in terms of other units	Symbol
Area	square meter	m^2	
Volume	cubic meter	m^3	
	liter	$dm^3 = 10^{-3}\ m^3$	L or l
Mass	unified atomic mass unit	$(6.022 \times 10^{23})^{-1}\ g$	u or Da
Time	minute	60 s	min
	hour	60 min = 3600 s	h
	day	24 h = 86400 s	d
Speed	meter per second	m/s	
Acceleration	meter per second squared	m/s^2	
Temperature*	degree Celsius	K	°C
Mass density	gram per liter	$g/L = 1\ kg/m^3$	
Amount-of-substance concentration (molarity†)	molar	mol/L	M
Molality‡	molal	mol/kg	*m*
Chemical reaction rate	molar per second†	M/s = mol/(L•s)	
Force	newton	$m \cdot kg/s^2$	N
Pressure	pascal	$N/m^2 = kg/(m \cdot s^2)$	Pa
	standard atmosphere§	101325 Pa	atm
Energy, Work, Heat	joule	$N \cdot m = m^3 \cdot Pa = m^2 \cdot kg/s^2$	J
	nutritional calorie§	4184 J	Cal
Heat (molar)	joule per mole	J/mol	
Heat capacity, entropy	joule per kelvin	J/K	
Heat capacity (molar), entropy (molar)	joule per mole kelvin	J/(mol•K)	
Specific heat	joule per kilogram kelvin	J/(kg•K)	
Power	watt	J/s	W
Electric charge	coulomb	s•A	C
Electric potential, electromotive force	volt	W/A	V
Viscosity	pascal second	Pa•s	
Surface tension	newton per meter	N/m	

*Temperature differences in kelvin are the same as those differences in degrees Celsius. To obtain degrees Celsius from Kelvin, subtract 273.15.

†Molarity is considered to be an obsolete unit by some physicists.

‡Molality, *m*, is often considered obsolete. Differentiate *m* and meters (m) by context.

§These are commonly used non-SI units.

Decimal multiples of SI units are named by attaching a **prefix** directly before the unit and a symbol prefix directly before the unit symbol. SI prefixes range from 10^{-24} to 10^{24}. The most common prefixes you are likely to encounter in chemistry are shown below:

Factor	Prefix	Symbol	Factor	Prefix	Symbol
10^9	giga—	G	10^{-1}	deci—	d
10^6	mega—	M	10^{-2}	centi—	c
10^3	kilo—	k	10^{-3}	milli—	m
10^2	hecto—	h	10^{-6}	micro—	μ
10^1	deca—	da	10^{-9}	nano—	n
			10^{-12}	pico—	p

Example: The distance, 0.0000004355 meters is equal to both 4.355×10^{-7} m and 435.5×10^{-9} m. This length is also equal to 435.5 nm (nanometers).

Example: Find a unit to express the volume of a cubic crystal that is 0.2 mm on each side so that the number before the unit is between 1 and 1000.

Solution: Volume is equal to length x width x height, so this volume is 0.0002 m^3 or $8 \times 10^{-12} \text{ m}^3$. Conversions of volumes and areas using powers of units of length must take the power into account. Therefore:
$$1 \text{ m}^3 = 10^3 \text{ dm}^3 = 10^6 \text{ cm}^3 = 10^9 \text{ mm}^3 = 10^{18} \text{ μm}^3$$

The length 0.0002 m is 2×10^2 μm, so the volume is also $8 \times 10^6 \text{ μm}^3$. This volume could also be expressed as $8 \times 10^{-3} \text{ mm}^3$, but none of these numbers are between 1 and 1000.
Expressing volume in liters is helpful in cases like these. There is no power on the unit of liters, therefore: $1 \text{ L} = 10^3 \text{ mL} = 10^6 \text{ μL} = 10^9 \text{ nL}$.

Converting cubic meters to liters gives:
$$8 \times 10^{-12} \text{ m}^3 \times \frac{10^3 \text{ L}}{1 \text{ m}^3} = 8 \times 10^{-9} \text{ L}.$$
The crystal's volume is 8 nanoliters (8 nL).

Example: Determine the ideal gas constant, R, in L•atm/(mol•K) from its SI value of 8.3144 J/(mol•K).

Solution: One joule is identical to one m^3•Pa (see the table on the previous page).
$$8.3144 \frac{\text{m}^3 \bullet \text{Pa}}{\text{mol} \bullet \text{K}} \times \frac{1000 \text{ L}}{1 \text{ m}^3} \times \frac{1 \text{ atm}}{101325 \text{ Pa}} = 0.082057 \frac{\text{L} \bullet \text{atm}}{\text{mol} \bullet \text{K}}$$

Skill 7.4   Distinguish between accuracy and precision and between systematic and random error.

A measurement is **precise** when individual measurements of the same quantity agree with one another. A measurement is **accurate** when they agree with the true value of the quantity being measured. An **accurate** measurement is **valid**. We get the right answer. A **precise** measurement is **reproducible**, meaning that we get a similar answer each time. These terms are related to **sources of error** in a measurement.

Precise measurements are near the **arithmetic mean** of the values. The arithmetic mean is the sum of the measurements divided by the number of measurements. The **arithmetic mean** is commonly called the **average**. It is the **best estimate** of the quantity based on the measurements taken.

Random error results from **limitations in equipment or techniques**. **Random error decreases precision**. Remember that all measurements reported to a proper number of significant digits contain an imprecise final digit to reflect random error.

Systematic error results from **imperfect equipment or technique**. **Systematic error decreases accuracy**. Instead of a random error with random fluctuations, there is a biased result that, on average, is too large or small.

Example: An environmental engineering company creates a solution of 5.00 ng/L of a toxin and distributes it to four toxicology labs to test their protocols. Each lab tests the material 5 times. Their results are charted as points on the number lines below. Interpret these data in terms of precision, accuracy, and type of error.

Solution: Results from lab 1 are both accurate and precise when compared to results from the other labs. Results from lab 2 are less precise than those from lab 1. Lab 2 seems to use a protocol that contains a greater random error. However, the mean result from lab 2 is still close to the known value. Lab 3 returned results that were about as precise as lab 1 but inaccurate compared to labs 1 and 2. Lab 3 most likely uses a protocol that yields a systematic error. The data from lab 4 is both imprecise and inaccurate. Systematic and random errors are larger than in lab 1.

Skill 7.5 **Apply the correct number of significant figures in measurements or calculations.**

Significant figures or **significant digits** are the digits indicating the **precision of a measurement**. There is uncertainty **only** in the last digit.

Example: You measure an object with a ruler marked in millimeters. The reading on the ruler is found to be about 2/3 of the way between 12 and 13 mm. What value should be recorded for its length?

Solution: Recording 13 mm does not give all the information that you found.

Recording $12\frac{2}{3}$ mm implies that an exact ratio was determined.

Recording 12.666 mm gives more information than you found. A value of 12.7 mm or 12.6 mm should be recorded because there is uncertainty only in the last digit.

There are five rules for determining the **number of significant digits** in a quantity.

1) All nonzero digits are significant and all zeros between nonzero digits are significant.
   Example: 4.521 kJ and 7002 u both have four significant digits.

2) Zeros to the left of the first nonzero digit are not significant.
   Example: 0.0002 m contains one significant digit.

3) Zeros to the right of a nonzero digit and the decimal point are significant figures.
   Example: 32.500 g contains five significant digits.

4) The significance of numbers ending in zeros that are not to the right of the decimal point can be unclear, so **this situation should be avoided** by using scientific notation or a different decimal prefix. Sometimes a decimal point is used as a placeholder to indicate the units-digit is significant. A word like "thousand" or "million" may be used in informal contexts to indicate the remaining digits are not significant.

   Example: 12000 Pa would be considered to have five significant digits by many scientists, but in the context, "The pressure rose from 11000 Pa to 12000 Pa," it almost certainly only has two. "12 thousand pascal" only has two significant figures, but 12000. Pa has five because of the decimal point. The value should be represented as 1.2×10^4 Pa (or 1.2000×10^4 Pa). The best alternative would be to use 12 kPa or 12.000 kPa.

5) Exact numbers have no uncertainty and contain an infinite number of significant digits. These relationships are **definitions**. They are not measurements.

> **Example**: There are exactly 1000 L in one cubic meter.

There are four rules for **rounding off significant digits**.
1) If the leftmost digit to be removed is a four or less, then round down. The last remaining digit stays as it was.
Example: Round 43.4 g to 2 significant figures. Answer: 43 g

2) If the leftmost digit to be removed is a six or more, then round up. The last remaining digit increases by one.
Example: Round 6.772 to 2 significant figures. Answer: 6.8 g

3) If the leftmost digit to be removed is a five that is followed by nonzero digits, then round up. The last remaining digit increases by one.
Example: Round 18.502 to 2 significant figures. Answer 19 g

4) If the leftmost digit to be removed is a five followed by nothing or by only zeros, force the last remaining digit to be even. If it is odd then round up by increasing it by one. If it is even (including zero) then it stays as it was.
Examples: Round 18.50 g and 19.5 g to 2 significant figures.
Answers: 18.50 g rounds off to 18 g and 19.5 g rounds off to 20 g

There are three rules for **calculating with significant digits**.
1) For multiplication or division, the result has the same number of significant digits as the term with the least number of significant digits.
Example: What is the volume of a compartment in the shape of a rectangular prism 1.2 cm long, 2.4 cm high and 0.9 cm deep?

> **Solution**: Volume=length x height x width
> Volume = 1.2 cm $\times$ 2.4 cm $\times$ 0.9 cm = 2.592 cm (as read on a calculator)
> Round to one digit because 0.9 cm has only one significant digit.
> Volume = 3 cm^3

2) For addition or subtraction, the result has the same number of digits after the decimal point as the term with the least number of digits after the decimal point.

Example: Volumes of 250.0 mL, 26 µL, and 4.73 mL are added to a flask. What is the total volume in the flask?

Solution: Only identical units may be added to each other, so 26 µL is first converted to 0.026 mL.

Volume = 250.0 mL + 0.026 mL + 4.73 mL = 254.756 mL (calculator value)

Round to one digit after the decimal because 250.0 mL has only one digit after the decimal. Volume = 254.8 mL.

3) For multi-step calculations, maintain all significant digits when using a calculator or computer and round off the final value to the appropriate number of significant digits after the calculation. When calculating by hand or when writing down an intermediate value in a multi-step calculation, maintain the first insignificant digit. In this text, insignificant digits in intermediate calculations are shown in italics except in the examples for the two rules above.

Skill 7.6 Relate the Celsius, Fahrenheit, and Kelvin temperature scales as they pertain to the physical properties of water.

The degree Fahrenheit (°F), a non-metric temperature scale, was proposed in 1724 by Gabriel Fahrenheit, who was looking to improve upon Galileo's thermometer by changing from an enclosed gas to a mercury system. Mercury has a large uniform thermal expansion, does not adhere to the glass, and its silvery color makes it easy to read. He calibrated his thermometer by:

"placing the thermometer in a mixture of salt ammoniac or sea salt, ice, and water a point on the scale will be found which is denoted as zero. A second point is obtained if the same mixture is used without salt. Denote this position as 30. A third point, designated as 96, is obtained if the thermometer is placed in the mouth so as to acquire the heat of a healthy man." (D. G. Fahrenheit, Phil. Trans. (London) 33, 78, 1724)

On his scale, he found the temperature of boiling water to be 212°. He adjusted the freezing point temperature for water to 32° so that the interval between freezing and boiling would be a rational number (180).

The centigrade scale, designed so that the freezing point of water is zero (0° C) and the boiling point of water is at 100° C, was proposed about twenty years later. Anders Celsius reversed the scale when he proposed the Celsius scale. Both the centigrade and Celsius scales have 100 degrees between the boiling point temperature and freezing point temperature of pure water at standard atmospheric conditions. These scales came from dividing the range of temperature between freezing and boiling temperatures of pure water into exactly 100 parts.

In 1948, the 9th General Conference on Weights and Measures (CGPM) changed the name of the centigrade scale to the Celsius scale and adopted its use. As a result, the Celsius scale is now defined by the following two rules.

1. The triple point of water is defined to be 0.01° C.
2. One degree Celsius equals the same temperature change as one degree on the ideal-gas scale, now called the Kelvin scale.

On the Celsius scale, the boiling point of water at standard atmospheric pressure is 99.975° C, in contrast to the 100 degrees defined by the centigrade scale.

The use of the Celsius or Fahrenheit scale means having to use negative numbers when measuring low temperatures. This proves to be inconvenient, so in the late 1800's Lord Kelvin suggested a new temperature scale. This temperature scale is based on a theoretical absolute zero, the temperature at which a material has lost all heat (or the point at which all molecular motion ceases). This temperature is the basis for the Kelvin scale and the value zero kelvin is assigned to it. At sea level, water freezes at 273.15 K and boils at 373.15 K. Notice, there are still 100 degrees between the freezing and boiling point temperatures on the Kelvin scale as well.

Temperatures on this scale are called **kelvins**, *not* degrees kelvin; kelvin is *not* capitalized, and the symbol (K) stands alone with no degree symbol. In 1967, the new official name "kelvin" and symbol "K" were set by the 13th General Conference on Weights and Measures (CGPM).

Conversions between scales are simple but require a little math.

Example: To convert from Celsius to Fahrenheit: multiply by 1.8 and add 32.

° F = 1.8° C + 32

Or, from Fahrenheit to Celsius: subtract 32 and divide by 1.8.

° C = (°F - 32.) / 1.8

Example: To convert from Celsius to Kelvin: add 273.15.

K = ° C + 273.15

Or, from Kelvin to Celsius: subtract 273.15.

° C = K -273.15

Baseline temperatures in the three temperature scales:

temperature	kelvin	degree Celsius	degree Fahrenheit
symbol	K	°C	°F
boiling point of water	373.15	100.	212.
melting point of ice	273.15	0.	32.
absolute zero	0.	-273.15	-459.67

Common temperature comparisons:

temperature	degree Celsius	degree Fahrenheit
symbol	°C	°F
boiling point of water	100.	212.
average human body temperature	37.	98.6
average room temperature	20. to 25.	68. to 77.
melting point of ice	0.	32.

Skill 7.7 Convert between different units of energy.

Energy is an important concept in the study of chemistry. Energy units used to related changes in a system vary, but they include calories and joules. The SI unit is joule but conversions between the two units can be made.

The **joule** (J) is the SI unit for energy and represents energy as **a force times a distance**. Since force is a mass times an acceleration, one joule is equal to one $kg \cdot m^2/s^2$.

A common reference to energy is **calorie**, as in "my Big Mac has 560 Calories." This unit is a nutritional unit and refers to a **kilocalorie (kc or C)**. A **chemical calorie** (cal) is defined as **the amount of energy required to raise 1 gram of water 1°C**. One thousand chemistry calories (kcal) equal one nutritional calorie.

Converting between joule and calorie is easy when using dimensional analysis (see skill 7.1). Note that **1 cal = 4.184 j**.

Example: How many joules are in a Big Mac that contains 560 Calories?

Solution: Since nutritional units are kilocalories,

560 calories = 560 kilocalories = 560,000 chemistry calories.

$$560\ 000\ \text{cal} \times \frac{4.184}{1} \frac{\text{j}}{\text{cal}} = 2{,}343{,}040\ \text{cal or 2,343 kJ}$$

COMPETENCY 8.0 KNOWLEDGE OF APPROPRIATE LABORATORY USE AND PROCEDURES

5%

*"While reading a textbook of chemistry I came upon the statement, nitric acid acts upon copper. I was getting tired of reading such absurd stuff and I was determined to see what this meant. Copper was more or less familiar to me, for copper cents were then in use. I had seen a bottle marked nitric acid on a table in the doctor's office where I was then doing time. I did not know its peculiarities, but the spirit of adventure was upon me. Having nitric acid and copper, I had only to learn what the words **acts upon** meant. The statement nitric acid acts upon copper would be something more than mere words. All was still. In the interest of knowledge I was even willing to sacrifice one of the few copper cents then in my possession. I put one of them on the table, opened the bottle marked nitric acid, poured some of the liquid on the copper and prepared to make an observation.*

But what was this wonderful thing which I beheld? The cent was already changed and it was no small change either. A green-blue liquid foamed and fumed over the cent and over the table. The air in the neighborhood of the performance became colored dark red. A great colored cloud arose. This was disagreeable and suffocating. How should I stop this? I tried to get rid of the objectionable mess by picking it up and throwing it out of the window. I learned another fact. Nitric acid not only acts upon copper, but it acts upon fingers. The pain led to another unpremeditated experiment. I drew my fingers across my trousers and another fact was discovered. Nitric acid acts upon trousers. Taking everything into consideration, this was the most impressive experiment and relatively probably the most costly experiment I have ever performed... It was a revelation to me. It resulted in a desire on my part to learn more about that remarkable kind of action. Plainly, the only way to learn more about it was to see its results, to experiment, to work in a laboratory."

Ira Remsen Story
Department of Chemistry
Johns Hopkins University

Skill 8.1 Identify appropriate chemistry laboratory procedures for the safe storage, use, and disposal of materials and equipment.

Disclaimer: The information presented is intended as a starting point for identification purposes only and should not be regarded as a comprehensive guide for recognizing hazardous substances and reactions. It is the responsibility of the readers of this book to obtain the required information about chemical hazards in their laboratory.

Chemical purchase, use, and disposal

- Inventory all chemicals on hand at least annually. Keep the list up-to-date as chemicals are consumed and replacement chemicals are received.
- If possible, limit the purchase of chemicals to quantities that will be consumed within one year and that are packaged in small containers suitable for direct use in the lab without transfer to other containers.
- Label all chemicals to be stored with date of receipt or preparation and have labels initialed by the person responsible.
- Generally, bottles of chemicals should not remain:
  - Unused on shelves in the lab for more than one week. Move these chemicals to the storeroom or main stockroom.
  - Unused in the storeroom near the lab for more than one month. Move these chemicals to the main stockroom.
  - Check shelf life of chemicals. Properly dispose of any out-dated chemicals.
- Ensure that the disposal procedures for waste chemicals conform to environmental protection requirements.
- Do not purchase or store large quantities of flammable liquids. Fire department officials can recommend the maximum quantities that may be kept on hand.
- Never open a chemical container until you understand the label and the relevant portions of the MSDS.

Chemical storage plan for laboratories

- Chemicals should be stored according to hazard class (ex. flammables, oxidizers, health hazards/toxins, corrosives, etc.).
- Store chemicals away from direct sunlight or localized heat.
- All chemical containers should be properly labeled, dated upon receipt, and dated upon opening.
- Store hazardous chemicals below shoulder height of the shortest person working in the lab.
- Shelves should be painted or covered with chemical-resistant paint or chemical-resistant coating.
- Shelves should be secure and strong enough to hold chemicals being stored on them. Do not overload shelves.
- Personnel should be aware of the hazards associated with all hazardous materials.
- Separate solids from liquids.

Chemicals that require extreme care or should not be in schools

Materials that react with air or water

The risks of using these materials is considered to exceed their educational utility:
- **Picric acid** (must be kept wet, explosive when dry)
- Sodium metal (reacts with water, ignites in dry air)
- Phosphorus (white form reacts with air. Red form becomes white upon heating)

Extremely corrosive materials

These materials should not be in high school laboratories.
- **Hydrofluoric acid** (even dilute solutions cause adverse internal effects).
- **Perchloric acid** (also causes explosive products)
- Bromine

Highly toxic materials

These materials should not be in high school laboratories.
- **Carbon disulfide** (also explosive)
- Cyanide compounds
- Benzene and toluene
- Mercury and mercury compounds
- Cadmium, chromium, and arsenic compounds
- Carbon tetrachloride and chloroform

Recognize acid/base reactions and redox reactions

Many hazardous reactions are simply **acid/base reactions or redox reactions with concentrated, powerful reagents.** For acid/base reactions, see **0019.** Also see **0016** for inorganic and organic acid nomenclature. For redox reactions, see **0020.**

Recognize the impact of reagent concentration on hazard level
Recognize that a more dilute acid, base, oxidizer, or reducer presents a lower hazard level and requires a lower level of protection in the laboratory.

Organic peroxides and peroxide-forming materials

Organic peroxides have the general structure: R–O–O–R', where R and/or R' are organic substituents. These compounds are **very unstable** and may self-react in a **violent explosion** when triggered by heat, impact, friction, light, or vibration. **Benzoyl peroxide** and other organic peroxides should not be present in high school chemistry labs.

Peroxide-forming compounds are chemicals with the potential to form organic peroxides when they react with oxygen in the air (as the chemical is concentrated) and/or become vaporized either by **erroneous boiling** or over time by **evaporation from a poorly sealed container**.

A peroxide-forming compound should be treated as a **potential explosive** and the local fire chief should be called if it:
- Is discolored
- Contains layering
- Contains crystals

Peroxide crystals may **form within the threads of the cap**, and the act of removing the cap may cause a fatal detonation. A bomb squad may be required.

Many high-risk peroxide-formers were used in high school chemistry in the past. In general, the risks of using the following materials is now thought to exceed their educational utility:
- Nearly all **ethers** including diisopropyl ether (the highest risk peroxide-forming compound), **ethyl ether**, and methyl ether.
- **Potassium metal** (also reacts with water)
- Tetrohydrofuran (THF)
- Cyclohexene and cyclohexanol
- Dioxanes

Several lower-risk peroxide-forming compounds are still commonly used in high schools. These materials **should never be concentrated by boiling (i.e. distilled)**:
- Isopropanol, 2-butanol, other secondary alcohols
- Ethylene glycol
- Acetaldehyde

A list of substances judged to have an excessive risk compared to their educational utility is found here:
http://www.govlink.org/hazwaste/publications/highrisktable.pdf

Below are examples of chemical groups that can be used to categorize storage. Use these groups as examples when separating chemicals for compatibility. Please note: reactive chemicals must be more closely analyzed since they have a greater potential for violent reactions. Contact Laboratory Safety if you have any questions concerning chemical storage.

Acids

- Make sure that all acids are stored by compatibility (ex. separate inorganics from organics).
- Store concentrated acids on lower shelves in chemical-resistant trays or in a corrosives cabinet. This will temporarily contain spills or leaks and protect shelving from residue.
- Separate acids from incompatible materials such as bases, active metals (ex. sodium, magnesium, potassium) and from chemicals which can generate toxic gases when combined (ex. sodium cyanide and iron sulfide).

Bases

- Store bases away from acids.
- Store concentrated bases on lower shelves in chemical-resistant trays or in a corrosives cabinet. This will temporarily contain spills or leaks and protect shelving from residue.

Flammables

- Approved flammable storage cabinets should be used for flammable liquid storage.
- You may store 20 gallons of flammable liquids per 100 sq. ft. in a properly fire separated lab. The maximum allowable quantity for flammable liquid storage in any size lab is not to exceed 120 gallons.
- You may store up to 10 gallons of flammable liquids outside of approved flammable storage cabinets.
- An additional 25 gallons may be stored outside of an approved storage cabinet if it is stored in approved safety cans not to exceed 2 gallons in size.
- Use only explosion-proof or intrinsically safe refrigerators and freezers for storing flammable liquids.

Peroxide-forming chemicals

- Peroxide-forming chemicals should be stored in airtight containers in a dark, cool, and dry place.
- Unstable chemicals such as peroxide-formers must always be labeled with date received, date opened, and disposal/expiration date.
- Peroxide-forming chemicals should be properly disposed of before the date of expected peroxide formation (typically 6-12 months after opening).
- Suspicion of peroxide contamination should be immediately investigated. Contact Laboratory Safety for procedures.

Water-reactive chemicals

- Water-reactive chemicals should be stored in a cool, dry place.
- Do not store water-reactive chemicals under sinks or near water baths.
- Class D fire extinguishers for the specific water-reactive chemical being stored should be made available.

Oxidizers

- Make sure that all oxidizers are stored by compatibility.
- Store oxidizers away from flammables, combustibles, and reducing agents.

Toxins

- Toxic compounds should be stored according to the nature of the chemical, with appropriate security employed when necessary.
- A "Poison Control Network" telephone number should be posted in the laboratory where toxins are stored. Color coded labeling systems that may be found in your lab are shown below.

Hazard	Color Code
Flammables	Red
Health Hazards/Toxins	Blue
Reactives/Oxidizers	Yellow
Contact Hazards	White
General Storage	Gray, Green, Orange

Please Note: Chemicals with labels that are colored and striped may react with other chemicals in the same hazard class. See MSDS for more information. Chemical containers which are not color-coded should have hazard information on the label. Read the label carefully and store accordingly.

The Florida Department of Education provides chemical storage and hazardous waste disposal guidelines on its website:
http://www.firn.edu/doe/curriculum/sc3/sc3dgc.html

Disposal of chemical waste

Schools are regulated by the Environmental Protection Agency, as well as state and local agencies, when it comes to disposing of chemical waste. Check with your state science supervisor, local college or university environmental health and safety specialists, and the Laboratory Safety Workshop for advice on the disposal of chemical waste. The American Chemical Society publishes an excellent guidebook, *Laboratory Waste Management, A Guidebook* (1994).

The following are basic guidelines for disposing of chemical waste.
You may dispose of hazardous waste as outlined below. It is the responsibility of the generator to ensure hazardous waste does not end up in ground water, soil or the atmosphere through improper disposal.

1. **Sanitary Sewer** - Some chemicals (acids or bases) may be neutralized and disposed to the sanitary sewer. This disposal option must be approved by the local waste water treatment authority prior to disposal. This may not be an option for some small communities that do not have sufficient treatment capacity at the waste water treatment plant for these types of wastes. Hazardous waste may NOT be disposed of in this manner. This includes heavy metals.

2. **Household Hazardous Waste Facility** - Waste chemicals may be disposed through a county household hazardous waste facility (HHW) or through a county contracted household hazardous waste disposal company. Not all counties have a program to accept waste from schools. Verify with your county HHW facility that they can handle your waste prior to making arrangements.

3. **Disposal through a Contractor** - A contractor may be used for the disposal of the waste chemicals. Remember that you must keep documentation of your hazardous waste disposal for at least three years. This information must include a waste manifest, reclamation agreement or any written record which describes the waste and how much was disposed, where it was disposed and when it was disposed. Waste analysis records must also be kept when it is necessary to making a determination of whether waste is hazardous is necessary. **Any unknown chemicals should be considered hazardous!** The Bureau of Solid & Hazardous Waste can be reached at 850-245-8707.

Skill 8.2   Choose the correct laboratory equipment for a particular procedure.

The descriptions and diagrams in this skill are included to help you **identify** the techniques. They are **not meant as a guide to perform the techniques** in the lab.

Handling liquids

A **beaker** (below left) is a cylindrical cup with a notch at the top. Beakers are often used for making solutions. An **Erlenmeyer** flask (below center) is a conical flask. A liquid in an Erlenmeyer flask will evaporate more slowly than when it is in a beaker and it is easier to swirl about. A **round-bottom flask** (below-right) is also called a Florence flask. It is designed for uniform heating, but it requires a stand to keep it upright.

A **test tube** has a rounded bottom and is designed to hold and to heat small volumes of liquid. A **Pasteur pipet** is a small glass tube with a long thin capillary tip and a latex suction bulb, and it is used for transferring small amounts of liquid from one container to another.

A **crucible** is a cup-shaped container made of porcelain or metal for holding chemical compounds when heating them to very high temperatures. A **watch glass** is a concave circular piece of glass that is usually used as surface for evaporating a liquid and observing precipitates or crystallization. A **Dewar flask** is a double walled vacuum flask with a metallic coating to provide good thermal insulation and short term storage of liquid nitrogen.

Fitting and cleaning glassware

If a thermometer, glass tube, or funnel must be threaded through a stopper or a piece of tubing and it won't fit, either make the hole larger or use a smaller piece of glass. Use soapy water or glycerol to lubricate the glass before inserting it. Hold the glass piece as close as possible to the stopper during insertion. It's also good practice to wrap a towel around the glass and the stopper during this procedure. **Never apply undue pressure**.

Glassware sometimes contains **tapered ground-glass joints** to allow direct glass-to-glass connections. A thin layer of joint **grease** must be applied when assembling an apparatus with ground-glass joints. Too much grease will contaminate the experiment, and too little will cause the components to become tightly locked together. Disassemble the glassware with a **twisting** motion immediately after the experiment is over.

Cleaning glassware becomes more difficult with time, so it should be cleaned soon after the experiment is completed. Wipe off any lubricant with paper towel moistened in a solvent like hexane before washing the glassware. Use a brush with lab soap and water. Acetone may be used to dissolve most organic residues. Spent solvents should be transferred to a waste container for proper disposal.

Heating

A **hot plate** (shown below) is used to heat Erlenmeyer flasks, beakers and other containers with a flat bottom. Hot plates often have a built-in **magnetic stirrer**. A **heating mantle** has a hemispherical cavity that is used to heat round-bottom flasks. A **Bunsen burner** is designed to burn natural gas. Bunsen burners are useful for heating high-boiling point liquids, water, or solutions of non-flammable materials. They are also used for bending glass tubing. Smooth boiling is achieved by adding **boiling stones** to a liquid.

Boiling and melting point determination

The **boiling point** is determined by heating a liquid along with a boiling stone in a clamped test tube with a clamped thermometer positioned just above the liquid surface and away from the tube walls. The thermometer measures the temperature of the vapor above the liquid, which is at the same temperature as the liquid while boiling. The constant highest constant-value temperature reading after boiling is achieved is the boiling point.

The **melting point** is determined by placing a pulverized solid in a capillary tube and using a rubber band to fasten the capillary to a thermometer so that the sample is at the level of the thermometer bulb. The thermometer and sample are inserted into a **Thiele tube** filled with mineral or silicon oil. The Thiele tube has a sidearm that is heated with a Bunsen burner to create a flow of hot oil. This flow maintains an even temperature during heating. The melting point is read when the sample turns into a liquid. Many electric melting point devices are also available that heat the sample more slowly to give more accurate results. These are also safer to use than a Thiele tube with a Bunsen burner.

Centrifugation

A **centrifuge** separates two immiscible phases by spinning the mixture (placed in a **centrifuge tube**) at high speeds. A **microfuge** or microcentrifuge is a small centrifuge. The weight of material placed in a centrifuge must be **balanced**, so if one sample is placed in a centrifuge, a tube with roughly an equal mass of water should be placed opposite the sample.

Filtration

The goal of **gravity filtration** is to remove solids from a liquid and obtain a liquid without solid particulates. Filter paper is folded, placed in a funnel on top of a flask, and wetted with the solvent to seal it to the funnel. Next the mixture is poured through, and the solid-free liquid is collected from the flask.

The goal of **vacuum filtration** is usually to remove liquids from a solid to obtain a solid that is dry. An **aspirator** or a **vacuum pump** is used to provide suction though a rubber tube to a **filter trap**. The trap is attached to a **filter flask** (shown to the right) by a second rubber tube. The filter flask is an Erlenmeyer flask with a thick wall and a hose barb for the vacuum tube. Filter flasks are used to filter material using a **Büchner funnel** (shown to the right) or a smaller **Hirsch funnel**. These porcelain or plastic funnels hold a circular piece of filter paper. A single-hole rubber stopper supports the funnel in the flask while maintaining suction.

Mixing

Heterogeneous reaction mixtures in flasks are often mixed by **swirling**. To use a magnetic stirrer, a bar magnet coated with Teflon called a flea or a **stir bar** is placed into the container, and the container is placed on the stirrer. The container should be moved and the stir speed adjusted for smooth mixing. Mechanical stirring paddles, agitators, vortexers, or rockers are also used for mixing.

Decanting

When a coarse solid has settled at the bottom of a flask of liquid, **decanting** the solution simply means pouring out the liquid and leaving the solid behind.

Extraction

Compounds in solution are often separated based on their **solubility differences**. During **liquid-liquid extraction** (also called **solvent extraction**), a second solvent immiscible to the first is added to the solution in a **separatory funnel** (shown at right). Usually one solvent is nonpolar and the other is a polar solvent like water. The two solvents are immiscible and separate from each other after the mixture is shaken to allow solute exchange. One layer contains the compound of interest, and the other contains impurities to be discarded. The solutions in the two layers are separated from each other by draining liquid through the stopcock.

Titration

Titration is described in **Skill 4.15**

Distillation

Liquids in solution are often separated based on their **boiling point differences**. During simple **distillation**, the solution is placed in a round-bottom flask called the **distillation flask** or **still pot**, and boiling stones are added. The apparatus shown below is assembled (note that clamps and stands are not shown), and the still pot is heated using a heating mantle.

While boiling, hot vapor escapes through the **distillation head**, enters the **condenser**, and is cooled and condensed back to a liquid. The vapor loses its heat to water flowing through the outside of the condenser. The condensate or **distillate** falls into the **receiving flask**. The apparatus is open to the atmosphere through a vent above the receiving flask. The distillate contains a higher concentration of the liquid with the lower boiling point. The less volatile liquid reaches a high concentration in the still pot. Head temperature is monitored during the process.

Distillation may also be used to remove a solid from a pure liquid by boiling and condensing the liquid into the receiving flask.

Skill 8.3 **Identify emergency procedures and safety equipment needed in the science laboratory and classroom.**

Disclaimer: The information presented below is intended as a starting point for identification purposes only and should not be regarded as a comprehensive guide for safety procedures in the laboratory. It is the responsibility of the readers of this book to consult with professional advisers about safety procedures in their laboratory.

1013 f.s. **Educational Facilities** is implemented by the Florida Board of Education Administrative Rule 6A-2.0010 (http://www.firn.edu/doe/rules/6a-2.htm).

This rule establishes requirements found in the Florida Building Code: http://www2.iccsafe.org/florida_building_code/changed/ch-4/Sec%20423.pdf

The following list is a summary of the requirements for chemical laboratories contained in the above documents:

1) A dousing shower and eye-wash with a floor drain are required where students handle potentially dangerous materials.

2) Accessible fully-charged fire extinguishers of the appropriate type and fire blankets must be present if a fire hazard exists.

3) There must be a master control valve or switch accessible to and within 15 feet of the instructor's station for emergency cut-off of all gas cocks, compressed air valves, water, or electrical services accessible to students. Valves must completely shut off with a one-quarter turn. This master control is in addition to the regular main gas supply cut-off, and the main supply cut-off must be shut down upon activation of the fire alarm system.

4) A high capacity emergency exhaust system with a source of positive ventilation must be installed, and signs providing instructions must be permanently installed at the emergency exhaust system fan switch.

5) Fume hoods must contain supply fans that automatically shut down when the emergency exhaust fan is turned on.

6) Rooms and/or cabinets for chemical storage must have limited student access and ventilation to the exterior of the building separate from the air-conditioning system. The rooms should be kept at moderate temperature, be well-illuminated, and contain doors lockable from the outside and operable at all times from the inside. Cabinet shelves must have a half-inch lip on the front and be constructed of non-corrosive material.

7) Appropriate caution signs must be placed at hazardous work and storage areas.

Therefore, all chemistry laboratories should be equipped with the following safety equipment. Both teachers and students should be familiar with the operation of this equipment.

Fire extinguisher

Fire extinguishers are rated for the type of fires they will extinguish. Chemical laboratories should have a combination ABC extinguisher along with a type D fire extinguisher. If a type D extinguisher is not available, a bucket of dry sand will do. Make sure you are trained to use the type of extinguisher available in your setting.

- **Class A** fires are ordinary materials like burning paper, lumber, cardboard, plastics etc.

- **Class B** fires involve flammable or combustible liquids such as gasoline, kerosene, and common organic solvents used in the laboratory.

- **Class C** fires involve energized electrical equipment, such as appliances, switches, panel boxes, power tools, hot plates and stirrers. Water is usually a dangerous extinguishing medium for class C fires because of the risk of electrical shock unless a specialized water mist extinguisher is used.

- **Class D** fires involve combustible metals, such as magnesium, titanium, potassium and sodium as well as pyrophoric organometallic reagents such as alkyllithiums, Grignards and diethylzinc. These materials burn at high temperatures and will react violently with water, air, and/or other chemicals. Handle with care!!

- **Class K** fires are kitchen fires. This class was added to the NFPA portable extinguishers Standard 10 in 1998. Kitchen extinguishers installed before June 30, 1998 are "grandfathered" into the standard.

Some fires may be a combination of these! Your fire extinguishers should have ABC ratings on them. These ratings are determined under ANSI/UL Standard 711 and look something like "3-A:40-B:C." Higher numbers mean more firefighting power. In this example, the extinguisher has a good firefighting capacity for Class A, B and C fires. NFPA has a brief description of UL 711 if you want to know more.

Fire blanket

A fire blanket can be used to smother a fire. However, use caution when using a fire blanket on a clothing fire. Some fabrics are polymers that melt onto the skin. Stop, Drop and Roll is the best method for extinguishing clothing on fire.

Safety shower

Use a safety shower in the event of a chemical spill or fire. Pull the overhead handle and remove clothing that may be contaminated with chemicals, to allow the skin to be rinsed.

Eye protection

Everyone present must wear eye protection whenever anyone in the laboratory is performing any of the following activities:

1) Handling hazardous chemicals
2) Handling laboratory glassware
3) Using an open flame.

Safety glasses do not offer protection from splashing liquids. Safety glasses appear similar to ordinary glasses and may be used in an environment that only requires protection from **flying fragments**. Safety glasses with side-shields offer additional protection from **flying fragments approaching from the side**.

Safety goggles offer protection from both flying fragments and splashing liquids. **Only safety goggles** are suitable for eye protection where **hazardous chemicals** are used and handled. Safety goggles with no ventilation (type G) or with indirect ventilation (type H) are both acceptable. Goggles should be marked "Z87" to show they meet federal standards.

Eyewash

In the event of an eye injury or chemical splash, use the eyewash immediately. Help the injured person by holding their eyelids open while rinsing. Rinse copiously and have the eyes checked by a physician afterwards.

Skin protection

Wear **gloves** made of a material known to resist penetration by the chemical being handled. Check gloves for holes and the absence of interior contamination. Wash hands and arms and clean under fingernails after working in a laboratory.

Wear a lab coat or apron. Wear footwear that completely covers the feet.

Ventilation - Using a Fume Hood

A fume hood carries away vapors from reagents or reactions you may be working with. Using a fume hood correctly will reduce your personal exposure to potentially harmful fumes or vapors. When using a fume hood, keep the following in mind.

• Place equipment or reactions as far back in the hood as is practical. This will improve the efficiency of fume collection and removal.

• Turn on the light inside the hood using the switch on the outside panel, near the electrical outlets.

• The glass sash of the hood is a safety shield. The sash will fall automatically to the appropriate height for efficient operation and should not be raised above this level, except to move equipment in and out of the hood. Keep the sash between your body and the inside of the hood. If the height of the automatic stop is too high to protect your face and body, lower the sash below this point. Do not stick your head inside a hood or climb inside a hood.

• Wipe up all spills immediately. Clean the glass of your hood, if a splash occurs.

• When you are finished using a hood, lower the sash to the level marked by the sticker on the side.

Work habits

- Never work alone in a laboratory or storage area.
- Never eat, drink, smoke, apply cosmetics, chew gum or tobacco, or store food or beverages in a laboratory environment or storage area.
- Keep containers closed when they are not in use.
- Never pipet by mouth.
- Restrain loose clothing and long hair and remove dangling jewelry.
- Tape all Dewar flasks with fabric-based tape.
- Check all glassware before use. Discard if chips or star cracks are present.
- Never leave heat sources unattended.
- Do not store chemicals and/or apparatus on the lab bench or on the floor or aisles of the lab or storage room.
- Keep lab shelves organized.
- Never place a chemical, not even water, near the edges of a lab bench.
- Use a fume hood that is known to be in operating condition when working with toxic, flammable, and/or volatile substances.
- Never put your head inside a fume hood.
- Never store anything in a fume hood.
- Obtain, read, and be sure you understand the MSDS (see below) for each chemical that is to be used before allowing students to begin an experiment.
- Analyze new lab procedures and student-designed lab procedures in advance to identify any hazardous aspects. Minimize and/or eliminate these components before proceeding. Ask yourself these questions:
  - What are the hazards?
  - What are the worst possible things that could go wrong?
  - How will I deal with them?
  - What are the prudent practices, protective facilities and equipment necessary to minimize the risk of exposure to the hazards?
- Analyze close calls and accidents to eliminate their causes and prevent them from occurring again.
- Identify which chemicals may be disposed of in the drain by consulting the MSDS or the supplier. Clear one chemical down the drain by flushing with water before introducing the next chemical.
- Preplan for emergencies.
  - Keep the fire department informed of your chemical inventory and its location.
  - Consult with a local physician about toxins used in the lab and ensure that your area is prepared in advance to treat victims of toxic exposure.
  - Identify devices that should be shut off if possible in an emergency.
  - Inform your students of the designated escape route and alternate route.

Substitutions

- When feasible, substitute less hazardous chemicals for chemicals with greater hazards in experiments.
- Dilute substances when possible instead of using concentrated solutions.
- Use lesser quantities instead of greater quantities in experiments when possible.
- Use films, videotapes, computer displays, and other methods rather than experiments involving hazardous substances.

Label information

Chemical labels contain safety information in four parts:
1) There will be a signal word. From most to least potentially dangerous, this word will be "Danger!" "Warning!" or "Caution."
2) Statements of hazard (e.g., "Flammable," "May Cause Irritation") follow the signal word. Target organs may be specified.
3) Precautionary measures are listed such as "Keep away from ignition sources" or "Use only with adequate ventilation."
4) First aid information is usually included, such as whether to induce vomiting and how to induce vomiting if the chemical is ingested.

Chemical hazard pictorial

Several different pictorials are used on labels to indicate the level of a chemical hazard. The most common is the **"fire diamond" NFPA (National Fire Prevention Association) pictorial** shown at left. A zero indicates a minimal hazard and a four indicates a severe risk. Special information includes if the chemical reacts with water, **OX** for an oxidizer, **COR ACID** for a corrosive acid, and **COR ALK** for a corrosive base. The "Health" hazard level is for **acute toxicity only**.

Pictorials are designed for **quick reference in emergency situations**, but they are also useful as minimal summaries of safety information for a chemical. They are not required on chemicals you purchase, so it's a good idea to add a label pictorial to every chemical you receive if one is not already present. **The entrance to areas where chemicals are stored should carry a fire diamond label** to represent the materials present.

Procedures for flammable materials: minimize fire risk

The vapors of a flammable liquid **or solid** may travel across the room to an ignition source and cause a fire or explosion.

- Store flammables in an approved safety cabinet for flammable liquids. Store in safety cans if possible.
- Minimize volumes and concentrations used in an experiment with flammables.
- Minimize the time containers are open.
- Minimize ignition sources in the laboratory.
- Ensure that there is good air movement in the laboratory before the experiment.
- Check the fire extinguishers and be certain that you know how to use them.
- Tell the students that the "Stop, Drop, and Roll" technique is best for a clothing fire outside the lab, but in the lab they should walk calmly to the safety shower and use it. Practice this procedure with students in drills.
- A fire blanket should not be used for clothing fires because clothes often contain polymers that melt onto the skin. Pressing these fabrics into the skin with a blanket increases burn damage.
- If a demonstration of an exploding gas or vapor is performed, it should be done behind a safety shield using glass vessels taped with fabric tape.

Procedures for corrosive materials: minimize risk of contact

Corrosive materials **destroy or permanently change living tissue** through chemical action. **Irritants** cause inflammation due to an immune response but not through chemical action. The effect is usually reversible but can be severe and long lasting. **Sensitizers** are irritants that cause no symptoms after the first exposure but may cause irritation during a later exposure to the same or a different chemical.

- Always store corrosives below eye level.
- Only diluted corrosives should be used in pre-high school laboratories and their use at full-strength in high school should be limited.
- Dilute corrosive materials by slowly and carefully **adding them to water**. Adding water to a concentrated acid or base can cause rapid boiling and splashing.
- Wear goggles and face shield when handling hazardous corrosives. The face, ears, and neck should be protected.
- Wear gloves known to be impervious to the chemical. Wear sleeve gauntlets and a lab apron made of impervious material if splashing is likely.
- Always wash your hands after handling corrosives.

- Splashes on skin should be flushed with flowing water for 15 minutes while a doctor is called.
- If a corrosive material is splashed on their clothing:
    - First use the safety shower with clothing on.
    - Remove all clothing while under the safety shower including shoes and socks. This is no time for modesty.
    - Stay under the shower for 15 minutes while a doctor is called.
- Splashes in eyes should be dealt with as follows:
    - Go to the eyewash fountain within 30 seconds.
    - Have someone else hold their eyelids open with thumb and forefinger and use the eyewash.
    - Continuously move the eyeballs during 15 minutes of rinsing to cleanse the optic nerve at the back of the eye. A doctor should be called.

Procedures for toxic materials: minimize exposure

Toxic effects are either **chronic** or **acute**. Chronic effects are seen after repeated exposures or after one long exposure. Acute effects occur within a few hours at most.

- Use the smallest amount needed at the lowest concentration for the shortest period of time possible. Weigh the risks against the educational benefits.
- Be aware of the five different routes of exposure
    1) Inhalation – the ability to smell a toxin is not a proper indication of unsafe exposure. Work in the fume hood when using toxins. Minimize dusts and mists by cleaning often, cleaning spills rapidly, and maintaining good ventilation in the lab.
    2) Absorption through intact skin – always wear impervious gloves if the MSDS indicates this route of exposure.
    3) Ingestion
    4) Absorption through other body orifices such as ear canal and eye socket.
    5) Injection by a cut from broken contaminated glassware or other sharp equipment.
- Be aware of the first symptoms of overexposure described by the MSDS. Often these are headache, nausea, and dizziness. Get to fresh air and do not return until the symptoms have passed. If the symptom returns when you come back into the lab, contact a physician and have the space tested.
- Be aware of whether vomiting should be induced in case of ingestion
- Be aware of the recommended procedure in case of unconsciousness.

Procedures for reactive materials to minimize incompatibility

Many chemicals are **self-reactive**. For example, they explode when dried out or when disturbed under certain conditions or they react with components of air. These materials generally **should not be allowed into the high school**. Other precautions must be taken to minimize reactions between **incompatible pairs**.

- Store fuels and oxidizers separately.
- Store reducing agents and oxidizing agents separately.
- Store acids and bases separately.
- Store chemicals that react with fire-fighting materials (i.e., water or carbon dioxide) under conditions that minimize the possibility of a reaction if a fire is being fought in the storage area.
- MSDSs list other incompatible pairs.
- Never store chemicals in alphabetical order by name.
- When incompatible pairs must be supplied to students, do so under direct supervision with very dilute solutions and/or small quantities.

Material Safety Data Sheet (MSDS) information

Many chemicals have a mixture of toxic, corrosive, flammable, and reactive risks. The **Material Safety Data Sheet** or **MSDS** for a chemical contains detailed safety information beyond that presented on the label. This includes acute and chronic health effects, first aid and firefighting measures, what to do in case of a spill, and ecological and disposal considerations.

The MSDS will state whether the chemical is a known or suspected carcinogen, mutagen, or teratogen. A **carcinogen** is a compound that causes cancer (malignant tumors). A **mutagen** alters DNA with the potential effects of causing cancer or birth defects children not yet conceived. A **teratogen** produces birth defects and acts during fetal development

There are many parts of an MSDS that are not written for the layperson. Their level of detail and technical content may be difficult for many people outside the fields of toxicology and industrial safety to understand. In a high school chemistry lab, the value of an MSDS is in the words and not in the numerical data it contains, but some knowledge of the numbers is useful for comparing the dangers of one chemical to another. Numerical results of animal toxicity studies are often presented in the form of **LD_{50} values**. These represent the **dose required to kill 50% of animals** tested.

Exposure limits via inhalation may be presented in three ways:

1) PEL (Permissible Exposure Limit) or TLV-TWA (Threshold Limit Value-Time Weighted Average). This is the maximum permitted concentration of the airborne chemical in volume parts per million (ppm) for a **worker exposed 8 hours daily**.
2) TLV-STEL (Threshold Limit Value-Short Term Exposure Limit). This is the maximum concentration permitted for a 15-minute exposure period.
3) TLV-C (Threshold Limit Value-Ceiling). This is the concentration that should never be exceeded at any moment.

http://hazard.com/msds/index.php contains a large database of MSDSs. http://www.ilpi.com/msds/ref/demystify.html contains a useful "MSDS demystifier." Cut and paste an MSDS into the web page, and hypertext links will appear to a glossary of terms.

Facilities and equipment

- Use separate labeled containers for general trash, broken glass, and for each type of hazardous chemical waste—ignitable, corrosive, reactive, and toxic.
- Keep the floor area around safety showers, eyewash fountains, and fire extinguishers clear of all obstructions.
- Never block escape routes.
- Never prop open a fire door.
- Provide safety guards for all moving belts and pulleys.
- Instruct everyone in the lab on the proper use of the safety shower and eyewash fountain (see corrosive materials above). Most portable eyewash devices cannot maintain the required flow for 15 minutes. A permanent eyewash fountain is preferred.
- If contamination is suspected in the breathing air, arrange for sampling to take place.
- Regularly inspect fire blankets, if present, for rips and holes. Maintain a record of inspection.
- Regularly check safety showers and eyewash fountains for proper rate of flow. Maintain a record of inspection.
- Keep up-to-date emergency phone numbers posted next to the telephone.
- Place fire extinguishers near an escape route.
- Regularly maintain fire extinguishers and maintain a record of inspection. Arrange with the local fire department for training of teachers and administrators in the proper use of extinguishers.
- Regularly check fume hoods for proper airflow. Ensure that fume hood exhaust is not drawn back into the intake for general building ventilation.
- Secure compressed gas cylinders at all times and transport them only while secured on a hand truck.

- Restrict the use and handling of compressed gas to those who have received formal training.
- Install chemical storage shelves with lips. Never use stacked boxes for storage instead of shelves.
- Only use an explosion-proof refrigerator for chemical storage.
- Have appropriate equipment and materials available in advance for spill control and cleanup. Consult the MSDS for each chemical to determine what is required. Replace these materials when they become outdated.
- Provide an appropriate supply of first aid equipment and instruction on its proper use.

Additional comments: teach safety to students

- Weigh the risks and benefits inherent in lab work, inform students of the hazards and precautions involved in their assignment, and involve students in discussions about safety before every assignment.
- If an incident happens, it can be used to improve lab safety via student participation. Ask the student involved. The student's own words about what occurred should be included in the report.
- Safety information supplied by the manufacturer on a chemical container should be seen by students who actually use the chemical. If you distribute chemicals in smaller containers to be used by students, copy the hazard and precautionary information from the original label onto the labels for the students' containers. Students interested in graphic design may be able to help you perform this task. Labels for many common chemicals may be found here: http://beta.ehs.cornell.edu/labels/cgi-bin/label_selection.pl
- Organize a student safety committee whose task is to conduct one safety inspection and present a report. A different committee may be organized each month or every other month.

Additional comments: General

- Any chemical can be hazardous. The way it is used determines the probability of harm.
- Every person is individually and personally responsible for the safe use of chemicals.
- If an accident might happen, it will eventually happen. Proper precautions will ensure the consequences are minimized when it does occur.
- Accidents are often predicted by one or more close calls in which nobody is injured and no property is damaged but something out of the ordinary occurs. Examples might be a student briefly touching a hot surface and saying "Ouch!" with no injury, two students engaged in horseplay, or a student briefly removing safety goggles to read a meniscus level. **Eliminate the cause of a close call to prevent a future accident.**

Also see:
http://www.labsafety.org/40steps.htm,
http://www.flinnsci.com/Sections/Safety/safety.asp,
and the American Chemical Society safety publications listed under References.

Skill 8.4   Identify the areas of teacher liability and responsibility in science-related activities.

Today's chemistry's teachers must not only act responsibly, they must also be prepared to prove to others how they acted responsibly. Here are a few ideas you can use in your classroom to document that you are a responsible chemistry teacher.

Safety contracts

Safety contracts are a good way for you to establish the importance of good safety work habits. A student safety contract is a detailed listing of all of the rules of the chemistry laboratory. Review the safety contract with your students, and have them sign and date it. Additionally, students should then take the contract home so their parents or guardians can review and sign the contract as well. This will establish a good understanding of how important following all the course safety rules are. Most science departments have general safety contracts that you can use or modify.

Lesson plans

In your daily lesson plans, you can document that you discussed with your students the safety rules that apply to the experiment that they will be doing on that day. Your lesson plans are a journal which documents all of the activities you have done in class for the entire school year. Safety rules must be reinforced every time a laboratory experiment is done with you students.

Safety posters

Commercial safety posters can be purchased which reinforce the most important safety rules, such as, wearing goggles and aprons, no horseplay, and notifying your instructor whenever there has been an accident. These posters can be placed in strategic locations around the chemistry laboratory.

Goggle policy

There is only one policy on goggles that needs to be enforced. "Any time chemicals, glassware, or heat is used, you must wear your laboratory goggles. No exceptions!" If you don't wear your goggles then you must leave the lab.

Chemical terms

Many chemistry experiments include in safety instructions terms like corrosive, flammable, oxidizer, reducer, etc. Make sure that your students understand the meaning of these terms.

Document safety violations

It is a good idea to write in your lesson plans the name of the student and the safety violation that occurred on that day. Have the student sign your plan book acknowledging their violation.

A prudent attitude toward dealing with hazards in the laboratory is characterized by a determination to make every effort to be informed about risks and reduce them to a minimum, while recognizing that the notion of "zero risk" in laboratory operations (or any other workplace) is an impossible ideal.

If you can reasonably foresee the consequences of what you are about to do, or not do, you will be deemed responsible. Begin to implement some of the ideas suggested. These will all go a long way in helping to prove you are a responsible chemistry teacher.

Skill 8.5   Demonstrate knowledge of pertinent legislation and national guidelines regarding laboratory safety, hazardous materials, experimentation, and accommodations for special needs students (e.g., American Chemical Society, National Science Teachers Association).

It is the responsibility of the teacher to stay up to date on information affecting the classroom, whether new guidelines are prescribed by a professional organization such as the National Science Teachers Association or new laws are enacted on the national or state level. Information regarding legislation and national guidelines is available from a number of sources. Consult the following for current information:

Florida Department of Education: http://www.fldoestem.org/center13.aspx

The American Chemical Society: http://portal.acs.org/portal/acs/corg/content

The National Science Teachers Association: http://www.nsta.org/

A good printed source of current regulations is found in *Prudent Practices in the Laboratory: Handling and Disposal of Chemicals* (1995) published by the National Academies Press. An overview is available at: http://www.nap.edu/html/prudent/overview.html The book may be purchased through Amazon at: http://www.amazon.com/Prudent-Practices-Laboratory-Handling-Chemicals/dp/030905229

Sample Test

Directions: Read each item and select the best response.

1. A piston compresses a gas at constant temperature. Which gas properties increase?

   I. Average speed of molecules
   II. Pressure
   III. Molecular collisions with container walls per second

   A. I and II
   B. I and III
   C. II and III
   D. I, II, and III

2. The temperature of a liquid is raised at atmospheric pressure. Which liquid property increases?

   A. critical pressure
   B. vapor pressure
   C. surface tension
   D. viscosity

3. Potassium crystallizes with two atoms contained in each unit cell. What is the mass of potassium found in a lattice 1.00×10^6 unit cells wide, 2.00×10^6 unit cells high, and 5.00×10^5 unit cells deep?

   A. 85.0 ng
   B. 32.5 μg
   C. 64.9 μg
   D. 130. μg

4. A gas is heated in a sealed container. Which of the following occur?

   A. gas pressure rises
   B. gas density decreases
   C. the average distance between molecules increases
   D. all of the above

5. How many molecules are in 2.20 pg of a protein with a molecular weight of 150. kDa?

   A. 8.83×10^9
   B. 1.82×10^9
   C. 8.83×10^6
   D. 1.82×10^6

6. At STP, 20. μL of O_2 contain 5.4×10^{16} molecules. According to Avogadro's hypothesis, how many molecules are in 20. μL of Ne?

   A. 5.4×10^{15}
   B. 1.0×10^{16}
   C. 2.7×10^{16}
   D. 5.4×10^{16}

7. An ideal gas at 50.0 °C and 3.00 atm is in a 300. cm³ cylinder. The cylinder volume changes by moving a piston until the gas is at 50.0 °C and 1.00 atm. What is the final volume?

   A. 100. cm³
   B. 450. cm³
   C. 900. cm³
   D. 1.20 dm³

8. Which gas law may be used to solve the previous question?

   A. Charles's law
   B. Boyle's law
   C. Graham's law
   D. Avogadro's law

9. A blimp is filled with 5000. m³ of helium at 28.0 °C and 99.7 kPa. What is the mass of helium used?

   $$R = 8.3144 \frac{J}{mol-K}$$

   A. 797 kg
   B. 810. kg
   C. 879 kg
   D. 8.57×10^3 kg

10. Which of the following are able to flow from one place to another?

    I. Gases
    II. Liquids
    III. Solids
    IV. Supercritical fluids

    A. I and II
    B. II only
    C. I, II, and IV
    D. I, II, III, and IV

11. One mole of an ideal gas at STP occupies 22.4 L. At what temperature will one mole of an ideal gas at one atm occupy 31.0 L?

    A. 34.6 °C
    B. 105 °C
    C. 378 °C
    D. 442 °C

12. Why does $CaCl_2$ have a higher normal melting point than NH_3?

    A. Covalent bonds are stronger than London dispersion forces.
    B. Covalent bonds are stronger than hydrogen bonds.
    C. Ionic bonds are stronger than London dispersion forces.
    D. Ionic bonds are stronger than hydrogen bonds.

13. Which intermolecular attraction explains the following trend in straight-chain alkanes?

Condensed structural formula	Boiling point (°C)
CH_4	-161.5
CH_3CH_3	-88.6
$CH_3CH_2CH_3$	-42.1
$CH_3CH_2CH_2CH_3$	-0.5
$CH_3CH_2CH_2CH_2CH_3$	36.0
$CH_3CH_2CH_2CH_2CH_2CH_3$	68.7

A. London dispersion forces
B. Dipole-dipole interactions
C. Hydrogen bonding
D. Ion-induced dipole interactions

14. List the substances NH_3, PH_3, $MgCl_2$, Ne, and N_2 in order of increasing melting point.

A. $N_2 < Ne < PH_3 < NH_3 < MgCl_2$
B. $N_2 < NH_3 < Ne < MgCl_2 < PH_3$
C. $Ne < N_2 < NH_3 < PH_3 < MgCl_2$
D. $Ne < N_2 < PH_3 < NH_3 < MgCl_2$

15. 1-butanol, ethanol, methanol, and 1-propanol are all liquids at room temperature. Rank them in order of increasing viscosity.

A. 1-butanol < 1-propanol < ethanol < methanol
B. methanol < ethanol < 1-propanol < 1-butanol
C. methanol < ethanol < 1-butanol < 1-propanol
D. 1-propanol < 1-butanol < ethanol < methanol

16. Which gas has a diffusion rate of 25% the rate for hydrogen?

A. helium
B. methane
C. nitrogen
D. oxygen

17. 2.00 L of an unknown gas at 1500. mm Hg and a temperature of 25.0 °C weighs 7.52 g. Assuming the ideal gas equation, what is the molecular mass of the gas?

760 mm Hg=1 atm
R=0.08206 L-atm/(mol-K)

A. 21.6 u
B. 23.3 u
C. 46.6 u
D. 93.2 u

18. Which substance is most likely to be a gas at room temperature?

A. SeO_2
B. F_2
C. $CaCl_2$
D. I_2

19. What pressure is exerted by a mixture of 2.7 g of H_2 and 59 g of Xe at STP on a 50. L container?

A. 0.69 atm
B. 0.76 atm
C. 0.80 atm
D. 0.97 atm

20. A few minutes after opening a bottle of perfume, the scent is detected on the other side of the room. What law relates to this phenomenon?

A. Graham's law
B. Dalton's law
C. Boyle's law
D. Avogadro's law

21. Which of the following are true?

A. Solids have no vapor pressure.
B. Dissolving a solute in a liquid increases its vapor pressure.
C. The vapor pressure of a pure substance is characteristic of that substance and its temperature.
D. All of the above

22. Find the partial pressure of N_2 in a container at 150. kPa holding H_2O and N_2 at 50 °C. The vapor pressure of H_2O at 50 °C is 12 kPa.

A. 12 kPa
B. 138 kPa
C. 162 kPa
D. The value cannot be determined.

23. The normal boiling point of water on the Kelvin scale is closest to:

A. 112 K
B. 212 K
C. 273 K
D. 373 K
E.

24. Which phase may be present at the triple point of a substance?

I. Gas
II. Liquid
III. Solid
IV. Supercritical fluid

A. I, II, and III
B. I, II, and IV
C. II, III, and IV
D. I, II, III, and IV

25. In the following phase diagram, _____ occurs as P is decreased from A to B at constant T and _____ occurs as T is increased from C to D at constant P.

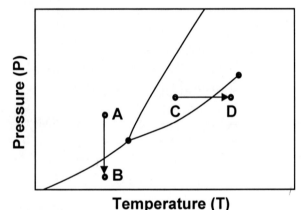

A. deposition, melting
B. sublimation, melting
C. deposition, vaporization
D. sublimation, vaporization

26. Heat is added to a pure solid at its melting point until it all becomes liquid at its freezing point. Which of the following occur?

A. Intermolecular attractions are weakened.
B. The kinetic energy of the molecules does not change.
C. The freedom of the molecules to move about increases.
D. All of the above.

27. Which of the following occur when NaCl dissolves in water?

A. Heat is required to break bonds in the NaCl crystal lattice.
B. Heat is released when hydrogen bonds in water are broken.
C. Heat is required to form bonds of hydration.
D. The oxygen end of the water molecule is attracted to the Cl^- ion.

28. The solubility of $CoCl_2$ is 54 g per 100 g of ethanol. Three flasks each contain 100 g of ethanol. Flask #1 also contains 40 g $CoCl_2$ in solution. Flask #2 contains 56 g $CoCl_2$ in solution. Flask #3 contains 5 g of solid $CoCl_2$ in equilibrium with 54 g $CoCl_2$ in solution. Which of the following describe the solutions present in the liquid phase of the flasks?

A. #1-saturated, #2-supersaturated, #3-unsaturated.
B. #1-unsaturated, #2-miscible, #3-saturated.
C. #1-unsaturated, #2-supersaturated, #3-saturated.
D. #1-unsaturated, #2-not at equilibrium, #3-miscible.

29. The solubility at 1.0 atm of pure CO_2 in water at 25 °C is 0.034 M. According to Henry's law, what is the solubility at 4.0 atm of pure CO_2 in water at 25 °C? Assume no chemical reaction occurs between CO_2 and H_2O.

A. 0.0085 M
B. 0.034 M
C. 0.14 M
D. 0.25 M

30. Carbonated water is bottled at 25 °C under pure CO_2 at 4.0 atm. Later the bottle is opened at 4 °C under air at 1.0 atm that has a partial pressure of 3×10^{-4} atm CO_2. Why do CO_2 bubbles form when the bottle is opened?

   A. CO_2 falls out of solution due to a drop in solubility at the lower total pressure.
   B. CO_2 falls out of solution due to a drop in solubility at the lower CO_2 pressure.
   C. CO_2 falls out of solution due to a drop in solubility at the lower temperature.
   D. CO_2 is formed by the decomposition of carbonic acid.

31. When KNO_3 dissolves in water, the water grows slightly colder. An increase in temperature will _____ the solubility of KNO_3.

   A. increase
   B. decrease
   C. have no effect on
   D. have an unknown effect with the information given on

32. An experiment requires 100. mL of a 0.500 M solution of $MgBr_2$. How many grams of $MgBr_2$ will be present in this solution?

   A. 9.21 g
   B. 11.7 g
   C. 12.4 g
   D. 15.6 g

33. 500. mg of RbOH are added to 500. g of ethanol (C_2H_6O) resulting in 395 mL of solution. Determine the molarity and molality of RbOH.

   A. 0.0124 M, 0.00488 m
   B. 0.0124 M, 0.00976 m
   C. 0.0223 M, 0.00488 m
   D. 0.0223 M, 0. 00976 m

34. 20.0 g H_3PO_4 in 1.5 L of solution are intended to react with KOH according to the following reaction:
   $$H_3PO_4 + 3\,KOH \rightarrow K_3PO_4 + 3\,H_2O$$
   What is the molarity and normality of the H_3PO_4 solution?

   A. 0.41 M, 1.22 N
   B. 0.41 M, 0.20 N
   C. 0.14 M, 0.045 N
   D. 0.14 M, 0. 41 N

35. Aluminum sulfate is a strong electrolyte. What is the concentration of all species in a 0.2 M solution of aluminum sulfate?

   A. 0.2 M Al^{3+}, 0.2 M SO_4^{2-}
   B. 0.4 M Al^{3+}, 0.6 M SO_4^{2-}
   C. 0.6 M Al^{3+}, 0.4 M SO_4^{2-}
   D. 0.2 M $Al_2(SO_4)_3$

36. 15 g of formaldehyde (CH_2O) are dissolved in 100 g of water. Calculate the weight percentage and mole fraction of formaldehyde in the solution.

A. 13%, 0.090
B. 15%, 0.090
C. 13%, 0.083
D. 15%, 0.083

37. Which of the following would make the best solvent for Br_2?

A. H_2O
B. CS_2
C. NH_3
D. molten NaCl

38. Which of the following is most likely to dissolve in water?

A. H_2
B. CCl_4
C. SF_6
D. CH_3OH

39. Which of the following is not a colligative property?

A. Viscosity lowering
B. Freezing point lowering
C. Boiling point elevation
D. Vapor pressure lowering

40. $$BaCl_2(aq) + Na_2SO_4(aq) \rightarrow$$
$$BaSO_4(s) + 2NaCl(aq)$$
is an example of a _____ reaction.

A. acid-base
B. precipitation
C. redox
D. nuclear

41. List the following aqueous solutions in order of increasing boiling point.

I. 0.050 m $AlCl_3$
II. 0.080 m $Ba(NO_3)_2$
III. 0.090 m NaCl
IV. 0.12 m ethylene glycol ($C_2H_6O_2$)

A. I < II < III < IV
B. I < III < IV < II
C. IV < III < I < II
D. IV < III < II < I

42. Osmotic pressure is the pressure required to prevent _____ flowing from low to high _____ concentration across a semipermeable membrane.

A. solute, solute
B. solute, solvent
C. solvent, solute
D. solvent, solvent

43. A solution of NaCl in water is heated on a mountain in an open container until it boils at 100. °C. The air pressure on the mountain is 0.92 atm. According to Raoult's law, what mole fraction of Na^+ and Cl^- are present in the solution?

A. 0.04 Na^+, 0.04 Cl^-
B. 0.08 Na^+, 0.08 Cl^-
C. 0.46 Na^+, 0.46 Cl^-
D. 0.92 Na^+, 0.92 Cl^-

44. Write a balanced nuclear equation for the emission of an alpha particle by polonium-209.

A. $^{209}_{84}Po \rightarrow ^{205}_{81}Pb + ^{4}_{2}He$
B. $^{209}_{84}Po \rightarrow ^{205}_{82}Bi + ^{4}_{2}He$
C. $^{209}_{84}Po \rightarrow ^{209}_{85}At + ^{0}_{-1}e$
D. $^{209}_{84}Po \rightarrow ^{205}_{82}Pb + ^{4}_{2}He$

45. Write a balanced nuclear equation for the decay of calcium-45 to scandium-45.

A. $^{45}_{20}Ca \rightarrow ^{41}_{18}Sc + ^{4}_{2}He$
B. $^{45}_{20}Ca + ^{0}_{1}e \rightarrow ^{45}_{21}Sc$
C. $^{45}_{20}Ca \rightarrow ^{45}_{21}Sc + ^{0}_{-1}e$
D. $^{45}_{20}Ca + ^{0}_{-1}p \rightarrow ^{45}_{21}Sc$

46. $^{3}_{1}H$ decays with a half-life of 12 years. 3.0 g of pure $^{3}_{1}H$ were placed in a sealed container 24 years ago. How many grams of $^{3}_{1}H$ remain?

A. 0.38 g
B. 0.75 g
C. 1.5 g
D. 3.0 g

47. Oxygen-15 has a half-life of 122 seconds. What percentage of a sample of oxygen-15 has decayed after 300. seconds?

A. 18.2%
B. 21.3%
C. 78.7%
D. 81.8%

48. Which of the following isotopes is commonly used for medical imaging in the diagnose of diseases?

A. cobalt-60
B. technetium-99m
C. tin-117m
D. plutonium-238

49. Carbon-14 dating would be useful in obtaining the age of which object?

A. a 20th century Picasso painting
B. a mummy from ancient Egypt
C. a dinosaur fossil
D. all of the above

50. Which of the following isotopes can create a chain reaction of nuclear fission?

A. uranium-235
B. uranium-238
C. plutonium-238
D. all of the above

51. List the following scientists in chronological order from earliest to most recent with respect to their most significant contribution to atomic theory:

I. John Dalton
II. Niels Bohr
III. J. J. Thomson
IV. Ernest Rutherford

A. I, III, II, IV
B. I, III, IV, II
C. I, IV, III, II
D. III, I, II, IV

52. Match the theory with the scientist who first proposed it:

I. Electrons, atoms, and all objects with momentum also exist as waves.
II. Electron density may be accurately described by a single mathematical equation.
III. There is an inherent indeterminacy in the position and momentum of particles.
IV. Radiant energy is transferred between particles in exact multiples of a discrete unit.

A. I-de Broglie, II-Planck, III-Schrödinger, IV-Thomson
B. I-Dalton, II-Bohr, III-Planck, IV-de Broglie
C. I-Henry, II-Bohr, III-Heisenberg, IV-Schrödinger
D. I-de Broglie, II-Schrödinger, III-Heisenberg, IV-Planck

53. How many neutrons are in $^{60}_{27}$Co ?

A. 27
B. 33
C. 60
D. 87

54. The terrestrial composition of an element is: 50.7% as an isotope with an atomic mass of 78.9 u and 49.3% as an isotope with an atomic mass of 80.9 u. Both isotopes are stable. Calculate the atomic mass of the element.
    A. 79.0 u
    B. 79.8 u
    C. 79.9 u
    D. 80.8 u

55. Which of the following is a correct electron arrangement for oxygen?
    A.
1s	2s	2p
↑↓	↑↓	↑↓ ↑↓

    B. $1s^2 1p^2 2s^2 2p^2$
    C. 2, 2, 4
    D. none of the above

56. Which of the following statements about radiant energy is **not** true?

    A. The energy change of an electron transition is directly proportional to the wavelength of the emitted or absorbed photon.
    B. The energy of an electron in a hydrogen atom depends only on the principle quantum number.
    C. The frequency of photons striking a metal determines whether the photoelectric effect will occur.
    D. The frequency of a wave of electromagnetic radiation is inversely proportional to its wavelength

57. Match the orbital diagram for the ground state of carbon with the rule/principle it violates:

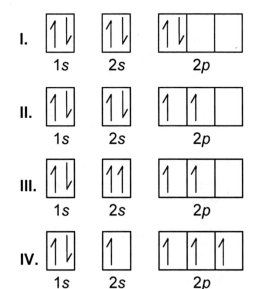

    A. I-Pauli exclusion, II-Aufbau, III-no violation, IV-Hund's
    B. I-Aufbau, II-Pauli exclusion, III-no violation, IV-Hund's
    C. I-Hund's, II-no violation, III-Pauli exclusion, IV-Aufbau
    D. I-Hund's, II-no violation, III-Aufbau, IV-Pauli exclusion

58. Select the list of atoms that are arranged in order of increasing size.

    A. Mg, Na, Si, Cl
    B. Si, Cl, Mg, Na
    C. Cl, Si, Mg, Na
    D. Na, Mg, Si, Cl

59. Based on trends in the periodic table, which of the following properties would you expect to be greater for Rb than for K?

I. Density
II. Melting point
III. Ionization energy
IV. Oxidation number in a compound with chlorine

A. I only
B. I, II, and III
C. II and III
D. I, II, III, and IV

60. Which oxide forms the strongest acid in water?

A. Al_2O_3
B. Cl_2O_7
C. As_2O_5
D. CO_2

61. Rank the following bonds from least to most polar:

C-H, C-Cl, H-H, C-F

A. C-H < H-H < C-F < C-Cl
B. H-H < C-H < C-F < C-Cl
C. C-F < C-Cl < C-H < H-H
D. H-H < C-H < C-Cl < C-F

62. At room temperature, $CaBr_2$ is expected to be:

A. a ductile solid
B. a brittle solid
C. a soft solid
D. a gas

63. Which of the following is a proper Lewis dot structure of CHClO?

A.

B.

C.

D.

64. In C_2H_2, each carbon atom contains the following valence orbitals:

A. p only
B. p and sp hybrids
C. p and sp^2 hybrids
D. sp^3 hybrids only

65. Which statement about molecular structures is false?

A. is a conjugated molecule

B. A bonding σ orbital connects two atoms by the straight line between them.

C. A bonding π orbital connects two atoms in a separate region from the straight line between them.

D. The anion with resonance forms

will always exist in one form or the other.

66. What is the shape of the PH_3 molecule? Use the VSEPR model.

A. Trigonal pyramidal
B. Trigonal bipyramidal
C. Trigonal planar
D. Tetrahedral

67. What is the chemical composition of magnesium nitrate?

A. 11.1% Mg, 22.2% N, 66.7% O
B. 16.4% Mg, 18.9% N, 64.7% O
C. 20.9% Mg, 24.1% N, 55.0% O
D. 28.2% Mg, 16.2% N, 55.7% O

68. The IUPAC name for Cu_2SO_3 is:

A. Dicopper sulfur trioxide
B. Copper (II) sulfate
C. Copper (I) sulfite
D. Copper (II) sulfite

69. Which name or formula is **not** represented properly?

A. Cl_4S
B. $KClO_3$
C. Calcium dihydrogen phosphate
D. Sulfurous acid

70. Household "chlorine bleach" is sodium hypochlorite. Which of the following best represent the production of sodium hypochlorite, sodium chloride, and water by bubbling chlorine gas through aqueous sodium hydroxide?

A. $4Cl(g) + 4NaOH(aq) \rightarrow$
   $NaClO_2(aq) + 3NaCl(aq) + 2H_2O(l)$

B. $2Cl_2(g) + 4NaOH(aq) \rightarrow$
   $NaClO_2(aq) + 3NaCl(aq) + 2H_2O(l)$

C. $2Cl(g) + 2NaOH(aq) \rightarrow$
   $NaClO(aq) + NaCl(aq) + H_2O(l)$

D. $Cl_2(g) + 2NaOH(aq) \rightarrow$
   $NaClO(aq) + NaCl(aq) + H_2O(l)$

71. Balance the equation for the neutralization reaction between phosphoric acid and calcium hydroxide by filling in the blank stoichiometric coefficients.

___H_3PO_4 + ___$Ca(OH)_2$ →

___$Ca_3(PO_4)_2$ + ___H_2O

A. 4, 3, 1, 4
B. 2, 3, 1, 8
C. 2, 3, 1, 6
D. 2, 1, 1, 2

72. Write an equation showing the reaction between calcium nitrate and lithium sulfate in aqueous solution. Include all products.

A. $CaNO_3(aq)$ + $Li_2SO_4(aq)$ → $CaSO_4(s)$ + $Li_2NO_3(aq)$

B. $Ca(NO_3)_2(aq)$ + $Li_2SO_4(aq)$ → $CaSO_4(s)$ + $2LiNO_3(aq)$

C. $Ca(NO_3)_2(aq)$ + $Li_2SO_4(aq)$ → $2LiNO_3(s)$ + $CaSO_4(aq)$

D. $Ca(NO_3)_2(aq)$ + $Li_2SO_4(aq)$ + $2H_2O(l)$ → $2LiNO_3(aq)$ + $Ca(OH)_2(aq)$ + $H_2SO_4(aq)$

73. Find the mass of CO_2 produced by the combustion of 15 kg of isopropyl alcohol in the reaction:

$$2C_3H_7OH + 9O_2 → 6CO_2 + 8H_2O$$

A. 33 kg
B. 44 kg
C. 50 kg
D. 60 kg

74. What is the density of nitrogen gas at STP? Assume an ideal gas and a value of 0.08206 L•atm/(mol•K) for the gas constant.

A. 0.62 g/L
B. 1.14 g/L
C. 1.25 g/L
D. 2.03 g/L

75. Find the volume of methane that will produce 12 m³ of hydrogen in the reaction:

$$CH_4(g) + H_2O(g) → CO(g) + 3H_2(g)$$

Assume temperature and pressure remain constant.

A. 4.0 m³
B. 32 m³
C. 36 m³
D. 64 m³

76. A 100 L vessel of pure O_2 at 500. kPa and 20. °C is used for the combustion of butane:

$$2C_4H_{10} + 13O_2 \rightarrow 8CO_2 + 10H_2O$$

Find the mass of butane to consume all the O_2 in the vessel. Assume O_2 is an ideal gas and use a value of $R =$ 8.314 J/(mol•K).

A. 183 g
B. 467 g
C. 1.83 kg
D. 7.75 kg

77. Consider the reaction between iron and hydrogen chloride gas:

$$Fe(s) + 2HCl(g) \rightarrow FeCl_2(s) + H_2(g)$$

7 moles of iron and 10 moles of HCl react until the limiting reagent is consumed. Which statements are true?

I. HCl is the excess reagent
II. HCl is the limiting reagent
III. 7 moles of H_2 are produced
IV. 2 moles of the excess reagent remain

A. I and III
B. I and IV
C. II and III
D. II and IV

78. 32.0 g of hydrogen and 32.0 grams of oxygen react to form water until the limiting reagent is consumed. What is present in the vessel after the reaction is complete?

A. 16.0 g O_2 and 48.0 g H_2O
B. 24.0 g H_2 and 40.0 g H_2O
C. 28.0 g H_2 and 36.0 g H_2O
D. 28.0 g H_2 and 34.0 g H_2O

79. Three experiments were performed at the same initial temperature and pressure to determine the rate of the reaction

$$2ClO_2(g) + F_2(g) \rightarrow 2ClO_2F(g)$$

Results are shown in the table below. Concentrations are given in millimoles per liter (mM).

Exp.	Initial $[ClO_2]$ (mM)	Initial $[F_2]$ (mM)	Initial rate of $[ClO_2F]$ increase (mM/sec)
1	5.0	5.0	0.63
2	5.0	20	2.5
3	10	10	2.5

What is the rate law for this reaction?

A. Rate $= k\left[F_2\right]$

B. Rate $= k\left[ClO_2\right]\left[F_2\right]$

C. Rate $= k\left[ClO_2\right]^2\left[F_2\right]$

D. Rate $= k\left[ClO_2\right]\left[F_2\right]^2$

80. The reaction

$(CH_3)_3CBr(aq) + OH^-(aq) \rightarrow$

$(CH_3)_3COH(aq) + Br^-(aq)$

occurs in three elementary steps:

$(CH_3)_3CBr \rightarrow (CH_3)_3C^+ + Br^-$ is slow

$(CH_3)_3C^+ + H_2O \rightarrow (CH_3)_3COH_2^+$ is fast

$(CH_3)_3COH_2^+ + OH^- \rightarrow$
$(CH_3)_3COH + H_2O$ is fast

What is the rate law for this reaction?

A. $Rate = k[(CH_3)_3CBr]$

B. $Rate = k[OH^-]$

C. $Rate = k[(CH_3)_3CBr][OH^-]$

D. $Rate = k[(CH_3)_3CBr]^2$

81. Which statement about equilibrium is not true?

A. Equilibrium shifts to minimize the impact of changes.
B. Forward and reverse reactions have equal rates at equilibrium.
C. A closed container of air and water is at a vapor-liquid equilibrium if the humidity is constant.
D. The equilibrium between solid and dissolved forms is maintained when salt is added to an unsaturated solution.

82. Which statements about reaction rates are true?

I. Catalysts shift an equilibrium to favor product formation.
II. Catalysts increase the rate of forward and reverse reactions.
III. A greater temperature increases the chance that a molecular collision will overcome a reaction's activation energy.
IV. A catalytic converter contains a homogeneous catalyst.

A. I and II
B. II and III
C. II, III, and IV
D. I, III, and IV

83. Write the equilibrium expression K_{eq} for the reaction

$$CO_2(g) + H_2(g) \rightleftharpoons CO(g) + H_2O(l)$$

A. $\dfrac{[CO][H_2O]}{[CO_2][H_2]^2}$

B. $\dfrac{[CO_2][H_2]}{[CO][H_2O]}$

C. $\dfrac{[CO][H_2O]}{[CO_2][H_2]}$

D. $\dfrac{[CO]}{[CO_2][H_2]}$

84. What could cause this change in the energy diagram of a reaction?

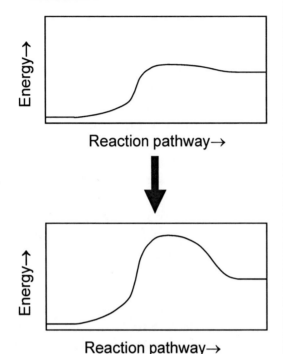

Reaction pathway→

Reaction pathway→

A. Adding catalyst to an endothermic reaction
B. Removing catalyst from an endothermic reaction
C. Adding catalyst to an exothermic reaction
D. Removing catalyst from an exothermic reaction

85. BaSO$_4$ (K_{sp} = 1X10^{-10}) is added to pure H$_2$O. How much is dissolved in 1 L of saturated solution?

A. 2 mg
B. 10 μg
C. 2 μg
D. 100 pg

86. The exothermic reaction
2NO(g) + Br$_2$(g) $\rightleftharpoons$ 2NOBr(g) is at equilibrium. According to LeChatelier's principle:

A. Adding Br$_2$ will increase [NO].
B. An increase in container volume (with T constant) will increase [NOBr].
C. An increase in pressure (with T constant) will increase [NOBr].
D. An increase in temperature (with P constant) will increase [NOBr].

87. At a certain temperature, *T*, the equilibrium constant for the reaction
2NO(g) $\rightleftharpoons$ N$_2$(g) + O$_2$(g) is K_{eq} = 2X10^3. If a 1.0 L container at this temperature contains 90 mM N$_2$, 20 mM O$_2$, and 5 mM NO, what will occur?

A. The reaction will make more N$_2$ and O$_2$.
B. The reaction is at equilibrium.
C. The reaction will make more NO.
D. The temperature, *T*, is required to solve this problem.

88. Which statement about acids and bases is <u>not</u> true?

A. All strong acids ionize in water.
B. All Lewis acids accept an electron pair.
C. All Brønsted bases use OH$^-$ as a proton acceptor
D. All Arrhenius acids form H$^+$ ions in water.

89. Which of the following are listed from weakest to strongest acid?

   A. H_2SO_3, H_2SeO_3, H_2TeO_3
   B. $HBrO$, $HBrO_2$, $HBrO_3$, $HBrO_4$
   C. HI, HBr, HCl, HF
   D. H_3PO_4, $H_2PO_4^-$, HPO_4^{2-}

90. NH_4F is dissolved in water. Which of the following are conjugate acid/base pairs present in the solution?

   I. NH_4^+/NH_4OH
   II. HF/F^-
   III. H_3O^+/H_2O
   IV. H_2O/OH^-

   A. I, II, and III
   B. I, III, and IV
   C. II and IV
   D. II, III, and IV

91. What are the pH and the pOH of 0.010 M $HNO_3(aq)$?

   A. pH = 1.0, pOH = 9.0
   B. pH = 2.0, pOH = 12.0
   C. pH = 2.0, pOH = 8.0
   D. pH = 8.0, pOH = 6.0

92. What is the pH of a buffer made of 0.128 M sodium formate (HCOONa) and 0.072 M formic acid (HCOOH)? The pK_a of formic acid is 3.75.

   A. 2.0
   B. 3.0
   C. 4.0
   D. 5.0

93. A sample of 50.0 ml KOH is titrated with 0.100 M $HClO_4$. The initial buret reading is 1.6 ml and the reading at the endpoint is 22.4 ml. What is [KOH]?

   A. 0.0416 M
   B. 0.0481 M
   C. 0.0832 M
   D. 0.0962 mM

94. Rank the following from lowest to highest pH. Assume a small volume for the component given in moles:

   I. 0.01 mol HCl added to 1 L H_2O
   II. 0.01 mol HI added to 1 L of an acetic acid/sodium acetate solution at pH 4.0
   III. 0.01 mol NH_3 added to 1 L H_2O
   IV. 0.1 mol HNO_3 added to 1 L of a 0.1 M $Ca(OH)_2$ solution

   A. I < II < III < IV
   B. I < II < IV < III
   C. II < I < III < IV
   D. II < I < IV < III

95. The curve below resulted from the titration of a _____ _____ with a _____ _____ titrant.

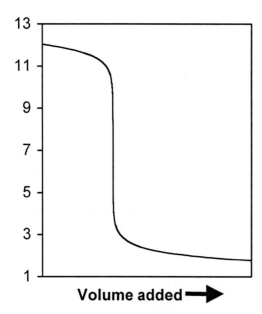

Volume added →

A. weak acid, strong base
B. weak base, strong acid
C. strong acid, strong base
D. strong base, strong acid

96. Which statement about thermochemistry is true?

A. Particles in a system move about less freely at high entropy
B. Water at 100 °C has the same internal energy as water vapor at 100°C
C. A decrease in the order of a system corresponds to an increase in entropy.
D. At its sublimation temperature, dry ice has a higher entropy than gaseous CO_2

97. What is the heat change of 36.0 g H_2O at atmospheric pressure when its temperature is reduced from 125 °C to 40. °C? Use the following data:

Values for water

Heat capacity of solid	37.6 J/mol•°C
Heat capacity of liquid	75.3 J/mol•°C
Heat capacity of gas	33.1 J/mol•°C
Heat of fusion	6.02 kJ/mol
Heat of vaporization	40.67 kJ/mol

A. −92.0 kJ
B. −10.8 kJ
C. 10.8 kJ
D. 92.0 kJ

98. What is the standard heat of combustion of $CH_4(g)$? Use the following data:

Standard heats of formation

$CH_4(g)$	−74.8 kJ/mol
$CO_2(g)$	−393.5 kJ/mol
$H_2O(l)$	−285.8 kJ/mol

A. −890.3 kJ/mol
B. −604.6 kJ/mol
C. −252.9 kJ/mol
D. −182.5 kJ/mol

99. Which reaction creates products at a lower total entropy than the reactants?

A. Dissolution of table salt:
$NaCl(s) \rightarrow Na^+(aq) + Cl^S(aq)$
B. Oxidation of iron:
$4Fe(s) + 3O_2(g) \rightarrow 2Fe_2O_3(s)$
C. Dissociation of ozone:
$O_3(g) \rightarrow O_2(g) + O(g)$
D. Vaporization of butane:
$C_4H_{10}(l) \rightarrow C_4H_{10}(g)$

100. Which statement about reactions is true?

A. All spontaneous reactions are both exothermic and cause an increase in entropy.
B. An endothermic reaction that increases the order of the system cannot be spontaneous.
C. A reaction can be non-spontaneous in one direction and also non-spontaneous in the opposite direction.
D. Melting snow is an exothermic process.

101. 10 kJ of heat are added to one kilogram of Iron at 10. °C. What is its final temperature? The specific heat of iron is 0.45 J/g•°C.

A. 22 °C
B. 27 °C
C. 32 °C
D. 37 °C

102. Which reaction is not a redox process?

A. Combustion of octane:
$2C_8H_{18} + 25O_2 \rightarrow 16CO_2 + 18H_2O$
B. Depletion of a lithium battery:
$Li + MnO_2 \rightarrow LiMnO_2$
C. Corrosion of aluminum by acid:
$2Al + 6HCl \rightarrow 2AlCl_3 + 3H_2$
D. Taking an antacid for heartburn:
$CaCO_3 + 2HCl \rightarrow CaCl_2 + H_2CO_3$
$\rightarrow CaCl_2 + CO_2 + H_2O$

103. Given the following heats of reaction:
$\Delta H = -0.3 \text{ kJ/mol}$ for
$Fe(s) + CO_2(g) \rightarrow FeO(s) + CO(g)$
$\Delta H = 5.7 \text{ kJ/mol}$ for
$2Fe(s) + 3CO_2(g) \rightarrow Fe_2O_3(s) + 3CO(g)$
and $\Delta H = 4.5 \text{ kJ/mol}$ for
$3FeO(s) + CO_2(g) \rightarrow Fe_3O_4(s) + CO(g)$

use Hess's Law to determine the heat of reaction for:

$3Fe_2O_3(s) + CO(g) \rightarrow 2Fe_3O_4(s) + CO_2(g)$

A. −10.8 kJ/mol
B. −9.9 kJ/mol
C. −9.0 kJ/mol
D. −8.1 kJ/mol

104. What is the oxidant in the reaction:

$$2H_2S + SO_2 \rightarrow 3S + 2H_2O ?$$

A. H_2S
B. SO_2
C. S
D. H_2O

105. Molten NaCl is subjected to electrolysis. What reaction takes place at the cathode?

A. $2Cl^-(l) \rightarrow Cl_2(g) + 2e^-$
B. $Cl_2(g) + 2e^- \rightarrow 2Cl^-(l)$
C. $Na^+(l) + e^- \rightarrow Na(l)$
D. $Na^+(l) \rightarrow Na(l) + e^-$

106. What is the purpose of the salt bridge in an electrochemical cell?

A. To receive electrons from the oxidation half-reaction
B. To relieve the buildup of positive charge in the anode half-cell
C. To conduct electron flow
D. To permit positive ions to flow from the cathode half-cell to the anode half-cell

107. Given:
$E°=-2.37V$ for $Mg^{2+}(aq)+2e^- \rightarrow Mg(s)$

and

$E°=0.80$ V for $Ag^+(aq)+e^- \rightarrow Ag(s)$,

what is the standard potential of a voltaic cell composed of a piece of magnesium dipped in a 1 M Ag^+ solution and a piece of silver dipped in 1 M Mg^{2+}?

A. 0.77 V
B. 1.57 V
C. 3.17 V
D. 3.97 V

108.

A proper name for this hydrocarbon is:

A. 4,5-dimethyl-6-hexene
B. 2,3-dimethyl-1-hexene
C. 4,5-dimethyl-6-hexyne
D. 2-methyl-3-propyl-1-butene

109. An IUPAC approved name for this molecule is:

A. butanal
B. propanal
C. butanoic acid
D. propanoic acid

110. Which molecule has a systematic name of methyl ethanoate?

A.

B.

C.

D.

111. This compound contains an:

A. alkene, carboxylic acid, ester, and ketone
B. aldehyde, alkyne, ester, and ketone
C. aldehyde, alkene, carboxylic acid, and ester
D. acid anhydride, aldehyde, alkene, and amine

112. Which group of scientists made contributions in the same area of chemistry?

A. Volta, Kekulé, Faraday, London
B. Hess, Joule, Kelvin, Gibbs
C. Boyle, Charles, Arrhenius, Pauli
D. Davy, Mendeleev, Ramsay, Galvani

113. Which of the following pairs are isomers?

I.

II.   pentanal 2-pentanone

III.

IV.

A. I and IV
B. II and III
C. I, II, and III
D. I, II, III, and IV

114. Which instrument would be most useful for separating two different proteins from a mixture?

A. UV/Vis spectrophotometer
B. Mass spectrometer
C. Gas chromatograph
D. Liquid chromatograph

115. Classify these biochemicals.

I.

II.

III.

IV.

A. I-nucleotide, II-sugar, III-peptide, IV-fat
B. I-disaccharide, II-sugar, III-fatty acid, IV-polypeptide
C. I-disaccharide, II-amino acid, III-fatty acid, IV-polysaccharide
D. I I-nucleotide, II-sugar, III-triacylglyceride, and IV-DNA

116. You create a solution of 2.00 μg/ml of a pigment and divide the solution into 12 samples. You give four samples each to three teams of students. They use a spectrophotometer to determine the pigment concentration. Here is their data:

Team	Concentration (μg/ml)			
	sample 1	sample 2	sample 3	sample 4
1	1.98	1.93	1.92	1.88
2	1.70	1.72	1.69	1.70
3	1.78	1.99	2.87	2.20

Which of the following are true?

A. Team 1 has the most precise data
B. Team 3 has the most accurate data in spite of it having low precision
C. The data from team 2 is characteristic of a systematic error
D. The data from team 1 is more characteristic of random error than the data from team 3.

117. Which pair of measurements have an identical meaning?

A. 32 micrograms and 0.032 g
B. 26 nm and 2.60×10^{-8} m
C. 3.01×10^{-5} m^3 and 30.1 ml
D. 0.0020 L and 20 cm^3

118. Match the instrument with the quantity it measures

II. eudiometer
III. calorimeter
IV. manometer
V. hygrometer

A. I-volume, II-mass, III-radioactivity, IV-humidity
B. I-volume, II-heat, III-pressure, IV-humidity
C. I-viscosity, II-mass, III-pressure, IV-surface tension
D. I-viscosity, II-heat, III-radioactivity, IV-surface tension

119. Four nearly identical gems from the same mineral are weighed using different balances. Their masses are:

3.4533 g, 3.459 g, 3.4656 g, 3.464 g

The four gems are then collected and added to a volumetric cylinder containing 10.00 ml of liquid, and a new volume of 14.97 ml is read. What is the average mass of the four stones and what is the density of the mineral?

A. 3.460 g, and 2.78 g/ml
B. 3.460 g and 2.79 g/ml
C. 3.4605 g and 2.78 g/ml
D. 3.461 g and 2.79 g/ml

120. Which list includes equipment that would **not** be used in vacuum filtration.

    A. Rubber tubing, Florence flask, Büchner funnel

    B. Vacuum pump, Hirsch funnel, rubber stopper with a single hole

    C. Aspirator, filter paper, filter flask

    D. Lab stand, clamp, filter trap

121. Which of the following statements about lab safety is **not** true?

    A. Corrosive chemicals should be stored below eye level.

    B. A chemical splash on the eye or skin should be rinsed for 15 minutes in cold water.

    C. MSDS means "Material Safety Data Sheet."

    D. A student should "stop, drop, and roll" if their clothing catches fire in the lab.

122. Which of the following lists consists entirely of chemicals that are considered safe enough to be in a high school lab?

    A. hydrochloric acid, lauric acid, potassium permanganate, calcium hydroxide

    B. ethyl ether, nitric acid, sodium benzoate, methanol

    C. cobalt (II) sulfide, ethylene glycol, benzoyl peroxide, ammonium chloride

    D. picric acid, hydrofluoric acid, cadmium chloride, carbon disulfide.

123. The following procedure was developed to find the specific heat capacity of metals:

1. Place pieces of the metals in an ice-water bath so their initial temperature is 0 °C.
2. Weigh a styrofoam cup.
3. Add water at room temperature to the cup and weigh it again
4. Add a cold metal from the bath to the cup and weigh the cup a third time.
5. Monitor the temperature drop of the water until a final temperature at thermal equilibrium is found.

_____ is also required as additional information in order to obtain heat capacities for the metals. The best control would be to follow the same protocol except to use _____ in step 4 instead of a cold metal.

    A. The heat capacity of water / a metal at 100 °C

    B. The heat of formation of water / ice from the 0 °C bath

    C. The heat of capacity of ice / glass at 0 °C

    D. The heat capacity of water / water from the 0 °C bath

124. Which statement about the impact of chemistry on society is <u>not</u> true?

A. Partial hydrogenation creates *trans* fat.
B. The Haber Process incorporates nitrogen from the air into molecules for agricultural use.
C. The CO_2 concentration in the atmosphere has decreased in the last ten years.
D. The concentration of ozone-destroying chemicals in the stratosphere has decreased in the last ten years.

125. Which statement about everyday applications of chemistry is <u>true</u>?

A. Rainwater found near sources of air pollution will most likely be basic.
B. Batteries run down more quickly at low temperatures because chemical reactions are proceeding more slowly.
C. Benzyl alcohol is a detergent used in shampoo.
D. Adding salt decreases the time required for water to boil.

Answer Key

1.	C	26.	D	51.	B	76.	A	101.	C
2.	B	27.	A	52.	D	77.	D	102.	D
3.	D	28.	C	53.	B	78.	C	103.	B
4.	A	29.	C	54.	C	79.	B	104.	B
5.	C	30.	B	55.	D	80.	A	105.	C
6.	D	31.	A	56.	A	81.	D	106.	D
7.	C	32.	A	57.	C	82.	B	107.	C
8.	B	33.	B	58.	C	83.	D	108.	B
9.	A	34.	D	59.	A	84.	B	109.	C
10.	C	35.	B	60.	B	85.	A	110.	A
11.	B	36.	C	61.	D	86.	C	111.	C
12.	D	37.	B	62.	B	87.	A	112.	B
13.	A	38.	D	63.	C	88.	C	113.	B
14.	D	39.	A	64.	B	89.	B	114.	D
15.	B	40.	B	65.	D	90.	D	115.	A
16.	D	41.	C	66.	A	91.	B	116.	C
17.	C	42.	C	67.	B	92.	C	117.	C
18.	B	43.	A	68.	C	93.	A	118.	B
19.	C	44.	D	69.	A	94.	A	119.	B
20.	A	45.	C	70.	D	95.	D	120.	A
21.	C	46.	B	71.	C	96.	C	121.	D
22.	B	47.	D	72.	B	97.	A	122.	A
23.	D	48.	B	73.	A	98.	A	123.	D
24.	A	49.	B	74.	C	99.	B	124.	C
25.	D	50.	A	75.	A	100.	B	125.	B

Rationales with Sample Questions

Note: The first insignificant digit should be carried through intermediate calculations. This digit is shown using *italics* in the solutions below.

1. **A piston compresses a gas at constant temperature. Which gas properties increase?**

   II. Average speed of molecules
   III. Pressure
   IV. Molecular collisions with container walls per second

   A. I and II
   B. I and III
   C. II and III
   D. I, II, and III

C. A decrease in volume (V) occurs at constant temperature (T). Average molecular speed is determined only by temperature and will be constant. V and P are inversely related, so pressure will increase. With less wall area and at higher pressure, more collisions occur per second.

2. **The temperature of a liquid is raised at atmospheric pressure. Which liquid property increases?**

   A. critical pressure
   B. vapor pressure
   C. surface tension
   D. viscosity

B. The critical pressure of a liquid is its vapor pressure at the critical temperature and is always a constant value. A rising temperature increases the kinetic energy of molecules and decreases the importance of intermolecular attraction. More molecules will be free to escape to the vapor phase (vapor pressure increases), but the effect of attractions at the liquid-gas interface will fall (surface tension decreases) and molecules will flow against each other more easily (viscosity decreases).

3. **Potassium crystallizes with two atoms contained in each unit cell. What is the mass of potassium found in a lattice 1.00×10^6 unit cells wide, 2.00×10^6 unit cells high, and 5.00×10^5 unit cells deep?**

   A. 85.0 ng
   B. 32.5 μg
   C. 64.9 μg
   D. 130. μg

D. First we find the number of unit cells in the lattice by multiplying the number in each row, stack, and column:

1.00×10^6 unit cell lengths $\times 2.00 \times 10^6$ unit cell lengths $\times 5.00 \times 10^5$ unit cell lengths

$= 1.00 \times 10^{18}$ unit cells

Avogadro's number and the molecular weight of potassium (K) are used in the solution:

$$1.00 \times 10^{18} \text{ unit cells} \times \frac{2 \text{ atoms of K}}{\text{unit cell}} \times \frac{1 \text{ mole of K}}{6.02 \times 10^{23} \text{ atoms of K}} \times \frac{39.098 \text{ g K}}{1 \text{ mole of K}}$$

$$= 1.30 \times 10^{-4} \text{ g}$$

$$= 130. \text{ μg}$$

4. **A gas is heated in a sealed container. Which of the following occur?**

   A. gas pressure rises
   B. gas density decreases
   C. the average distance between molecules increases
   D. all of the above

A. The same material is kept in a constant volume, so neither density nor the distance between molecules will change. Pressure will rise because of increasing molecular kinetic energy impacting container walls.

5. **How many molecules are in 2.20 pg of a protein with a molecular weight of 150. kDa?**

   A. 8.83×10^9
   B. 1.82×10^9
   C. 8.83×10^6
   D. 1.82×10^6

C. The prefix "p" for "pico-" indicates 10^{-12}. A kilodalton is 1000 atomic mass units.

$$2.20 \text{ pg protein} \times \frac{10^{-12} \text{ g}}{1 \text{ pg}} \times \frac{1 \text{ mole protein}}{150 \times 10^3 \text{ g protein}} \times \frac{6.02 \times 10^{23} \text{ molecules protein}}{1 \text{ mole protein}} =$$
$$= 8.83 \times 10^6 \text{ molecules}$$

6. **At STP, 20. μL of O_2 contain 5.4×10^{16} molecules. According to Avogadro's hypothesis, how many molecules are in 20. μL of Ne at STP?**

   A. 5.4×10^{15}
   B. 1.0×10^{16}
   C. 2.7×10^{16}
   D. 5.4×10^{16}

D. Avogadro's hypothesis states that equal volumes of different gases at the same temperature and pressure contain equal numbers of molecules.

7. **An ideal gas at 50.0 °C and 3.00 atm is in a 300. cm³ cylinder. The cylinder volume changes by moving a piston until the gas is at 50.0 °C and 1.00 atm. What is the final volume?**

   A. 100. cm³
   B. 450. cm³
   C. 900. cm³
   D. 1.20 dm³

C. A three-fold decrease in pressure of a constant quantity of gas at constant temperature will cause a three-fold increase in gas volume.

8. **Which gas law may be used to solve the previous question?**

    A. Charles's law
    B. Boyle's law
    C. Graham's law
    D. Avogadro's law

B. The inverse relationship between volume and pressure is Boyle's law.

9. **A blimp is filled with 5000. m^3 of helium at 28.0 °C and 99.7 kPa. What is the mass of helium used?**

$$R = 8.3144 \frac{J}{mol - K}$$

    A. 797 kg
    B. 810. kg
    C. 1.99×10^3 kg
    D. 8.57×10^3 kg

A. First the ideal gas law is manipulated to solve for moles.

$$PV = nRT \implies n = \frac{PV}{RT}$$

Temperature must be expressed in Kelvin: $T = (28.0 + 273.15) K = 301.15 K$.

The ideal gas law is then used with the knowledge that joules are equivalent to Pa-m^3:

$$n = \frac{PV}{RT} = \frac{(99.7 \times 10^3 \ Pa)(5000. \ m^3)}{\left(8.3144 \frac{m^3 \text{-} Pa}{mol \text{-} K}\right)(301.15 \ K)} = 1.991 \times 10^3 \ mol \ He .$$

Moles are then converted to grams using the molecular weight of helium:

$$1.991 \times 10^3 \ mol \ He \times \frac{4.0026 \ g \ He}{1 \ mol \ He} = 797 \times 10^3 \ g \ He = 797 \ kg \ He .$$

7.97×10^5
or
A. 797×10^3 kg

10. Which of the following are able to flow from one place to another?

   I. Gases
   II. Liquids
   III. Solids
   IV. Supercritical fluids

   A. I and II
   B. II only
   C. I, II, and IV
   D. I, II, III, and IV

C. Gases and liquids both flow. Supercritical fluids have some traits in common with gases and some in common with liquids, and so they flow also. Solids have a fixed volume and shape.

11. One mole of an ideal gas at STP occupies 22.4 L. At what temperature will one mole of an ideal gas at one atm occupy 31.0 L?

   A. 34.6 °C
   B. 105 °C
   C. 378 °C
   D. 442 °C

B. Either Charles's law, the combined gas law, or the ideal gas law may be used with temperature in Kelvin.

Charles's law or the combined gas law with $P_1 = P_2$ may be manipulated to equate a ratio between temperature and volume when P and n are constant.

$$V \propto T \text{ or } \frac{P_1 V_1}{T_1} = \frac{P_2 V_2}{T_2} \Rightarrow \frac{T_1}{V_1} = \frac{T_2}{V_2} \Rightarrow T_2 = V_2 \frac{T_1}{V_1}$$

$$T_2 = 31.0 \text{ L} \frac{273.15 \text{ K}}{22.4 \text{ L}} = 378 \text{ K} = 105 \text{ °C}.$$

The ideal gas law may also be used with the appropriate gas constant:

$$PV = nRT \Rightarrow T = \frac{PV}{nR}$$

$$T = \frac{(1 \text{ atm})(31.0 \text{ L})}{(1 \text{ mol})\left(0.08206 \frac{\text{L-atm}}{\text{mol-K}}\right)} = 378 \text{ K} = 105 \text{ °C}.$$

12. **Why does CaCl$_2$ have a higher normal melting point than NH$_3$?**

   A. London dispersion forces in CaCl$_2$ are stronger than covalent bonds in NH$_3$.
   B. Covalent bonds in NH$_3$ are stronger than dipole-dipole bonds in CaCl$_2$.
   C. Ionic bonds in CaCl$_2$ are stronger than London dispersion forces in NH$_3$.
   D. Ionic bonds in CaCl$_2$ are stronger than hydrogen bonds in NH$_3$.

D. London dispersion forces are weaker than covalent bonds, eliminating choice A. A higher melting point will result from stronger intermolecular bonds, eliminating choice B. CaCl$_2$ is an ionic solid resulting from a cation on the left and an anion on the right of the periodic table. The dominant attractive forces between NH$_3$ molecules are hydrogen bonds.

13. **Which intermolecular attraction explains the following trend in straight-chain alkanes?**

Condensed structural formula	Boiling point (°C)
CH$_4$	-161.5
CH$_3$CH$_3$	-88.6
CH$_3$CH$_2$CH$_3$	-42.1
CH$_3$CH$_2$CH$_2$CH$_3$	-0.5
CH$_3$CH$_2$CH$_2$CH$_2$CH$_3$	36.0
CH$_3$CH$_2$CH$_2$CH$_2$CH$_2$CH$_3$	68.7

   A. London dispersion forces
   B. Dipole-dipole interactions
   C. Hydrogen bonding
   D. Ion-induced dipole interactions

A. Alkanes are composed entirely of non-polar C-C and C-H bonds, resulting in no dipole interactions or hydrogen bonding. London dispersion forces increase with the size of the molecule, resulting in a higher temperature requirement to break these bonds and a higher boiling point.

14. List NH_3, PH_3, $MgCl_2$, Ne, and N_2 in order of increasing melting point.

    A. $N_2 < Ne < PH_3 < NH_3 < MgCl_2$
    B. $N_2 < NH_3 < Ne < MgCl_2 < PH_3$
    C. $Ne < N_2 < NH_3 < PH_3 < MgCl_2$
    D. $Ne < N_2 < PH_3 < NH_3 < MgCl_2$

D. Higher melting points result from stronger intermolecular forces. $MgCl_2$ is the only material listed with ionic bonds and will have the highest melting point. Dipole-dipole interactions are present in NH_3 and PH_3 but not in Ne and N_2. Ne and N_2 are also small molecules expected to have very weak London dispersion forces and so will have lower melting points than NH_3 and PH_3. NH_3 will have stronger intermolecular attractions and a higher melting point than PH_3 because hydrogen bonding occurs in NH_3. Ne has a molecular weight of 20 and a spherical shape and N_2 has a molecular weight of 28 and is not spherical. Both of these factors predict stronger London dispersion forces and a higher melting point for N_2. Actual melting points are: Ne (25 K) < N_2 (63 K) < PH_3 (140 K) < NH_3 (195 K) < $MgCl_2$ (987 K).

15. 1-butanol, ethanol, methanol, and 1-propanol are all liquids at room temperature. Rank them in order of increasing viscosity.

    A. 1-butanol < 1-propanol < ethanol < methanol
    B. methanol < ethanol < 1-propanol < 1-butanol
    C. methanol < ethanol < 1-butanol < 1-propanol
    D. 1-propanol < 1-butanol < ethanol < methanol

B. Higher viscosities result from stronger intermolecular attractive forces. The molecules listed are all alcohols with the -OH functional group attached to the end of a straight-chain alkane. In other words, they all have the formula $CH_3(CH_2)_{n-1}OH$. The only difference between the molecules is the length of the alkane corresponding to the value of n. With all else identical, larger molecules have greater intermolecular attractive forces due to a greater molecular surface for the attractions. Therefore the viscosities are ranked: methanol (CH_3OH) < ethanol (CH_3CH_2OH) < 1-propanol ($CH_3CH_2CH_2OH$) < 1-butanol ($CH_3CH_2CH_2CH_2OH$).

16. Which gas has a diffusion rate of 25% the rate for hydrogen?

    A. helium
    B. methane
    C. nitrogen
    D. oxygen

D. Graham's law of diffusion states:

$$\frac{r_1}{r_2} = \sqrt{\frac{M_2}{M_1}} \ .$$

Hydrogen (H_2) has molecular weight of 2.0158 u. Using the unknown for material #1 and hydrogen for material #2 in the equation for Graham's law, the ratio of rates is:

$$\frac{r_{unknown}}{r_{hydrogen}} = \sqrt{\frac{2.0158 \ u}{M_{unknown}}} = 0.25. \quad \text{Squaring both sides yields} \quad \frac{2.0158 \ u}{M_{unknown}} = 0.0625 \ .$$

Solving for $M_{unknown}$ gives:

$$M_{unknown} = \frac{2.0158 \ u}{0.0625} = 32 \ u \ .$$

The given possibilities are: He (4.0 u), CH_4 (16 u), N_2 (28 u), and O_2 (32 u).

17. **2.00 L of an unknown gas at 1500. mm Hg and a temperature of 25.0 °C weighs 7.52 g. Assuming the ideal gas equation, what is the molecular weight of the gas?**

760 mm Hg=1 atm
R=0.08206 L-atm/(mol-K)

A. 21.6 u
B. 23.3 u
C. 46.6 u
D. 93.2 u

C. Pressure and temperature must be expressed in the proper units. Next the ideal gas law is used to find the number of moles of gas.

$$P = 1500 \text{ mm Hg} \times \frac{1 \text{ atm}}{760 \text{ mm Hg}} = 1.974 \text{ atm and } T = 25.0 + 273.15 = 298.15 \text{ K}$$

$$PV = nRT \implies n = \frac{PV}{RT}$$

$$n = \frac{(1.974 \text{ atm})(2.00 \text{ L})}{\left(0.08206 \frac{\text{L-atm}}{\text{mol-K}}\right)(298.15 \text{ K})} = 0.1613 \text{ mol.}$$

The molecular mass may be found from the mass of one mole.

$$\frac{7.52 \text{ g}}{0.1613 \text{ mol}} = 46.6 \frac{\text{g}}{\text{mol}} \implies 46.6 \text{ u}$$

18. **Which substance is most likely to be a gas at STP?**

A. SeO_2
B. F_2
C. $CaCl_2$
D. I_2

B. A gas at STP has a normal boiling point under 0 °C. The substance with the lowest boiling point will have the weakest intermolecular attractive forces and will be the most likely gas at STP. F_2 has the lowest molecular weight, is not a salt, metal, or covalent network solid, and is non-polar, indicating the weakest intermolecular attractive forces of the four choices. F_2 actually is a gas at STP, and the other three are solids.

19. What pressure is exerted by a mixture of 2.7 g of H2 and 59 g of Xe at 0 °C on a 50. L container?

    A. 0.69 atm
    B. 0.76 atm
    C. 0.80 atm
    D. 0.97 atm

C. Grams of gas are first converted to moles:

$$2.7 \text{ g H}_2 \times \frac{1 \text{ mol H}_2}{2 \times 1.0079 \text{ g H}_2} = 1.33 \text{ mol H}_2 \quad \text{and} \quad 59 \text{ g Xe} \times \frac{1 \text{ mol H}_2}{131.29 \text{ g H}_2} = 0.449 \text{ mol Xe}$$

Dalton's law of partial pressures for an ideal gas is used to find the pressure of the mixture:

$$P_{total}V = \left(n_{H_2} + n_{Xe}\right)RT \Rightarrow P_{total} = \frac{\left(n_{H_2} + n_{Xe}\right)RT}{V}$$

$$P_{total} = \frac{(1.33 \text{ mol} + 0.449 \text{ mol})\left(0.08206 \frac{\text{L-atm}}{\text{mol-K}}\right)(273.15 \text{ K})}{50. \text{ L}} = 0.80 \text{ atm.}$$

20. A few minutes after opening a bottle of perfume, the scent is detected on the other side of the room. What law relates to this phenomenon?

    A. Graham's law
    B. Dalton's law
    C. Boyle's law
    D. Avogadro's law

A. Graham's law describes the rate of diffusion (or effusion) of a gas, in this instance, the rate of diffusion of molecules in perfume vapor.

21. Which of the following statements are true of vapor pressure at equilibrium?

    A. Solids have no vapor pressure.
    B. Dissolving a solute in a liquid increases its vapor pressure.
    C. The vapor pressure of a pure substance is characteristic of that substance and its temperature.
    D. All of the above

C. Only temperature and the identity of the substance determine vapor pressure. Solids have a vapor pressure, and solutes decrease vapor pressure.

22. Find the partial pressure of N_2 in a container holding H_2O and N_2 at 150. kPa and 50 °C. The vapor pressure of H_2O at 50 °C is 12 kPa.

    A. 12 kPa
    B. 138 kPa
    C. 162 kPa
    D. The value cannot be determined.

B. The partial pressure of H_2O vapor in the container is its vapor pressure. The partial pressure of N_2 may be found by manipulating Dalton's law:

$$P_{total} = P_{H_2O} + P_{N_2} \Rightarrow P_{N_2} = P_{total} - P_{H_2O}$$
$$P_{N_2} = P_{total} - P_{H_2O} = 150.\ \text{kPa} - 12\ \text{kPa} = 138\ \text{kPa}$$

23. The normal boiling point of water on the Kelvin scale is closest to:

    A. 112 K
    B. 212 K
    C. 273 K
    D. 373 K

D. Temperature in Kelvin are equal to Celsius temperatures plus 273.15. Since the normal boiling point of water is 100 °C, it will boil at 373.15 K, corresponding to answer D.

24. **Which phase may be present at the triple point of a substance?**

    I. **Gas**
    II. **Liquid**
    III. **Solid**
    IV. **Supercritical fluid**

    A. I, II, and III
    B. I, II, and IV
    C. II, III, and IV
    D. I, II, III, and IV

A. Gas, liquid and solid may exist together at the triple point.

25. **In the following phase diagram, _____ occurs as P is decreased from A to B at constant T and _____ occurs as T is increased from C to D at constant P.**

    A. deposition, melting
    B. sublimation, melting
    C. deposition, vaporization
    D. sublimation, vaporization

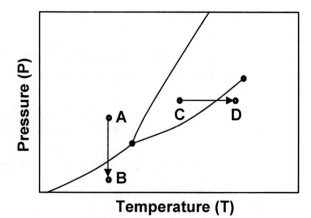

D. Point A is located in the solid phase, point C is located in the liquid phase. Points B and D are located in the gas phase. The transition from solid to gas is sublimation and the transition from liquid to gas is vaporization.

26. **Heat is added to a pure solid at its melting point until it all becomes liquid at its freezing point. Which of the following occur?**

    A. Intermolecular attractions are weakened.
    B. The kinetic energy of the molecules does not change.
    C. The freedom of the molecules to move about increases.
    D. All of the above

D. Intermolecular attractions are lessened during melting. This permits molecules to move about more freely, but there is no change in the kinetic energy of the molecules because the temperature has remained the same.

27. Which of the following occur when NaCl dissolves in water?

    A. Heat is required to break bonds in the NaCl crystal lattice.
    B. Heat is released when hydrogen bonds in water are broken.
    C. Heat is required to form bonds of hydration.
    D. The oxygen end of the water molecule is attracted to the Cl^- ion.

A. The lattice does break apart, H-bonds in water are broken, and bonds of hydration are formed, but the first and second process require heat while the third process releases heat. The oxygen end of the water molecule has a partial negative charge and is attracted to the Na^+ ion.

28. The solubility of $CoCl_2$ is 54 g per 100 g of ethanol. Three flasks each contain 100 g of ethanol. Flask #1 also contains 40 g $CoCl_2$ in solution. Flask #2 contains 56 g $CoCl_2$ in solution. Flask #3 contains 5 g of solid $CoCl_2$ in equilibrium with 54 g $CoCl_2$ in solution. Which of the following describe the solutions present in the liquid phase of the flasks?

    A. #1-saturated, #2-supersaturated, #3-unsaturated.
    B. #1-unsaturated, #2-miscible, #3-saturated.
    C. #1-unsaturated, #2-supersaturated, #3-saturated.
    D. #1-unsaturated, #2-not at equilibrium, #3-miscible.

C. Flask #1 contains less solute than the solubility limit, and is unsaturated. Flask #2 contains more solute than the solubility limit, and is supersaturated and also not at equilibrium. Flask #3 contains the solubility limit and is a saturated solution. The term "miscible" applies only to liquids that mix together in all proportions.

29. The solubility at 1.0 atm of pure CO_2 in water at 25 °C is 0.034 M. According to Henry's law, what is the solubility at 4.0 atm of pure CO_2 in water at 25 °C? Assume no chemical reaction occurs between CO_2 and H_2O.

    A. 0.0085 M
    B. 0.034 M
    C. 0.14 M
    D. 0.25 M

C. Henry's law states that CO_2 solubility in M (mol/L) will be proportional to the partial pressure of the gas. A four-fold increase in pressure from 1.0 atm to 4.0 atm will increase solubility four-fold from 0.034 M to 0.14 M.

30. Carbonated water is bottled at 25 °C under pure CO_2 at 4.0 atm. Later the bottle is opened at 4 °C under air at 1.0 atm that has a partial pressure of 3×10^{-4} atm CO_2. Why do CO_2 bubbles form when the bottle is opened?

    A. CO_2 leaves the solution due to a drop in solubility at the lower total pressure.
    B. CO_2 leaves the solution due to a drop in solubility at the lower CO_2 pressure.
    C. CO_2 leaves the solution due to a drop in solubility at the lower temperature.
    D. CO_2 is formed by the decomposition of carbonic acid.

B. A is incorrect because if the water were bottled under a different gas at a high pressure, it would not be carbonated. CO_2 partial pressure is the important factor in solubility. C is incorrect because a decrease in temperature will increase solubility, and the chance from 298 K to 277 K is relatively small. D may occur, but this represents a small fraction of the gas released.

31. When KNO_3 dissolves in water, the water grows slightly colder. An increase in temperature will _____ the solubility of KNO_3.

    A. increase
    B. decrease
    C. have no effect on
    D. have an unknown effect with the information given on

A. The decline in water temperature indicates that the net solution process is endothermic (requiring heat). A temperature increase supplying more heat will favor the solution and increase solubility according to Le Chatelier's principle.

32. An experiment requires 100. mL of a 0.500 M solution of $MgBr_2$. How many grams of $MgBr_2$ will be present in this solution?

    A. 9.21 g
    B. 11.7 g
    C. 12.4 g
    D. 15.6 g

A.

$$0.100 \text{ L solution} \times \frac{0.500 \text{ mol MgBr}_2}{\text{L}} \times \frac{(24.305 + 2 \times 79.904) \text{ g MgBr}_2}{\text{mol MgBr}_2} = 9.21 \text{ g MgBr}_2$$

33. **500. mg of RbOH are added to 500. g of ethanol (C_2H_6O) resulting in 395 mL of solution. Determine the molarity and molality of RbOH.**

   A. 0.0124 M, 0.00488 *m*
   B. 0.0124 M, 0.00976 *m*
   C. 0.0223 M, 0.00488 *m*
   D. 0.0223 M, 0. 00976 *m*

B. First we determine the moles of solute present:

$$0.500 \text{ g RbOH} \times \frac{1 \text{ mol RbOH}}{(85.468 + 15.999 + 1.0079) \text{ g RbOH}} = 0.004879 \text{ mol RbOH}.$$

This value is used to calculate molarity and molality:

$$\frac{0.04879 \text{ mol RbOH}}{0.395 \text{ L solution}} = 0.0124 \text{ M RbOH}$$

and

$$\frac{0.04879 \text{ mol RbOH}}{0.500 \text{ kg ethanol}} = 0.00976 \text{ } m \text{ RbOH}.$$

34. 20.0 g H_3PO_4 in 1.5 L of solution are intended to react with KOH according to the following reaction: $H_3PO_4 + 3KOH \rightarrow K_3PO_4 + 3H_2O$. What is the molarity and normality of the H_3PO_4 solution?

    A. 0.41 M, 1.22 N
    B. 0.41 M, 0.20 N
    C. 0.14 M, 0.045 N
    D. 0.14 M, 0. 41 N

D. We use two methods to solve this problem. In the first method, we determine the moles of solute present and use it to calculate molarity and normality:

$$20.0 \text{ g } H_3PO_4 \times \frac{1 \text{ mol } H_3PO_4}{(3 \times 1.0079 + 30.974 + 4 \times 15.999) \text{ g } H_3PO_4} = 0.204 \text{ mol } H_3PO_4.$$

$$\frac{0.204 \text{ mol } H_3PO_4}{1.5 \text{ L solution}} = 0.136 \frac{\text{mol } H_3PO_4}{L} = 0.14 \text{ M } H_3PO_4$$

and

$$\frac{0.204 \text{ mol } H_3PO_4}{1.5 \text{ L solution}} \times \frac{3 \text{ reaction equivalents}}{1 \text{ mol } H_3PO_4} = 0.408 \frac{\text{reaction equivalents}}{L} = 0.41 \text{ N } H_3PO_4.$$

Alternatively, molarity may be found in one step and normality may be determined from the molarity:

$$\frac{20.0 \text{ g } H_3PO_4}{1.5 \text{ L}} \times \frac{1 \text{ mol } H_3PO_4}{(3 \times 1.0079 + 30.974 + 4 \times 15.999) \text{ g } H_3PO_4} = 0.136 \frac{\text{mol } H_3PO_4}{L} = 0.14 \text{ M } H_3PO_4$$

and

$$0.136 \frac{\text{mol } H_3PO_4}{L} \times \frac{3 \text{ reaction equivalents}}{1 \text{ mol } H_3PO_4} = 0.408 \frac{\text{reaction equivalents}}{L} = 0.41 \text{ N.}$$

what are Rxn equivalents

35. Aluminum sulfate is a strong electrolyte. What is the concentration of all species in a 0.2 M solution of aluminum sulfate?

A. 0.2 M Al^{3+}, 0.2 M $SO_4{}^{2-}$
B. 0.4 M Al^{3+}, 0.6 M $SO_4{}^{2-}$
C. 0.6 M Al^{3+}, 0.4 M $SO_4{}^{2-}$
D. 0.2 M $Al_2(SO_4)_3$

B. A strong electrolyte will completely ionize into its cation and anion. Aluminum sulfate is $Al_2(SO_4)_3$. Each mole of aluminum sulfate ionizes into 2 moles of Al^{3+} and 3 moles of $SO_4{}^{2-}$:

$$0.2\,\frac{\text{mol }Al_2(SO_4)_3}{L} \times \frac{2 \text{ mol }Al^{3+}}{\text{mol }Al_2(SO_4)_3} = 0.4\,\frac{\text{mol }Al^{3+}}{L} \text{ and}$$

$$0.2\,\frac{\text{mol }Al_2(SO_4)_3}{L} \times \frac{3 \text{ mol }SO_4{}^{2-}}{\text{mol }Al_2(SO_4)_3} = 0.6\,\frac{\text{mol }SO_4{}^{2-}}{L}.$$

36. 15 g of formaldehyde (CH_2O) are dissolved in 100. g of water. Calculate the weight percentage and mole fraction of formaldehyde in the solution.

A. 13%, 0.090
B. 15%, 0.090
C. 13%, 0.083
D. 15%, 0.083

C. Remember to use the total amounts in the denominator.

For weight percentage: $\dfrac{15 \text{ g }CH_2O}{(15+100) \text{ g total}} = 0.13 = 13\%$.

For mole fraction, first convert grams of each substance to moles:

$$15 \text{ g }CH_2O \times \frac{\text{mol }CH_2O}{(12.011+2\times1.0079+15.999) \text{ g }CH_2O} = 0.4996 \text{ mol }CH_2O$$

$$100 \text{ g }H_2O \times \frac{\text{mol }H_2O}{(2\times1.0079+15.999) \text{ g }H_2O} = 5.551 \text{ mol }H_2O.$$

Again use the total amount in the denominator $\dfrac{0.4996 \text{ mol }CH_2O}{(0.4996 + 5.551) \text{ mol total}} = 0.083$.

37. Which of the following would make the best solvent for Br_2?

    A. H_2O
    B. CS_2
    C. NH_3
    D. molten NaCl

B. The best solvents for a solute have intermolecular bonds of similar strength to the solute ("like dissolves like"). Bromine is a non-polar molecule with intermolecular attractions due to weak London dispersion forces. The relatively strong hydrogen bonding in H_2O and NH_3 and the very strong electrostatic attractions in molten NaCl would make each of them a poor solvent for Br_2 because these molecules would prefer to remain attracted to one another. CS_2 is a fairly small non-polar molecule.

38. Which of the following is most likely to dissolve in water?

    A. H_2
    B. CCl_4
    C. $(SiO_2)_n$
    D. CH_3OH

D. The best solutes for a solvent have intermolecular bonds of similar strength to the solvent. H_2O molecules are connected by fairly strong hydrogen bonds. H_2 and CCl_4 are molecules with intermolecular attractions due to weak London dispersion forces. $(SiO_2)_n$ is a covalent network solid and is essentially one large molecule with bonds that much stronger than hydrogen bonds. CH_3OH (methanol) is miscible with water because it contains hydrogen bonds between molecules.

39. Which of the following is <u>not</u> a colligative property?

    A. Viscosity lowering
    B. Freezing point lowering
    C. Boiling point elevation
    D. Vapor pressure lowering

A. Vapor pressure lowering, boiling point elevation, and freezing point lowering may all be visualized as a result of solute particles interfering with the interface between phases in a consistent way. This is not the case for viscosity.

40. $BaCl_2(aq) + Na_2SO_4(aq) \rightarrow BaSO_4(s) + 2NaCl(aq)$ is an example of a _____ reaction.

    A. acid-base
    B. precipitation
    C. redox
    D. nuclear

B. $BaSO_4$ falls out of the solution as a precipitate, but the charges on Ba^{2+} and SO_4^{2-} remain unchanged, so this is not a redox reaction. Neither $BaCl_2$ nor Na_2SO_4 are acids or bases, and the nuclei involved also remain unaltered

41. List the following aqueous solutions in order of increasing boiling point.

    I.   0.050 *m* $AlCl_3$
    II. 0.080 *m* $Ba(NO_3)_2$
    III. 0.090 *m* NaCl
    IV. 0.12 *m* ethylene glycol ($C_2H_6O_2$)

    A. I < II < III < IV
    B. I < III < IV < II
    C. IV < III < I < II
    D. IV < III < II < I

C. <u>Particles</u> in solution determine colligative properties. The first three materials are strong electrolyte salts, and $C_2H_6O_2$ is a non-electrolyte.

$AlCl_3(aq)$ is Al^{3+} +3 Cl^-. So $0.050\ \dfrac{\text{mol } AlCl_3}{\text{kg } H_2O} \times \dfrac{4 \text{ mol particles}}{\text{mol } AlCl_3} = 0.200\ m$ particles

$Ba(NO_3)_2(aq)$ is Ba^{2+} +2 NO_3^-. So $0.080\ \dfrac{\text{mol } Ba(NO_3)_2}{\text{kg } H_2O} \times \dfrac{3 \text{ mol particles}}{\text{mol } Ba(NO_3)_2} = 0.240\ m$ particles

$NaCl(aq)$ is Na^+ +Cl^-. So $0.090\ \dfrac{\text{mol } NaCl}{\text{kg } H_2O} \times \dfrac{2 \text{ mol particles}}{\text{mol } NaCl} = 0.180\ m$ particles

$C_2H_6O_2(aq)$ is not an electrolyte. So $0.12\ \dfrac{\text{mol } C_2H_6O_2}{\text{kg } H_2O} \times \dfrac{1 \text{ mol particles}}{\text{mol } C_2H_6O_2} = 0.12\ m$ particles

The greater the number of dissolved particles, the greater the boiling point elevation.

42. Osmotic pressure is the pressure required to prevent _____ flowing from low to high _____ concentration across a semipermeable membrane.

    A. solute, solute
    B. solute, solvent
    C. solvent, solute
    D. solvent, solvent

C. Osmotic pressure is the pressure required to prevent osmosis, which is the flow of solvent across the membrane from low to high solute concentration. This is also the direction from high to low solvent concentration.

43. A solution of NaCl in water is heated on a mountain in an open container until it boils at 100. °C. The air pressure on the mountain is 0.92 atm. According to Raoult's law, what mole fraction of Na^+ and Cl^- are present in the solution?

    A. 0.04 Na^+, 0.04 Cl^-
    B. 0.08 Na^+, 0.08 Cl^-
    C. 0.46 Na^+, 0.46 Cl^-
    D. 0.92 Na^+, 0.92 Cl^-

A. The vapor pressure of H_2O at 100. °C is exactly 1 atm. Boiling point decreases with external pressure, so the boiling point of pure H_2O at 0.9 atm will be less than 100. °C. Adding salt raises the boiling point at 0.92 atm to 100. °C by decreasing vapor pressure to 0.92 atm. According to Raoult's law:

$$P^{vapor}_{solution} = P^{vapor}_{pure\ solvent}\left(mole\ fraction\right)_{solvent} \Rightarrow \left(mole\ fraction\right)_{solvent} = \frac{P^{vapor}_{solution}}{P^{vapor}_{pure\ solvent}}.$$

$$\text{Therefore, } \left(mole\ fraction\right)_{H_2O} = \frac{0.92\ atm\ at\ 100.\ °C}{1.0\ atm\ at\ 100.\ °C} = 0.92\ \frac{mol\ H_2O}{mol\ total}.$$

The remaining 0.08 mole fraction of solute is evenly divided between the two ions:

$$\left(mole\ fraction\right)_{solute} = 1 - \left(mole\ fraction\right)_{H_2O} = 1 - 0.92 = 0.08\ \frac{mol\ solute\ particles}{mol\ total}$$

$$\left(mole\ fraction\right)_{Na^+} = 0.08\ \frac{mol\ solute\ particles}{mol\ total} \times \frac{1\ mol\ Na^+}{2\ mol\ solute\ particles} = 0.04\ \frac{mol\ Na^+}{mol\ total}$$

$$\left(mole\ fraction\right)_{Cl^-} = 0.08\ \frac{mol\ solute\ particles}{mol\ total} \times \frac{1\ mol\ Cl^-}{2\ mol\ solute\ particles} = 0.04\ \frac{mol\ Cl^-}{mol\ total}.$$

44. Write a balanced nuclear equation for the emission of an alpha particle by polonium-209.

A. $^{209}_{84}\text{Po} \rightarrow {}^{205}_{81}\text{Pb} + {}^{4}_{2}\text{He}$

B. $^{209}_{84}\text{Po} \rightarrow {}^{205}_{82}\text{Bi} + {}^{4}_{2}\text{He}$

C. $^{209}_{84}\text{Po} \rightarrow {}^{209}_{85}\text{At} + {}^{0}_{-1}\text{e}$

D. $^{209}_{84}\text{Po} \rightarrow {}^{205}_{82}\text{Pb} + {}^{4}_{2}\text{He}$

D. The periodic table before skill 1.1 shows that polonium has an atomic number of 84. The emission of an alpha particle, $^{4}_{2}\text{He}$ (eliminating choice C), will leave an atom with an atomic number of 82 and a mass number of 205 (eliminating choice A). The periodic table identifies this element as lead, $^{205}_{82}\text{Pb}$, not bismuth (eliminating choice B).

45. Write a balanced nuclear equation for the decay of calcium-45 to scandium-45.

A. $^{45}_{20}\text{Ca} \rightarrow {}^{41}_{18}\text{Sc} + {}^{4}_{2}\text{He}$

B. $^{45}_{20}\text{Ca} + {}^{0}_{1}\text{e} \rightarrow {}^{45}_{21}\text{Sc}$

C. $^{45}_{20}\text{Ca} \rightarrow {}^{45}_{21}\text{Sc} + {}^{0}_{-1}\text{e}$

D. $^{45}_{20}\text{Ca} + {}^{0}_{1}\text{p} \rightarrow {}^{45}_{21}\text{Sc}$

C. All four choices are balanced mathematically. "A" leaves scandium-41 as a decay product, not scandium-45. "B" and "D" require the addition of particles not normally present in the atom. If these reactions do occur, they are not decay reactions because they are not spontaneous. "C" involves the common decay mechanism of beta emission.

46. $^{3}_{1}\text{H}$ decays with a half-life of 12 years. 3.0 g of pure $^{3}_{1}\text{H}$ were placed in a sealed container 24 years ago. How many grams of $^{3}_{1}\text{H}$ remain?

A. 0.38 g
B. 0.75 g
C. 1.5 g
D. 3.0 g

B. Every 12 years, the amount remaining is cut in half. After 12 years, 1.5 g will remain. After another 12 years, 0.75 g will remain.

47. Oxygen-15 has a half-life of 122 seconds. What percentage of a sample of oxygen-15 has decayed after 300. seconds?

    A. 18.2%
    B. 21.3%
    C. 78.7%
    D. 81.8%

D. We may assume a convenient number (like 100.0 g) for a sample size. The amount remaining may be found from:

$$A_{remaining} = A_{initially} \left(\frac{1}{2}\right)^{\frac{t}{t_{halflife}}}$$

$$= 100.0 \text{ g } {}^{15}O \left(\frac{1}{2}\right)^{\frac{300. \text{ seconds}}{122 \text{ seconds}}} = 18.2 \text{ g } {}^{15}O$$

We are asked to determine the percentage that has decayed. This will be 100.0 g – 18.2 g = 81.8 g or 81.8% of the initial sample.

48. Which of the following isotopes is commonly used for medical imaging in the diagnose of diseases?

    A. cobalt-60
    B. technetium-99m
    C. tin-117m
    D. plutonium-238

B. The other three isotopes have limited medical applications (tin-117m has been used for the relief of bone cancer pain), but only Tc-99m is used routinely for imaging.

49. Carbon-14 dating would be useful in obtaining the age of which object?

    A. a 20th century Picasso painting
    B. a mummy from ancient Egypt
    C. a dinosaur fossil
    D. all of the above

B. C-14 is used in archeology because its half-life is 5730 years. Too little C-14 would have decayed from the painting and nearly all of the C-14 would have decayed from the fossil. In both cases, an estimate of age would be impossible with this isotope.

50. **Which of the following isotopes can create a chain reaction of nuclear fission?**

    A. uranium-235
    B. uranium-238
    C. plutonium-238
    D. all of the above

A. Uranium-235 and plutonium-239 are the two fissile isotopes used for nuclear power. ^{238}U is the most common uranium isotope. ^{238}Pu is used as a heat source for energy in space probes and some pacemakers.

51. **List the following scientists in chronological order from earliest to most recent with respect to their most significant contribution to atomic theory:**

    I. John Dalton
    II. Niels Bohr
    III. J. J. Thomson
    IV. Ernest Rutherford

    A. I, III, II, IV
    B. I, III, IV, II
    C. I, IV, III, II
    D. III, I, II, IV

B. Dalton founded modern atomic theory. J.J. Thomson determined that the electron is a subatomic particle but he placed it in the center of the atom. Rutherford discovered that electrons surround a small dense nucleus. Bohr determined that electrons may only occupy discrete positions around the nucleus.

52. Match the theory with the scientist who first proposed it:

   I. Electrons, atoms, and all objects with momentum also exist as waves.
   II. Electron density may be accurately described by a single mathematical equation.
   III. There is an inherent indeterminacy in the position and momentum of particles.
   IV. Radiant energy is transferred between particles in exact multiples of a discrete unit.

   A. I-de Broglie, II-Planck, III-Schrödinger, IV-Thomson
   B. I-Dalton, II-Bohr, III-Planck, IV-de Broglie
   C. I-Henry, II-Bohr, III-Heisenberg, IV-Schrödinger
   D. I-de Broglie, II-Schrödinger, III-Heisenberg, IV-Planck

D. Henry's law relates gas partial pressure to liquid solubility.

53. How many neutrons are in $_{27}^{60}\text{Co}$?

   A. 27
   B. 33
   C. 60
   D. 87

B. The number of neutrons is found by subtracting the atomic number (27) from the mass number (60).

54. The terrestrial composition of an element is: 50.7% as an isotope with an atomic mass of 78.9 u and 49.3% as an isotope with an atomic mass of 80.9 u. Both isotopes are stable. Calculate the atomic mass of the element.

   A. 79.0 u
   B. 79.8 u
   C. 79.9 u
   D. 80.8 u

C.

Atomic mass of element = (Fraction as 1st isotope) (Atomic mass of 1st isotope)

\+

(Fraction as 2nd isotope) (Atomic mass of 2nd isotope)

= (0.507) (78.9 u) + (0.493) (80.9 u) = 79.89 u = 79.9 u

40.0

39.9 = 79.9

55. Which of the following is a correct electron arrangement for oxygen?

A.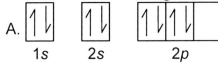

1s   2s   2p

B. $1s^2 1p^2 2s^2 2p^2$
C. 2, 2, 4
D. none of the above

D. Choice A violates Hund's rule. The two electrons on the far right should occupy the final two orbitals. B should be $1s^2 2s^2 2p^4$. There is no $1p$ subshell. C should be 2, 6. Number lists indicate electrons in shells.

56. Which of the following statements about radiant energy is not true?

    A. The energy change of an electron transition is directly proportional to the wavelength of the emitted or absorbed photon.
    B. The energy of an electron in a hydrogen atom depends only on the principle quantum number.
    C. The frequency of photons striking a metal determines whether the photoelectric effect will occur.
    D. The frequency of a wave of electromagnetic radiation is inversely proportional to its wavelength.

A. The energy change (ΔE) is <u>inversely</u> proportional to the wavelength (λ) of the photon according the equations:

$$\Delta E = \frac{hc}{\lambda}.$$

where h is Planck's constant and c is the speed of light.

Choice B is true for hydrogen. Atoms with more than one electron are more complex. The frequency of individual photons, not the number of photons determines whether the photoelectric effect occurs, so choice C is true. Choice D is true. The proportionality constant is the speed of light according to the equation:

$$v = \frac{c}{\lambda}.$$

57. Match the orbital diagram for the ground state of carbon with the rule/principle it violates:

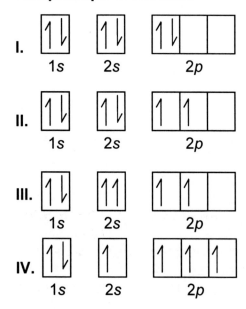

I. 1s 2s 2p

II. 1s 2s 2p

III. 1s 2s 2p

IV. 1s 2s 2p

   A. I-Pauli exclusion, II-Aufbau, III-no violation, IV-Hund's
   B. I-Aufbau, II-Pauli exclusion, III-no violation, IV-Hund's
   C. I-Hund's, II-no violation, III-Pauli exclusion, IV-Aufbau
   D. I-Hund's, II-no violation, III-Aufbau, IV-Pauli exclusion

C. Diagram I violates Hund's rule because a second electron is added to a degenerate orbital before all orbitals in the subshell have one electron. Diagram III violates the Pauli exclusion principle because both electrons in the 2s orbital have the same spin. They would have the same 4 quantum numbers. Diagram IV violates the Aufbau principle because an electron occupies the higher energy 2p orbital before 2s orbital has been filled; this configuration is not at the ground state.

58. Select the list of atoms that are arranged in order of increasing size.

   A. Mg, Na, Si, Cl
   B. Si, Cl, Mg, Na
   C. Cl, Si, Mg, Na
   D. Na, Mg, Si, Cl

C. These atoms are all in the same row of the periodic table. Size increases further to the left for atoms in the same row.

59. Based on trends in the periodic table, which of the following properties would you expect to be greater for Rb than for K?

I. Density
II. Melting point
III. Ionization energy
IV. Oxidation number in a compound with chlorine

A. I only
B. I, II, and III
C. II and III
D. I, II, III, and IV

A. Rb is underneath K in the alkali metal column (group 1) of the periodic table. There is a general trend for density to increase lower on the table for elements in the same row, so we select choice I. Rb and K experience metallic bonds for intermolecular forces and the strength of metallic bonds decreases for larger atoms further down the periodic table resulting in a lower melting point for Rb, so we do not choose II. Ionization energy decreases for larger atoms further down the periodic table, so we do not choose III. Both Rb and K would be expected to have a charge of +1 and therefore an oxidation number of +1 in a compound with chlorine, so we do not choose IV.

60. Which oxide forms the strongest acid in water?

A. Al_2O_3
B. Cl_2O_7
C. As_2O_5
D. CO_2

B. The strength of acids formed from oxides increases with electronegativity and with oxidation state. We know Cl has a greater electronegativity than Al, As, and C because it is closer to the top right of the periodic table. The oxidation numbers of our choices are +3 for Al, +7 for Cl, +5 for As, and +4 for C. Both its electronegativity and its oxidation state indicate Cl_2O_7 will form the strongest acid.

61. Rank the following bonds from least to most polar:

C-H, C-Cl, H-H, C-F

    A. C-H < H-H < C-F < C-Cl
    B. H-H < C-H < C-F < C-Cl
    C. C-F < C-Cl < C-H < H-H
    D. H-H < C-H < C-Cl < C-F

D. Bonds between atoms of the same element are completely non-polar, so H-H is the least polar bond in the list, eliminating choices A and C. The C-H bond is considered to be non-polar even though the electrons of the bond are slightly unequally shared. C-Cl and C-F are both polar covalent bonds, but C-F is more strongly polar because F has a greater electronegativity.

62. At room temperature, $CaBr_2$ is expected to be:

    A. a ductile solid
    B. a brittle solid
    C. a soft solid
    D. a gas

B. Ca is a metal because it is on the left of the periodic table, and Br is a non-metal because it is on the right. The compound they form together will be an ionic salt, and ionic salts are brittle solids (choice B) at room temperature. NaCl is another example.

63. Which of the following is a proper Lewis dot structure of CHClO?

C. C has 4 valence shell electrons, H has 1, Cl has 7, and O has 6. The molecule has a total of 18 valence shell electrons. This eliminates choice B which has 24. Choice B is also incorrect because has an octet around a hydrogen atom instead of 2 electrons and because there are only six electrons surrounding the central carbon. A single bond connecting all atoms would give choice A. This is incorrect because there are only 6 electrons surrounding the central carbon. A double bond between C and O gives the correct answer, C. A double bond between C and O and also between C and Cl would give choice D. This is incorrect because there are 10 electrons surrounding the central carbon.

64. In C_2H_2, each carbon atom contains the following valence orbitals:

A. *p* only
B. *p* and *sp* hybrids
C. *p* and sp^2 hybrids
D. sp^3 hybrids only

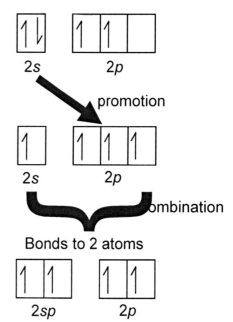

B. An isolated C has the valence electron configuration $2s^2 2p^2$. Before bonding, one *s* electron is promoted to an empty *p* orbital. In C_2H_2, each C atom bonds to 2 other atoms. Bonding to two other atoms is achieved by combination into two *p* orbitals and two *sp* hybrids.

65. Which statement about molecular structures is false?

A.   is a conjugated molecule.

B. A bonding σ orbital connects two atoms by the straight line between them.
C. A bonding π orbital connects two atoms in a separate region from the straight line between them.
D. The anion with resonance forms will always exist in one form or the other.

D. A conjugated molecule is a molecule with double bonds on adjacent atoms such as the molecule shown in A. Choice B and C give the definition of sigma and pi molecular orbitals. D is false because a resonance form is one of multiple equivalent Lewis structures, but these structures do not describe the actual state of the molecule. The anion will exist in a state between the two forms.

66. What is the shape of the PH₃ molecule? Use the VSEPR model.

    A. Trigonal pyramidal
    B. Trigonal bipyramidal
    C. Trigonal planar
    D. Tetrahedral

A. The Lewis structure for PH₃ is given to the right. This structure contains 4 electron pairs around the central atom, so the geometral arrangement is tetrahedral. However, the shape of a molecule is given by its atom locations, and there are only three atoms so choice D is not correct. Four electrons pairs with one unshared pair (3 bonds and one lone pair) give a trigonal pyramidal shape as shown to the left.

67. What is the chemical composition of magnesium nitrate?

    A. 11.1% Mg, 22.2% N, 66.7% O
    B. 16.4% Mg, 18.9% N, 64.7% O
    C. 20.9% Mg, 24.1% N, 55.0% O
    D. 28.2% Mg, 16.2% N, 55.7% O

B. First find the formula for magnesium nitrate. Mg is an alkali earth metal (**Skill 3.1**) and will always have a 2+ charge. The nitrate ion is NO_3^- (**Skill 5.2**). Two nitrate ions are required for each Mg^{2+} ion. Therefore the formula is $Mg(NO_3)_2$

    Skill 5.1 describes determination chemical composition.
    1) Determine the number of atoms for elements in $Mg(NO_3)_2$: 1 Mg, 2 N, 6 O.
    2) Multiply by the molecular weight of the elements to determine the grams of each in one mole of the formula.

$$\frac{1 \text{ mol Mg}}{\text{mol Mg(NO}_3)_2} \times \frac{24.3 \text{ g Mg}}{\text{mol Mg}} = 24.3 \text{ g Mg/mol Mg(NO}_3)_2$$

$$2(14.0) = 28.0 \text{ g N/mol Mg(NO}_3)_2$$

$$6(16.0) = 96.0 \text{ g O/mol Mg(NO}_3)_2$$

    3) Determine formula mass $148.3 \text{ g Mg(NO}_3)_2/\text{mol Mg(NO}_3)_2$
    4) Divide to determine % composition

$$\%Mg = \frac{24.3 \text{ g Mg/mol Mg(NO}_3)_2}{148.3 \text{ g Mg(NO}_3)_2/\text{mol Mg(NO}_3)_2} = 0.164 \text{ g Mg/g Mg(NO}_3)_2 \times 100\% = 16.4\%$$

$$\%N = \frac{28.0}{148.3} \times 100\% = 18.9\% \qquad \%O = \frac{96.0}{148.3} \times 100\% = 64.7\%$$

Answer A is the fractional representation of the presence of each atom in the formula. Composition is based on mass percentage. Answer C is the chemical composition of $Mg(NO_2)_2$, magnesium nitrite. Answer D is the chemical composition of "$MgNO_3$", a formula that results from not balancing charges.

68. The IUPAC name for Cu_2SO_3 is:

A. Dicopper sulfur trioxide
B. Copper (II) sulfate
C. Copper (I) sulfite
D. Copper (II) sulfite

C. Cu_2SO_3 is an ionic compound containing copper cation and the SO_3 anion. Choice A is wrong because it uses the naming system for molecular compounds. The SO_3 anion is 2– and is named sulfite. It takes two copper cations in to neutralize this charge, so Cu has a charge of 1+, and the name is copper (I) sulfite.

69. Which name or formula is not represented properly?

A. Cl_4S
B. $KClO_3$
C. Calcium dihydrogen phosphate
D. Sulfurous acid

A A is the answer because the atoms in the sulfur tetrachloride molecule are placed in order of increasing electronegativity. This formla is properly written as SCl_4. B is a proper formula for potassium chlorate. Calcium dihydrogen phosphate is $Ca(H_2PO_4)_2$. It derives its name from the Ca^{2+} cation in combination with an anion composed of a phosphate anion (PO_4^{3-}) that is doubly protonated to give a $H_2PO_4^-$ ion. Sulfurous acid is $H_2SO_3(aq)$.

70. Household "chlorine bleach" is sodium hypochlorite. Which of the following best represent the production of sodium hypochlorite, sodium chloride, and water by bubbling chlorine gas through aqueous sodium hydroxide?

A. $4Cl(g) + 4NaOH(aq) \rightarrow NaClO_2(aq) + 3NaCl(aq) + 2H_2O(l)$
B. $2Cl_2(g) + 4NaOH(aq) \rightarrow NaClO_2(aq) + 3NaCl(aq) + 2H_2O(l)$
C. $2Cl(g) + 2NaOH(aq) \rightarrow NaClO(aq) + NaCl(aq) + H_2O(l)$
D. $Cl_2(g) + 2NaOH(aq) \rightarrow NaClO(aq) + NaCl(aq) + H_2O(l)$

D. Chlorine gas is a diatomic molecule, eliminating choices A and C. The hypochlorite ion is ClO^- eliminating choices A and B. All of the equations are properly balanced.

71. Balance the equation for the neutralization reaction between phosphoric acid and calcium hydroxide by filling in the blank stoichiometric coefficients.

$$\_\_H_3PO_4 + \_\_Ca(OH)_2 \rightarrow \_\_Ca_3(PO_4)_2 + \_\_H_2O$$

A. 4, 3, 1, 4
B. 2, 3, 1, 8
C. 2, 3, 1, 6
D. 2, 1, 1, 2

C. We are given the unbalanced equation (**step 1**).

Next we determine the number of atoms on each side (**step 2**). For reactants (left of the arrow): 5H, 1P, 6O, and 1Ca. For products: 2H, 2P, 9O, and 3Ca.

We assume that the molecule with the most atoms—i.e. $Ca_3(PO_4)_2$—has a coefficient of one, and find the other coefficients required to have the same number of atoms on each side of the equation (**step 3**). Assuming $Ca_3(PO_4)_2$ has a coefficient of one means that there will be 3 Ca and 2 P on the right because H_2O has no Ca or P. A balanced equation would also have 3 Ca and 2 P on the left. This is achieved with a coefficient of 2 for H_3PO_4 and 3 for $Ca(OH)_2$. Now we have:

$$2H_3PO_4 + 3Ca(OH)_2 \rightarrow Ca_3(PO_4)_2 + ?H_2O$$

The coefficient for H_2O is found by a balance on H or on O. Whichever one is chosen, the other atom should be checked to confirm that a balance actually occurs. For H, there are 6 H from $2H_3PO_4$ and 6 from $3Ca(OH)_2$ for a total of 12 H on the left. There must be 12 H on the right for balance. None are accounted for by $Ca_3(PO_4)_2$, so all 12 H must occur on H_2O. It has a coefficient of 6.

$$2H_3PO_4 + 3Ca(OH)_2 \rightarrow Ca_3(PO_4)_2 + 6H_2O$$

This is choice C, but if time is available, it is best to check that the remaining atom is balanced. There are 8 O from $2H_3PO_4$ and 6 from $3Ca(OH)_2$ for a total of 14 on the left, and 8 O from $Ca_3(PO_4)_2$ and 6 from $6H_2O$ for a total of 14 on the right. The equation is balanced.

Mulitplication by a whole number (**step 4**) is not required because the stoichiometric coefficients from step 3 already are whole numbers.

An alternative method would be to try the coefficients given for answer A, answer B, etc. until we recognize a properly balanced equation.

72. Write an equation showing the reaction between calcium nitrate and lithium sulfate in aqueous solution. Include all products.

A. $CaNO_3(aq) + Li_2SO_4(aq) \rightarrow CaSO_4(s) + Li_2NO_3(aq)$

B. $Ca(NO_3)_2(aq) + Li_2SO_4(aq) \rightarrow CaSO_4(s) + 2LiNO_3(aq)$

C. $Ca(NO_3)_2(aq) + Li_2SO_4(aq) \rightarrow 2LiNO_3(s) + CaSO_4(aq)$

D. $Ca(NO_3)_2(aq) + Li_2SO_4(aq) + 2H_2O(l) \rightarrow 2LiNO_3(aq) + Ca(OH)_2(aq) + H_2SO_4(aq)$

B. When two ionic compounds are in solution, a precipitation reaction should be considered. We can determine from their names that the two reactants are the ionic compounds $Ca(NO_3)_2$ and Li_2SO_4. The compounds are present in aqueous solution as their four component ions Ca^{2+}, NO_3^-, Li^+, and SO_4^{2-}. Solubility rules indicate that nitrates are always soluble but sulfate will form a solid precipitate with Ca^{2+} forming $CaSO_4(s)$. Choice A results from assuming that the nitrate anion has a 2– charge instead of its 1– charge. B is correct. C assumes lithium nitrate is the precipitate. Choice D includes the reverse of a neutralization reaction. Water would not decompose due to the addition of these salts.

73. Find the mass of CO_2 produced by the combustion of 15 kg of isopropyl alcohol in the reaction:

$$2C_3H_7OH + 9O_2 \rightarrow 6CO_2 + 8H_2O$$

A. 33 kg
B. 44 kg
C. 50 kg
D. 60 kg

A Remember "grams to moles to moles to grams." Step 1 converts mass to moles for the known value. In this case, kg and kmol are used. Step 2 relates moles of the known value to moles of the unknown value by their stoichiometry coefficients. Step 3 converts moles off the unknown value to a mass.

$$15 \times 10^3 \text{ g } C_4H_8O \times \underset{\text{step 1}}{\frac{1 \text{ mol } C_4H_8O}{60 \text{ g } C_4H_8O}} \times \underset{\text{step 2}}{\frac{6 \text{ mol } CO_2}{2 \text{ mol } C_4H_8O}} \times \underset{\text{step 3}}{\frac{44 \text{ g } CO_2}{1 \text{ mol } CO_2}} = 33 \times 10^3 \text{ g } CO_2$$

$$= 33 \text{ kg } CO_2$$

74. What is the density of nitrogen gas at STP? Assume an ideal gas and a value of 0.08206 L-atm/(mol-K) for the gas constant.

    A. 0.62 g/L
    B. 1.14 g/L
    C. 1.25 g/L
    D. 2.03 g/L

C The molecular mass M of N_2 is 28.0 g/mol.

$$d = \frac{nM}{V} = \frac{PM}{RT} = \frac{(1\,\text{atm})\left(28.0\,\frac{g}{mol}\right)}{\left(0.08206\,\frac{L\cdot atm}{mol\cdot K}\right)(273.15\,\text{K})} = 1.25\frac{g}{L}$$

Choice A results from forgetting that nitrogen is a diatomic gas. Choice B results from using a value of 25 °C for standard temperature. This is the thermodynamic standard temperature, but not STP.

A faster method is to recall that one mole of an ideal gas at STP occupies 22.4 L.

$$d\,(\text{in }\frac{g}{L}) = \frac{M\,(\text{in }\frac{g}{mol})}{22.4\,\frac{L}{mol}} = \frac{28.0\,\frac{g}{mol}}{22.4\,\frac{L}{mol}} = 1.25\frac{g}{L}.$$

75. Find the volume of methane that will produce 12 m³ of hydrogen in the reaction: $CH_4(g) + H_2O(g) \rightarrow CO(g) + 3H_2(g)$. Assume temperature and pressure remain constant.

    A. 4.0 m³
    B. 32 m³
    C. 36 m³
    D. 64 m³

A Stoichiometric coefficients may be used directly for ideal gas volumes at constant T and P because of Avogadro's Law.

$$12\,\text{m}^3\,H_2 \times \frac{1\,\text{m}^3\,CH_4}{3\,\text{m}^3\,H_2} = 4.0\,\text{m}^3\,CH_4$$

12 g of H_2 will be produced from 32 g of CH_4 (incorrect choice B).

76. A 100. L vessel of pure O_2 at 500. kPa and 20. °C is used for the combustion of butane:

$$2C_4H_{10} + 13O_2 \rightarrow 8CO_2 + 10H_2O.$$

Find the mass of butane to consume all the O_2 in the vessel. Assume O_2 is an ideal gas and use a value of $R = 8.314$ J/(mol·K).

A. 183 g
B. 467 g
C. 1.83 kg
D. 7.75 kg

A We are given a volume and asked for a mass. The steps will be "volume to moles to moles to mass."

"Volume to moles..." requires the ideal gas law, but first several units must be altered.

    Units of joules are identical to $m^3 \cdot Pa$.
    500 kPa is 500×10^3 Pa.
    100 L is 0.100 m^3.
    20 °C is 293.15 K.

$J = m^3 \, Pa$

$PV = nRT$ is rearranged to give:

$$n = \frac{PV}{RT} = \frac{(500 \times 10^3 \ Pa)(0.100 \ m^3 \ O_2)}{\left(8.314 \ \dfrac{m^3 \cdot Pa}{mol \cdot K}\right)(293.15 \ K)} = 20.51 \ mol \ O_2$$

"...to moles to mass" utilizes stoichiometry. The molecular weight of butane is 58.1 u.

$$20.51 \ mol \ O_2 \times \frac{2 \ mol \ C_4H_{10}}{13 \ mol \ O_2} \times \frac{58.1 \ g \ C_4H_{10}}{1 \ mol \ C_4H_{10}} = 183 \ g \ C_4H_{10}$$

77. Consider the reaction between iron and hydrogen chloride gas:

$$Fe(s) + 2HCl(g) \rightarrow FeCl_2(s) + H_2(g) \ .$$

7 moles of iron and 10 moles of HCl react until the limiting reagent is consumed. Which statements are true?

I. HCl is the excess reagent
II. HCl is the limiting reagent
III. 7 moles of H_2 are produced
IV. 2 moles of the excess reagent remain

A. I and III
B. I and IV
C. II and III
D. II and IV

D The limiting reagent is found by dividing the number of moles of each reactant by its stoichiometric coefficient. The lowest result is the limiting reagent.

$$7 \text{ mol Fe} \times \frac{1 \text{ mol reaction}}{1 \text{ mol Fe}} = 7 \text{ mol reaction if Fe is limiting}$$

$$10 \text{ mol HCl} \times \frac{1 \text{ mol reaction}}{2 \text{ mol HCl}} = 5 \text{ mol reaction if HCl is limiting.}$$

Therefore, HCl is the limiting reagent (II is true) and Fe is the excess reagent.

5 moles of the reaction take place, so 5 moles of H_2 are produced, and of the 7 moles of Fe supplied, 5 are consumed, leaving 2 moles of the excess reagent (IV is true).

78. 32.0 g of hydrogen and 32.0 grams of oxygen react to form water until the limiting reagent is consumed. What is present in the vessel after the reaction is complete?

A. 16.0 g O_2 and 48.0 g H_2O
B. 24.0 g H_2 and 40.0 g H_2O
C. 28.0 g H_2 and 36.0 g H_2O
D. 28.0 g H_2 and 34.0 g H_2O

C First the equation must be constructed:

$$2H_2 + O_2 \rightarrow 2H_2O$$

A fast and intuitive solution would be to recognize that:
1) One mole of H_2 is about 2.0 g, so about 16 moles of H_2 are present.
2) One mole of O_2 is 32.0 g, so one mole of is O_2 is present
3) Imagine the 16 moles of H_2 reacting with one mole of O_2. 2 moles of H_2 will be consumed before the one mole of O_2 is gone. O_2 is limiting. (Eliminate choice A.)
4) 16 moles less 2 leaves 14 moles of H_2 or about 28 g. (Eliminate choice B.)
5) The reaction began with 64.0 g total. Conservation of mass for chemical reactions forces the total final mass to be 64.0 g also. (Eliminate choice D.)

A more standard solution is presented next. First, mass is converted to moles:

$$32.0 \text{ g } H_2 \times \frac{1 \text{ mol } H_2}{2.016 \text{ g } H_2} = 15.87 \text{ mol } H_2 \quad \text{and} \quad 32.0 \text{ g } O_2 \times \frac{1 \text{ mol } O_2}{32.00 \text{ g } O_2} = 1.000 \text{ mol } O_2$$

Dividing by stoichiometric coefficients give

$$15.87 \text{ mol } H_2 \times \frac{1 \text{ mol reaction}}{2 \text{ mol } H_2} = 7.935 \text{ mol reaction if } H_2 \text{ is limiting}$$

$$1.000 \text{ mol } O_2 \times \frac{1 \text{ mol reaction}}{1 \text{ mol } O_2} = 1.000 \text{ mol reaction if } O_2 \text{ is limiting.}$$

O_2 is the limiting reagent, so no O_2 will remain in the vessel.

$$1.000 \text{ mol } O_2 \text{ consumed} \times \frac{2 \text{ mol } H_2O \text{ produced}}{1 \text{ mol } O_2} \times \frac{18.016 \text{ g } H_2O}{1 \text{ mol } H_2O} = 36.0 \text{ g } H_2O \text{ produced}$$

$$1.000 \text{ mol } O_2 \text{ consumed} \times \frac{2 \text{ mol } H_2 \text{ consumed}}{1 \text{ mol } O_2} \times \frac{2.016 \text{ g } H_2}{1 \text{ mol } H_2} = 4.03 \text{ g } H_2 \text{ consumed}$$

Remaining H_2 is found from:

$$32.0 \text{ g } H_2 \text{ initially} - 4.03 \text{ g } H_2 \text{ consumed} = 28.0 \text{ g } H_2 \text{ remain.}$$

79. Three experiments were performed at the same initial temperature and pressure to determine the rate of the reaction

$$2ClO_2(g) + F_2(g) \rightarrow 2ClO_2F(g).$$

Results are shown in the table below. Concentrations are given in millimoles per liter (mM).

Exp.	Initial $[ClO_2]$ (mM)	Initial $[F_2]$ (mM)	Initial rate of $[ClO_2F]$ increase (mM/sec)
1	5.0	5.0	0.63
2	5.0	20	2.5
3	10	10	2.5

What is the rate law for this reaction?

A. $Rate = k \left[F_2 \right]$

B. $Rate = k \left[ClO_2 \right] \left[F_2 \right]$

C. $Rate = k \left[ClO_2 \right]^2 \left[F_2 \right]$

D. $Rate = k \left[ClO_2 \right] \left[F_2 \right]^2$

B A four-fold increase in $[F_2]$ at constant $[ClO_2]$ between experiment one and two caused a four-fold increase in rate. Rate is therefore proportional to $[F_2]$ at constant $[ClO_2]$, eliminating choice D (Choice D predicts rate to increase by a factor of 16).

Between experiment 1 and 3, $[F_2]$ and $[ClO_2]$ both double in value. Once again, there is a four-fold increase in rate. If rate were only dependent on $[F_2]$ (choice A), there would be a two-fold increase. The correct answer, B, attributes a two-fold increase in rate to the doubling of $[F_2]$ and a two-fold increase to the doubling of $[ClO_2]$, resulting in a net four-fold increase. Choice C predicts a rate increase by a factor of 8.

If this were an elementary reaction describing a collision event between three molecules, choice C would be expected, but stoichiometry cannot be used to predict a rate law.

80. The reaction
$$(CH_3)_3CBr(aq) + OH^-(aq) \rightarrow (CH_3)_3COH(aq) + Br^-(aq)$$
occurs in three elementary steps:
$$(CH_3)_3CBr \rightarrow (CH_3)_3C^+ + Br^- \text{ is slow}$$
$$(CH_3)_3C^+ + H_2O \rightarrow (CH_3)_3COH_2^+ \text{ is fast}$$
$$(CH_3)_3COH_2^+ + OH^- \rightarrow (CH_3)_3COH + H_2O \text{ is fast}$$
What is the rate law for this reaction?

A. $\text{Rate} = k\left[(CH_3)_3CBr\right]$

B. $\text{Rate} = k\left[OH^-\right]$

C. $\text{Rate} = k\left[(CH_3)_3CBr\right]\left[OH^-\right]$

D. $\text{Rate} = k\left[(CH_3)_3CBr\right]^2$

A The first step will be rate-limiting. It will determine the rate for the entire reaction because it is slower than the other steps. This step is a unimolecular process with the rate given by answer A. Choice C would be correct if the reaction as a whole were one elementary step instead of three, but the stoichiometry of a reaction composed of multiple elementary steps cannot be used to predict a rate law.

81. Which statement about equilibrium is <u>not</u> true?

A. Equilibrium shifts to minimize the impact of changes.
B. Forward and reverse reactions have equal rates at equilibrium.
C. A closed container of air and water is at a vapor-liquid equilibrium if the humidity is constant.
D. The equilibrium between solid and dissolved forms is maintained when salt is added to an unsaturated solution.

D Choice A is a restatement of Le Chatelier's Principle. B is a definition of equilibrium. A constant humidity (Choice C) occurs if the rate of vaporization and condensation are equal, indicating equilibrium. No solid is present in an **un**saturated solution. If solid is added, all of it dissolves indicating a lack of equilibrium. D would be true for a saturated soution.

82. Which statements about reaction rates are true?

I. A catalyst will shift an equilibrium to favor product formation.
II. Catalysts increase the rate of forward and reverse reactions.
III. A greater temperature increases the chance that a molecular collision will overcome a reaction's activation energy.
IV. A catalytic converter contains a homogeneous catalyst.

A. I and II
B. II and III
C. II, III and IV
D. I, III, and IV

B Catalysts provide an alternate mechanism in both directions, but do not alter equilibrium (I is false, II is true). The kinetic energy of molecules increases with temperature, so the energy of their collisions increases also (III is true). Catalytic converters contain a heterogeneous catalyst (IV is false).

83. Write the equilibrium expression K_{eq} for the reaction
$$CO_2(g) + H_2(g) \rightleftharpoons CO(g) + H_2O(l)$$

A. $\dfrac{[CO][H_2O]}{[CO_2][H_2]^2}$

B. $\dfrac{[CO_2][H_2]}{[CO][H_2O]}$

C. $\dfrac{[CO][H_2O]}{[CO_2][H_2]}$

D. $\dfrac{[CO]}{[CO_2][H_2]}$

D Product concentrations are multiplied together in the numerator and reactant concentrations in the denominator, eliminating choice B. The stoichiometric coefficient of H_2 is one, eliminating choice A. For heterogeneous reactions, concentrations of pure liquids or solids are absent from the expression because they are constant, eliminating choice C. D is correct.

84. What could cause this change in the energy diagram of a reaction?

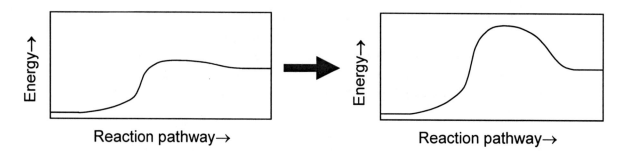

A. Adding catalyst to an endothermic reaction
B. Removing catalyst from an endothermic reaction
C. Adding catalyst to an exothermic reaction
D. Removing catalyst from an exothermic reaction

B The products at the end of the reaction pathway are at a greater energy than the reactants, so the reaction is endothermic (narrowing down the answer to A or B). The maximum height on the diagram corresponds to activation energy. An increase in activation energy could be caused by removing a heterogeneous catalyst.

85. BaSO$_4$ (K_{sp} = 1X10^{-10}) is added to pure H$_2$O. How much is dissolved in 1 L of saturated solution?

A. 2 mg
B. 10 µg
C. 2 µg
D. 100 pg

A $BaSO_4(s) \rightleftharpoons Ba^{2+}(aq) + SO_4^{2-}(aq)$, therefore: $K_{sp} = \left[Ba^{2+}\right]\left[SO_4^{2-}\right]$.

In a saturated solution: $\left[Ba^{2+}\right] = \left[SO_4^{2-}\right] = \sqrt{1 \times 10^{-10}} = 1 \times 10^{-5}$ M.

The mass in one liter is found from the molarity:

$$1 \times 10^{-5} \frac{\text{mol } Ba^{2+} \text{ or } SO_4^{2-}}{L} \times \frac{1 \text{ mol dissolved } BaSO_4}{1 \text{ mol } Ba^{2+} \text{ or } SO_4^{2-}} \times \frac{\overset{223}{(137+32+4 \times 16)}\text{g } BaSO_4}{1 \text{ mol } BaSO_4}$$

$$= 0.002 \frac{g}{L} BaSO_4 \times 1 \text{ L solution} \times \frac{1000 \text{ mg}}{g} = 2 \text{ mg } BaSO_4$$

86. The exothermic reaction $2NO(g) + Br_2(g) \rightleftharpoons 2NOBr(g)$ is at equilibrium. According to LeChatelier's principle:

    A. Adding Br_2 will increase [NO].
    B. An increase in container volume (with T constant) will increase [NOBr].
    C. An increase in pressure (with T constant) will increase [NOBr].
    D. An increase in temperature (with P constant) will increase [NOBr].

C LeChatelier's principle predicts that equilibrium will shift to partially offset any change. Adding Br_2 will be partially offset by reducing [Br_2] and [NO] via a shift to the right (not choice A). For the remaining possibilities, we may write the reaction as: 3 moles $\rightleftharpoons$ 2 moles + heat. An increase in container volume will decrease pressure. This change will be partially offset by increasing the number of moles present, shifting the reaction to the left (not choice B). An increase in pressure will be offset by a decrease the number of moles present, shifting the reaction to the right (choice C, correct). Raising the temperature by adding heat will shift the reaction to the left (not choice D).

87. At a certain temperature, T, the equilibrium constant for the reaction $2NO(g) \rightleftharpoons N_2(g) + O_2(g)$ is $K_{eq} = 2 \times 10^3$. If a 1.0 L container at this temperature contains 90 mM N_2, 20 mM O_2, and 5 mM NO, what will occur?

    A. The reaction will make more N_2 and O_2.
    B. The reaction is at equilibrium.
    C. The reaction will make more NO.
    D. The temperature, T, is required to solve this problem.

A Calculate the reaction quotient at the actual conditions:

$$Q = \frac{\left[N_2\right]\left[O_2\right]}{\left[NO\right]^2} = \frac{(0.090 \text{ M})(0.020 \text{ M})}{(0.005 \text{ M})^2} = 72$$

This value is less than K_{eq}: $72 < 2 \times 10^3$, therefore $Q < K_{eq}$. To achieve equilibrium, the numerator of Q must be larger relative to the denominator. This occurs when products turn into reactants. Therefore NO will react to make more N_2 and O_2.

88. Which statement about acids and bases is <u>not</u> true?

    A. All strong acids ionize in water.
    B. All Lewis acids accept an electron pair.
    C. All Brønsted bases use OH^- as a proton acceptor.
    D. All Arrhenius acids form H^+ ions in water.

C   Choice A is the definition of a strong acid, choice B is the definition of a Lewis acid, and choice D is the definition of an Arrhenius acid. By definition, all Arrhenius bases form OH^- ions in water, and all Brønsted bases are proton acceptors. But not all Brønsted bases use OH^- as a proton acceptor. NH_3 is a Brønsted base for example.

89. Which of the following are listed from weakest to strongest acid?

    A. H_2SO_3, H_2SeO_3, H_2TeO_3
    B. $HBrO$, $HBrO_2$, $HBrO_3$, $HBrO_4$
    C. HI, HBr, HCl, HF
    D. H_3PO_4, $H_2PO_4^-$, HPO_4^{2-}

B   The electronegativity of the central atom decreases from S to Se to Te as period number increases in the same periodic table group. The acidity of the oxide also decreases. Choice B is correct because acid strength increases with the oxidation state of the central atom. C is wrong because HI, HBr, and HCl are all strong acids but HF is a weak acid. D is wrong because acid strength is greater for polyprotic acids.

(A) acid strength↑ w/ oxidation state of central atom

(B) acid strength↑ (I guess!) w/ electroneg? → but what abt F⁻

90. NH$_4$F is dissolved in water. Which of the following are conjugate acid/base pairs present in the solution?

   I.   NH$_4^+$/NH$_4$OH
   II. HF/F$^-$
   III. H$_3$O$^+$/H$_2$O
   IV. H$_2$O/OH$^-$

   A. I, II, and III
   B. I, III, and IV
   C. II and IV
   D. II, III, and IV

D NH$_4$F is soluble in water and completely dissociates to NH$_4^+$ and F$^-$. F$^-$ is a weak base with HF as its conjugate acid (**II**). NH$_4^+$ is a weak acid with NH$_3$ as its conjugate base. A conjugate acid/base pair must have the form HX/X (where X is one lower charge than HX). NH$_4^+$/NH$_4$OH (**I**) is not a conjugate acid/base pair, eliminating choice A and B. H$_3$O$^+$/H$_2$O and H$_2$O/OH$^-$ (**III** and **IV**) are always present in water and in all aqueous solutions as conjugate acid/base pairs. All of the following equilibrium reactions occur in NH$_4$F(aq):

$$NH_4^+(aq) + OH^-(aq) \rightleftharpoons NH_3(aq) + H_2O(l)$$
$$F^-(aq) + H_3O^+(aq) \rightleftharpoons HF(aq) + H_2O(l)$$
$$2H_2O(l) \rightleftharpoons H_3O^+(aq) + OH^-(aq)$$

91. What are the pH and the pOH of 0.010 M HNO$_3$(aq)?

   A. pH = 1.0, pOH = 9.0
   B. pH = 2.0, pOH = 12.0
   C. pH = 2.0, pOH = 8.0
   D. pH = 8.0, pOH = 6.0

B HNO$_3$ is a strong acid, so it completely dissociates:

$$\left[H^+\right] = 0.010 \text{ M} = 1.0 \times 10^{-2} \text{ M.}$$
$$pH = -\log_{10}\left[H^+\right] = -\log_{10}\left(1.0 \times 10^{-2}\right) = 2.0 \text{ (choices B or C).}$$
$$\text{From pH} + pOH = 14: \quad pOH = 12.0 \text{ (choice B).}$$

92. What is the pH of a buffer made of 0.128 M sodium formate (HCOONa) and 0.072 M formic acid (HCOOH)? The pK_a of formic acid is 3.75.

    A. 2.0
    B. 3.0
    C. 4.0
    D. 5.0

C From the pK_a, we may find the K_a of formic acid:
$$K_a = 10^{-pK_a} = 10^{-3.75} = 1.78 \times 10^{-4}$$
This is the equilibrium constant:
$$K_a = \frac{\left[H^+\right]\left[HCOO^-\right]}{\left[HCOOH\right]} = 1.78 \times 10^{-4} \text{ for the dissociation:}$$
$$HCOOH \rightleftharpoons H^+ + HCOO^-.$$
The pH is found by solving for the H^+ concentration:
$$\left[H^+\right] = K_a \frac{\left[HCOOH\right]}{\left[HCOO^-\right]} = (1.78 \times 10^{-4})\frac{0.072}{0.128} = 1.0 \times 10^{-4} \text{ M}$$
$$pH = -\log_{10}\left[H^+\right] = -\log_{10}\left(1.0 \times 10^{-4}\right) = 4.0 \text{ (choice C)}$$

93. A sample of 50.0 ml KOH is titrated with 0.100 M $HClO_4$. The initial buret reading is 1.6 ml and the reading at the endpoint is 22.4 ml. What is [KOH]?

    A. 0.0416 M
    B. 0.0481 M
    C. 0.0832 M
    D. 0.0962 M

A $HClO_4$ and KOH are both strong electrolytes. If you are good at memorizing formulas, solve the problem this way:
$$C_{unknown} = \frac{C_{known}\left(V_{final} - V_{initial}\right)}{V_{unknown}} = \frac{0.100 \text{ M }(22.4 \text{ ml} - 1.6 \text{ ml})}{50.0 \text{ ml}} = 0.0416 \text{ M}.$$
The problem may also be solved by finding the moles of known substance:
$$0.100 \frac{mol}{L} \times \frac{1 L}{1000 \text{ mL}} \times \left(22.4 \text{ mL} - 1.6 \text{ mL}\right) = 0.00208 \text{ mol } HClO_4$$
This will neutralize 0.00208 mol KOH, and $\dfrac{0.00208 \text{ mol}}{0.0500 \text{ L}} = 0.0416 \text{ M}$

94. Rank the following from lowest to highest pH. Assume a small volume for the added component:

I. 0.01 mol HCl added to 1 L H_2O
II. 0.01 mol HI added to 1 L of an acetic acid/sodium acetate solution at pH 4.0
III. 0.01 mol NH_3 added to 1 L H_2O
IV. 0.1 mol HNO_3 added to 1 L of a 0.1 M $Ca(OH)_2$ solution ˀ

A. I < II < III < IV
B. I < II < IV < III
C. II < I < III < IV
D. II < I < IV < III

A HCl is a strong acid. Therefore solution I has a <u>pH of 2</u> because

$$pH = -\log_{10}\left[H^+\right] = -\log_{10}(0.01) = 2.$$

HI is also a strong acid and would have a pH of 2 at this concentration in water, but the buffer will prevent pH from dropping this low. Solution II will have a pH <u>above 2</u> and below 4, eliminating choices C and D.

If a strong base were in solution III, its pOH would be 2. Using the equation pH + pOH = 14, its pH would be 12. Because NH_3 is a weak base, the pH of solution III will be greater than 7 and <u>less than 12</u>.

A neutralization reaction occurs in solution IV between 0.1 mol of H^+ from the strong acid HNO_3 and <u>0.2 mol of OH^-</u> from the strong base $Ca(OH)_2$. Each mole of $Ca(OH)_2$ contributes two base equivalents for the neutralization reaction. The base is the excess reagent, and 0.1 mol of OH^- remain after the reaction. This resulting solution will have a pOH of 1 and a <u>pH of 13</u>.

A is correct because: 2 < between 2 and 4 < between 7 and 12 < 13

95. The curve below resulted from the titration of a _____ _____ with a _____ _____ titrant.

A. weak acid, strong base
B. weak base, strong acid
C. strong acid, strong base
D. strong base, strong acid

D The pH is above 7 initially and decreases, so an acid titrant is neutralizing a base. This eliminates A and C. The maximum slope (equivalence point) at the neutral pH of 7 indicates a strong base titrated with a strong acid, D.

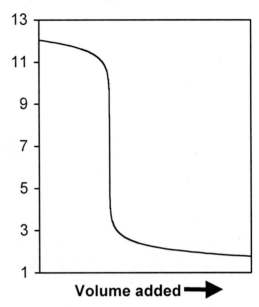

Volume added ➡

96. Which statement about thermochemistry is true?

A. Particles in a system move about less freely at high entropy
B. Water at 100 °C has the same internal energy as water vapor at 100°C
C. A decrease in the order of a system corresponds to an increase in entropy.
D. At its sublimation temperature, dry ice has a higher entropy than gaseous CO_2

C At high entropy, particles have a large freedom of molecular motion (A is false). Water and water vapor at 100 °C contain the same translational kinetic energy, but water vapor has additional internal energy in the form of resisting the intermolecular attractions between molecules (B is false). We also know water vapor has a higher internal energy because heat must be added to boil water. Entropy may be thought of as the disorder in a system (C is correct). Sublimation is the phase change from solid to gas, and there is less freedom of motion for particles in solids than in gases. Solid CO_2 (dry ice) has a lower entropy than gaseous CO_2 because entropy decreases during a phase change that prevents molecular motion (D is false).

97. What is the heat change of 36.0 g H_2O at atmospheric pressure when its temperature is reduced from 125 °C to 40. °C? Use the following data:

A. −92.0 kJ
B. −10.8 kJ
C. 10.8 kJ
D. 92.0 kJ

Values for water	
Heat capacity of solid	37.6 J/mol•°C
Heat capacity of liquid	75.3 J/mol•°C
Heat capacity of gas	33.1 J/mol•°C
Heat of fusion	6.02 kJ/mol
Heat of vaporization	40.67 kJ/mol

[handwritten notes: 100 − 40; vap to 100; 100 condeny to h2o]

A Heat is evolved from the substance as it cools, so the heat change will be negative, eliminating choices C and D. Data in the table are given using moles, so the first step is to convert the mass of water to moles:

$$36.0 \text{ g } H_2O \times \frac{1 \text{ mol } H_2O}{18.02 \text{ g } H_2O} = 2.00 \text{ mol } H_2O$$

There are three contributions to the heat evolved. First, the heat evolved when cooling the vapor from 125 °C to 100 °C is found from the heat capacity of the gas:

$$q_1 = n \times C \times \Delta T = 2.00 \text{ mol } H_2O(g) \times 33.1 \frac{J}{mol \text{ °C}} \times (100 \text{ °C} - 125 \text{ °C})$$

$$= -1655 \text{ J to cool vapor}$$

Next, the heat evolved during condensation is found from the heat of vaporization:

$$q_2 = n \times (-\Delta H_{vaporization}) = 2.00 \text{ mol } H_2O \times (-40.67 \frac{kJ}{mol})$$

$$= -81.34 \text{ kJ to condense vapor}$$

Incorrect answer B results from using a heat of vaporization of 40.67 J/mol instead of kJ/mol.

Finally, the heat evolved when cooling the liquid from 100 °C to 40 °C is found from the heat capacity of the liquid:

$$q_3 = n \times C \times \Delta T = 2.00 \text{ mol } H_2O(g) \times 75.3 \frac{J}{mol \text{ °C}} \times (40 \text{ °C} - 100 \text{ °C})$$

$$= -9036 \text{ J to cool liquid}$$

The total heat change is the sum of these contributions:

$$q = q_1 + q_2 + q_3 = -1.655 \text{ kJ} + (-81.34 \text{ kJ}) + (-9.036 \text{ kJ}) = -92.03 \text{ kJ}$$

$$= -92.0 \text{ kJ (Choice A)}$$

98. **What is the standard heat of combustion of CH₄(g)? Use the following data:**

A. −890.3 kJ/mol
B. −604.5 kJ/mol
C. −252.9 kJ/mol
D. −182.5 kJ/mol

Standard heats of formation

$CH_4(g)$	−74.8 kJ/mol
$CO_2(g)$	−393.5 kJ/mol
$H_2O(l)$	−285.8 kJ/mol

A First we must write a balanced equation for the combustion of CH₄. The balanced equation is:

$$CH_4(g) + 2O_2(g) \rightarrow CO_2(g) + 2H_2O(l).$$

The heat of combustion may be found from the sum of the productions minus the sum of the reactants of the heats of formation:

$$\Delta H_{rxn} = H_{product\ 1} + H_{product\ 2} + \ldots - \left(H_{reactant\ 1} + H_{reactant\ 2} + \ldots \right)$$

$$= \Delta H_f^\circ (CO_2) + 2\Delta H_f^\circ (H_2O) - \left(\Delta H_f^\circ (CH_4) + 2\Delta H_f^\circ (O_2) \right)$$

The heat of formation of an element in its most stable form is zero by definition, so $\Delta H_f^\circ (O_2(g)) = 0 \ \dfrac{kJ}{mol}$, and the remaining values are found from the table:

$$\Delta H_{rxn} = -393.5 \ \frac{kJ}{mol} + 2(-285.8 \ \frac{kJ}{mol}) - \left(-74.8 \ \frac{kJ}{mol} + 2(0) \right) = -890.3 \ \frac{kJ}{mol} \ \text{(choice A)}$$

99. **Which reaction creates products at a lower total entropy than the reactants?**

A. Dissolution of table salt: $NaCl(s) \rightarrow Na^+(aq) + Cl^-(aq)$
B. Oxidation of iron: $4Fe(s) + 3O_2(g) \rightarrow 2Fe_2O_3(s)$
C. Dissociation of ozone: $O_3(g) \rightarrow O_2(g) + O(g)$
D. Vaporization of butane: $C_4H_{10}(l) \rightarrow C_4H_{10}(g)$

B Choice A is incorrect because two particles are at a greater entropy than one and because ions in solution have more freedom of motion than a solid. For B (the correct answer), the products are at a lower entropy than the reactants because there are fewer product molecules and they are all in the solid form but one of the reactants is a gas. Reaction B is still spontaneous because it is highly exothermic. For C, there are more product molecules than reactants, and for D, the gas phase is always at a higher entropy than the liquid.

100. Which statement about reactions is true?

   A. All spontaneous reactions are both exothermic and cause an increase in entropy.
   B. An endothermic reaction that increases the order of the system cannot be spontaneous.
   C. A reaction can be non-spontaneous in one direction and also non-spontaneous in the opposite direction.
   D. Melting snow is an exothermic process

B All reactions that are both exothermic and cause an increase in entropy will be spontaneous, but the converse (choice A) is not true. Some spontaneous reactions are exothermic but decrease entropy and some are endothermic and increase entropy. Choice B is correct. The reverse reaction of a non-spontaneous reaction (choice C) will be spontaneous. Melting snow (choice D) requires heat. Therefore it is an endothermic process

101. 10. kJ of heat are added to one kilogram of Iron at 10. °C. What is its final temperature? The specific heat of iron is 0.45 J/g•°C.

   A. 22 °C
   B. 27 °C
   C. 32 °C
   D. 37 °C

C The expression for heat as a function of temperature change:
$$q = n \times C \times \Delta T$$
may be rearranged to solve for the temperature change:
$$\Delta T = \frac{q}{n \times C}.$$
In this case, n is a mass and C is the specific heat of iron:
$$\Delta T = \frac{10000 \text{ J}}{1000 \text{ g} \times 0.45 \ \dfrac{\text{J}}{\text{g} \ ^\circ\text{C}}} = 22 \ ^\circ\text{C}.$$
This is not the final temperature (choice A is incorrect). It is the temperature difference between the initial and final temperature.
$$\Delta T = T_{final} - T_{initial} = 22 \ ^\circ\text{C}$$
Solving for the final temperature gives us:
$$T_{final} = \Delta T + T_{initial} = 22 \ ^\circ\text{C} + 10 \ ^\circ\text{C} = 32 \ ^\circ\text{C} \text{ (Choice C)}$$

102. Which reaction is <u>not</u> a redox process?

    A. Combustion of octane: $2C_8H_{18} + 25O_2 \rightarrow 16CO_2 + 18H_2O$

    B. Depletion of a lithium battery: $Li + MnO_2 \rightarrow LiMnO_2$

    C. Corrosion of aluminum by acid: $2Al + 6HCl \rightarrow 2AlCl_3 + 3H_2$

    D. Taking an antacid for heartburn:
       $CaCO_3 + 2HCl \rightarrow CaCl_2 + H_2CO_3 \rightarrow CaCl_2 + CO_2 + H_2O$

D The oxidation state of atoms is altered in a redox process. During combustion (choice A), the carbon atoms are oxidized from an oxidation number of –4 to +4. Oxygen atoms are reduced from an oxidation number of 0 to –2. All batteries (choice B) generate electricity by forcing electrons from a redox process through a circuit. Li is oxidized from 0 in the metal to +1 in the $LiMnO_2$ salt. Mn is reduced from +4 in manganese(IV) oxide to +3 in lithium manganese(III) oxide salt. Corrosion (choice C) is due to oxidation. Al is oxidized from 0 to +3. H is reduced from +1 to 0. Acid-base neutralization (choice D) transfers a proton (an H atom with an oxidation state of +1) from an acid to a base. The oxidation state of all atoms remains unchanged (Ca at +2, C at +4, O at –2, H at +1, and Cl at –1), so D is correct. Note that choices C and D both involve an acid. The availability of electrons in aluminum metal favors electron transfer but the availability of CO_3^{2-} as a proton acceptor favors proton transfer.

103. Given the following heats of reaction:

$\Delta H = -0.3$ kJ / mol for $\quad Fe(s) + CO_2(g) \rightarrow FeO(s) + CO(g)$

$\Delta H = 5.7$ kJ / mol for $\quad 2Fe(s) + 3CO_2(g) \rightarrow Fe_2O_3(s) + 3CO(g)$

and $\Delta H = 4.5$ kJ / mol for $\quad 3FeO(s) + CO_2(g) \rightarrow Fe_3O_4(s) + CO(g)$

use Hess's Law to determine the heat of reaction for:

$$3Fe_2O_3(s) + CO(g) \rightarrow 2Fe_3O_4(s) + CO_2(g)?$$

A. −10.8 kJ/mol
B. −9.9 kJ/mol
C. −9.0 kJ/mol
D. −8.1 kJ/mol

B We are interested in $3Fe_2O_3$ as a reactant. Only the second reaction contains this molecule, so we will take three times the opposite of the second reaction. We are interested in $2Fe_3O_4$ as a product, so we will take two times the third reaction. An intermediate result is:

$3Fe_2O_3(s) + 9CO(g) \rightarrow 6Fe(s) + 9CO_2(g) \qquad \Delta H = -3 \times 5.7$ kJ/mol $= -17.1$ kJ/mol

$6FeO(s) + 2CO_2(g) \rightarrow 2Fe_3O_4(s) + 2CO(g) \qquad \Delta H = 2 \times 4.5$ kJ/mol $= 9.0$ kJ/mol

_____

$3Fe_2O_3(s) + 6FeO(s) + 7CO(g) \rightarrow$

$\qquad 2Fe_3O_4(s) + 6Fe(s) + 7CO_2(g)$ $\qquad \Delta H = (-17.1 + 9.0)$ kJ/mol $= -8.1$ kJ/mol

However, D is not the correct answer because it is not ΔH for the reaction of the problem statement. We may use six times the first reaction to eliminate both FeO and Fe from the intermediate result and obtain the reaction of interest:

$3Fe_2O_3(s) + 6FeO(s) + 7CO(g) \rightarrow$

$\qquad 2Fe_3O_4(s) + 6Fe(s) + 7CO_2(g)$ $\qquad \Delta H = -8.1$ kJ/mol

$6Fe(s) + 6CO_2(g) \rightarrow 6FeO(s) + 6CO(g) \qquad \Delta H = 6 \times (-0.3$ kJ/mol$) = -1.8$ kJ/mol

_____

$3Fe_2O_3(s) + CO(g) \rightarrow 2Fe_3O_4(s) + CO(g)$ $\qquad \Delta H = (-8.1 + -1.8)$ kJ/mol

$\qquad = -9.9$ kJ/mol (choice B)

104. What is the oxidant in the reaction: $2H_2S + SO_2 \rightarrow 3S + 2H_2O$?

    A. H_2S
    B. SO_2
    C. S
    D. H_2O

B The S atom in H_2S has an oxidation number of –2 and is oxidized by SO_2 (the oxidant, choice B) to elemental sulfer (oxidation number = 0). The S atom in SO_2 has an oxidation number of +4 and is reduced. The two half-reactions are:

$$SO_2 + 4e^- + 4H^+ \xrightarrow{\text{reduction}} S + 2H_2O$$

$$2H_2S \xrightarrow{\text{oxidation}} 2S + 4e^- + 4H^+$$

105. Molten NaCl is subjected to electrolysis. What reaction takes place at the cathode?

    A. $2Cl^-(l) \rightarrow Cl_2(g) + 2e^-$
    B. $Cl_2(g) + 2e^- \rightarrow 2Cl^-(l)$
    C. $Na^+(l) + e^- \rightarrow Na(l)$
    D. $Na^+(l) \rightarrow Na(l) + e^-$

C Reduction (choices B and C) always occurs at the cathode. Molten NaCl is composed of ions in liquid form before electrolysis (answer C). A and D are oxidation reactions, and D is also not properly balanced because a +1 charge is on the left and a –1 charge is on the right. The two half-reactions are:

$$Na^+(l) + e^- \xrightarrow{\text{reduction at cathode}} Na(l)$$

$$2Cl^-(l) \xrightarrow{\text{oxidation at anode}} Cl_2(g) + 2e^-$$

The net reaction is:

$$2NaCl(l) \rightarrow 2Na(l) + Cl_2(g)$$

106. What is the purpose of the salt bridge in a voltaic cell?

    A. To receive electrons from the oxidation half-reaction
    B. To relieve the buildup of positive charge in the anode half-cell
    C. To conduct electron flow
    D. To permit positive ions to flow from the cathode half-cell to the anode half-cell

D The anode receives electrons from the oxidation half-reaction (choice A) and the circuit conducts electron flow (choice C) to the cathode which supplies electrons for the reduction half-reaction. This flow of electrons from the anode to the cathode is relieved by a flow of ions through the salt bridge from the cathode to the anode (answer D). The salt bridge relieves the buildup of positive charge in the cathode half-cell (choice B is incorrect).

107. Given $E°=-2.37$ V for $Mg^{2+}(aq)+2e^-\rightarrow Mg(s)$ and $E°=0.80$ V for $Ag^+(aq)+e^-$ $\rightarrow Ag(s)$, what is the standard potential of a voltaic cell composed of a piece of magnesium dipped in a 1 M Ag^+ solution and a piece of silver dipped in 1 M Mg^{2+}?

    A. 0.77 V
    B. 1.57 V
    C. 3.17 V
    D. 3.97 V

C $Ag^+(aq)+e^-\rightarrow Ag(s)$ has a larger value for $E°$ (reduction potential) than $Mg^{2+}(aq)+2e^-\rightarrow Mg(s)$. Therefore, in the cell described, reduction will occur at the Ag electrode and it will be the cathode. Using the equation:

$$E°_{cell} = E°(\text{cathode}) - E°(\text{anode}), \text{ we obtain:}$$

$$E°_{cell} = 0.80 \text{ V} - (-2.37 \text{ V}) = 3.17 \text{ V (Answer C)}.$$

Choice D results from the incorrect assumption that electrode potentials depend on the amount of material present. The balanced net reaction for the cell is:

$$Mg(s) \rightarrow Mg^{2+}(aq) + 2e^- \qquad\qquad E°_{ox} = 2.37 \text{ V}$$

$$2Ag^+(aq) + 2e^- \rightarrow 2Ag(s) \qquad\qquad E°_{red} = 0.80 \text{ V (not 1.60 V)}$$

$$Mg(s) + 2Ag^+(aq) \rightarrow 2Ag(s) + Mg^{2+}(aq) \qquad E°_{cell} = 3.17 \text{ V (not 3.97 V)}$$

108. A proper name for this hydrocarbon is:

A. 4,5-dimethyl-6-hexene
B. 2,3-dimethyl-1-hexene
C. 4,5-dimethyl-6-hexyne
D. 2-methyl-3-propyl-1-butene

B The hydrocarbon contains a double bond and no triple bonds, so it is an alkene. Choice C describes an alkyne. The longest carbon chain is six carbons long, corresponding to a parent molecule of 1-hexene (circled to the left). Choice D is an improper name because it names the molecule as a substituted butane, using a shorter chain as the parent molecule. Finally, the lowest possible set of locant numbers must be used. Choice A is an improper name because the larger possible set of locant numbers is chosen.

109. An IUPAC approved name for this molecule is:

A. butanal
B. propanal
C. butanoic acid
D. propanoic acid

C The COOH group means that the molecule is a carboxylic acid and its name will use the suffix –oic acid. The presence of 4 carbon atoms means the prefix butan- will be used. An alternate name for the molecule is butyric acid. Choices A and B would be used for aldehydes (CHO group). Choices B and D would be used for 3 carbon atoms:

butanal (also called butyraldehyde):

propanal (also called propionaldehyde):

propanoic acid (also called propionic acid):

110. Which molecule has a systematic name of methyl ethanoate?

A.

B.

C.

D.

A The suffix –*oate* is used for esters. The ester group is shown to the right. Choice C is a ketone (ethyl methyl ketone or 2-butanone). The ketone group is shown to the left. Choice D is an acid anhydride (ethanoic methanoic anhydride). The acid anhydride group is shown below to the right. A and B are both esters. The hydrocarbon R_2 with the carbonyl group receives the –*oate* suffix and the hydrocarbon R_1 with the -*yl* suffix is attached to the other oxygen. Choice B is ethyl methanoate and A is correct.

111. This compound contains an:

A. alkene, carboxylic acid, ester, and ketone
B. aldehyde, alkyne, ester, and ketone
C. aldehyde, alkene, carboxylic acid, and ester
D. acid anhydride, aldehyde, alkene, and amine

C The derivatives are circled below:

Choice A is wrong because there are no ketones in the molecule. A ketone has a carbonyl group linked to two hydrocarbons as shown to the right. All the carbonyls in the molecule are linked to at least one oxygen atom. Choice B is wrong because there are no ketones and no alkynes in the molecule. An alkyne contains a C≡C triple bond. Choice D is wrong because there are no acid anhydrides (shown to the left) and no amines (shown to the right). Amines require at least one N-C bond and there are no nitrogen atoms in the molecule.

112. Which group of scientists made contributions in the same area of chemistry?

A. Volta, Kekulé, Faraday, London
B. Hess, Joule, Kelvin, Gibbs
C. Boyle, Charles, Arrhenius, Pauli
D. Davy, Mendeleev, Ramsay, Galvani

B Hess, Joule, Kelvin, and Gibbs all contributed to thermochemistry and have thermodynamic entities named after them. Volta, Faraday, and Galvani (choice D) contributed to electrochemistry, Kekulé to organic chemistry, London to chemical bonding, Boyle and Charles to gas laws, Arrhenius to acid/base chemistry and thermochemstry, Pauli to quantum theory, Davy and Ramsay to element isolation, and Mendeleev to the periodic table.

113. Which of the following pairs are isomers?

I.

II. pentanal 2-pentanone

III.

IV.

A. I and IV
B. II and III
C. I, II, and III
D. I, II, III, and IV

B In pair I, the N—N bond may freely rotate in the molecule because it is not a double bond. The identical molecule is represented twice.

For pair II, pentanal is

and 2-pentanone is:

Both molecules are $C_5H_{10}O$, and they are isomers because they have the same formula with a different arrangement of atoms.

In pair III, both molecules are 1,3-dibromocyclopentane, $C_5H_8Br_2$. In the first molecule, the bromines are in a *trans* configuration, and in the second molecule, they are *cis*. The two molecules are also viewed from different perspectives. Unlike pair I, no bond rotation may occur because the intervening atoms are locked into place by the ring, so they are different arrangements and are isomers.

In pair IV (1-fluoroethanol), there is a chiral center, so stereoisomers are possible, but as in pair I, the same molecule is represented twice. Rotating the C-O bond indicates that the two structures are superimposable. This molecule: to the right is a stereoisomer to the molecule represented in IV. The answer is B (pairs II and III).

114. Which instrument would be most useful for separating two different proteins from a mixture?

    A. UV/Vis spectrophotometer
    B. Mass spectrometer
    C. Gas chromatograph
    D. Liquid chromatograph

D UV/Vis spectrophotometry measures the light at ultraviolet and visible wavelengths that can pass through the mixture, and mass spectrometry determines molecular weights. Both might be used to find the concentration of each protein, but neither is a separation technique. Gas chromatography is used for small molecules in the gas phase. Proteins are too large to exist in the gas phase. Liquid chromatography (answer D) is used to separate large molecules.

115. Classify these biochemicals.

I.

II.

III.

IV.

    A. I-nucleotide, II-sugar, III-peptide, IV-fat
    B. I-disaccharide, II-sugar, III-fatty acid, IV-polypeptide
    C. I-disaccharide, II-amino acid, III-fatty acid, IV- polysaccharide
    D. I-nucleotide, II-sugar, III-triacylglyceride, and IV-DNA

A I is a phosphate (PO_4) linked to a sugar and an amine: a nucleotide. II has the formula $C_nH_{2n}O_n$, indicative of a sugar. III contains three amino acids linked with peptide bonds. It is a tripeptide. IV is a triacylglyceride, a fat molecule.

116. You create a solution of 2.00 μg/ml of a pigment and divide the solution into 12 samples. You give four samples each to three teams of students. They use a spectrophotometer to determine the pigment concentration. Here is their data:

	Concentration (μg/ml)			
Team	sample 1	sample 2	sample 3	sample 4
1	1.98	1.93	1.92	1.88
2	1.70	1.72	1.69	1.70
3	1.78	1.99	2.87	2.20

Which of the following are true?

A. Team 1 has the most precise data
B. Team 3 has the most accurate data in spite of it having low precision
C. The data from team 2 is characteristic of a systematic error
D. The data from team 1 is more characteristic of random error than the data from team 3.

C For choice A, the data from team 2 are closer to the mean for team 2 than the data from team 1 are to its mean. Therefore, team 1's data does not have the most precision.

For choice B, the mean from team 1 is near 1.9 μg/ml (we don't need to calculate exact values). It differs from the actual value by 0.1 μg/ml. The mean from team 2 is near 1.7 μg/ml and is inaccurate by 0.3 μg/ml. The mean from team 3 is not obvious, but it may be calculated as 2.21 μg/ml, differing from the actual value by about 0.2 μg/ml. Team 3's data is less accurate than the data from team 1.

The data from team 2 is clustered close to a central value but this value is wrong. Low accuracy with high precision is indicative of a systematic error. (C is correct).

For choice D, a lack of precision is indicative of random error, and the data from team 1 is more precise than the data from team 3.

117. Which pair of measurements have an identical meaning?

    A. 32 micrometers and 0.032 g
    B. 26 nm and 2.60×10^{-8} m
    C. 3.01×10^{-5} m^3 and 30.1 ml
    D. 0.0020 L and 20 cm^3

C For A, the prefix *micro—* indicates 10^{-6}. 32 micrograms is 0.000032 g. For B, the two measurements do not have the same meaning because they differ in the number of significant figures. 26 nm is 2.6×10^{-8} m. The symbol "n" for *nano—* indicates 10^{-9}. For C and D, unit conversions between cubic meters and liters are required.

$$\text{For C: } 3.01 \times 10^{-5} \text{ m}^3 \times \frac{1000 \text{ L}}{1 \text{ m}^3} \times \frac{1000 \text{ ml}}{1 \text{ L}} = 30.1 \text{ ml (C is correct).}$$

$$\text{For D: } 0.0020 \text{ L} \times \frac{1 \text{ m}^3}{1000 \text{ L}} \times \frac{(100)^3 \text{ cm}^3}{1 \text{ m}^3} = 2.0 \text{ cm}^3 \text{ (D is incorrect).}$$

118. Match the instrument with the quantity it measures

    I. eudiometer
    II. calorimeter
    III. manometer
    IV. hygrometer

    A. I-volume, II-mass, III-radioactivity, IV-humidity
    B. I-volume, II-heat, III-pressure, IV-humidity
    C. I-viscosity, II-mass, III-pressure, IV-surface tension
    D. I-viscosity, II-heat, III-radioactivity, IV-surface tension

B A eudiometer is a straight tube used to measure gas volume by liquid exclusion. A calorimeter is a device used to measure changes in heat. A manometer is a U-shaped tube used to measure pressure. A hygrometer measures humidity (Answer B). Mass is measured with a balance, radioactivity is measured with a Geiger counter or scintillation counter. Viscosity is measured with a viscometer, surface tension is measured by several different techniques.

119. Four nearly identical gems from the same mineral are weighed using different balances. Their masses are:

3.4533 g, 3.459 g, 3.4656 g, 3.464 g.

The four gems are then collected and added to a volumetric cylinder containing 10.00 ml of liquid, and a new volume of 14.97 ml is read. What is the average mass of the four stones and what is the density of the mineral?

A. 3.460 g, and 2.78 g/ml
B. 3.460 g and 2.79 g/ml
C. 3.4605 g and 2.78 g/ml
D. 3.461 g and 2.79 g/ml

B The average mass is the sum of the four readings divided by four:

$(3.4533 \text{ g} + 3.459 \text{ g} + 3.4656 \text{ g} + 3.464 \text{ g})/4 = 3.460475 \text{ g}$ (caculator value)

This value must be rounded off to three significant digits <u>after the decimal point</u> because this is the lowest precision of the added values. The four is an exact number. This means rounding downwards to 3.460 g, eliminating choices C and D. The volume of the collected stones is found from the increase in the level read off the cylinder:

$14.97 \text{ ml} - 10.00 \text{ ml} = 4.97 \text{ ml}$

The density is found by dividing the sum of the masses by this volume:

$$\frac{3.4533 \text{ g} + 3.459 \text{ g} + 3.4656 \text{ g} + 3.464 \text{ g}}{4.97 \text{ ml}} = \frac{13.8419 \text{ g}}{4.97 \text{ ml}} = 2.7850905 \text{ g/ml} \text{ (caculator value)}$$

This value must be rounded off to three <u>total</u> significant digits because this is the lower precision of the numerator and the denominator. The first insignificant digit is a 5. In this case there are additional non-zero digits after the 5, so rounding occurs upwards to 2.79 g/ml (answer B).

120. Which list includes equipment that would <u>not</u> be used in vacuum filtration.

    A. Rubber tubing, Florence flask, Büchner funnel
    B. Vacuum pump, Hirsch funnel, rubber stopper with a single hole
    C. Aspirator, filter paper, filter flask
    D. Lab stand, clamp, filter trap

A Florence flasks are round-bottomed and are used for uniform heating. They do not have the hose barb or the thick wall needed to serve as a filter flask during vacuum filtration. Only a designated filter flask should be used during vacuum filtration. Every other piece of equipment could be used in filtration. A spatula is often used to scrape dried product off of filter paper.

121. Which of the following statements about lab safety is <u>not</u> true?

    A. Corrosive chemicals should be stored below eye level.
    B. A chemical splash on the eye or skin should be rinsed for 15 minutes in cold water.
    C. MSDS means "Material Safety Data Sheet."
    D. A student should "stop, drop, and roll" if their clothing catches fire in the lab.

D In the lab, the safety shower should be used.

122. Which of the following lists consists entirely of chemicals that are considered safe enough to be in a high school lab?

    A. hydrochloric acid, lauric acid, potassium permanganate, calcium hydroxide
    B. ethyl ether, nitric acid, sodium benzoate, methanol
    C. cobalt (II) sulfide, ethylene glycol, benzoyl peroxide, ammonium chloride
    D. picric acid, hydrofluoric acid, cadmium chloride, carbon disulfide.

A Hydrochloric acid (HCl) is a common acid reagent in high school chemistry. Lauric acid is the fatty acid $CH_3(CH_2)_{10}COOH$ also known as dodecanoic acid. Potassium permanganate ($KMnO_4$) is a strong oxidizer. Calcium hydroxide ($Ca(OH)_2$) is a strong base. These chemicals in their pure state are hazardous, but they are considered safe enough to be in high schools. Ethyl ether (Choice B) should not be in high schools because it may form highly explosive organic peroxides over time. Benzoyl peroxide (choice C) at low concentrations in gel form is an acne medication, but the pure compound is highly explosive. Choice D consists entirely of chemicals that are too dangerous for high schools. Picric acid is highly explosive, hydrofluoric acid is very corrosive and very toxic, all cadmium compounds are highly toxic, and carbon disulfide is explosive and toxic.

123. The following procedure was developed to find the specific heat capacity of metals:

1. Place pieces of the metals in an ice-water bath so their initial temperature is 0 °C.
2. Weigh a styrofoam cup.
3. Add water at room temperature to the cup and weigh it again
4. Add a cold metal from the bath to the cup and weigh the cup a third time.
5. Monitor the temperature drop of the water until a final temperature at thermal equilibrium is found.

_____ is also required as additional information in order to obtain heat capacities for the metals. The best control would be to follow the same protocol except to use _____ in step 4 instead of a cold metal.

A. The heat capacity of water / a metal at 100 °C
B. The heat of formation of water / ice from the 0 °C bath
C. The heat of capacity of ice / glass at 0 °C
D. The heat capacity of water / water from the 0 °C bath

D The equation:

$$q = n \times C \times \Delta T$$

is used to determine what additional information is needed. The specific heat, C, of the metals may be found from the heat added, the amount of material, and the temperature change. The amount of metal is found from the difference in weight between steps 3 and 4, and the temperature change is found from the difference between the final temperature and 0 °C. The additional value required is the heat added, q. This may be found from the heat removed from the water if the amount of water, the heat capacity of water, and the temperature change of water are known. The amount of water is found from the difference in weight between step 2 and 3, and the temperature change is found from the difference between the final temperature and room temperature. The only additional information required is the heat capacity of water, eliminating choices B and C. Heat of formation (choice B) is only used for chemical reactions.

A good control simplifies only the one aspect under study without adding anything new. Metal at 100 °C (choice A) would alter the temperature of the experiment and glass (choice C) would add an additional material to the study. Ice (choice B) would require consideration of the heat of fusion. Choice D is an ideal control because the impact of water at 0 °C on room temperature water is simpler than the impact of metals at 0 °C on room temperature water, and nothing new is added.

124. Which statement about the impact of chemistry on society is <u>not</u> true?

    A. Partial hydrogenation creates *trans* fat.
    B. The Haber Process incorporates nitrogen from the air into molecules for agricultural use.
    C. The CO_2 concentration in the atmosphere has decreased in the last ten years.
    D. The concentration of ozone-destroying chemicals in the stratosphere has decreased in the last ten years.

C CO_2 concentrations in the atmosphere continue to increase (answer C), but the concentration of ozone destroying chemicals has fallen (answer D) due to international agreements.

125. Which statement about everyday applications of chemistry is <u>true</u>?

    A. Rainwater found near sources of air pollution will most likely be basic.
    B. Batteries run down more quickly at low temperatures because chemical reactions are proceeding more slowly.
    C. Benzyl alcohol is a detergent used in shampoo.
    D. Adding salt decreases the time required for water to boil.

B   Sources of air pollution (choice A) will most likely cause acid rain.

Low temperatures decrease reaction rates, and this is also true of electrochemical reactions in batteries. At low temperature, less current is supplied and the effect will be a short life for applications that demand current. (Answer B is correct).

Benzyl alcohol (choice C) has the formula shown to the right. Like detergents, this molecule has a non-polar region (the benzene ring) and a polar region (the hydroxyl group). But, unlike detergents, the non-polar region for benzyl alcohol is small and short. Detergents have long, "tail-like" non-polar regions that can surround oils and grease. Benzyl alcohol is sometimes included in shampoo to prevent itching and bacterial growth.

Adding salt (choice D) increases the boiling point of water, thus increasing the time required for water to boil. It decreases the time required to cook food once boiling occurs.

XAMonline, INC. 21 Orient Ave. Melrose, MA 02176

Toll Free number 800-509-4128

TO ORDER Fax 781-662-9268 OR www.XAMonline.com

<u>FLORIDA TEACHER CERTIFICATION</u>

<u>EXAMINATIONS</u>   <u>- FTCE - 2008</u>

PO#   Store/School:

Bill to Address 1   Ship to address

City, State Zip

Credit card number_____-_____-_____-_____ expiration____

EMAIL _____

PHONE   **FAX**

13# ISBN 2007	TITLE	Qty	Retail	Total
978-1-58197-900-8	Art Sample Test K-12			
978-1-58197-689-2	Biology 6-12			
978-1-58197-099-9	Chemistry 6-12			
978-1-58197-572-7	Earth/Space Science 6-12			
978-1-58197-578-9	Educational Media Specialist PK-12			
978-1-58197-347-1	Elementary Education K-6			
978-1-58197-292-4	English 6-12			
978-1-58197-274-0	Exceptional Student Ed. K-12			
978-1-58197-294-8	FELE Florida Ed. Leadership			
978-1-58197-919-0	French Sample Test 6-12			
978-1-58197-615-1	General Knowledge			
978-1-58197-586-4	Guidance and Counseling PK-12			
978-1-58197-045-6	Humanities K-12			
978-1-58197-640-3	Mathematics 6-12			
978-1-58197-597-0	Middle Grades English 5-9			
978-1-58197-662-5	Middle Grades General Science 5-9			
978-1-58197-286-3	Middle Grades Integrated Curriculum			
978-1-58197-284-9	Middle Grades Math 5-9			
978-1-58197-590-1	Middle Grades Social Science 5-9			
978-1-58197-616-8	Physical Education K-12			
978-1-58197-044-9	Physics 6-12			
978-1-58197-657-1	Prekindergarten/Primary PK-3			
978-1-58197-695-3	Professional Educator			
978-1-58197-659-5	Reading K-12			
978-1-58197-270-2	Social Science 6-12			
978-1-58197-583-3	Spanish K-12			
			SUBTOTAL	
b/handling $8.25 one title, $11.00 two titles, $15.00 three or more titles				
			TOTAL	

Normality

LaVergne, TN USA
10 June 2010

185661LV00001B/36/P

9 781581 970463